I couldn't put this book down! Brent has done an amazing job at capturing the challenges that traders face on a daily basis and how best to navigate today's markets. It is an essential read for anyone who is interested in managing money and the behavioral psychology behind those who "make the market!" Brent shows himself to be as skillful an author as he has been one of the leading players in global foreign exchange. Well done!

—Ben Melkman,
founder and CIO of Light Sky Macro

Brent has been on my must-read list for years. This book is no exception. **ALPHA TRADER is an instant trading classic.**

—John Mauldin,
president of Mauldin Economics

Brent is a smart, balanced and hyper-pragmatic trader. I have known and worked with him for years, and his constant search for new paradigms is what sets him apart. **ALPHA TRADER is a very, very valuable book** which may save young (and old) traders from significant emotional (and monetary) pain.

—Jens Nordvig,
world-renowned currency strategist,
economist and founder of Exante Data

Alpha Trader is one of the most intuitive books about applied trading psychology and rational behavior. **It is a masterpiece that puts you in control of your trading.**

—Saed Abukarsh,
partner at Ark Capital Management (Dubai)

Brent's book is an honest assessment of what is required to be successful in the markets. Successful traders have a process that is not canned or rigid... Because markets are not. If you are serious about making it as a full-time trader, **ALPHA TRADER is the book you need to read**. It's an honest take on what you will need to do and expect to make it like a pro.

—Dave Floyd,
founder of the Aspen Trading Group

Brent has been trading for 20 years and you should listen to anyone who has been trading that long. Over the course of a 20-year career, a trader will experience at least 50 major panics, crashes, and dislocations. Having the wrong exposure to one of these means the end of your career. Trading isn't about getting rich; it's about staying alive.

—Jared Dillian,
publisher of the Daily Dirtnap
and regular Bloomberg contributor

Alpha Trader

The Mindset, Methodology and
Mathematics of Professional Trading

Brent Donnelly

First edition 2021

Editing: Stephen K. Donnelly
Cover design: Emir Orucevic
Interior layout: KUHN Design Group
Author photo: Christine Donnelly

ISBN 978-1-7367398-0-8 (hardcover)
ISBN 978-1-7367398-1-5 (softcover)
ISBN 978-17367398-3-9 (ebook)

For more information go to: www.brentdonnelly.com

This book is dedicated to
the small bird who carries us all on her back.

CONTENTS

PART ONE: WHY DO SOME TRADERS SUCCEED, BUT MOST FAIL?

PART TWO: THE ALPHA TRADER MINDSET

PART THREE: METHODOLOGY AND MATHEMATICS

PART FOUR: ADAPTATION AND ATTITUDE

FOREWORD

If you're reading this foreword, you're probably considering whether or not to buy this book. You also probably have a professional or semi-professional connection to financial markets. Maybe you already work on a trading desk. Maybe you work in sales at one of those too-big-to-fail outfits and trade in your personal account. Maybe you don't currently work in the financial industry at all, but you've been spending a lot of hours on Robinhood and you're thinking about taking your involvement "to the next level", whatever that means to you. In any event, you're reading this foreword for clues as to whether this book will make you a *better* trader. Whether it will help you make *more* money.

It will.

Why will *Alpha Trader* help you become a better trader? Not because it tells you WHAT to think as a successful trader. Not because it gives you instructions on trading this or trading that. No, no, no. It's because *Alpha Trader* teaches you HOW to think as a successful trader. And that's what makes all the difference. It's the *only* thing that makes a difference, in every game that we humans play.

Here, I'll give you an example of what I mean.

If you're not a serious chess player, you've never heard of Aron Nimzowitsch. If you *are* a serious chess player, you undoubtedly have a dog-eared copy of his groundbreaking book – *My System* – first published in 1925. What was so revolutionary about Nimzowitsch's book? It wasn't a collection of openings. It wasn't a list of moves and countermoves that you should memorize. It wasn't a manual full of instructions. No, no, no. Nimzowitsch's book doesn't tell you *what* to think about chess. It teaches you *how* to think about chess. How to think about position. How to think about the flow of the game. How to think about risk-taking and aggression. How to think about edge and strategic dynamics. Sounds pretty dry, right? Not in the least. *My System* is written with wit, with a point of view. *My System* is chock-full of examples and illustrations, but presented as annotated stories of personal experience, not constructed applications of pure theory.

These are the same topics covered in *Alpha Trader* – position, flow, risk-taking, edge, strategic dynamics – all amplified by Brent Donnelly's keen understanding of the pervasive role of variance and chance, the crucial difference that makes the game of markets so much more difficult than the game of chess.

This is the same format and style of *Alpha Trader* – wit, a point of view, annotated personal experiences – all in service to illuminating a frame of thought rather than rote instruction.

I think that *Alpha Trader* and Brent Donnelly are to the game of markets what *My System* and Aron Nimzowitsch are to the game of chess. Truly revolutionary. Truly useful. Books and authors that will change forever HOW you think about playing their games with mastery.

But wait, there's more.

Yes, *Alpha Trader* will help all you professional and semi-professional and professional-wannabe traders become better traders. This book will help you make more money. You should buy this book and you should read it cover to cover.

And then you should give this book to your partner or your father or your daughter or your close friend … someone who has never traded a day in their life, someone who has no professional or semi-professional connection to financial markets whatsoever … and ask them to read this book. Please.

Because *Alpha Trader* won't only make you a better trader. It won't only help you make more money from trading. It will make you a better player of games.

Back in 1988, Iain M. Banks wrote a book titled *The Player of Games*, part of a wonderful series of science fiction novels that describe The Culture, a super-advanced galactic civilization. In this book, The Culture sends a representative to negotiate with a less advanced civilization where everyone's social and political status is determined by how well they play a very complicated game. The Culture's representative enters the global tournament himself, and despite only a few years to study a game that all of the inhabitants of this civilization spend their lives playing, he manages (spoiler alert!) to win the game. How? Because anyone can master the rules, even the intricacies of the rules, of any game. There's nothing special in that. There's no edge. What IS special, however, and where there IS edge comes in the very personal and very human understanding of position, informational flow, variance, risk-taking and strategic dynamics that shape ALL games.

And ... not to burst anyone's bubble, but that less advanced civilization where everyone's social and political status is determined by how well they play a very complicated game? That's us. That's Earth. That's the modern human civilization. That's the very complicated game of markets and politics and social interactions that we all play, all the time, in ways both large and small.

It's the single-most important determinant for success in our financialized and casino-fied and gamified world, regardless of where you sit or what you do in that world: *are you an effective player of games?*

I think that *Alpha Trader* can help anyone – trader or not – become a more effective player of games.

It sure did for me.

Dr. Ben Hunt
Co-founder and CIO
Epsilon Theory

A QUICK STORY
BEFORE WE START

The Connecticut air is cold and damp. The trader moves in silence. He steps quietly through the pitch-black darkness of his Colonial McMansion and toward the door. As he disarms the home security system, the BEEP BEEP BEEP of the keypad code he enters is impossibly loud in the quiet of the pre-dawn morning. He steps out of the house, closes and locks the door, and hops into his car.

As he rolls down the driveway and into the foggy morning, he inserts a Deadmau5 CD and blasts it at high volume in an effort to wake up and get pumped for another day of trading. But this will not just be another day of trading. This will be one of the most insane trading days of his career.

It has been a frustrating year so far. The Eurozone Crisis has been smoldering for months but the trader's attempts to sell the euro have been met with massive countertrend rallies as the Fed embarks on another round of USD-negative quantitative easing (QE). They call EURUSD a collision of two garbage trucks. The trader struggles to steer clear of the wreckage.

His strongest view recently has been lower USDJPY. There is risk aversion popping up all over the place as markets worry about a domino effect where Greece crashes out of the Eurozone, followed by Spain, Portugal, Ireland and then finally Italy. Everyone is bearish stocks as the S&P 500 rally from 666 in March 2009 to 1050 now is seen as a mirage; the side effect of a money printing magic trick performed by central bankers. Totally unsustainable.

EURUSD opened the year at 1.4500 and now trades sub-1.25 so the short trade is hard to stomach. Even when you know it's the right thing to do, it takes a lot of courage to sell something down >15%. So the trader has shifted his attention to USDJPY and he expects it to go substantially lower as global risk aversion remains elevated and safe haven currencies like the yen should find demand.

USDJPY has been inexplicably well-bid given recent risk aversion and the Fed "money printing". It just rallied from 90 to 94 on air over the last two weeks. Meanwhile, the best leading indicator for USDJPY is always US bond yields and they have been plummeting for a month. USDJPY looks completely wrong.

The trader stares at Figure 0.1, which shows US 10-year bond yields and

Figure 0.1: USDJPY vs. US 10-year rates November 2009 to May 5, 2010

The chart covers the period up to May 5. This story takes place May 6.
Chart courtesy of Refinitiv

USDJPY. The black bars are USDJPY and the dotted line shows US bond yields. Note they usually follow in lockstep. The divergence is a strong signal to the trader that he should be short USDJPY.

If you look in the top right corner, you can see that USDJPY is a bit off the highs, but not much. Two days in a row, the high has been 94.99 and USDJPY is now bouncing aimlessly around 93.80 as he rolls into the hedge fund parking lot. It is still early so there are only three Porsche 911s in the lot right now. More will arrive later.

This USDJPY trade has been tiring and painful as the trader got short at 94.00 with a stop loss at 95.05 and those two daily highs mean he has come within a hair (6 pips, or 0.064%) of getting stopped out, two days in a row. Holding on to a trade like this is exhausting as his fight-or-flight stress system remains activated for long stretches. Cortisol overload.

Now, he can relax a bit and let things play out. His target is 91.00. Average daily range has been about 1 yen (100 pips) lately so he figures we might get there in the next week or so.

10:45 AM

It has been a boring morning with USDJPY in a tight range. The sun comes out and it's almost shorts weather outside so the trader decides to go for a run before lunch. Less than a mile into his run, he gets his first indication that this is not a random, ordinary day. His Blackberry rings. Bank sales on the line to tell him that USDJPY has just dumped 100 points in 15 minutes. Trading 92.80 now... Odd. He turns around and sprints back to the office, Spidey-sense tingling.

By the time he grabs a quick shower and returns to the desk, USDJPY is 91.50. He is short $100 million USDJPY so that puts his profit (aka P&L or profit and loss) around +$2.8 million on the day. That's more P&L than this trader typically makes in an excellent month. A huge haul. He scans the headlines and Bloomberg chats and finds no good explanation for what is going on. The stock market is down, but not enough to explain the move in USDJPY. This makes no sense. When a trade shows a big profit that makes no sense, he likes to cover it and move on.

The trader buys 100 million USDJPY at 91.50. He is back to flat with no position and nearly 3 bucks of P&L in the bank.

He sits there calmly and processes what has happened. He allows himself to feel happy, just for a second. He stuck to his plan and had the patience to sit with a decent-sized position for three days. He relaxes and basks in the satisfaction of a job well done.

Then… Some dumb voice in his brain says:

2.8 million dollars is an amazing day. But…
Maybe I can make 5 million today?

And his hands, as if possessed by some mischievous or evil force, move slowly toward the BUY and SELL buttons. For no reason. And like a moron… He goes long USDJPY.

First, he buys $50 million at 91.50 and then another $50 million at 91.25. These are impulsive trades with no rationale. His planned stop loss is 90.85 but before he has time to input a stop loss order, he notices S&Ps lurch lower on a huge volume surge. He puts on his headset and fires up the S&P squawk to see what's going on.

> If you want to hear the soundtrack to what happens
> next, Google "Flash crash stock market 2010 squawk"
> and select one of the YouTube replay videos

The announcer's voice is strained as he narrates an unexplained fall in stocks from 1150 to 1120. USDJPY skips through 91.00 and the trader's P&L shrinks to $2.0 million. He tries to sell at 90.80 and whiffs. USDJPY is suddenly in freefall. 90.10 trades. 90.00 breaks. USDJPY has just dropped more than four percent in a few hours. A monster move. The trader's eyes flick over to his P&L which has now shrunk back to six digits. Two-thirds of three days' work, gone in 60 seconds.

And then… Stocks sell off hard out of nowhere. Like… REALLY HARD. The S&P squawk guy is losing it. Screaming. 1100 breaks in the S&P. 1080, 1070, 1060. USDJPY is a waterfall. The squawk loses his mind as he yells:

"We have some BIG paper sellers here… 7 evens are trading. 6 evens are trading! 5 EVENS ARE TRADING!!! New lows here…"

USDJPY breaks 89.00 and the trader has still sold only 23 million USD, leaving him stuck with a position of 77 million USD. It is a fast market, nearly impossible to transact. He picks up a phone to two different banks and neither one answers. He tries to hit the 88.60 and gets a reject notice from the aggregator. The price feed is stale and crossed now; it shows 89.00 / 88.10, which is not possible. The trader is now down on the day. In the red. His face is hot and feels red like his P&L. Urge to slam fist on desk is rising. The trader feels like he is falling, falling::::::::::::::::::::in cinematic slow-mo.

USDJPY stabilizes a bit even as the S&P squawk continues to go nuts.

"65 even offered! 60 trades... 60 even bid, this is the widest we have seen in years," his voice cracks, he's yelling like the announcer at Churchill Downs as the horses turn for the stretch.

"60s trading! 50s trading! 50 at 70 now! We are twenty wide!"

1060 trades in S&Ps now, down just about 10% today, on zero news. Nobody knows what the hell is going on and there is panic in the air. The squawk dude continues to scream. He is pouring gasoline on the trader's agitation.

The trader's P&L is now six figures in the red. Sadness. Anger. He is furious with himself because he had the right trade, waited patiently for almost three days for it to work, caught the move perfectly according to plan ... And then flipped the other way on a whim, for no reason and gave everything and more back in half an hour. $2.8 million is a good month for this trader. He just made and lost that much in less than two hours.

I am an idiot. How did I get into this mess?

He needs to make a decision here and quick but he realizes that he is flooded. It is impossible to make a good trading decision when you're flooded. He needs a second to clear his mind. He tears off the headphones, drops them on his desk, and stands up.

He walks over to the window and tries to find a moment of lucid calm. He has been through these emotional storms before and knows how to get back to shore. He stares over the waters of the Long Island Sound. Gradually, his heart rate lowers. Clarity slowly, slowwwwly returns. His lizard brain retreats and his rational mind takes over. He talks to himself:

*It doesn't matter how you got here. What are you going to do about it? 88.00 was the low in March. It's a massive level. The panic is fading. USDJPY is down 700 points in two days and now bonds are reversing lower. **This is the place to buy USDJPY, not sell.***

He returns to his keyboard, puts his headphones back on. The squawk guy has stopped screaming. He is noticeably more composed. S&P futures have bottomed within a whisker of limit down. They are stable but have not rebounded significantly. The bid/offer is super wide so it's hard to tell whether they are moving higher or just bouncing along the bottom.

The trader looks around the room and sees the panic and electricity levels have dropped. Not as many phones are ringing. Voices in the room are no longer frantic. He buys 50 million USDJPY at 88.85. And another 73 million at 88.95. Max long now, long $200 million USDJPY. But this time it's thought out, not random, and he feels good about what he is doing. He feels confident but fully in control. He calmly thinks forward: *USDJPY could easily rally to 92.50 from here. When you catch a turn like this, you can be greedy.*

He leaves a stop loss for half his position (sell 100 million USDJPY at 87.94) and then sits back to let things play out. He has his plan and now he knows all he can do is watch and see if it works. There is one more frenetic whipsaw and USDJPY briefly prints to a low of 87.95. One pip from his 100 million USD stop loss. Amazing luck. Seconds later, stocks stabilize, and then it's like everyone realizes all at once that whatever the heck just happened... It's over.

USDJPY is paid at 88.70, then up through 89.50. It breaks 90.00 and as it hits 90.40, the trader flicks his eyes to the P&L. It is almost exactly back to the level where it peaked earlier: $2.8 million. He praises the trading gods and squares up. NICE!

Figure 0.2: USDJPY May 3-7, 2010 (US stock market Flash Crash was May 6)

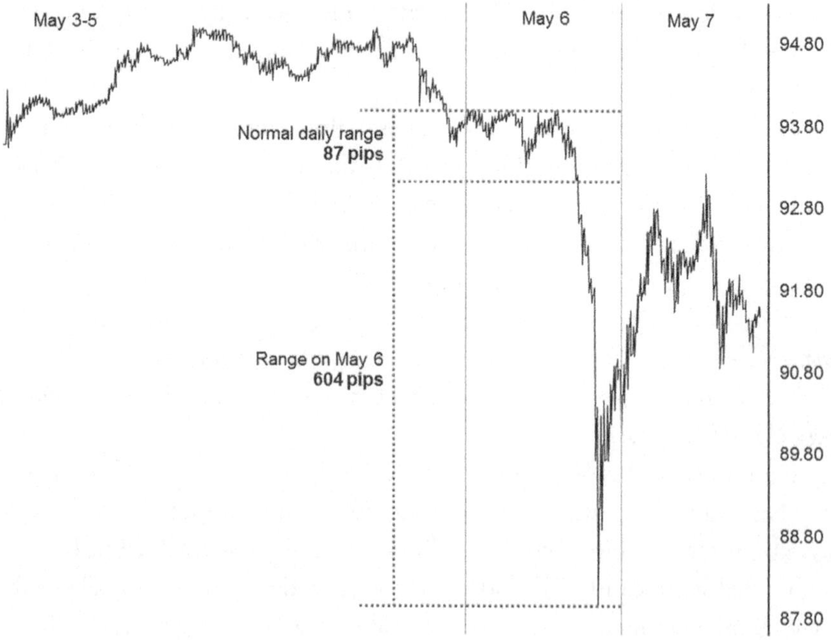

Too bad he didn't stick with his plan on the way back up, either. A few hours later, USDJPY hit the trader's original target of 92.50.

Check out Figure 0.2 for the price action in USDJPY that day.

The trader made a multitude of both good and bad decisions in the three hours around the 2010 Flash Crash. The trading described in this story is a microcosm of everything that can go right and wrong in trading. Traders make good, careful decisions and get rewarded, they make bad decisions and get punished … but then sometimes a good decision leads to a bad outcome … or a bad decision is rescued by good luck. Every trader is a steaming hot bowl of bias stew and must maintain self-awareness and lucidity behind the screens as the trading day oscillates between boredom and terror.

• • •

That story of the 2010 Flash Crash, just like this book, is all about the razor thin line that separates success and failure in trading. Alpha Trader is written to help you understand markets but also, more importantly, to help you better understand yourself as a trader. It is about great decisions and dumb mistakes. It is about how to be rational and why smart people do stupid things. All the time.

The book is written for traders at every skill level. I wrote it to be understood by noobs, but I also aimed to write something that will resonate with experienced trading professionals.

Alpha Traders are smart, rational, disciplined, flexible, patient, and aggressive… They have the endurance to handle unending ups, downs, hills, and valleys. They come in fired up each day to solve the ultimate puzzle and they get paid incredibly well if they succeed. Alpha Traders work hard (even when they don't feel like it), seek to continuously improve, and love markets more than they love money.

Thank you for taking the time to read my book. I hope you find it entertaining and useful. I hope it helps you unlock your maximum trading potential.

By the way, I plan to publish future updates, fresh trading stories and new lessons, tactics and strategies, exclusively for readers of *Alpha Trader*. If you are interested, please sign up at brentdonnelly.com.

Enjoy.
Brent

alpha ADJECTIVE

the strongest, smartest, highest ranking members of a group.

alpha NOUN

abnormal returns in investing or trading; the edge of a strategy in excess of the broad market or benchmark return.

INTRODUCTION

Trading is a complex, chaotic, loosely-structured game played by the smartest minds and most expensive computers in the world. It is the ultimate puzzle. Few can trade at an elite level for an extended period. The game is constantly changing and the rules, mechanics and probabilities are difficult to observe and forever in flux. Just when you think you've got a plan: BAM.

You get punched in the mouth.

Trading is hard. Many people do not have the skills or knowledge to consistently make money. Those who do have the skills often cannot monetize them because they are irrational and poorly disciplined. Markets are like a giant battlefield crawling with heavily-armed humans and cyborgs all searching for and fighting over scattered chunks of gold. High-speed and ultra-competitive.

Trading attracts intelligent, driven individuals who see enormous financial rewards and few barriers to entry. But no amount of intelligence or skill is enough if you are irrational, undisciplined, or overconfident. The best analysis is useless if you can't resist the urge to self-destruct.

From the 20-something professional poker player who trades momentum stocks in the back of a casino between tournaments, to the grizzled 60-year-old industry veteran launching a new systematic strategy out of a sleek glass building in bucolic Connecticut, everyone is battling for a slice of the same finite pie. How does a tiny group of traders stay on top and profit, year after year, while most fail? How do you excel in this high-stakes competition? How do you unleash the alpha?

The answer is mindset, methodology, and math.

This book is for traders of every skill and experience level. The kid who just opened a Robinhood account with $100 of birthday money faces many of the same challenges and psychological hurdles as the veteran portfolio manager running billions of dollars of currency risk for a London asset management firm. I have been trading, managing other traders, and mentoring for 25 years. But I still make mistakes. All the time.

Plugging leaks, building on strengths, and neutralizing weaknesses is a lifelong battle.

To write this book, I sifted through thousands of pages of academic research, talked to dozens of veteran traders, and dug through 25 years of my own memories and experience, all in an effort to define the ideal trader. No one can achieve trading perfection; that is not the goal. To achieve excellence, though, we must first identify what perfection looks like, then head in that direction.

This is not a behavioral economics textbook and it is not a boring, theoretical deep dive into trading psychology. It's a practical guide full of actionable information, concisely distilled research, exciting and relevant trading floor stories, and real-life examples that explain and reinforce critical concepts.

Trading involves a deeply personal journey of struggle, continuous adaptation, and self-improvement. The journey never ends because whenever you think you've almost mastered the game, the game changes.

No book can fully describe the individual path that each trader will follow, so take what resonates for you and reject what does not. I am not all-knowing. This book documents the thinking of one person. What works for me is not guaranteed to work for you. As Bruce Lee said:

Research your own experience.
Absorb what is useful, reject what is useless…
… and add what is essentially your own.

Alpha Trader will help you take an honest look at yourself and help you identify your strengths, weaknesses, and edge. The book will explain how irrational behavior and bias are trader kryptonite. It will teach you specific rules, realistic techniques and practical habits that will help you evolve into a more successful and profitable trader.

Be rational and self-aware. Learn, improve, and grow. Unleash the Alpha.

• • •

My goal is to keep this book as punchy and practical as possible. Here is how it is structured:

Part One digs into the equation that determines success or failure in trading. I review the research and my own experience and try to find the general equation for trading success. When you read Part One, think about where you match up or diverge from the Alpha Trader profile. This section is a short look at the general recipe for success before we dig into the specific ingredients.

Part Two goes into more depth as I unpack the specific qualities of winning and losing traders. I hope you will identify some of these winning traits and kryptonite in your own character and learn from the strategies I present to build on strengths and iron out weaknesses. Part Two ends with a look at how smart people do stupid things and provides a ton of examples and perspective on trader bias.

Part Three is the most fun. There, we will talk about how to become an expert in your product and how to achieve sustainable, long-term professional trading success. We dig deep into topics like microstructure, market narrative, technical analysis, sentiment and positioning, self-discipline, and risk management. Then, we spend a chapter bringing it all together with a detailed walkthrough of a real trade, giving you a direct look into my thought process from start to finish. By the end of Part Three, you will have detailed knowledge of how I structure trades and you can use that knowledge to develop or improve your own methodology.

Finally, Part Four is all about healthy mindset. There, I write about how you can adapt and continuously improve with a focus on self-awareness, perspective, and metacognition.

Now that you have an overview of how the book is structured, let's go!

PART ONE

WHY DO SOME
TRADERS SUCCEED,
BUT MOST FAIL?

Part One is a quick look at success in general and at success in trading more specifically. We start with a look inward as I ask you to evaluate yourself and establish a baseline of your current strengths and weaknesses as a trader. In Chapter 2, we look at how incredibly difficult it is to achieve lasting trading success. Chapter 3 is a scan of the research on success in the world outside of trading. Then, in Chapter 4, we take this information and study the research on trading to solve for the more specific equation of trading success.

As you read Part One, think about where you match up or diverge from the Alpha Trader profile, and take notes. The point of Part One is to study, understand and define the factors that lead to trading success and then start an iterative process where you repeatedly learn, plan, execute, analyze, and improve to get there.

CHAPTER 1

KNOW YOURSELF

Good traders are introspective and self-aware

I n trading, the enemy is not bad luck. It's not other traders, or the market. The enemy is not the algos or the central banks or the goldbugs or sales or your manager or the HODLers or Dave Portnoy or QE. When it comes to trading, enemy number one is you.

Know the enemy and know yourself.
SUN TZU

I like that Sun Tzu quote for Chapter One of a book about trading because it has a cool circularity. In trading, the enemy and the self are one.

**You will not succeed in trading
without self-awareness and discipline.**

The biggest challenge in trading is not choosing what asset class to trade, or when to buy and sell, or what percentage of your capital to risk on each trade. The biggest challenge in trading is to manage your *self*. You are a bundle of emotions, memories, history, knowledge, and bias. You can be smart and do stupid things. You can make a hard job impossible by making irrational and compulsive decisions.

The first step toward becoming a better trader is to get a firm handle on who you are right now. Therefore, before we delve into what makes a successful trader, I want you to complete a quick quiz. It will help you set a personal baseline and take an inventory of your attributes. It will give you a snapshot of how you see yourself as a trader before we jump in.

DO THE QUIZ NOW! Don't be lazy. It will take you five minutes or less.

Instructions

Rate yourself in each category of the trader assessment below by putting an X in the appropriate box in each row. Be honest. Don't think about your best or worst moments. Your answers should reflect how you see yourself as a trader on an average day. Do the test privately without any chance of your boss or co-workers seeing. Otherwise, you may be tempted to stretch the truth or exaggerate your positive traits.

If you have never traded before, that's fine. Most people have a pretty good idea of their likely strengths and weaknesses even before they start trading, so just fill out how you see yourself, or how you think you will act as a trader. Don't think about your ideal self; just record the current reality. Sure, there will be some bias and uncertainty and subjectivity and probably overconfidence as you complete the grid. That's fine. Just do your best.

Trader self-assessment

		1	2	3	4	5	6	7	8	9	10	
Risk averse	A											Risk seeking
Not very confident	B											Extremely confident
Firmly held opinions	C											Intellectually flexible
Contrarian	D											Tend to follow others
		1	2	3	4	5	6	7	8	9	10	
Impulsive	E											Rational
Can snap under stress	F											Copes with high stress
Poor self-control	G											Excellent willpower
Average math skill	H											Quantitative superstar
Procrastinator	I											Doer
Loves money	J											Loves trading
Acts on gut feel	K											Acts on logic
Rarely positive	L											Always positive
		1	2	3	4	5	6	7	8	9	10	
Lucky	M											Unlucky
Limitless energy	N											Often exhausted
Highly creative	O											Average imagination
I control my life	P											I don't control my life
Decisive	Q											Hesitant
Adapts well to change	R											Not great with change
Focused	S											Scattered
Always very curious	T											Not all that curious
Organized	U											Disorganized
Trading experience	V											No trading experience
		1	2	3	4	5	6	7	8	9	10	
Highly emotional	W											Robotic
Loner	X											Social
Masculine	Y											Feminine
Introvert	Z											Extrovert

You may have noticed something when filling out the quiz: The traits are arranged in a specific way. Each of the four sections has its own logic.

Here is how the groups are arranged:

Group 1 (A to D): These traits are on a continuum where both extremes are bad. You need a lot—but not too much—of many traits to succeed in trading. For example, an Alpha Trader must be risk seeking but not reckless. She must be confident but not overconfident. She must be nimble but not constantly changing her mind. An independent thinker but not a reflexive contrarian.

Finding the fine balance is part of what makes trading so hard. Too careful and you'll never make any money. Not careful enough, you'll blow up. It is hard for many to find the middle ground on the continuum of particular attributes.

Group 2 (E to L): Successful traders tend to score on the high end (right hand side) of this scale.

Group 3 (M to V): Successful traders tend to score on the low end (left hand side) of this scale.

Group 4 (W to Z): These traits influence you as a trader but there is no strictly better place to land on the scale.

Now let's look at the ideal trader. Keep in mind, this ideal trader does not exist. This is an abstraction to help you see where you are vs. the ideal. Also keep in mind that I am not the holder of absolute truth on this topic. I have decades of experience and I have done extensive research on this topic but it is possible for reasonable people to disagree about the importance of many of these personality traits as they pertain to trading success. The research is not conclusive; in fact, it's often contradictory.

For example, the research on the importance of gut feel in trading is all over the place. Much of it uses experiments with small sample sizes to make general but unconvincing conclusions. Some of it uses methodology that I find uninspired. The fact that the research on gut feel in trading is mixed probably tells you something about the relative importance of gut feel. Unlike rational thinking, which all research deems to be critically important, gut feel is less clearly an important part of trading success.

In fact, relying on your gut can often be detrimental. Intuition can be the aggregation of data and patterns processed at a subconscious level to reach useful conclusions, or it can be a bunch of sloppy heuristics and emotion that produces biased, irrational decisions.

After working on various trading floors for many years and studying the research on trader success and failure, here are my best estimates for the ideal characteristics of the Alpha Trader:

Trader self-assessment

		1	2	3	4	5	6	7	8	9	10	
Risk averse	A							X				Risk seeking
Not very confident	B								X			Extremely confident
Firmly held opinions	C				X							Intellectually flexible
Contrarian	D				X							Tend to follow others
Impulsive	E										X	Rational
Can snap under stress	F										X	Copes with high stress
Poor self-control	G										X	Excellent willpower
Average math skill	H									X		Quantitative superstar
Procrastinator	I										X	Doer
Loves money	J										X	Loves trading
Acts on gut feel	K									X		Acts on logic
Rarely positive	L								X			Always positive
Lucky	M	X										Unlucky
Limitless energy	N	X										Often exhausted
Highly creative	O			X								Average imagination
I control my life	P	X										I don't control my life
Decisive	Q			X								Hesitant
Adapts well to change	R	X										Not great with change
Focused	S			X								Scattered
Always very curious	T	X										Not all that curious
Organized	U	X										Disorganized
Trading experience	V	X										No trading experience
Highly emotional	W							X				Robotic
Loner	X							X				Social
Masculine	Y							X				Feminine
Introvert	Z					X						Extrovert

How do your scores match up to the Alpha Trader? Where do your scores diverge? Does this divergence concern you or does it make perfect sense? Some divergences might be worrisome, and some might just identify how you are unique. Remember, this is a thought experiment not a math problem.

Each trait will be discussed more fully later on, so I will not take a lot of time explaining them here. I'll give you just enough to satisfy your curiosity since I'm sure you're wondering about a few of my answers.

A: Risk seeking is a natural fit for trading, but too much leads to recklessness and ruin.

B: Confidence is good, but overconfidence is kryptonite.

C: "Strong opinions, weakly held." If you don't know this concept, don't worry. We'll cover it in Chapter 5.

D: You need to think for yourself but not reflexively go against the crowd. The crowd is correct more often, and for longer, than many contrarians expect.

E: Rational, high-quality thinking is the #1 characteristic of an Alpha Trader.

F: Trading is stressful. Can you handle it?

G: Self-control and willpower are critical. Making rules is easy. Sticking to them is hard.

H: Trading is a quantitative game full of estimated probability, hidden mathematics, and incomplete information. Math and statistics knowledge are a huge edge.

I: Trading is hard. Simply doing the work is a big advantage in a world where even professional traders can sometimes be lazy.

J: A passion for trading is the motivation that will lead you to success: not a passion for money. Trading is too hard and too grueling to do just for the money.

K: Logic trumps gut feel most of the time.

L: Losing streaks and big losses hurt. A positive attitude helps you bounce back when you inevitably hit a rough patch. A negative outlook can pull you into a downward spiral when markets inevitably fail to cooperate.

M: Good traders seem to be luckier than bad traders. *Hmmm.*

N: Trading is a marathon. You need endurance to keep running.

O: One edge in markets is to look at the world differently than others. But if you are extremely creative, you may find that trading is not a good enough outlet for that creativity.

P: The Trading Gods are not pushing the market against you. The more you believe that you are in control of your life, the better your odds of trading success.

Q: Traders need to be decisive, but extreme decisiveness may border on impulsiveness and that can lead to overconfidence and overtrading.

R: Adapt or die. Markets are always changing. Can you keep up?

S: Trading in the zone requires focus. But you need to be able to multi-task a bit as well. Singular focus is not usually possible in trading as you must toggle between various markets, reading research, monitoring Twitter, and actual trading activity.

T: Curiosity leads to learning. Learning makes you more knowledgeable. Superior knowledge is an edge.

U: An organized trader has a clear process. She collects data and approaches the task of trading methodically. That's a good thing!

V: Nothing beats experience. If you never make the same mistake twice, you won't make many mistakes after 20 years.

W: Emotion is not a good or bad thing in trading. All kinds of emotional types can succeed in finance. That said, emotion and irrational behavior tend to go together so if you're emotional you need to be unusually self-aware, too.

X: There are some advantages to having a network of contacts but a trader can easily succeed completely on his own.

Y: A wide body of research shows women perform better at trading than men. This is mostly because men trade more than women due to overconfidence.

Z:　Extroverts and introverts might have different styles but neither one is better or worse at trading.

Your scores on the quiz should take you one small or perhaps medium-sized step closer to self-awareness. Self-knowledge comes from experience and from data, but it can also come from focused introspection.

Keep in mind that you are probably overconfident in your self-assessment. Whatever grades you gave yourself are probably somewhat inflated relative to reality because human beings pretty much always overrate themselves. In a survey I conducted in 2016, for example (see figure 1.1), 70% of traders said they were better than average while just 5% rated themselves worse than average. Not possible! You are almost certainly not quite as good as you think you are.

Men are especially prone to overconfidence. But even if you overrated yourself on every positive variable in this quiz, the relative distinctions you make

Figure 1.1: Results of a survey I conducted in 2016

Question: How would you compare yourself to others in your role?

Sample size = 319

between traits (not the absolute numbers you assign) are the most important thing. This will reveal your strengths, expose some weaknesses, and help you find avenues for continuous improvement.

The harsh reality of trading is that it is insanely difficult (but not impossible!) to succeed. If you have been trading for a while, you have a good sense of the enormous challenge presented by trading. If you are new here, I want to give you a realistic view of the success rate.

Success in trading is only possible for a small group of individuals, but those individuals are rewarded with an incredible adventure and extraordinary financial upside. The more worthwhile and lucrative a goal is in this world, the harder the achievement of the goal is likely to be. Trading certainly fits that relationship. It is a business with an extremely high level of difficulty but massive reward potential.

Now that you have taken a few minutes to think about your trader personality, let's head to Chapter 2 and look at just how difficult it is to achieve persistent trading success.

IF IT WAS EASY, IT WOULDN'T PAY SO WELL

*Research shows success in trading is
hard to achieve and harder to sustain*

Trading for a living is like becoming a pro athlete or a famous author or a professional poker player. There are few barriers to entry and no specific credentials are required. And the financial rewards are potentially astronomical. Anyone can dream of making it big in these fields. But only a tiny fraction of those who go after the dream will succeed at any point. An even smaller fraction will achieve sustained success over many decades. The goal of this book is to help you become one of the very few who thrives—and survives.

Intelligence and drive are the keys to success in most business pursuits, but this is not strictly true in trading. Intelligence and drive are necessary, but not sufficient conditions for trading success.

Many people think of trading as a zero-sum game and that makes them feel optimistic. Since almost everyone believes themselves to be better than average in almost all pursuits, the thought is that if something is a zero-sum game, all you have to do is be better than the next guy to win. *Wrong.*

Trading is a negative sum game.

When I was day trading equities, most traders were gross positive and net negative in most periods. They could take money out of the market, but not enough to cover their brokerage, bid/offer spread and other slippage. Transaction costs and slippage are a significant drag for traders at every level.

Therefore, you need a significant edge to not only make money, but also to make enough money to exceed execution, technology, and operational costs. Further, grinding out tiny profits still isn't enough. There is so much risk and uncertainty involved in trading that for it to make any sense, you need to significantly exceed the income you could make in a lower risk profession. The bar for success in trading is high.

WHAT PERCENTAGE OF TRADERS SUCCEED?

The word "succeed" can mean many things, but based on various metrics, my conclusion from the research and my own observation over the years is that the success rate for independent day traders is probably between 3% and 5%. For institutional traders, the success rate is much, much higher because:

- there are many barriers to entry that one must overcome before earning a role on an institutional trading desk so the pool of entrants is much more highly qualified and well-vetted than a random selection of independent traders;

- traders at a bank receive significant training and are surrounded by experienced mentors; and

- market making has a built-in edge which gives new traders at a bank more runway.

In my experience, of all the individuals who manage to get one of the few trading seats available at a bank, about 50% succeed as traders. I define "succeed" as: still employed and profitable three years after starting.

For traders at a hedge fund, the success rate is higher than retail but lower than bank traders. Most hedge funds don't have elaborate training programs or the edge from market making that banks do, but most traders hired by hedge funds already have substantial experience, so the sample is biased. You are usually already successful by the time you get a job at a hedge fund.

Cory Mitchell of day trading firm Vantage Point Trading wrote a nice blog post on this topic[1]. He defined success as "producing consistent profits for

---

1. https://vantagepointtrading.com/whats-the-day-trading-success-rate-the-thorough-answer/

multiple years" and after studying a meaningful sample size he estimated the observed success rate at Vantage Point was between 3.5% and 4.5%.

When I worked as a day trader in Toronto in the late 1990s, the success rate was about the same. I sat on a trading floor that held 50 people and almost the entire floor turned over three times in the three years I was there. Anyone that lasted, I got to know well because we spent so much time together in the office.

Of the ~150 traders that came and went, 8 made money consistently for two years or more. Most bombed out in three to six months and the remainder struggled for one or two years but could never grind out enough money to call it a job. 8 out of 150 is 5.3%, and that low success rate came despite a mandatory (and excellent) 2-week training course.

The low success rate makes sense and is roughly consistent with success rates in other sought-after skill-based professions with low barriers to entry such as fiction writing and pro sports. About 2.6% of published books sell more than 5,000 copies[2]. 3% to 7% of high school athletes make the NCAA in most sports while about 2% of NCAA athletes go pro[3].

If you're new to trading, you need to understand going in that the success rate is low. You will need a ton of innate skill, the energy to work hard every single day and rare levels of perseverance to have any chance whatsoever. It's not a matter of flicking through a few charts, drawing a couple of trendlines or using some automated *Charty McChart Chart POWERIndicator*™.

Brad Barber, Yi-Sung Lee, Terrence Odean, Ke Zhang and Yu-Jane Liu studied this topic in a 2017 research paper: "Do individual day traders make money? Evidence from Taiwan." Day trading was extremely popular in Taiwan in the late 1990s (as it was in many other countries). 20% of all trading volume in Taiwanese stocks at that time was attributable to individual day traders.

Here are the takeaways from their study:

- One percent of individual investors accounted for half of day trading volume in Taiwan.

- Heavy day traders made gross profits but not enough to cover transaction costs and thus they were net negative P&L.

---

2. https://www.publishersweekly.com/pw/by-topic/columns-and-blogs/soapbox/article/6153-a-bookselling-tail.html

3. http://www.ncaa.org/about/resources/research/estimated-probability-competing-college-athletics

- Over any particular 6-month period, 8 out of 10 day traders lost money.

- A small group of day traders had persistent ability to generate net profit, in excess of transaction costs.

- Many traders sustained losses for long periods before quitting.

- About 1% of traders generated consistent profits through skill.

This quote from an article about the study captures the long odds of success they uncovered[4]:

> The vast, vast majority of day traders were losing money. Unless you really had a strong reason to think that your ability to day trade was much greater than that of most people, it made no sense to start day trading in the first place. It'd be like, to some extent, going into a casino and saying I'm really good at roulette; even though I know everyone else loses money at roulette, I'm going to win.

For the record, professional investors have a very low success rate too. Here's a typical stat, from a January 2020 Financial Times article[5]: "Just 28 per cent of US equity fund managers investing in large companies managed to beat the US stock market last year, and over the past decade a mere 11 per cent managed to do so, according to Bank of America." This result emerges in study after study.

A random group of unskilled investors should beat the market 50% of the time. Yet a significant majority of investors consistently underperform a simple index or benchmark. Solving for how to generate alpha in highly-efficient markets is one of the toughest puzzles on earth.

Markets are extremely (but not perfectly) efficient.

Knowing that success in trading is rare, let's look at how to achieve it. The next chapter is twenty pages or so. It's a short discussion of the research on success in general. Then, in Chapter 4, we will apply these lessons about achievement in general to the more specific subject of trading success.

---

4. https://www.aaii.com/journal/article/trading-more-frequently-leads-to-worse-returns

5. https://www.ft.com/content/a7e20d96-318c-11ea-9703-eea0cae3f0de

CHAPTER 3

UNDERSTANDING SUCCESS

*Success and high performance
in the world outside of trading*

This short chapter will give you some background on the main determinants of success in the world in general, outside of trading. Since trading is both a business and a skilled pursuit, it is worth doing a quick review of what leads to success in similar fields, before we zoom in on trading more specifically in Chapter 4.

Success is a squishy noun that can mean different things to different people. Most research frames success in terms of one or more of the following:

- Income
- Educational achievement
- Ranking or achievement in sport
- Happiness, health, and longevity
- Avoidance of negative outcomes like criminality, addiction, and divorce

We'll focus on the first three since those are the outcomes that relate most closely to trading. Let's look at some measures and characteristics of personality and how they relate to success.

Figure 3.1: The relationship between IQ and income

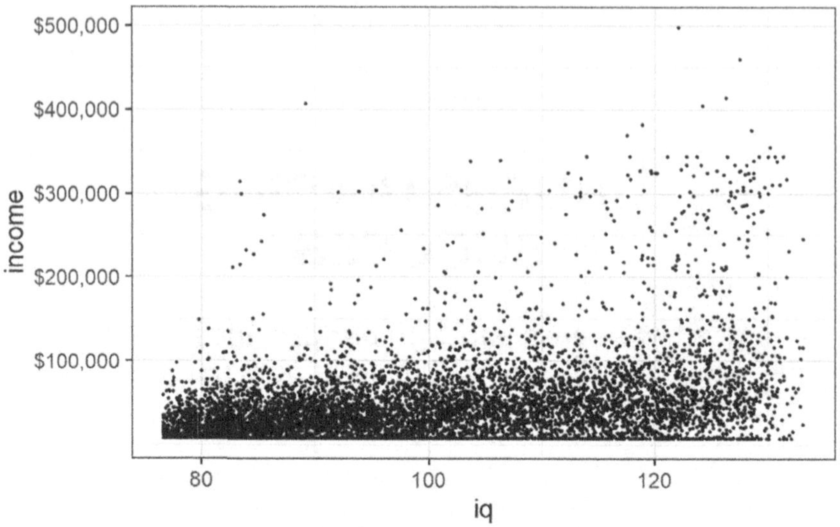

This and next two images courtesy of Jonatan Pallesen
https://jsmp.dk/posts/2019-06-16-talebiq/

IQ (Intelligence Quotient)

IQ is a controversial topic in the world of psychology and there is heated debate over what exactly it measures. This quote captures a few of the shortcomings of IQ, in simple language:

> Just to clear the air, let's note first that whatever an intelligence test measures it is not quite the same thing as we usually mean by intelligence. It neglects such important things as leadership and creative imagination. It takes no account of social judgement or musical or artistic or other aptitudes, to say nothing of such personality matters as diligence and emotional balance.
>
> **DARRELL HUFF,** How to Lie with Statistics

There is plenty of controversy when researchers try to correlate IQ with various measures of success. It is hard to control for all the other factors that go into whatever form of success one is trying to measure. That said, most research finds some link between IQ and success. For example, an excellent paper by Jay Zagorsky of Boston University[6] comes to this conclusion:

---

6. Jay Zagorsky, "Do you have to be smart to be rich?" (Elsevier, 2007)

... results confirm other researchers' findings that IQ test scores and income are related. Depending on the method of analysis used and specific factors held constant, each point increase in IQ test scores is associated with $202 to $616 more income per year. This means the average income difference between a person with an IQ score in the normal range (100) and someone in the top 2% of society (130) is currently between $6,000 and $18,500 per year.

Figure 3.1 from data blogger Jonatan Pallesen shows the relationship between IQ and income using 10 years of data.

You can see the relationship slopes up and to the right and the very high incomes are much more common in the top right quadrant than in the top left quadrant. If we are defining success as income, IQ is an important predictor.

Figure 3.2 offers a nice clear visual. Pallesen breaks IQ into three groups (low, middle, high) to show how the median and right tails of the income distribution relate to IQ:

Figure 3.2: The distribution of incomes for low, median, and high IQs

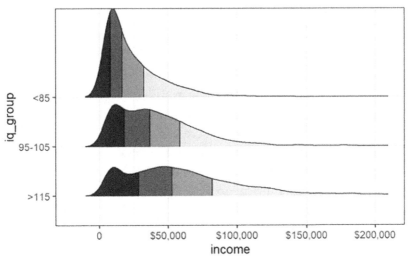

Source: https://jsmp.dk/posts/2019-06-16-talebiq/

IQ also correlates with most other measures of success like mortality, longevity, crime and (somewhat obviously) academic grades:

I included a chart of academic grades vs. IQ (Figure 3.3) so you can see that even a measure of success directly connected to IQ (doing well in school) still

Figure 3.3: Academic Grades and IQ

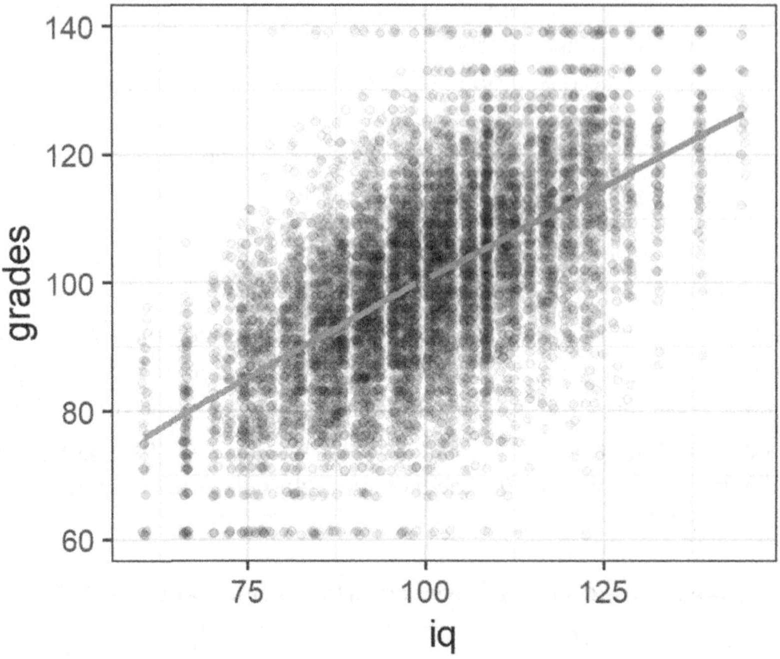

Source: https://jsmp.dk/posts/2019-06-16-talebiq/

has significant volatility around the trend line. There are plenty of high IQ students with poor grades and low IQ students with good grades. Academic success depends on far more than intelligence.

After IQ, the next big driver of success is personality. There is so much research on the connections between personality and life outcomes that no individual could process it all in one lifetime. In the next few pages, I will do my best to succinctly summarize some of the key relationships between personality and success.

The Big Five

Most studies of personality and its impact on life outcomes use the Big Five Personality Traits[7]. These are the five personality traits that dominate the literature on personality. The five traits use common language descriptors to classify

---

7. You can take a free Big Five test here: https://openpsychometrics.org/tests/IPIP-BFFM/. It is not an adware or promotional site, it's just the test. There is another slightly different one here: https://projects.fivethirtyeight.com/personality-quiz/.

people on five key domains. These five domains incorporate nearly all aspects of human personality, and extensive research shows that these five factors explain the majority of human character. The model is sometimes known as OCEAN because the five traits are:

- **Openness to experience** (*inventive/curious* **vs.** *consistent/cautious*)

- **Conscientiousness** (*efficient/organized* **vs.** *easy-going/careless*)

- **Extraversion** (*outgoing/energetic* **vs.** *solitary/reserved*)

- **Agreeableness** (*friendly/compassionate* **vs.** *challenging/detached*)

- **Neuroticism** (*sensitive/nervous* **vs.** *secure/confident*)

The Big Five is better than Myers-Briggs (MBTI) according to nearly all researchers and psychologists because it is scientific and repeatable. In contrast, Myers-Briggs was created in the 1920s by non-experts without any scientific process or empirical inputs. MBTI often yields two different results for the same person, even if the person takes the test twice in a short span of time.

MBTI is fun and may have some practical applications, but it has no empirical or scientific basis. As Wharton psychology professor Adam Grant says in his Psychology Today article, Goodbye to MBTI, the fad that won't die[8]:

> If we're going to divide people into categories, those categories ought to be meaningful. In social science, we use four standards: Are the categories reliable, valid, independent, and comprehensive? For the MBTI, the evidence says: Not very, no, no, and not really.

Scientists and experts strongly prefer the Big Five to MBTI so that is what we'll use here.

Each Big Five trait runs on a continuum. The five traits capture most or all aspects of human personality, and there are many facets or more specific traits that fall under each heading. Some of these traits are more relevant to us than others. For example, I want to highlight grit and self-control as critical facets under the heading of conscientiousness, because those are important in trading.

Grit captures characteristics like perseverance, resilience, ambition, and the pursuit of long-term goals. Multiple studies show that grit is highly correlated

---

8. https://www.psychologytoday.com/us/blog/give-and-take/201309/goodbye-mbti-the-fad-won-t-die

with conscientiousness[9] so it falls under that heading, but I think it is specifically important to trading and thus worth mentioning separately. Same story with self-control, which has a lower correlation with conscientiousness than grit, but still falls in the same bucket[10]. We will discuss these more later.

Most research shows that the Big Five traits are fairly stable over a person's lifetime. There is just one trait that changes significantly over the lifetime of an average person: conscientiousness. There is a steady and meaningful rise in conscientiousness as we age. Figure 3.4, made with data provided by Christopher Soto, paints the picture[11].

Remember though, this is an average. Averages camouflage the substantial variance within a sample. Conscientiousness evolves differently in specific individuals over time. Some people will massively increase their conscientiousness as they grow. Some will flatline their entire life or even become less conscientious.

Figure 3.4: Conscientiousness by age (average of male and female scores)

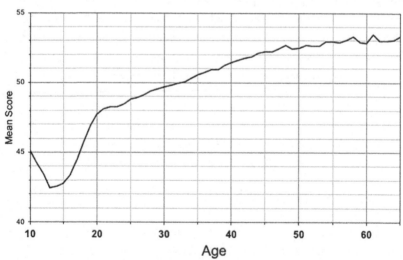

Image: Donnelly, data provided by Christopher Soto

9. For example, Rimfeld et. al 2016 shows the proportion of variance that grit and conscientiousness share due to genetic causes is 0.86 https://www.ncbi.nlm.nih.gov/pmc/articles/PMC4981570/

10. See: Deborah Cobb-Clark et al., "Self-Control: Determinants, Life Outcomes and Intergenerational Implications", *IZA Discussion Paper Series* 2019 and Kaitlin Werner et al., "Grit, Self-Control and Conscientiousness", (2020)

11. Christopher Soto et al., "Age Differences in Personality Traits from 10 to 65", Journal of Personality and Social Psychology (2011). Thank you, Chris, for generously sharing your data.

Untangling the connections between the Big Five traits and future success is incredibly complex because of the need to control for so many other factors (parental income, birthplace, sex, education, cross-correlation between the traits themselves, etc.) but the multitude of studies on the Big Five converge on some consistent conclusions[12].

THE BIG FIVE AND FINANCIAL SUCCESS

Income has a strong positive correlation with conscientiousness and extraversion. It has a weak negative relationship with agreeableness and neuroticism. Openness results look inconclusive to me as they have a negative coefficient in some studies and a positive coefficient in others.

Figure 3.5, an excellent diagram from Miriam Gensowski's 2014 paper, shows how she found the Big Five influenced men's incomes, by age.

As one might expect, neuroticism correlates with many negative outcomes including lower income and higher incidence of mental disorder and general health problems. Note that the negative impact of neuroticism on income is not large.

Agreeableness, perhaps surprisingly, shows up in more than a half-dozen research papers as a *negative* influence on income. It consistently reduces average earnings by 2%-6%[13]. Being nice doesn't pay!

Besides the simple linear relationship between personality and income, the fit between a job and the personality of the employee also matters. Linear regression gives a brute force look at how personality influences income, but a more nuanced approach is to match a worker's personality to an expert's views on what personality traits are necessary in that person's job. Research shows that a good fit between a person and their job leads to higher income for the worker[14].

This last observation is important when we think about trading. Knowing that job / personality fit is an important driver of income, we will spend some time in Chapter 4 looking at how the Big Five relate to trading success. This will help you understand if your personality is a good fit with trading and where you might need to monitor a potential personality mismatch.

---

12. Miriam Gensowski, "Personality, IQ and lifetime earnings" (2014).

13. Braakmann 2009; Denissen, Bleidorn and Hennecke 2018; Heineck 2007; Nandi and Nikoletti 2014; Mueller and Plug 2006; Judge, Livingston, and Hurst 2012; Nyhus and Pons 2005.

14. Jaap Denissen et al., "Uncovering the power of personality to shape income" (2017).

Figure 3.5: The Direct Effect of Personality and IQ on earnings (men)

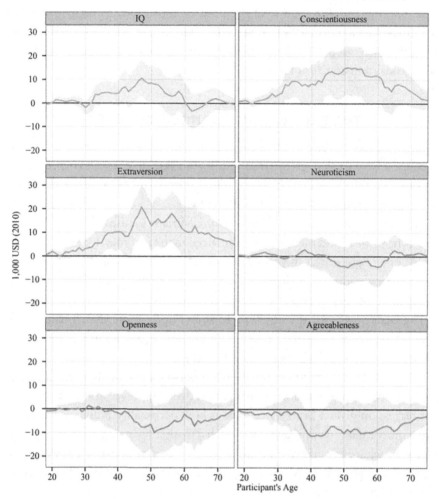

To summarize, here is how the Big Five personality traits relate to income:

Trait	Correlation with income
Openness	None
Conscientiousness	Strong positive
Extraversion	Small positive
Agreeableness	Moderate negative
Neuroticism	Small negative

Obviously, income is just one way to measure success. Let's look at two others.

Success in sports

Athletic competition is similar to trading in many ways. Sports and trading both present fast-moving, high-pressure environments with quick decision-making and (usually) incomplete information. They present a competitive atmosphere with well-defined rules, objective numerical feedback, and clear winners and losers.

In sport, the trait that consistently correlates with high performance is, once again, conscientiousness. This finding is consistent across many papers[15] and pushes conscientiousness to the top of the charts in terms of our best guess of what might matter for trading at this point. If conscientiousness leads to higher income and better performance in sports, it is logical to think it matters for trading too.

Academic success

Academic environments also have some similarity to trading. School and trading both generally present intellectually challenging, problem-solving environments where feedback is immediate and objective (academic grades = P&L[16]). Once again, the number one trait that correlates with academic performance is conscientiousness. And once again, neuroticism correlates negatively.

It is worth mentioning here that academic grades and test scores are a better predictor of career and social success than IQ[17]. This is because outcomes like grades and test scores are a combination of not just intelligence, but also hard work, conscientiousness, grit, self-control, and perseverance. Intelligence is a necessary but not sufficient condition for good grades, high test scores and future success. IQ by itself is not enough.

While the Big Five also have some predictive power when it comes to happiness, health, mortality, divorce, criminality and other facets of life, those realms are not measures of success that are as relevant to trading. We know how the

---

15. Examples: Tran 2012, which looked at American football rankings vs. the Big Five; Allen, et al 2011, which looked at athlete coping and performance vs. the Big Five; and Fasold et al. 2019 which showed a relationship between conscientiousness and handball goalkeeper performance.

16. P&L stands for profit and loss, the ultimate measure of trading success.

17. https://www.independent.co.uk/news/science/personality-iq-success-wealth-factors-determining-prospects-intelligence-careers-james-heckman-a7880376.html

Big Five predict income, sports performance, and academic success, three outcomes that I believe are correlated to trading success. The overall results are clear:

- Conscientiousness is the most important positive predictor of success.
- IQ is also an important positive predictor.
- Neuroticism is a less important, negative predictor of success.

Of course, we have only looked at innate traits so far. Another way of looking at success is to isolate effort or hard work. Most research on performance breaks down success into some combination of talent, skill, and effort. You can't just be smart and talented, you need to do the work. We will go into that concept later but for now we can file "effort" under "conscientiousness".

Another important variable when it comes to success is environment. Kids that grow up in supportive environments, like athletes with world-class coaches, perform better. This is relevant to trading too, and we will discuss the importance of a healthy trading environment later on. I have been in both the right trading environment and the wrong trading environment at various points in my career, and my belief is that trading is so difficult that it becomes almost impossible if you are not in a supportive setting.

Finally, luck is an extremely important contributor to success in any specific activity and in life overall. Many successful people do not fully appreciate or acknowledge the significant role luck played in their success. As E. B. White put it: "Luck is not something you can mention in the presence of self-made men."

Some examples of how luck influences success:

- More than 50% of the difference in income between any human being on earth is determined by where they were born[18]. As Warren Buffett put it:

  "Through dumb luck, Charlie and I were born in the United States, and we are forever grateful for the staggering advantages this accident of birth has given us."
  WARREN BUFFETT'S *2014 Shareholder Letter*

---

18. Branco Milanovic, "Global Inequality of Opportunity: How much of our income is determined by where we live?", (2015).

- People born in June and July are significantly less likely to become CEOs due to the relative age effect[19]. Schools group children together by age, regardless of their birth month, and the cutoff for most schools is July 31. Therefore, children born in June and July are disadvantaged through life because they are younger than their classmates born in other months and are perceived to be less mature, less intelligent, and lower potential than their peers.

- How about this completely insane true story from the early days of FedEx[20]:

  > By mid-July our funds were so meager that on Friday we were down to about $5,000 in the checking account, while we needed $24,000 for the jet fuel payment... When I arrived back in Memphis on Monday morning, much to my surprise, the bank balance stood at nearly $32,000. I asked Fred where the funds had come from, and he responded, "The meeting with the General Dynamics board was a bust and I knew we needed money for Monday, so I took a plane to Las Vegas and won $27,000 (playing blackjack)." I said, "You mean you took our last $5,000—how could you do that?" He shrugged his shoulders and said, "What difference does it make? Without the funds for the fuel companies, we couldn't have flown anyway."

- People born earlier in the year outperform those born later in the year in almost every sport where this has been studied. The foreground bars in Figure 3.6 show month of birth distribution for elite youth soccer players in Europe, with overall month of birth data for the entire population as the background bars.

Many simulations and studies show that luck plays an enormous role in success, especially in cases of extreme success. While moderate success can often be explained mostly by skill, effort and talent, extreme success usually also requires significant good luck.

While you cannot control luck, remember that effort and skill determine the slope of your life's path, even if luck determines the starting point and variance around that path. As Abraham Lincoln said: "The harder I work, the luckier

19. Du, Gao and Levi, "The Relative Age Effect and Career Success: Evidence from Corporate CEOs" (2012).

20. Robert Frock, "Changing how the world does business" (2006).

Figure 3.6: Month of birth distribution for players in qualifying teams for UEFA U17, U19 and U21 tournaments in 2010/11.

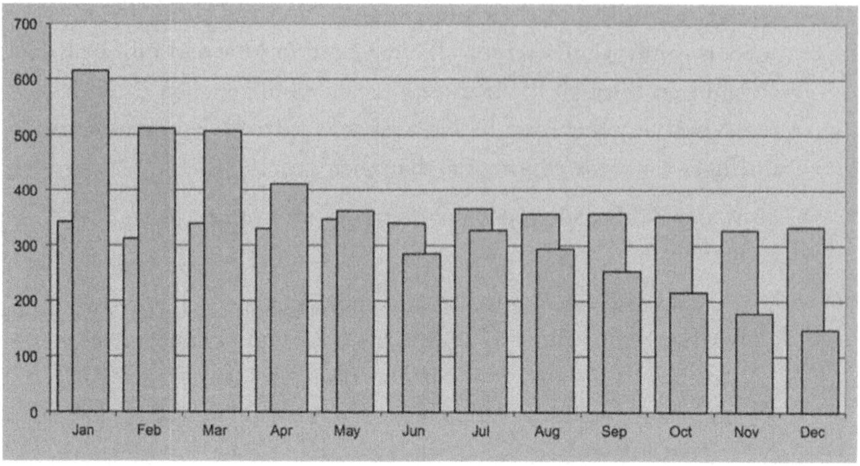

Image by Chemical287 via Creative Commons

I get." We will discuss this more in Chapter 15 and you will see that some of what we tend to call luck is more just a matter of being observant and seizing on opportunities that present themselves.

Fortunately, most varieties of luck are short-term and mean-reverting. The larger the sample, the more luck disappears and the true nature of a phenomenon is revealed. A coin might come up heads 10 times in a row but it's not going to come up heads 500,000 times in a row. A bad trader might make money 3 days in a row but she is unlikely to be profitable in any given year. A weak poker player might beat a professional in a one-hour session but he will go bust in a marathon cash game.

This discussion is important because luck plays a major role in trading. It operates through multiple channels like short-term variance and path dependence. In the Flash Crash story at the start of this book, there were multiple instances where the trader got lucky and if you re-ran that Flash Crash USD-JPY scenario a million times, there would be plenty of instances where the trader came out deep in the red.

What seems like luck in life is often just careful observation and the ability to capitalize on opportunity. Richard Wiseman, who has spent years researching luck, set up a variety of interesting experiments to show that luck is not really luck. In one experiment, he placed a $20-dollar bill on the ground in the path of students and found that those that self-identified as lucky were much more likely to notice and pick up the $20 bill than the others.

In another study, Wiseman gave volunteers a newspaper and told them to count the number of photos inside. On the second page, in large font, there was a box that said: "Stop counting—there are 43 photographs in this newspaper." Another box halfway through the paper read: "Stop counting, tell the experimenter you have seen this and win $250." Those who identified as lucky took just seconds to return their answer while those who viewed themselves as unlucky spent more than two minutes counting all the photos. Other studies reveal the same thing: What we perceive as luck is often just a combination of good observation skill and the ability to seize unexpected opportunities.

It is crucial that you understand the way luck influences trading, and how you can manage and reduce the negative impact of various forms of luck. This is discussed in Chapter 11.

Conscientiousness and neuroticism

Before we move on to Chapter 4, I want to talk a bit more about conscientiousness and neuroticism because they are most correlated to success, in arenas related to trading.

Neuroticism leads to many negative outcomes. It can be broken down into these facets:

- Irritability
- Insecurity
- Anxiety
- Hostility
- Depression
- Self-consciousness
- Impulsiveness
- Vulnerability

If you score high in any of those traits (they are all sub-traits of neuroticism), think about how you can reduce their presence or impact. Work on these negative traits using meditation, mindfulness, reframing, yoga, professional therapy, self-reflection, and other techniques. Neuroticism will make it harder for you to achieve your goals.

If neuroticism is kryptonite, conscientiousness is a superpower. Here is a breakdown of the facets or sub-traits that psychologists consider part of conscientiousness[21]:

- Orderliness / order / tidiness
- Industriousness / hard work / energy
- Reliability / responsibility
- Impulse control / self-control
- Decisiveness (opposite of procrastination)
- Persistence / perseverance

With the knowledge that these facets of conscientiousness are major predictors of life success, think about how you can improve in one or more of these areas. This will help you not just as a trader, but as a human being. This is especially true if you are young, because conscientiousness is the trait that can most easily be boosted over time.

My conscientiousness score is OK but not great. I am in the 60th percentile. That said, I have put a lot of work into trying to be more organized, reliable, and persistent. Over the years, I slowly learned that personality traits are not fixed, they can be molded and improved. I probably scored closer to 35 on conscientiousness when I was in my 20s. My self-control has never been great, and it is still not amazing. I accept this and try to work around it. Here are a few ways you can boost your conscientiousness:

1. Don't say things like: "I'm just like that" or "I'm really disorganized" or "That's just who I am" when it comes to conscientiousness. Being organized or on time or proactive is a choice. Think of your mind as plastic, not fixed.

2. Read the book: "Willpower: Rediscovering the Greatest Human Strength", by Roy Baumeister and John Tierney. It is packed with research and anecdotes about how to improve not just your willpower, but your organizational skills and your metacognition. I learned a ton of immediately applicable information from that book, including how to keep my inbox empty. It also taught me how we

---

21. MacCann, Duckworth and Roberts. "Empirical identification of the major facets of Conscientiousness," (2009).

have a finite supply of willpower each day and thus willpower often runs low, especially at night. And the book taught me the importance of Zeigarnik Loops[22].

3. Acknowledge your willpower is not perfect and create systems to protect yourself from this weakness. Create friction in places where you engage in activities you should not. An example of friction is when people turn off their phone while at dinner to avoid checking it. By making it a hassle, you are less likely to perform the habitual or addictive behavior. On the other hand, reduce friction to reinforce desirable habits. For example, if you want to get in shape, don't make yourself decide whether to work out or not each day. Work out every day. And go to bed in your workout gear so you have one less step to take in the morning before working out. When the decision is already made, there is less friction. In trading this means you need to build systems and install processes that protect you from unwanted behaviors like overtrading while working to automate desirable behaviors like stop loss discipline.

4. Set specific and realistic short-term action goals. Instead of saying: "Man, I need to get in shape." Say: "This month, I'm going to eat zero potato chips and work out 15 times."

5. Break long-term or difficult tasks into smaller chunks and focus on doing one chunk at a time. Writing a book is daunting. Writing a few pages is not. If you focus on writing a few pages each day, a few months later you magically have the rough draft of a book. Same thing in trading. Try not to focus on your YTD P&L too much. Come in each day and do your best. Each year is only around 250 trading days. Take them one at a time and do your very best each day. Let the YTD P&L take care of itself.

6. Make lists. Do not expect yourself to remember everything, even if you have an excellent memory. Outsource your memory to a notes app or a piece of paper.

7. Be on time. Even if you don't care about punctuality, many people do. It is rude to show up late for meetings, events, or dinner. It

---

22. Google it when you have time. Zeigarnik loops are interesting.

is sloppy and unprofessional to submit work after a deadline. Even if it doesn't bother you when others are late, forget about your own preferences. Your values around this topic are not the most important thing. Understand that punctuality is part of becoming a more considerate, thoughtful, and conscientious person. It is not OK to say "that's just who I am."

8. Adopt a continuous improvement mindset. You don't need to make huge changes all the time. Instead, be on the constant lookout for tiny improvements you can make that don't require Herculean effort. I try to do this with my daily newsletter, AM/FX. I will look at my charts and see if there is a way to display them a bit more clearly. I will think of new features that might appeal to different readers. I will ask my readers what they like and don't like and try to keep evolving the product through subtle improvements.

9. Learn about inbox zero. It sounds impossible at first, but it's not. Don't be one of those people with 1,431 unread messages who I have to contact three times before I get a reply. That is not good!

10. Turn off notifications for desktop e-mail and turn off nearly all notifications on your phone. You should check your e-mail once per hour or less. It is not that urgent. Each pop-up every time you get an e-mail is a pointless distraction and will take you out of the zone when you are trading. Access your technology when it makes sense to do so; don't be a puppet controlled by your apps.

Remember that most of your traits are not fixed. You can improve and evolve. You can increase your conscientiousness over time.

Conclusion

This chapter looked at research where success is defined as high income, exceptional sports performance, or high academic achievement. On these three measures, all of which have parallels to trading, the formula is:

Success = conscientiousness + IQ + talent/skill + luck - neuroticism

Everybody's story is different but that's the general formula for the overall population. The weighting of each factor varies by individual and over time. Now let's move on to Chapter 4 and see how closely success in the broader world parallels success in trading.

SO YOU'RE SAYING THERE'S A CHANCE?

Why some traders succeed but most fail

You don't need to be a rocket scientist. Investing is not a game where the guy with the 160 IQ beats the guy with a 130 IQ. Rationality is essential.[23]

WARREN BUFFETT

A s you will see in this chapter, that Buffett quote applies to trading too. There is a surprisingly large body of academic literature on trading. It is a profession that is of interest not just to those in finance, but also to psychologists, economists, statisticians, and sociologists. I spent weeks going through all this literature in an effort to find why some traders succeed but most fail.

This is not a formal review of the academic literature on trading success; it is my best effort to boil a ton of research down to a few key conclusions.

I don't want to bore you with superfluous information so I am going to jump straight to the conclusion and then explain it. After poring through all the research on trading success, two critical traits jump out:

1. **Rationality** is the human trait that best predicts trading success. People who are rational and do not jump to quick conclusions using mental shortcuts (heuristics) are more successful in trading. This characteristic can be measured as Rationality Quotient.

---

23. Janet Lowe, Warren Buffett Speaks, (Wiley 2007).

2. **Overconfidence** is the human trait that best predicts trading failure. People who overestimate their ability to outsmart the market perform worst.

Are you rational?

It makes a ton of sense that rational traders outperform those who are not. Good traders study behavioral finance because humans, as a group, act in predictably irrational ways and this predictable irrationality can be exploited for profit. So, by extension it seems reasonable to say that those who do not exhibit this irrationality will outperform.

Rationality can be measured with a simple three-question test called the Cognitive Reflection Test (CRT). More sophisticated tests of rationality are in development as well, such as Keith Stanovich's Comprehensive Assessment of Rational Thinking (CART)[24]. While IQ is meant to measure intelligence and EQ (Emotional Quotient) is meant to measure emotional intelligence, RQ (Rationality Quotient) measures how rational a person is.

RQ and IQ are correlated, but they are not the same thing. A nuanced understanding of probability along with the ability to avoid jumping to the first, most obvious conclusion are critical mental skills possessed by someone with high RQ but not necessarily by someone with high IQ.

Keith Stanovich is at the forefront of rationality research and he puts it this way:

> It is a profound historical irony of the behavioral sciences that the Nobel Prize was awarded for studies of cognitive characteristics (rational thinking skills) that are entirely missing from the most well-known mental assessment device in the behavioral sciences – the intelligence test. Intelligence tests measure important things, but not these – they do not assess the extent of rational thought. This might not be such an omission if it were the case that intelligence was an exceptionally strong predictor of rational thinking. However, research has found that it is a moderate predictor at best and that some rational thinking skills can be quite dissociated from intelligence[25].

24. Keith Stanovich, "The Comprehensive Assessment of Rational Thinking," (2013)

25. https://thepsychologist.bps.org.uk/volume-27/edition-2/what-intelligence-tests-miss

Stanovich and others have conducted a great deal of research on how rationality and intelligence relate and while the two are correlated, there are areas where particular types of rationality are totally uncorrelated to intelligence. For example, highly intelligent people suffer more from confirmation bias than less intelligent people. This is why experts often underperform laymen in tasks where one would expect the expert to outperform. Confident experts have trouble taking in new information if it contradicts their existing view of the world.

Here is more from an excerpt of an interview with Stanovich[26]:

> ... the correlations between measures of intelligence and various tasks from the cognitive psychology literature that measure aspects of rationality are surprisingly low. We use the term "surprisingly" here, because for many years it has been known that virtually all cognitive ability tasks correlate with each other. Indeed, many show quite high correlations. So, being psychologists, the surprise is in the context of this wide and vast cognitive ability literature, which has the technical name "Spearman's positive manifold." This positive manifold—that performance on cognitive tasks tends to correlate, and often quite highly—is more than 100 years old.

> ...Indeed, in restricted samples of educated adults this correlation can be virtually zero on certain tasks in the literature. Most often the correlation is positive, but, again, in light of 100 years of correlations between cognitive ability tasks, the correlations are often surprisingly low.

> Of course, one of the implications of this is that it will not be uncommon to find people whose intelligence and rationality are dissociated. That is, it will not be uncommon to find people with high levels of intelligence and low levels of rationality, and, to some extent, the converse.

There are entire books written about rationality and I will cover many specific forms of bias in Chapter 7, but for now we will review a few important ways that rational thinking differs from irrational thought.

---

26. https://jamiehalesblog.blogspot.com/2010/10/dysrationalia-intelligent-people.html

System 1 vs. System 2 thinking

The two systems concept was developed by Daniel Kahneman and is a major topic in his book "Thinking Fast and Slow".

System 1 (thinking fast) executes quickly without much thought. It is your lizard brain. It tends to be biased because it relies on speed, shortcuts, and heuristics. Speed sacrifices accuracy.

System 2 (thinking slow) requires conscious effort and thought and is less biased. System 2 is more rational than System 1.

Rational thinkers use System 2 more than System 1; they substitute methodical assessment for gut feel. If they use System 1, they follow up and double-check with System 2 afterwards before acting. System 1 is the crazy kid inside you. System 2 is the adult in the room.

Numeracy

Rational thinkers understand numbers.

- Rational thinkers understand probability. Irrational thinkers overestimate the chance of low probability events and underestimate the likelihood of high probability events.

- Irrational thinkers are often fooled by randomness and do not understand the human bias toward seeing patterns where none exist (apophenia).

- Rational thinkers are not influenced by how a problem is framed. If someone tells you there is a 1% chance you will die if you go skydiving, or they tell you there is a 99% chance you will live, you should feel the same about skydiving. In reality, the framing of the information matters and people are more likely to avoid the 1% chance of death and give the thumbs up to the 99% chance of living.

Logic

Rational thinkers act logically and consistently.

- Rational thinking shows consistent preferences. If you like A better than B and B better than C, you should like A better than C. There are many real-world examples where people don't follow this logic. Experiments show that many people do not have consistent preferences and will say they like (for example) bacon more than Skittles and Skittles more than Doritos but will then say they like Doritos more than bacon. This is not rational.

- Biased, irrational thinkers overweight short-term gains and overreact to recent or intense stimuli. When trading news, be aware of recency bias and don't overweight some random news item just because it's yelling at you in RED ALL CAPS on Bloomberg.

- Rational thinkers seek to understand alternative hypotheses, not just their own hypothesis. They accept evidence that contradicts their view. Irrational thinkers overweight confirming evidence and ignore contradictory evidence.

- Rational thinkers are not overconfident. They understand why it is funny that 80% of drivers think they are above average.

This is a short list of some of the differences between rational and irrational thought. There are hundreds of examples, enough to fill many books. We will go in depth on many of these forms of bias later. Now that you have a sense of rational vs. irrational thought patterns and methods, let's look at how to measure rationality.

Testing for rationality

The Cognitive Reflection Test (CRT) measures rationality using just three questions. It is a fairly new test, invented in 2005 by Shane Frederick. Here is one of the three questions[27] (the other two questions appear later in this book):

QUESTION: If it takes 5 machines 5 minutes to make 5 widgets, how long would it take 100 machines to make 100 widgets?

_____ minutes

Did you answer 100 minutes?

The correct answer is five minutes. Each machine makes one widget every five minutes. Therefore 100 machines can make 100 widgets in five minutes. Those who answer quickly use a shortcut to jump to the answer of 100 minutes. Those that use System 2 (slow down!) calculate the correct answer: Five minutes.

There are other, more in-depth rational thinking questionnaires. The CRT

---

27. Shane Frederick. "Cognitive Reflection and Decision Making". *Journal of Economic Perspectives*. (2005).

is valid and reliable but the three questions in the CRT have become somewhat well-known and if you already know about what is essentially a trick question, you are unlikely to answer it incorrectly the second time.

The best explanation for many of the deviations between efficient markets and reality come from the irrational behavior of the human beings interacting in markets. Therefore, one might reasonably assume a connection between rationality and trading.

Now, let's look at highlights from some of the most interesting research on success in trading.

Research Paper 1

"What Makes a Good Trader? On the Role of Quant Skills,
Behavioral Biases and Intuition on Trader Performance" (2015)
BRICE CORGNET, MARK DESANTIS, AND DAVID PORTER

This paper studied individual trader performance in an experimental setting. It then compared performance to participants' measures of financial literacy, cognitive skill, behavioral bias, and theory of mind. They conclude that behavioral bias (particularly overconfidence and the failure to understand random sampling) explains trader earnings while standard cognitive and theory of mind skills are of marginal importance.

Those that scored high on the CRT and exhibited less behavioral bias earned significantly more than those who did not. Standard intelligence and theory of mind ability were not important.

Rationality Quotient (RQ) is more important than IQ.

Here are a few quotes of interest from the paper, along with my thoughts:

> A common thread running through each of these [behavioral] biases is the individual's inability to refrain from using automatic responses and simple heuristics.

Bad traders think fast. Good traders think (a bit) slower. The paradox here is that sometimes you need to think fast when you are trading because speed can be an edge. If an important announcement hits the wires, you can't always sit around waiting for System 2 to deliver a verdict. If you don't hit the buttons right away, someone else will. In other words, some short-term trading requires a "Ready, Shoot, Aim" thinking style. That's OK.

If you are trading headlines, events, and quick reaction time trades, you can overcome the heuristic / fast thinking problem by trading in two steps.

Step 1: When you see a headline or something that makes you want to act... Go ahead and act. Go to market and get set on your position.

Step 2: Once you have the position on, take a step back and analyze your actions using System 2. Is this logical? Or is this a dumb idea? You need to have the force of mind to take a trade off right away, usually at a small loss, if your System 2 analysis says that your System 1 idea was wrong. This is hard because we tend to have trouble selling at a small loss and we tend to overvalue assets (or positions) we already own.

Note that if you enter trades using System 1 (reacting quickly to headlines, for example) then subsequently evaluate them more fully using System 2, you need to overcome both the endowment effect and anchoring bias in order to get out of bad trades quickly. If your System 2 analysis says "this is a bad trade", don't wait for the price to get back to break even. Cut the position and move on. Good short-term trading involves taking many small losses.

The endowment effect (a.k.a., divestiture aversion) says that when we own something, we value it more highly than if we did not already own it. Anchoring bias says we will attach importance to the price at which we entered a trade, even though that price is irrelevant once we have the trade on. We will talk about both these forms of trader bias (and many others) in Chapter 7.

Side note: Here's a funny-because-it's-true anecdote on the endowment effect from a 2019 blog post by Michael Batnick:

> Years ago when I was trading, probably 2010 or 2011, I had some fun trading weekly options around earnings releases. I was gambling, which is not something I only recently came to terms with. I knew it at the time which is why I never put a lot of money at risk. During one of these wagers I meant to buy calls, but by accident I bought puts. In that moment a funny thing happened. It wouldn't have been much trouble to unwind this trade, but instead I rationalized why puts were the right decision. "I guess I'm bearish now," I thought. My actions influenced my mindset. I was owned by my possessions.

The next quote of interest from the paper is:

> Individuals tend to mistakenly believe that they observe predict-
> able patterns in randomly generated data.

This is the failure to understand random sampling. Randomly generated data creates all sorts of patterns. Human beings are hard-wired to see patterns. We see faces in sockets, animals in the clouds, patterns in randomly-generated stock charts, and Jesus Christ on toast[28]. Humans see patterns even where there is often only randomness. This is why I tend to view technical analysis[29] with great skepticism—technical analysis pushes us toward pattern-seeking behavior when we should instead be fighting our bias to see patterns everywhere.

> Our studies show that people who are immune to commonly-known
> behavioral biases perform the best in experimental asset markets.

This is the conclusion of many studies. RQ is more important than IQ[30]. You are either part of the unbiased, efficient markets or you are creating exploitable inefficiency with your biased, irrational actions.

Research Paper 2

"Mental Capabilities, Trading Styles, and Asset
Market Bubbles: Theory and Experiment" (2016)

ANDREAS HEFTI, STEVE HEINKE AND FRÉDÉRIC SCHNEIDER

These researchers first did a series of experiments to evaluate participants on two dimensions, analyzing and mentalizing[31]. Then, they ran a typical asset market / trading experiment to see how different individuals would behave and perform. The core idea is that different actors behave differently in the market

---

28. See, for example: Liu, et al. "Seeing Jesus in toast: Neural and behavioral correlates of face pareido-lia," (2014).

29. Technical analysis is the study of financial markets using charts and patterns. This is a massive subject area that fills hundreds of books. There is even a designation one can earn as a certified technical analyst: Chartered Market Technician (CMT).

30. IQ is still important, though. There is plenty of research showing high-IQ investors outperform low-IQ investors. See, for example Grinblatt, Keloharju and Linnainmaa, "IQ and Stock Market Participation," (2011)

31. Mentalizing is a psychology term that relates to an individual's ability to think about and understand their own thoughts and the thoughts of others. It is conceptually similar (though not identical to) empathy or Theory of Mind. It essentially measures whether you can put yourself in someone else's shoes or see the world through their eyes.

and if we split individuals into groups we might see a pattern emerge in terms of trading success.

Analytical skill was measured as successful performance in mathematics, logic, and probability while mentalizing was defined as the ability to understand the mental states of others and predict their behavior. The traders were broken into four quadrants:

		Mentalizing	
		Low	High
Analytical	High	Technocratic	Sophisticated
	Low	Featureless	Semiotic

And here are the trading results:

		Mentalizing	
		Low	High
Analytical	High	**93**	**403**
	Low	(45)	(390)

Mathematics, logic and understanding of probability win. The ability to analyze the behavior of others has some power, but only if you have the rational and probabilistic thinking first. Analytical, rational thinking is necessary and sufficient to earn a profit, but the more well-rounded individual earns much more in this experiment.

Research Paper 3

"Good Thinking or Gut Feeling? Cognitive Reflection and Intuition in Traders, Bankers and Financial Non-Experts" (2015)

VOLKER THOMA, ELLIOTT WHITE, ASHA PANIGRAHI, VANESSA STROWGER, AND IRINA ANDERSON

This paper looks directly at CRT vs. intuition and comes to an unambiguous conclusion. Traders score higher on the CRT and favor the avoidance of mental shortcuts compared to non-traders. They rely more on System 2 than non-traders. Furthermore, the study found that traders do not rely on intuition any more than non-traders. To quote the study's conclusion:

> While traders are apparently no different in their use of 'intuition' or 'gut feeling' to other people, the majority of them are markedly improved in their propensity to engage in reflective thinking and less susceptible to 'cognitive impulsivity'.

The study also says that some would argue that high CRT scores could be equivalent to elevated numeracy. While there is overlap between high CRT scores, rationality and strong numeracy, other studies have shown that numeracy and CRT performance are not the same thing[32].

Research Paper 4

"Trader Personality and Trader Performance:
A Framework and Financial Market Experiment" (2008)

ARJEN VAN WITTELOOSTUIJN AND KATRIN MUEHLFELD

This paper involves an asset market trading experiment where results are compared to six personality traits: Locus of control, maximizing tendency, regret disposition, self-monitoring, sensation seeking and type A/type B behavior.

The primary conclusion of the paper is that those who trade less and those who work limit orders (i.e., act like market makers, not price takers) outperform those who trade more frequently and cross more spreads using market orders. The findings are consistent with many other papers and investigations which show that overtrading leads to worse performance[33].

The main driver of the underperformance from trading too much is transaction costs, but even in experiments where there are no transaction costs, *the subjects that trade most perform worst.* Good traders wait for outsized opportunities, they don't trade frenetically, reacting to every bit of flickering price action.

I say this as someone who must fight not to react to every bit of flickering price action.

---

32. Jordana Liberali et al., "Individual Differences in Numeracy and Cognitive Reflection, with Implications for Biases and Fallacies in Probability Judgment," (2011)

33. See, for example: Brad Barber and Terrance Odean, "Trading is Hazardous to Your Wealth," (2000) and "Boys Will be Boys: Gender, Overconfidence and Common Stock Investment," (2001).

While high CRT was a consistent variable in predicting the earnings of traders in many studies[34], the results of experiments and research on softer skills like Theory of Mind are mixed. For every research paper that found a positive connection between mentalizing or Theory of Mind and trader earnings, there was one that suggested the opposite[35].

My conclusion is that it is absolutely clear from the research that rational thinking is the number one trait of a successful trader. High intelligence, numeracy and financial literacy are also important. Trading with gut feel, intuition and similar soft skills is less important, and sometimes counterproductive.

Yes, gut and intuition can be the subconscious processing of reams of information, an amalgamation of disparate data and knowledge. It is common for people to know something without knowing how they know it. Then again, gut and intuition are often just the way fear, bias and other bad influences make their way into our thinking and behavior.

You may have seen breathless media reports in the mid-2010s with headlines like "Gut Instinct: Do Traders Have a Sixth Sense?[36]" trumpeting a few small studies that seemed to suggest trader intuition is of great importance. I read those studies. They generally had tiny sample sizes (10 to 20 traders) and were unconvincing, in my opinion.

Distilling all the research down to one formula, I get this new equation:

**Trading success = rational thinking + IQ +
self-control - overconfidence**

Recall from Chapter 3, the formula for general success (money, academic grades, and sports) was:

**Success = conscientiousness + IQ +
talent/skill + luck - neuroticism**

Combining it all together, we get this final equation:

---

34. See also: Brice Corgnet et al., "The Effect of Earned vs. House Money on Price Bubble Formation in Experimental Asset Markets", (2013), and Noussair, Tucker and Xu: "A Futures Market Reduces Bubbles but Allows Greater Profit for More Sophisticated Traders", (2014)

35. De Martino et al. "In the mind of the market: Theory of Mind biases value computation during financial bubbles" (2013)

36. https://www.cnbc.com/2016/09/20/gut-instinct-do-traders-have-a-sixth-sense.html

Alpha Trader = rational + intelligent + skilled + conscientious + calibrated confidence

Note my equation for trading success excludes some traits that are important but not critical to trading success. I did not include risk appetite, for example. People at each end of the risk-taking continuum (extremely risk averse or highly risk seeking) might underperform those in the middle, but risk appetite is not an important character trait in the literature on trading performance.

Furthermore, risk tolerance can be dialed up or down fairly easily with a simple set of rules. I have seen traders at every point on the risk-taking spectrum succeed.

Note that before the year 2000 or so, IQ was less important in trading because trading was more skill-based and less quantitative. Now, a higher level of intelligence is required although I would argue that Wall Street currently overvalues IQ and academics, and does not focus enough on grit, street smarts and fire in the belly.

My equation leaves out many positive attributes that most certainly make for better traders. It does not include positive attitude or ability to handle stress, for example. These are useful but not critical attributes when it comes to trading success. There are plenty of grumpy, stressed out traders that still make money. Sure, that's not ideal (and certainly does not meet my personal definition of success), but only the indispensable traits are in the equation. Many other attributes will help you succeed in trading but the formula I laid out is the mashed potatoes—everything else is gravy.

That concludes this chapter and our look into the research on trading success. I highlighted some specific papers because they capture the gist of the broader literature, but please note that I went through piles of research before I reached my conclusions. This chapter just shared a few highlights.

This is the end of Part One and our look at why some traders succeed but most fail.

In Part Two, we go deeper. We look at rationality, conscientiousness, and overconfidence in more detail, plus dig into many other important trader attributes to help you learn, evolve, adapt, and improve.

PART TWO

THE ALPHA
TRADER MINDSET

P art Two is a deeper look at the winning traits and negative attributes that combine to lead to trading riches or ruin. It is also an exploration of what it means to be rational and unbiased, a state of mind that can never be perfectly attained but which is always the goal.

Remember, nobody embodies every positive trait or is free from every negative aspect. The goal is to be brutally honest about your strengths and weaknesses and then work hard to boost positives, tame weaknesses, and plug leaks.

As you read the next three chapters, think about your own assets and limitations. Take notes. And never focus exclusively on fixing weaknesses. Awareness of your strengths, and the ability to build on those strengths, is just as important as the ability to identify and address weakness.

Part Two is divided into three chapters:

Chapter 5: Strengths and positive traits

Chapter 6: Weaknesses and leaks

Chapter 7: Rational, unbiased trading

Let's start with specific positive character traits that increase a trader's probability of success.

LEVEL UP

The traits and habits you need to succeed

There is no single x-factor in trading. Successful trading combines a variety of disparate skills and characteristics. Remember the formula from Chapter 4:

Alpha Trader = rational + intelligent + skilled + conscientious + calibrated confidence

As we unpack the essential traits, a broader list emerges. Let's go beyond the equation and dig into more detail to identify particular traits that I believe lead to success in trading. Here is my complete list of positive trader attributes:

Cognitive		Non-cognitive	Other
Rational	Curious	Disciplined	Raw trading instincts
Intelligent / Knowledgeable / Informed	Grit / perseverance	Adaptable	Experience
Quantitative	Growth mindset	Courageous	Passion for trading
Calibrated confidence	Organized / meticulous	Self-aware	Luck
Independent thinker	Process-oriented	Able to handle stress	Appropriate capital
Flexible and open-minded	Future-oriented	Focused	Healthy, supportive risk-taking environment
Creative	Healthy skeptic	Patient	
		Understands locus of control	
		Decisive	

That's a huge list!

Cognitive traits rely on intellectual effort, conscious thought, and reasoning. Most cognitive skills can be built up over time. Non-cognitive traits can be static or changeable[37]. As I showed in Chapter 3, conscientiousness generally increases with age, so take advantage of this and work especially hard on skills that come under that umbrella like organization, self-control, focus and preparedness.

Even if you cannot change some parts of who you are, understanding your fixed, innate characteristics can help you manage yourself better and avoid putting yourself in a position to fail. Whether you are a new trader or a wily veteran, the point of this section is to get you thinking about your own profile and areas where you can improve.

Nobody has every skill and characteristic in abundance. Many of the skills can be built, and weaknesses can be managed. Your goal is to know yourself well enough that you can take the actions needed to excel. Work on your weaknesses and level up your strengths using the methods and ideas in the chapters that follow.

I will discuss these traits individually but I won't waste time defining them, as I know that you know what all those words mean! This chapter will tell you what each trait means for trading and most importantly, give you specific ideas and tips on how you can level up in each area.

COGNITIVE TRAITS

Let's start with the cognitive traits (the first two columns of the table).

Rational

We talked a bit about rationality in the last chapter. Chapter 7 is a deep dive into all the ways humans act irrationally so I will leave the topic alone for now. Suffice it to say: Alpha traders think and act rationally. After analyzing heaps of research, thinking about all the traders I have worked with over many years, and studying my own best and worst trading periods, I feel strongly that the best way to describe the Alpha Trader in one word is: Rational.

---

37. Note: It is more difficult than you might expect to bucket skills as cognitive or non-cognitive; don't get mad at me if you think I put something under cognitive that you believe should fall under non-cognitive. For example, reasonable people might categorize "confidence" as either cognitive or non-cognitive.

Intelligent, knowledgeable, informed

Medium to high intelligence, especially as it relates to numbers, is important in trading. You need to do calculations on the fly, understand expected value and probability, know basic economics (micro and macro), solve puzzles, interpret stories, and understand or filter often conflicting and incomplete information. It's not rocket science… But it's also not shape sorting.

IQ is somewhat fixed, but knowledge and information can be accumulated over time to increase your edge.

Here are some ways to level up your knowledge:

- Think about areas you are weak and take courses online. For example, take a course or read a book about macroeconomics, options trading, technical analysis, financial history, or trading psychology. Branch out. Play the long game. Whether you are 25 or 50, keep learning. Don't just focus on your weaknesses. If you are strong in derivatives, keep getting better. Go deep into the topics you love but also explore areas where you lack familiarity. Become expert or near expert in as many domains as possible.

- Read more. The Economist, FT, WSJ, books & blogs (see recommendations in Appendix A). This is such a simple piece of advice but many people in finance say they are distracted at the desk all the time or it's too hard to find the time to read. If you read more than everyone else, you will be better informed than everyone else. And it's cumulative. You can up your efficiency by scanning a wider range of relevant blogs and news feeds. Even if you don't read every single word of every article, you capture the zeitgeist by scanning more sources.

- Think of a market adjacent to what you trade and learn about it. If you trade the Canadian dollar, study the oil market. If you trade S&P futures, read a book about SPX options. If you trade gold, read a book about platinum.

- E-mail or message someone who knows more than you do about a topic. If you read a blog and find it interesting, email the writer with a follow-up question. If you just read a book about markets, reach out to the author on LinkedIn and ask a specific question. If you trade USDJPY at a bank, walk over and talk to the person who trades 10-year bonds.

- Read financial history.

- Be thoughtful about your information sources and reduce redundancy. There is a major surplus of finance information and analysis out there. When I went to work at a hedge fund after my employer (Lehman Brothers) went under, I had 20 banks covering me at first. There was so much redundancy and useless information, I quickly narrowed my list down to five banks and found that was much more manageable. *How many overnight summaries does one person need?* There is plenty of good research on Wall Street, but there is also plenty of fluff. Get to know the strategists and researchers out there, read the best, and filter the rest.

  Thirty to fifty good Twitter follows are better than 350. You will find as you expand your media consumption, you get more and more redundant information, nonsense, and cut and paste headlines that just waste your time. If you work at a fund or institution, my estimate is you hit diminishing returns at about 3 to 5 coverage banks. After that, the duplication is probably not worth the odd bit of unique analysis that squeaks through.

The philosophy: Be curious, keep learning and build knowledge for the long run.

Quantitative

Many trading roles require in-depth knowledge of statistics and the ability to code or program (usually in Python). Even a trader in the most vanilla discretionary or short-term trading seat benefits from quantitative sophistication.

I will lump numeracy under this heading as well, because the ability to intuitively understand numbers helps traders enormously. For example, many market making roles require quick calculations (converting yen to dollars when a salesperson asks for a price in a fast market, for example). Traders that can do quick mental math have a small advantage over those that cannot.

How to level up your quantitative skills:

- Learn about expected value (EV) and decision trees. These are especially useful when trading economic or market events with discrete outcomes. For example:

  You think the Fed will cut rates today and the market has it priced as 80%/20%, in favor of a rate cut. A professional rates trader would say that 20 out of 25 basis points are priced in. You decide to risk $200,000 on the trade; you will make $50,000 if you are correct and the Fed cuts. If they don't cut, you lose your $200,000.

Many people will see this negative leverage as bad (risking 200 to make just 50) but it is not inherently good or bad[38]. It depends on the probabilities you assign to each outcome.

The tricky thing with market probabilities is that unlike probabilities in gambling, they are not known or measurable. You have to estimate them. Accurately estimating probabilities is a skill that gives you an edge in trading. Incomplete information is one of the challenging hallmarks of markets as an exercise in probability.

Back to our example. Let's say you think there is a 95% chance the Fed will cut rates. Here is the expected value of a $200,000 wager on this event:

	A	B	C	D
	$ at risk	Gain or loss	Odds of it happening	(B times C)
The Fed cuts	200,000	50,000	95%	47,500
The Fed does not cut	200,000	(200,000)	5%	(10,000)

Expected value of this trade	37,500
EV as a % of $ at risk	18.8%
18.8% is EV of 37,500 divided by $ at risk of 200,000	

So even though you are risking $200k to make $50k, this is an excellent trade idea. Clearly, though, your confidence in that 95% figure is key to making this bet. If you think it's more like 70% or 80%... Then stay away. Your view is about the same as the market.

---

38. See the section on favorite/longshot bias in Chapter 7. People tend to prefer longshots because optically they offer better payouts. But payouts depend not just on the odds the bet offers, but the probability of it paying out.

I assume that most people reading this book have a pretty clear understanding of EV, but if you are new to the game or you were sick the day this was taught in university statistics… Brush up! Go online and take a short course or do some reading about expected value. Good traders work comfortably with EV both explicitly and subconsciously.

- Learn Python. This is rapidly becoming the standard for data analysis in finance. Excel is fine but not as good as Python. Not even close.

- Take a course in statistics, probability, or data visualization.

- Read academic research papers about the assets you trade. Freely available academic research is a hugely underutilized resource. Most research can be found and read online. Go to Google Scholar and type in a topic you find interesting (e.g., stock market inefficiencies, trading psychology, currency valuation or high-frequency trading). If you find a good paper, go to the bibliography and read some of the papers cited.

- Learn about Bayes Theorem and Bayesian updating. There are many, many good websites on the topic (e.g., towardsdatascience.com). The basic idea of Bayesian updating is that good forecasters start with a prior probability and then update it as new information comes in. This is in contrast to people that form an opinion and then ignore new information. Good thinking and good forecasting are not possible without Bayesian updating.

A simple example:

> Your name is Bob. You are in high school and you estimate there is a 60% chance that Phoebe will go out on a date with you (once you finally get the guts to ask her). The next day, you say "Hi" to Phoebe as you both enter chem class. She says: "Hey, Tim!" and floats toward her desk, leaving a sweet cloud of vanilla scent in her wake. Using Bayesian updating, you take the new information (she doesn't know your name) and update your prior 60% estimate to 25%.

In contrast, someone who does not use Bayesian methods might ignore the new information because it does not fit his prior belief. This is known as confirmation bias, which we will discuss later in

Chapter 7. He might lie to himself and say "Oh it's fine… There was probably someone named Tim behind me and she was talking to him" even though there is nobody named Tim in chemistry class. This is how confirmation bias works. We trick ourselves and ignore information that doesn't fit our priors.

> UPDATE: Oh no! Phoebe just blew a kiss to Bad Boy Eric Cooper at the back of the class! You revise your probability that she will go on a date with you down to 0.84%.

One side benefit of using Bayes Theory, Bayesian updating and terms like "prior probability" and "updating your priors"… It makes you sound super smart. :]

- Read Superforecasting by Phil Tetlock and Dan Gardner. This is one of the best books on statistics and forecasting, and it has tons of applications both to the real world and to trading. The book also does an excellent job of explaining Bayes so you kill two bullet points with one stone if you read it. I would say Superforecasting is one of the books that has most influenced my quantitative thinking style (along with Fooled by Randomness by Nassim Taleb, Risk by Dan Gardner, and *Thinking in Bets* by Annie Duke). A full list of book recommendations appears in Appendix A.

- Backtest your ideas. If you notice that stocks tend to fall every Monday and rally every Tuesday, backtest it. If it feels like oil rallies every day from 2PM to 3PM, check it out. Is it true or false? Whenever a hypothesis appears in your head, dig in and figure out if it's true. Playing with ideas and data like this can inspire new ideas and a better understanding of the inner workings of the markets you trade. If you don't know how to backtest, just open Excel and start messing around. This is the kind of thing you can teach yourself with a bit of effort.

Calibrated confidence

Given the critical importance of confidence and (especially) overconfidence in trading, we will dig more deeply into this topic in Chapter 7. For now, I will just say that high confidence is required for trading but overconfidence is the worst leak.

Independent thinker

Important: An independent thinker is not someone who is contrarian all the time, disagrees with everyone, or loves playing devil's advocate. That is not independent thinking; that is reflexive opposition. That is not good!

Independent thinking means that you analyze information using your own framework and come to logical conclusions. You develop your own beliefs, incorporating as much information as possible. "Information" can include the curated beliefs of others.

Sometimes your conclusions agree with the crowd and you hop on the trend. Sometimes you are on the other side of consensus, so you take a contrarian view.

Many human beings are hardwired to conform. In a famous 1951 experiment by Solomon Asch, eight "subjects" were placed in a room. Seven were actors and the eighth was the true subject of the experiment. They were all shown the two cards in Figure 5.1 and asked to answer out loud which line (A, B, or C) was the same length as the line on the card on the left. The true subject was seated so that he or she would answer last.

Figure 5.1: The Cards Used in the Asch Conformity Experiments

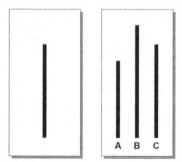

by Fred the Oyster, Creative Commons 4.0 (CC BY-SA 4.0)

In the test where the first seven in the group answer correctly, the subject answered correctly 99% of the time. On the other hand, when the group of actors all responded with the same wrong answer, the test subject gave the correct response only 63.2% of the time.

This result is surprising and unintuitive. You might say "Meh, that's dumb, I would never do that." Don't be so sure! This experiment has been replicated many times, and you have the benefit of being an outsider with complete information. Other experiments show that almost everyone conforms to social influence to a high degree.

When humans have incomplete knowledge, their instinct is to follow the group. Many people in the Asch experiment *did not* follow the group, but the experiment involved an easy question with an obvious answer. Everyone should have answered correctly yet almost 37% of people did not. Google "Stanford Prison Experiments" for another example of the astonishing levels of conformity observed in experimental settings.

In markets, where incomplete information and group behavior are an intrinsic part of the game, you need to make sure you are always thinking for yourself. Don't get caught up in the CNBC (bullish) or Twitter (bearish) hype or get sucked in by what the "smart guy at the big hedge fund" wrote in his opinion piece in the FT.

Think for yourself.

Also note that if your reaction when reading about the Asch experiment was: "I would never pick the wrong line in that experiment," you are just like almost everyone else who believes that bias is something that happens to everyone else, but not to them. Groupthink and conformity bias are real and impact smart people and dumb people alike![39]

When it comes to independent thinking, Peter Thiel nails it with this quote:

> *The most contrarian thing of all is not to oppose the crowd but to think for yourself.*

Flexible and open-minded

The cure for many forms of bias in trading (and in life) is to be flexible and open-minded. This is captured by the concept of "strong opinions, weakly held", a framework for thinking developed by technology forecaster and Stanford Scholar Paul Saffo. Here is his description of how to think[40]:

> Allow your intuition to guide you to a conclusion, no matter how imperfect — this is the "strong opinion" part. Then – and this is the "weakly held" part – prove yourself wrong. Engage in creative doubt.

39. Conformity bias is the human tendency to take cues for proper behavior in most contexts from the actions of others instead of exercising independent judgment.

40. https://www.saffo.com/02008/07/26/strong-opinions-weakly-held/

Look for information that doesn't fit, or indicators that point in an entirely different direction. Eventually your intuition will kick in and a new hypothesis will emerge out of the rubble, ready to be ruthlessly torn apart once again. You will be surprised by how quickly the sequence of faulty forecasts will deliver you to a useful result.

This sounds a lot like Bayesian updating, right? Start with a prior and update it as you get more information. It also sounds a lot like my discussion earlier of how to trade headlines with a "Ready, Shoot, Aim" approach. You react, using your System 1 or gut instinct, then you quickly analyze your action and look for confirming or (most critically) contradictory evidence. You look not just at your chosen hypothesis, but other competing ones.

I write a daily macro newsletter called AM/FX that goes out to a sizeable list of hedge fund and real money portfolio managers and strategists. One of the great benefits of sending out AM/FX is that when I publish my hypothesis, I have a few thousand people out there vetting it and consciously or unconsciously looking for alternatives. The e-mail responses I get make me aware of alternative ways of looking at the world that I might not have considered.

You can replicate this process by getting your hypothesis out there. If you have a strong view, share it with your coworkers and see what comes back. Drop it on Twitter (if you are thick-skinned enough to withstand the corrosive "SOMEBODY IS WRONG ON THE INTERNET!" culture there). Send an e-mail to a few traders you respect with your thesis laid out in one or two paragraphs.

If you are an introvert, don't feel like you have to remain an introvert forever. Push yourself to make new connections. I was a shy kid and pretty insecure in high school. I never liked meeting new people and I would consider myself an introvert by nature. I changed over time, though, as I saw the benefits of reaching out to people and making new connections and moving out of my comfort zone.

When you send your thesis out into the wild, the responses will inform you, not just by their content, but also by their tone. If you get a series of agitated replies with a bunch of rebuttals you can easily bat away, you are probably onto a good trade idea. Strong pushback indicates that people are positioned the other way. If you can easily refute their arguments, then happy days. On the other hand, sometimes you might get a bunch of well-reasoned replies that highlight facts you omitted from your analysis. Then it's time to reassess.

Exploring alternative hypotheses is
the bedrock of good thinking.

Start with a strong view and then try to step outside yourself as much as possible to look at alternative scenarios. This is part of why expected value and decision tree calculations (among many other forms of good thinking) add value. They force you to look at all the possible paths. You take multiple possible outcomes and attempt to weight them according to their probabilities. You don't just take a view and stick with it regardless of incoming or alternative information.

The book *Psychology of Intelligence Analysis* by Richards J. Heuer, Jr. is the best elucidation of good thinking I have read. The author worked for the CIA for 45 years in various roles including operations, counterintelligence, and intelligence analysis. The book explains how human bias impedes clear thinking. Much of it applies directly to trading.

The book is out of print but fortunately it is freely available on the CIA's website. Of particular relevance is "Part Two: Tools for Thinking", especially "Chapter 8: Analysis of Competing Hypotheses". If you want access to the full buffet of information, I suggest you read the whole book: it's less than 200 pages and it is not boring! If you want the quick meal, at least read Chapter 8. For now, here's an appetizer... My synopsis of Heuer's summary of Chapter 8[41].

STEP-BY-STEP OUTLINE OF ANALYSIS
OF COMPETING HYPOTHESES

1. Identify the possible hypotheses to be considered. Use a group of analysts with different perspectives to brainstorm the possibilities.

2. Make a list of significant evidence and arguments for and against each hypothesis.

3. Prepare a matrix with hypotheses across the top and evidence down the side. Analyze the "diagnosticity" of the evidence and arguments— that is, identify which items are most helpful in judging the relative likelihood of the hypotheses.

---

41. Abridged from: Richards J. Heuer, Psychology of Intelligence Analysis, Center for the Study of Intelligence, 1999

4. Refine the matrix. Reconsider the hypotheses and delete evidence and arguments that have no diagnostic value.

5. Draw tentative conclusions about the relative likelihood of each hypothesis. Proceed by trying to disprove the hypotheses rather than prove them.

6. Analyze how sensitive your conclusion is to a few critical items of evidence. Consider the consequences for your analysis if that evidence were wrong, misleading, or subject to a different interpretation.

7. Report conclusions. Discuss the relative likelihood of all the hypotheses, not just the most likely one.

8. Identify milestones for future observation that may indicate events are taking a different course than expected.

Be thoughtful and look at alternative hypotheses with an open mind. Lay out the arguments against your view and see how you feel about them. Do they make sense? Are they easily refuted?

Be aware that when you are in a position, you are not objective. You are under the influence of bias when you are in a trade. You own something (the trade and the view that led to it) and people don't like giving up what they own. Therefore, if you are feeling uncomfortable about a position, the best bet is to take it off. Then, once you're flat, you can analyze with an open, unbiased mind.

As I state in my first book[42]:

> Rule #7 of FX Trading: Flat is the strongest position. When in doubt: Get out.

It is easier to honestly evaluate competing hypotheses when you are flat, open-minded, and flexible.

Creative

People outside Wall Street don't generally associate the world of finance with creativity, but they should. Orthodox, follow-the-crowd thinking does not work in trading. Most of the legends of finance had some creative insight

---

42. Brent Donnelly, *The Art of Currency Trading*, John Wiley & Sons (2019). It is a tad meta for me to footnote my own book here. I acknowledge it feels a bit like I'm referring to myself in third person. Anyway, there is some overlap between my FX trading book and this book, so I will refer to that one in here a few times. I hope you don't mind. :)

that took them to another level. Examples include Milken's idea for high yield "junk" bonds, Paul Tudor Jones and Peter Borish's idea to overlay past and present chart patterns to predict the crash of 1987, George Soros' idea of reflexivity, and Ray Dalio's idea for the All-Weather portfolio which came to be known as Risk Parity.

Creative thinking does not have to mean you come up with ideas that completely revolutionize finance. Can you slice and dice data in a new and interesting way and thus create more accurate short-term market forecasts? Can you think outside the box to discover new variables that will help guide you through the noise?

For example, in 2006, it was fairly well-known that copper and gold prices could be used as predictors for the Australian dollar because those two commodities are significant Australian exports. Similarly, it was known that crude oil was a driver of the Canadian dollar because Canada exports huge amounts of crude. But there was no such variable for the New Zealand dollar for some reason, and my job at Lehman Brothers in those days was trading the AUD, CAD, and NZD.

So I Googled: "What are the major exports of New Zealand?" and the answer is: Milk products. Milk, butter, and cheese account for 25% of NZ exports and milk prices are an important marginal driver of NZ GDP[43]. So I overlaid a chart of dairy futures with the New Zealand dollar and DING! There was a pretty good fit. Correlation / causation yadda, yadda but when two things overlay and there is a logical connection between them in the real economy, you are probably onto something.

When I first published the overlay in 2006, I got a few *hahaha* emails in response. But eventually, the idea caught on and now it's a common variable for people to look at when assessing the fair value of the NZD. Recently, someone sent me a chart overlaying "Norwegian Spot Salmon Price" with the Norwegian Krona (NOK) and I was suitably impressed. There is still room for innovation in trading!

Try your best to think creatively about problems in finance. It is not always a brute force quantitative solution that is needed. To be creative does not mean you have to paint or write poems. It means you come at problems with imagination, and develop original ideas.

---

43. This website is great if you are interested in global import and exports data: https://oec.world/en/profile/country/nzl/

Circling back to Heuer[44]:

> ...[Think] of information in memory as somehow interconnected like a massive, multidimensional spider web. It is possible to connect any point within this web to any other point. When analysts connect the same points frequently, they form a path that makes it easier to take that route in the future. Once they start thinking along certain channels, they tend to continue thinking the same way and the path may become a rut. The path seems like the obvious and natural way to go.
>
> Information and concepts located near that path are readily available, so the same images keep coming up. Information not located near that path is less likely to come to mind. Talking about breaking mind-sets, or creativity, or even just openness to new information is really talking about spinning new links and new paths through the web of memory.
>
> These are links among facts and concepts, or between schemata for organizing facts or concepts, that were not directly connected or only weakly connected before. New ideas result from the association of old elements in new combinations. Previously remote elements of thought suddenly become associated in a new and useful combination. When the linkage is made, the light dawns. This ability to bring previously unrelated information and ideas together in meaningful ways is what marks the open-minded, imaginative, creative analyst.

How to be more creative in trading

1. Study other asset markets or businesses with linkages to your market. The more you understand the iron ore market, the better you can trade the Australian dollar. The more you understand American Airlines, the better you can trade the airlines ETF: JETS. Drill into the principal factors that drive your market and learn about them in detail.

2. Read about random and varied topics. It seems so obvious but I never really understood this until recently. If you read voraciously, you load new information into your mind and that information can then cross-pollenate with old information and spark new ideas.

---

44. Heuer (1999), abridged from p. 65.

Most ideas come from combining two forms of disparate knowledge. If you read about art, or outer space or fractals or whatever… Cool finance-related ideas may pop into your head from time to time thanks to the stimulation.

3. Go for a walk. Sitting at your desk staring at numbers going up and down will drop you into a rut at some point. Get up and go outside for a few minutes. I have had many moments of clarity on the way to the bathroom or on my way to pick up Panera for lunch.

4. Talk to people in your network. New ideas come from contact with new streams of thought. Don't be a taker, though. Offer ideas to your network. Don't be the guy that just emails ten people saying, "What you thinking?" To form a strong network, you need to both offer and receive information and ideas.

5. Be curious and develop interests outside finance. Learn some history. Listen to British rap music. Exercise your brain like it's a muscle.

Curious

Curious people are more interesting. Curiosity makes you smarter. It helps you learn. Some people are naturally more curious than others, but anyone can become more intentionally curious. It's not hard.

As one might expect, there is a direct link between curiosity and academic performance[45]. Curious kids learn more and perform better[46]. But research shows that information-seeking[47] and curiosity[48] also exert a positive influence on adult learning and job performance.

The simplest way to be curious is to simply ask "Why?" as much as possible. Back in the day, when everyone knew that apples fell from trees, Newton was the one to ask: "Why don't apples fall sideways? Why don't they fall upwards?"

When you see a phenomenon in the markets, ask why. This is particularly true when backtesting. When you discover a pattern that backtests successfully,

45. https://www.theatlantic.com/education/archive/2017/07/the-underrated-gift-of-curiosity/534573/

46. Hassinger-Das, B., Hirsh-Pasek, K., *Appetite for knowledge: curiosity and children's academic achievement* (2018)

47. Mussel, P., *Introducing the construct curiosity for predicting job performance* Journal of Organizational Behavior (2013)

48. Reio, T.G., Jr. and Wiswell, A., *Field investigation of the relationship among adult curiosity, workplace learning, and job performance*, Human Resource Development Quarterly (2000)

can you explain why it works? If you can, there is a much greater probability that what you discovered will work out of sample. Much of what you find sifting through data is just data snooping or data mining. But when you find patterns and can explain them logically, you have something much more powerful.

Part of being curious is also just not being lazy. When you see a term that you don't fully understand in a news article... Investigate. A few years ago, there was a headline saying the ECB might open up its OMT program, and a trader on another desk said out loud: "Huh... I wonder what OMT is," then went back to eating his sandwich. That's not good!

A curious trader would hear the announcement and then go off and do some research on OMT. That might lead them to the history of monetary financing and something epic like *Fiat Money in France*[49]. If you read that footnote, you are on the right track. You are showing intentional curiosity.

To be curious and conscientious is to be the kind of person that reads the footnotes. If you didn't read that last footnote, go and read it now. And then go download *Fiat Money in France* for free from the Mises Institute (the book is public domain). It is scary and entertaining stuff. France circa 1780 parallels the current era of infinite money printing, big time.

The Growth Mindset

If you have kids, you may be familiar with the idea of the growth mindset because it is a trendy topic in education right now. The idea was popularized by American psychologist Carol Dweck. Here is how she defines it in a 2012 interview:

> In a fixed mindset, students believe their basic abilities, their intelligence, their talents, are just fixed traits. They have a certain amount and that's that, and then their goal becomes to look smart all the time and never look dumb. In a growth mindset, students understand that their talents and abilities can be developed through effort, good teaching and persistence. They don't necessarily think everyone's the same or anyone can be Einstein, but they believe everyone can get smarter if they work at it.

---

49. *Fiat Money in France* by Andrew Dickson White is a classic 1876 book about how paper money can become worthless when governments print and spend irresponsibly. It is highly relevant in this era of unlimited money printing to finance unlimited government spending.

When you reflect on particular negative traits you possess and think "that's just who I am" or "that's just me", you cannot grow. Instead, embrace the surprising plasticity of the human brain and keep learning, evolving, and improving.

This concept is similar to the Japanese concept of Kaizen or "good change" which was a key ingredient in the superior quality and productivity of the Japanese automakers as they eclipsed North American car makers in the 1980s. With Kaizen or Growth Mindset (aka, continuous improvement), you always look to make incremental positive changes and continue to grow.

Without a growth mindset, this book is not going to help you much because you will wrongly believe that many of the traits, strengths, and weaknesses you possess are fixed or too difficult to change. That's not the right attitude. Pick a weakness, and work on it. You will notice improvement over time.

When someone says, "I'm not a people person" or "I'm not very good at math", that's a fixed mindset. Clearly people are predisposed a certain way by genetics, personality, and environment. That is your starting hand. A growth mindset says that you can overcome your starting hand by playing well, and thereby outperform your baseline or starting point.

Here's a quick summary of how the two mindsets contrast:

Growth mindset	Fixed mindset
Believes "I can change"	Believes "I am who I am"
Embraces challenges	Avoids challenges
Persists despite setbacks and failures	Retreats from obstacles
Learns from criticism	Rejects negative feedback
Inspired by the success of others	Threatened by the success of others

Even if you were the most disorganized kid in high school, all over the place in university and live like a pig now, you can still become an organized person. You have to drop the idea that you are a certain way and embrace positive change. You don't need to take radical action; make continuous small changes. Start small and keep improving every day.

Another hot topic in the world of education is *grit*.

Grit, perseverance, mental endurance

If you have kids, you have probably been bombarded with articles and parent coffees and TED Talks about building grit in your children. Fail early and fail fast and fail often and the marshmallow test and all that.

Here is how Angela Duckworth, who popularized the term "grit", defines it[50]:

> Grit is passion and perseverance for long-term goals. One way to think about grit is to consider what grit isn't. Grit isn't talent. Grit isn't luck. Grit isn't how intensely, for the moment, you want something.
>
> Instead, grit is about having what some researchers call an "ultimate concern"—a goal you care about so much that it organizes and gives meaning to almost everything you do. And grit is holding steadfast to that goal. Even when you fall down. Even when you screw up. Even when progress toward that goal is halting or slow.

Alpha traders have grit.

Duckworth's book: *Grit: The Power of Passion and Perseverance* is on every high-performing parent's bookshelf. Building grit in our kids is a strategy to combat the worry that helicopter parents have sheltered kids too much in recent years. The idea is that showering kids with praise and participation trophies instead of preparing them for the harsh realities of the cruel, cruel world makes them weaker, not stronger.

While my feeling is that grit has been overplayed and somewhat beaten to death as a trendy simple fix in educational circles, that does not mean it is not a valid and important topic. Grit is important in life and critically important in trading. One thing that many people fail to appreciate is just how grueling and demoralizing trading can be, even if you're good at it.

For example, I have been collecting data on my trading since 2006 and I make money almost exactly 50% of all days. Some years it's 52%, some years it's 49% but my win percentage is surprisingly stable. The variable that determines my yearly P&L is the magnitude of my up days relative to the magnitude of my down days.

Let's say you are a day trader that works 200 days per year. You are net profitable 50% of those days. If your average up day is $6,000 and your average down day is $2,800 (these stats are not unrealistic) ... Here is how much you make that year:

---

50. Check out the full Q&A (which is where this excerpt comes from) here: https://angeladuckworth.com/qa/

	A	B	D
	P&L	Number of days	
Up days	6,000	100	600,000
Down days	(2,800)	100	(280,000)
		P&L for the year	$320,000

OK, that's a pretty good income (depending on your location and lifestyle) but think about the emotional trajectory of that year. You lost money on 100 separate days, and losing days usually feel pretty bad. Forget about losing days, how about losing streaks? I just created a simulator in Excel that generates a series of 200 coin tosses which would be the same win/loss profile as a trader with a 50% win rate.

Almost every string of 200 coin tosses has a streak of at least 7 tails. Some of them have strings of 10 or even 15 tails in a row! That's a great deal of psychic pain to withstand, even if you are supremely confident that your win rate is truly 50%. If you have only been trading for three years and you think your win rate is 50%, then you hit 10 losing days in a row… Will you still be sure your win rate is 50%? Or will you start to worry you might have lost your edge… Or the market has changed… Or???

This is where grit and mental endurance come in. Sure, winning at trading is fun, but losing at trading is even more *un*fun. It is widely-accepted that humans will pay about twice as much to avoid a loss as they will pay for a gain. We will discuss this more in the section on bias.

Check out how the s-curve in Figure 5.2 deviates from the x-axis and you can see the pain of losses is twice as negative as the positive effect of same-sized gains. Knowing that this is the case, you need grit and mental endurance to withstand all the pain of all those losing days. I have come to terms with the distribution of probabilities at this stage of my career so now after a losing day, it is easier for me to move on than it used to be.

When I was in my 30's, there were a few bad days when I walked out of Lehman Brothers totally numb. One day was so bad I got on the subway going the wrong way and ended up in Kew Gardens before I realized what was going on. Now, I find it easier to say to myself something like: "Hills and valleys, buddy. Hills and valleys. Flush your mind and start fresh tomorrow."

That said, when I lose money nine days in a row (which still happens!) I can't

Figure 5.2: The pain of loss is 2X the pleasure from gain

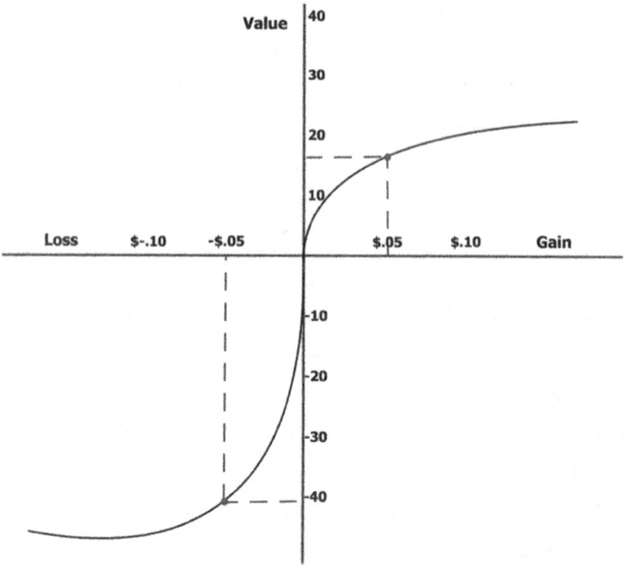

"Loss Aversion" by Laurenrosenberger, Creative Commons 4.0 (CC BY-SA 4.0)

help but get a little itchy and red-faced. In the middle of the ninth consecutive day I still might fantasize about turning my keyboard sideways and smashing it over the front edge of my desk.

But I don't do that, because I know it wouldn't help.

If you have ever played poker in a casino, you understand the concept of mental endurance. Sometimes (just like in trading) you have to sit there for hours and fold every hand because there is nothing to play. Then you finally get a good hand (AA) and play it perfectly only to lose to the drunk guy who hit trip 7's on the river. Can you internalize the fact that the other player got lucky and find strength in your own belief in process, not outcome? If you're good, you can.

Grit is about playing the long game.

Obviously there is overlap between grit and some of the other qualities and traits we have talked about. I wanted to single out grit because it's easy to understand and it captures so much in one 4-letter word[51].

---

51. Why is it that some four-letter words have so much more oomph than any 3 or 5 letter words? :]

Organized

Conscientious people are organized. This does not mean they were born organized. I struggled with organization and executive functioning right into my 30's and when I would miss a meeting or screw something up due to disorganization or bad planning I would just say "Well, that's how I am. Sorry." Then, at some point, I found that wasn't good enough. When you have a family, it becomes more difficult to just shrug and say "whoops".

Once you abandon the concept of "that's just the way I am" on any particular trait, you have taken a huge step towards evolution and improvement. Adopt the growth mindset: the belief that talent and character are not fixed. Science supports this idea. The human brain exhibits much more plasticity than we once thought. A growth mindset, instead of a fixed mindset opens up all sorts of upside for you as a person. Including… Becoming more organized.

The Baumeister and Gardner book on willpower that I referenced earlier is a good start if you want to become more organized. Also useful:

- *The Seven Habits of Highly Effective People* by Stephen Covey. Written in 1989 but still popular for a reason.

- *The Checklist Manifesto* by Atul Gawande. Pretty much exactly what it sounds like. Many interesting examples.

- *The Power of Habit* by Charles Duhigg. Almost everything about staying organized comes down to habit.

Note that these books can be boiled down into bullet points that will give you 80% of the benefit in 20% of the time. You can get summaries of most major books by googling "Summary, BOOK NAME", or by going to Goodreads, Blinkist and other websites. I find the distilled version of many nonfiction books is enough to get the point.

Another efficiency trick for non-fiction books: when you start an audiobook, set it to 2X normal speed and listen for two minutes. Then, set it to 1.5X normal speed, and it will sound normal. Efficiency!

Here is what being organized means in trading:

1. Have a plan each day

An excellent way to lose money consistently is to sit down at your computer and start hitting the BUY and SELL buttons with no plan. My plan comes together as I write AM/FX each day. For most of my career I have worked at a bank, so writing each day is a natural part of my job.

When I went to a hedge fund for a few years in the early 2010s, there was no reason to write (I had no one to write for) and I found my trading was sloppier and more random at first. Writing a quick plan in the morning anchors you and forces you to stop and think, before you start trading.

You don't have to write anything elaborate. It can be two sentences you send to your co-worker or it can be a detailed trade plan before each and every trade. The format is not the thing, the *doing it* is the thing.

A nice way to approach your plan for the day is to have a simple list that you check off each morning before you start trading. It can have 5 or 6 quick entries, for example:

1. Data and events today

2. Strong views

3. Big levels (sift through whatever charts and technical analysis you like and narrow it down to the big levels that might hit today)

4. My plan for the day. This does not have to be super-detailed. For an equity day trader, it might look something like:

   a. Buy 500 MSFT at 9:28 a.m. with a stop at $149.80 and re-evaluate at 3PM.

   b. Trade headlines with max risk of $4,000.

   c. Buy AAPL on break of $247.00, stop loss $244.80 and take profit at $249.99.

   d. Call Mom at 1:15 p.m.

   e. Workout 2 p.m. to 3 p.m. (biceps and back)

5. $ at risk (if you use a daily stop loss, how much are you risking today?)

6. Side projects (stuff you can do when the market is dead—reading, research, spreadsheet building, Python, etc.). Having a few of these at the ready will help you stay productive instead of sitting there when it's quiet going, "Hmm, what should I do?" or flicking through The Daily Mail. If you do your daily plan in Excel, you can carry over whatever side projects you did not complete yesterday into today's Daily Plan.

Try not to trade until all items on your Daily Plan have been filled in. Be ready for the day before you start trading. Don't be the guy who doesn't realize an economic number is coming out and yells, "Whoa! What happened!" when markets freak out at 10:00:00 a.m. Be prepared.

And don't watch any sports highlights until after 11 a.m. That's unprofessional. :]

2. Collect data

The best way to learn about and improve your trading is to collect data. What are your trading statistics? There will be a more complete discussion of what data to collect and how to analyze it in Chapter 11. For now, just know that good traders collect data and analyze it creatively.

3. Build and optimize your information network

Be thoughtful about what information you consume and how you connect with peers and mentors. Narrow down what you read regularly and cut out the garbage. There are a few analysts that I read religiously. On the other hand, when I find myself reading the super-smart analysis of someone who has been consistently bearish stocks since 2005, I know I am wasting my time.

Try to understand the motivations and bias behind anything you read. This is particularly important in the era of clickbait and markets-are-gonna-crash bear porn. I have spoken to good journalists who admit that they feel forced to sensationalize headlines and even entire stories in order to satisfy the institutionalized prioritization of clicks over quality.

If you read a story on Bloomberg or the WSJ that includes the phrase "unnamed sources", that is your first clue that the article could well be trash. A journalist can publish any sort of nonsense on the internet and there is very little consequence if it turns out to be inaccurate. The news cycle moves on and nobody goes back and rates reporters on their past accuracy. The #1 thing they get rated on is: number of clicks.

When you read stories and analysis about financial markets, it is important to know who wrote what you are reading. Finance stories are sometimes written by junior journalists with very little knowledge of financial markets. Many bank analysts and economists have strong worldviews and are committed to a directional bias. If an analyst is bullish, first ask: Is this analyst always bullish? Question the details and sources when reading news articles.

The unsourced and rumor-filled stories run by the major outlets during the China/US Trade War in 2018 and 2019 were particularly notable for their inaccuracy. After a while, the market caught on and stopped reacting to the non-stop, poorly-sourced stories with headlines like "Sources Say Trade Talks Hit Snag". Every news outlet publishes unsourced or poorly-sourced articles with headlines full of exaggeration at times. Be skeptical and weed them out as much as possible. If you react to a headline, read the actual story as quickly as possible afterwards because there might be less there than you think.

Just to be clear, there are plenty of excellent journalists in finance. My point is simply that you need to pay attention to who wrote whatever you are reading, and the more you know about their track record and biases, the clearer the lens you are reading through.

Next, think about your personal information network. Be thoughtful and efficient about who you talk to, what websites you read, who you follow on Twitter, and who you interact with. Can you prune the network a bit and get rid of some of the time-sucking or negative-value-add channels?

For example, I find reading tweets from a list of about 25 to 50 handles is a productive and useful way to acquire timely information. On the other hand, I know to refrain from reading replies and reactions to tweets; that is an incredible waste of time. And I try my best never to read or reply to political or trolling tweets.

Don't get sucked into the time-wasting negativity vortex of comments sections on social media or the web. They are time-sucking garbage dumps often representing the lowest form of humanity—the worst possible place to spend your limited and precious time. Twitter and Zerohedge, for example can be useful sources of information; just be sure to filter properly and avoid pointless time spent in the comments section rabbit hole.

4. Write it down, or type it out

Thoughts are abstract and fuzzy. Writing (with a pen or on a computer) is solid and concrete. If you think, "I'm going to cut my AAPL short at $285", that is completely different from writing **CUT AAPL 285** on a piece of paper and having those words stare up at you as the stock rallies from $282.50 to $284.75.

The same goes for any plans or ideas you have. There is so much noise in your head, so many competing voices vying for airtime. Don't assume you can formulate a plan in there and then execute it successfully without writing anything down. Again, this doesn't have to mean anything more than scratching a few notes down on a piece of paper or recording some thoughts in a spreadsheet.

**Research shows that when you write down
a goal, you are more likely to achieve it.**

When you write something down, it solidifies. It transforms from abstract into concrete. All the sludge falls away and only the important information is left. When you write something down, you have made a choice to select that particular information, goal, or action as more important than all the others. This highlights it for your brain. When you write something down, you signal to your brain "THIS IS IMPORTANT". Your brain records it as such.

The pathways and connections developed in your brain are different when you write something down because the encoding process is different. The encoding is stronger, more robust, and information is recalled more easily. If you want something to happen, write it down.

Another benefit of writing down stop losses, take profits, ideas and goals is that it is harder to wiggle out of them when they are staring right at you. You can't convince yourself that you *never really were going to stop out at $285 absolutely for sure* if you have a huge note on your desk that says **CUT AAPL @ 285**!!! It is your past self sending a message to your future self. Unambiguously. In black Sharpie.

5. Keep a trading journal.

A trading journal is the best way to keep track of your progress, especially early in your career. It can be a detailed record of every single trade you do, or it can be a few paragraphs you write at the end of the day. A trading journal can take whatever form you like. Record a few thoughts each day, or record the specifics of each trade you do. Either way, a journal will enhance your ability to analyze performance, and improve your process. You will start to notice repeated mistakes. You will identify bias in your views. *"Hmmm, I'm always short bonds and never long. That's probably not good. I need to be more flexible."*

Your journal entries should focus on your decision-making and process. What triggered the idea? How strongly did you feel about it? Was it all logic, or partly gut? Describe the specifics of the process and the route you took to develop, execute, and exit the trade.

To enforce the habit of journaling, I send an email to one of my peers on the desk at the end of each day. I call it 12-12, meaning 12 hours back and 12 hours forward. The 12 back part is a quick summary of how my day went, whether I stuck to the plan, whether I overtraded and so on. The 12 forward part is my overnight and next day trading plan including stop losses, dollars at risk and maximum position size.

Those are the five parts of what it means to be organized in trading. Now let's move to the next positive trait that leads to trading success.

Process oriented

There is a wide body of literature covering process vs. outcome. As a rule, you should view your trading P&L as a semi-random output of your process. You control the process, but you do not control the short-term outcome in trading. The sooner you understand this, the better. There is a tremendous amount of variance in trading and one of the best ways to handle this is to focus on your process. If the process is good, the results will eventually follow.

Think deeply about your process. Where do your trade ideas come from? Are you just flicking through a few charts and drawing some trendlines and expecting that to give you an edge? Or are you doing the heavy lifting by digging deep into the drivers, participants, and idiosyncrasies of your market, and uncovering unique insights that are likely not already in the price?

The best book that I have read on the topic of Process vs. Outcome is *Thinking in Bets* by Annie Duke. Duke used to be a professional poker player and while the book talks poker a fair bit, most of her insights also apply directly to trading. The book is about decision making with incomplete information, and that is the essence of trading.

Trading is like poker in that each decision relies on incomplete information and each outcome or trial is strongly influenced by luck. But like poker, in the long run, the luck evens out[52]. We will talk more about luck and variance in Chapter 11, but for now I just want you to understand that if you have a strong process, you will not be as worried about bad luck.

Your goals should mostly focus on process, not outcome. If you need to get to a particular outcome (say a $7,000,000 trading revenue budget), work

---

52. In finance, people prefer to say "variance" not "luck". It is more polite and sounds smarter. And seriously, there is a difference. Luck is what happens in a short sample. Variance is the fluctuation of a random variable around its mean. The better we can measure this variance, the less we worry about luck because in the long-run, luck disappears and variance can be predicted and managed.

backwards from there to set goals that are primarily related to process. Here are some examples of rules that might be part of a solid trading process:

- Complete 6-point Daily Plan every day before executing any trades.
- Maximum 10 trades per day.
- If I stop out of a trade, don't do the same trade again for 24 hours (and don't move stops to avoid triggering this rule!)
- Backtest and build a new trading system for the NASDAQ open.
- Contact three traders or other peers each day to share ideas or dialogue.

When you are confident in your process, you can ride out the inevitable losing streaks because you understand that outcomes are partially dictated by randomness in the short term. Obviously, in the end, it's the outcome that matters but **when you focus on process, the outcome "magically" takes care of itself**.

When evaluating trades, traders, and trading strategies, always refer to this matrix:

	Good outcome	Bad outcome
Good process, good decision	Winning. Feel happy, but not overconfident. How can we make the process even better?	Bad luck, nothing to feel bad about. On to the next trade.
Bad process, bad decision	Lucky. Undeserved success. Be thankful you were fortunate. Address the bad process.	Losing. Stop trading and fix your process.

Let's look at an example of bad decision / good outcome and see how traders with good thinking and bad thinking might respond.

Oil just dropped from $42 to $40 in ten minutes. Jimmy is caught long oil futures and the price is more than $1 through his original stop loss of $41. The market is in freefall but he has convinced himself to give it just a little bit more room because there is a big chart point right here that he hadn't noticed earlier when he first chose his stop loss.

Jimmy was originally long at $42 with a stop at $41 and a take profit at $43.80, risking $1.00 to make $1.80. This was a decent set up because he thought the odds of either side of the trade hitting were about 50/50. Fifty percent probability with a 1.8 : 1 payout = high expected value.

Now, he's down $2.00 on the trade and can't bring himself to cut it. The logical part of his brain says: "*Dude, you're way through your stop. Follow your own rules and get out.*" But there is another voice in his head saying: "*Jimmy-Boi... You know it's going higher; You just need to hold on just a little bit longer. This is the low, baby. Just hold on. You know you can do it...*" Then, before Jimmy has a chance to decide which voice to listen to, a headline hits:

*SAUDI ARABIA TO CUT OIL PRODUCTION 1M BBL/DAY AS ASIAN DEMAND FALLS

Boom! Oil spikes back up to $42 and Jimmy cuts the position at flat. He logs out of his trading software and starts scrolling through Facebook memes. Needless to say, crude rallies to $44 in a straight line afterwards as the Saudi news triggers a reassessment of the supply/demand equation.

Jimmy thinks: "I am so glad I held on and ignored my stop loss. That saved me a lot of money."

He does not understand bad process / bad decision / good outcome.

A good trader thinks: "Not only did I not follow my process, I failed to update my view when the headline came out. Instead of following a good process, I did everything wrong. Sure, I broke even but in the long run I am going to blow up or bleed out if I keep doing this.

"First, I need to automate my stop losses. My broker has a stop loss function that works perfectly fine. Second, when news comes out I need to analyze how it impacts my prior hypothesis, not just get out of the trade because it's back to flat. That's just dumb old reference dependence or anchoring bias. All I cared about was the level I got into the trade and my intraday P&L.

I should be making trading decisions based on market factors, not based on how I feel about my P&L or random, meaningless chart points. I don't deserve to be flat on this trade; I deserve to be down a cartload. I will count my blessings, reduce my risk for a day or two and spend some time working on my process."

On the flipside, if you do a bunch of analysis on a trade, execute according to your plan, then get blown out of the water by a random headline... Don't feel bad. That's just trading. Every trade has a probability of success and failure and unless you are Bobby Axelrod, the probability of success on a trade is never going to be 100%. As long as you stick to the plan and manage your risk appropriately, don't worry about losing trades. *Losing trades are part of the game.*

Think forward. Think forward. Think forward.

Spend most of your time thinking about the future path of markets and how you can predict and capitalize on that path. Spend as little time as possible thinking about trades that happened earlier today or yesterday or six weeks ago. The time to look back is when you are consciously in process-analysis mode, looking thoughtfully back on your trades and trading patterns in recent weeks or months. Otherwise, think forward.

Alpha Traders are future-oriented and don't spend much time on regret. There is nothing more tedious than a trader that constantly talks about what he was going to do, or should have done or was DEFINITELY going to do but then didn't because his phone rang or he got faked out by the price action or blah blah blah…

Hindsight Harry is annoying. Nobody likes Hindsight Harry. He bothers the heck out of the people he talks to because he has a negative mindset that emphasizes past outcomes when he should be focused on process and the future. Clear your mind of past trades and focus on the next opportunity. Good traders thoughtfully review their decisions in quiet moments, long after the fact. Bad traders say "woulda", "coulda", and "shoulda".

As Don Meredith, the American football announcer and player for the Dallas Cowboys once said:

If ifs and buts were candy and nuts, we'd all have a Merry Christmas.[53]

Healthy skeptic

Healthy skepticism is the ability to question the wisdom of the crowd, common knowledge, and experts while still maintaining the ability to incorporate information from respected sources. People sometimes confuse cynic with skeptic and it is important to know the difference.

The modern definition of cynicism is someone who is bitter, motivated by self-interest and/or distrustful of humanity in general. This is an unhealthy approach for markets as it leads to a persistently negative, inflexible, and bearish worldview.

Skeptic comes from the ancient Greek skeptikós, meaning thoughtful, inquiring or "I consider". It means someone who requires strong evidence before accepting a belief or claim. Skepticism is good.

---

53. You might also enjoy this Australian poem from 1937 which makes the same point: "Were 'ifs' and 'buts' just tents and huts / how gaily could we hide! / if 'buts' and 'ifs' were yachts and skiffs / how merrily we would ride! / but 'ifs' and 'buts' they interfere and spoil the whole affair / If it were not for 'ifs' and 'buts' / I'd be a millionaire! Source: https://trove.nla.gov.au/newspaper/article/58819878?searchTerm=%22ifs+and+buts%22

If someone tweets "Stocks are up 11 Mondays in a row!", the healthy skeptic reads that tweet, wonders if it's true, gathers the data and verifies the claim. Through this investigation, the trader might also discover other patterns in the data. Tuesdays are up even more, Fridays are quiet, Thursdays are busy, etc. A less independent and skeptical thinker retweets the original (possibly wrong) information and plans to buy stocks at 8 a.m. on Monday.

When you receive information, greet it with healthy skepticism. Is the information accurate? Is the person or organization disseminating the information biased? Are they always bearish, or frequently too optimistic? Are they trying to inform their readers, or generate clicks? Alpha traders are healthy skeptics. They require strong evidence before accepting a claim.

Don't believe the hype on CNBC. Ignore professional forecasters. Double-check any claim someone makes on FinTwit. Much of the "information" out there is biased or wrong.

This concludes our review of the cognitive traits from the first two columns of the table at the beginning of the chapter. Now we'll move on to the third column: *Non-cognitive traits.*

NON-COGNITIVE TRAITS

While cognitive traits like intelligence, rationality, quantitative skill, and properly-calibrated confidence are crucial for trading success, there are many non-cognitive traits that are equally important. Before we dig in, here is the complete list of traits we will cover:

1. Discipline and self-control

2. Adaptation

3. Courage

4. Self-awareness

5. Ability to handle stress

6. Focus

7. Patience

8. Locus of control

9. Decisiveness

Discipline and self-control

Discipline and self-control are facets of conscientiousness and are crucial to trading success. It is easy to learn the rules of trading but if you don't follow them, you will fail. Many sophisticated, intelligent, and knowledgeable traders fail because of poor discipline and bad self-control.

The fight to remain disciplined and fully in control of our actions is one of the great challenges faced by every human being. We all know that exercise and a healthy diet will keep us slim and healthy. Most people want to be slim and healthy. Yet 71.6% of US adults are overweight or obese[54]. *Understanding* what needs to be done and *doing* what needs to be done are two completely different things.

Self-discipline is the greatest edge in every aspect of life. Health, fitness, education, career success, productivity, marital longevity, and of course trading... They all require discipline. Improve your current level of discipline and you will increase your future levels of happiness and success. It's true in life, and in trading.

To start, understand where you are on the continuum of self-control. What score did you give yourself in the quiz from Chapter 1 (Row G)? If you are low in this category (as I am), this is the place to focus. The smartest trader in the world will not succeed if she has terrible self-control.

There are many traits and characteristics and ideas in this book but if you have a problem with self-discipline, I would make fixing that your first priority. Take action and learn to become more disciplined. Here are some suggestions on how to do that.

How to level up your self-discipline:

- If you have poor self-discipline, admit it. Then create systems to deal with it. Too many people just hope they will be stronger and more disciplined next time instead of creating friction to prevent unwanted actions, and automating desirable habits.

- Outsource discipline as much as possible. For example, every time you put on a trade, load up an automated stop loss right away. If you have a team that works for you, keep your hands off the buttons and let them get you in and out of trades according to parameters you set in advance. Remember that once you put a trade on, the bias kicks

---

54. That's a CDC stat from 2016.

in. You often start to overthink, overreact, and overanalyze. Stick with the parameters you selected when you entered, automate or outsource the stop loss, and take profit so that you do not overtrade.

- Create a clear set of risk management rules and keep them as simple as possible. If you have a daily stop loss of $100,000, it's easy to know when you are done for the day. On the other hand, if you use a very complex set of rules governing your risk management and have no clear eject button, you are more likely to crash. Always have either a daily, weekly, or monthly stop loss (or all three) to manage risk of ruin.

- Meditate or do yoga. A mind in a state of agitation has less self-control and less willpower. Learn about mindfulness. Check out dailystoic.com.

- Read books about willpower and self-control. It is a trait that is innate to some extent but can also be built. *Willpower: Rediscovering the Greatest Human Strength* by Roy Baumeister and John Tierney is excellent, as are *The Science of Self-Discipline* by Peter Hollins and *The Disciplined Trader* by Mark Douglas.

- When you are done reading these books, create a short list of take-aways: two or three actions you plan to take to improve your process and become more disciplined. Keep things as simple as possible.

- Get a coach. There are many levels of coaching available for traders. When I worked at a hedge fund, we had a coach that came in once a month and I found the process useful. I found I did most of the talking and the coach prompted me and helped me find my way. There are online trading coaches available too, but do your homework before hiring someone.

A majority of the trading advice, coaching, lessons, seminars, and products available online are worse than worthless. They are often scams or borderline scams, frauds offered up by individuals with marketing, not trading skills. Good trading coaches have some combination of experience in psychology, performance science and trading. Do some due diligence before you hire a trading coach.

Adaptation

Many traders are good in a specific type of market. Some are good break-out traders, or range traders or flow traders. Maybe they do well when stocks are falling but not when stocks rally. Some traders were great before the algos but have no idea how to trade algo-driven markets. The challenge is that markets are always changing. If you're really good at one type of market, it is almost guaranteed you will be a dinosaur at some point.

Adaptation is such an important part of long-term trading success that I devoted an entire chapter to it. See Chapter 14 for a full discussion of why and how excellent traders adapt.

Courage (but not recklessness)

Good trading requires courage. You need to be able to put on positions that go against what common knowledge, media hype and the smart guy on TV are saying. You need to take positions big enough that they make you feel legitimately at risk if things go wrong. You need to be able to drive the car fast enough to win the Grand Prix... But not so fast you slam into the wall.

Optimal risk appetite is the narrow balancing point between tight, risk-averse white-knuckling and sloppy overtrading. There is no such thing as a perfect trade. When you see a setup that looks amazing, commit the maximum capital possible under your risk management framework.

I use a three-level system for conviction and risk allocation. We will go in depth on sizing and conviction in Chapter 11 but for now just know that when it comes to your highest conviction trades, you should have enough risk on to make you feel uncomfortable, but not out of control. The biggest size you think is still rational, whether or not that makes your knees weak. If it makes your knees wobble a bit but the math is rational, that's perfect.

Varying bet size when huge opportunities come along is an important determinant of trading success.

Changing bet size is the way card counters beat the dealer in blackjack. They look for opportunities with abnormally good odds and then make large bets on those events. Obviously the big difference with trading is that you don't know the odds of any trade, you can only estimate them. But if you see a trade that you believe has a 90% chance of success and a payout of 2 : 1... You need the courage to bet big.

Good traders understand the importance of varying bet size based on opportunity, market volatility and their current performance. Bad traders always trade the same position size regardless of the opportunity set, volatility or P&L.

Remember, there is a continuum from chicken to crazy. You need to be courageous, but not reckless. Risk of ruin is the number one risk to manage—not risk of missing out. Not risk of falling behind budget or benchmark. Not risk of underperforming the guy next to you.

Take meaningful, courageous risk
but never look into the abyss.

Note that risk appetite for an individual is not constant. Many traders behave differently under different conditions. Here are three effects that influence trader risk appetite:

1. Zero-bound effect. Traders that are down on the year tend to trade more nervously than traders who are up. If you are up $4 million on the year and drop to $2.5 million (a loss of $1.5 million), that will feel different than going from plus $1 million to minus $500,000. You need to have the courage to take smart risk, even when you are down.

2. End-of-period effect. Traders tend to take less risk at the end of the year. If a trader has had a good year, they want to bank it. If they have had a bad year, they don't want to make it worse. This effect is why most hedge funds will not pay out more than once per year. Hedge funds that institute twice-yearly payouts find that trader risk appetite drops in both June and December, instead of just in December.

3. House money effect. Traders that are massively profitable in a given period will tend to take on extra risk. This is known as the house money effect, a bias that shows up in both experimental and real-world settings. The house money effect is especially strong immediately after large gains, and then it dissipates over time.

HOW IS YOUR RISK APPETITE?

How did you score yourself on the continuum from "Risk Averse" to "Sometimes Reckless" in the Chapter 1 quiz (row A)? If you scored 7 or 8 you are probably in the sweet spot. Below seven, you are probably not taking enough risk and could be trading below potential. 9 or 10? You may well be overtrading or pushing too hard.

Here is a quick discussion of different risk appetite scores, what they mean, and how to address problems related to specific ranges. I suggest you read all the sections, regardless of your risk appetite score, because there are tips and anecdotes in each section that apply to everyone.

Risk appetite score: 1-4
Risk averse trader

More traders than you would expect fall into the 1-4 range. That's OK! You can still succeed in trading if you are risk averse. But don't be in denial. Be self-aware and be honest about your score. A score between 1 and 4 signals you are a risk averse trader. Even if your risk appetite score is higher than four, please read this section.

The risk averse trader:

- Is afraid to lose money. It is impossible to trade successfully if you are afraid of losing money. You will always be weak. If your fear comes from within, you need to work on it. If your fear comes from inadequate capitalization, the irony is this: your fear of losing money means you are going to lose all your money. Wait until you are adequately capitalized and find another source of income until then. Traders with too little capital end up gambling. The biggest real risk in trading is that you will lose money. You need to understand and accept this risk before you can have any chance of success as a professional.

- Has trouble pulling the trigger.

- Always looks for the perfect trade.

- Needs many things to align before trading.

- Often feels much more comfortable having the same position as manager or peers. Rarely takes the opposite position.

- Looks for an excuse to take off a trade as soon as she puts it on. She will say things like "It should have gone up by now", "It's not trading well", "I don't like the price action" or "This idea isn't working" even when the security has barely moved. She will take a tiny loss or tiny profit using any possible excuse because fundamentally she is risk averse and her subconscious would prefer not to have the position (or any position)! There is a difference between taking risk and putting on positions. If you are always on edge the second you put on a position, you need to think about how to develop staying power. See the tips below.

Tips for risk averse traders

First of all, plenty of good traders are risk averse. They have many of the skills necessary to succeed in trading, and this is their main weakness. It is not the hardest weakness to overcome, but it requires a short list of rules that must be followed religiously:

1. **Set a minimum risk size for every trade.** With aggressive traders, you are more worried about maximum dollars at risk. With risk averse traders, you need to set minimums. Much as there is a speed limit on every highway, there is also a lesser-known minimum speed on many roads. If you are trading from home with a $50,000 account, risking $100 to make $200 is not going to move the needle. In that example, a trader could set a minimum of at least $500 of risk per trade, $1,000 if it's a high-quality idea. Minimum risk amounts ensure that you extract maximum value from your good ideas.

   Be thoughtful about what is a reasonable minimum. If you are a bank trader trying to make $10,000,000 of alpha in a year, risking $30,000 to make $50,000 is a waste of time unless you can find many of these trades each day. Reverse-engineer your minimum $ at risk per trade using your monthly or yearly P&L objective.

   Here is an example. You are trading from home and want to make $250,000 next year. You make money 50% of days and lose money 50% of days. Your average winning day is 1.6X your average losing day. Toss this into a spreadsheet and keep changing the "average winning day" amount until the year total is $250,000. That gives you a starting point for how much risk you will need to take.

			Notes
1	Trading days per year	252	
2	Average winning day	5,291	Modify this until yearly number (row 8) matches budget
3	% winning days	50%	Your best estimate. Use historical data if possible.
4	Win day : lose day P&L ratio	1.60	
5	Average losing day	3,307	Row 2 / Row 4
6	All winning day profits	666,666	Row 1 * Row 2 * Row 3
7	All losing days total	(416,666)	Row 1 * (1 - Row 3) * Row 5
8	Yearly P&L	**250,000**	Row 6 + Row 7

This concept can also be relevant to traders with high risk appetite scores. When I first worked at a hedge fund, I felt like a kid in a candy store because instead of just FX, I was able to trade every financial market under the sun. I could trade oil, wheat, bonds and whatever else I wanted.

At first, this led me to dabble in many markets. It was a great learning experience, but I found that I did a poor job of risk managing trades in secondary markets because they were much smaller than my core trades. I would risk $300,000 on an FX trade, but I might only risk $50,000 on an oil trade at first, because I felt I didn't know the market as well.

Thus, when an oil trade went against me, I would tend to show poor discipline because the P&L impact was minimal. I would drag my stop lower or even just cancel it because the losses didn't really hurt. In contrast, when a trade went my way, I had trouble taking profit at my target because the gain didn't feel big enough.

I might say to myself: "Man, that was a great idea, but I only made $65,000. Not even worth the mental capital. Maybe I can stretch it to $100,000 and at least make it worth the effort." Needless to say, after hitting the target, oil would reverse and I would cut at a small loss.

My trading in these products improved substantially when I set risk minimums for non-core markets. Instead of dabbling in oil or silver or other futures, I would only enter if I had a strong view and was willing to take meaningful risk (say $200,000 or more if my normal risk size in FX was $300,000). This ensured:

a. High conviction before entering a secondary market because meaningful capital was at stake; and

b. proper attention to the position and rigorous risk management since the position was big enough to matter, meaning

c. no too-small positions in non-core markets to distract or waste mental capital.

2. **Do not take off a trade until the stop loss, take profit, or some other predetermined reassessment trigger is hit.** I will explain the meaning of "reassessment trigger" throughout this book. The risk averse trader sees danger at every corner and is consciously or subconsciously looking for excuses to end the discomfort of being in a trade and get back to the relaxed state of flat. Remember: to be an Alpha Trader, you need to be OK with feeling uncomfortable sometimes.

If you are a risk averse trader (or you are managing a risk averse trader) simply institute a rule. When you put on a trade, list the reasons you will take it off: stop loss or take profit hit (of course). Time triggers are fine, as long as they are determined ahead of time. For example: I will reassess at 4 p.m. today (if it's a day trade) or at 3 p.m. Friday (if it's a multi-day trade). These are called reassessment triggers[55].

All reassessment triggers should be determined ahead of time. Any other reason to take off a trade is not acceptable. It looks bid! It's not going down! Some other market just blipped higher so I got nervous… etc. These are not good reasons to reduce risk.

Once you take a position, you are a gigantic drooling bias monster. Your weaknesses are multiplied by ten when you are in a trade. Set specific rules that will restrict your actions when the inevitable discomfort kicks in. Learn to live with the discomfort. That's what real risk feels like. Have courage. Stop white-knuckling every trade. Put

---

55. I first heard the term "reassessment trigger" while reading Bija Advisors notes online. So I give credit to Stephen Duneier for coining the term, though I'm not positive he invented it. It's a good term.

the trade on and let it cook. Do not take it off until one of your ex-ante triggers hits.

3. **Use trade quotas.** Set a number of trades that you plan to do in a given period and stick to it. Your first instinct might be: "What if there are not that many opportunities?" There are always opportunities. If they are only lower conviction opportunities, then just size them appropriately.

   The quota you set for yourself is highly contingent on your trading style, but if you are a short-term trader (but not a day trader or high-frequency trader), you might set a minimum of three trades per week. This forces you to get engaged and take risk, even when you are uncomfortable doing so. Sure, it might put you in a few lower EV trades, but the tradeoff is necessary to ensure you don't spend too much time underinvested on the sidelines.

   A basketball player who always waits for the perfect shot might shoot 100% from the field and score 4 points per game. That is not good! As a coach, you want that player to take 15 shots and miss 5 (and thus score ~20 points). Traders who are risk averse do not take enough shots, so implementing a quota forces them to find a better place on the continuum[56].

Risk appetite score: 5-7

Moderate risk trader

If you gave yourself a 5, 6 or 7 on the continuum of risk averse to risk seeking, you can probably up your game. Your risk aversion is not a weakness, but you might be able to stretch yourself a bit and avoid an early career plateau.

In the early 2000s, I worked for a bank that was generally risk averse. They ran a risk business model that is surprisingly common in banks: "take risk, but don't lose money". This is the optimal business model for a manager that wants to protect the bank but also allow for a bit of upside if trading conditions are optimal. This same business model is employed by many pod-based hedge funds. If you have 100 traders all working with very tight stops but some of

---

56. If you don't like the word quota, you can use "goal" but to me quota implies you must reach the number and goal implies you hope to reach it. So I like "quota" better.

those traders are still able to generate 20% returns in a year, the overall returns and Sharpe ratio of the hedge fund will be outstanding.

Some traders detest this business model because it makes them nervous. Taking risk without losing money sounds like an oxymoron. It really isn't. It just means that you need to behave like a call option. Take as much risk as you want when you are profitable, but play extremely tight when you are not. This is the logical approach for any conservative senior manager who views the traders working for him as a portfolio. It is a good business model even if it's not the most fun one to work in for traders with very strong risk appetite.

The moderate risk taker thrives in that sort of model because they deliver exactly what management wants: decent upside with limited downside. I have generally been fairly flexible in my approach but I definitely have concluded that this is the optimal strategy for most traders. Increase your risk when you have a strong P&L base and decrease your risk when you are near or below zero. This substantially reduces risk of ruin, allows for the right tail, and offers you the best chance at long-term success.

The trader with risk appetite in the 5-7 range struggles to produce the right tail of the distribution though, because they will more likely be satisfied once they hit their budget or goal. This is the kind of trader I was, when I worked at the generally risk-averse bank I mentioned. If my budget was $5 million and I got there eight months into the year, I was encouraged to "bank it" or "ring the register" or "take it easy into year end."

This makes sense on some level but greatly reduces your ability to see what kind of trader you can be, because despite the risks of the house money effect, most traders are at their best when they have a big base of P&L to work with but can remain patient and on the lookout for great opportunities worthy of a big bet.

Given the incentives and guidance from management, at that bank I acted like a trader with risk appetite of 5-7 even though my true risk appetite is much higher. High enough that it tends to be a weakness when I'm not at my best.

When I went to Lehman Brothers in 2006, I had a great start to the year. My budget was $6 million and I was up more than that by March. I went to my boss at the time and asked him how he felt I should proceed. I gave him the explanation of how things went at my last job and how they would tell me to "take it easy" once I hit my budget. Steam came out of his ears.

"No way, dude! This your chance to see what kind of trader you are! You have six million dollars in the bank! Set a stop loss at three million and go turn that six into ten."

I sat there thinking for a bit and he waved me out of his office.

"Go! Go make money!"

That year I made $50 million dollars and I am forever thankful to that manager for teaching me that lesson. The lesson was not: "You have money in the bank so go gamble it." The lesson was: "When you are in a strong capital position with chunky P&L, increase your risk in a methodical way and try to blow through the ceiling. The time to go for it is not January 1; the time to go for it is when you have money in the bank and markets are full of opportunity."

When you take this approach, it is crucial that you remain aware of downside and drawdown. Set a point at which you will go back to a more defensive approach. In the case outlined above, I was up $6 million and set my "go back to defensive" level at +$3m. This gives you ammo to push hard when you're doing well but also defines your downside so you don't just blow through all the money you've made.

This idea of pushing hard when you are in a strong position is 100% contingent on the opportunity set. You don't push just because you're doing well. You push because you're doing well *and* there are great opportunities.

Wait, wait, wait… Then pounce. Traders with risk appetite scores in the 5 to 7 range need permission and opportunity to push hard when they are doing well. If you are managing a trader like this… Push them to push themselves. Ask them: "Do you want to see what kind of trader you can be? This is your chance."

If you scored between 5 and 7 on risk appetite, here are some things to try:

- As described above: When you reach a P&L threshold where you would have been satisfied in the past (e.g., at budget, above budget, best YTD ever and it's only August…) don't look at it as an opportunity to chill. Think about an amount you could lose that would still leave you in a strong position. If your budget was $4 million and you are up $3 million in April, for example. Say to yourself: I'm going to wait for a really good opportunity or series of opportunities, and trade extra aggressively until I draw back down to $2 million. In other words, I'm going to be very aggressive with $1 million of my P&L if I see trades I believe in.

  If you draw back down to $2 million, reset and slow down. But if you are able to risk that $1 million to make $3 million, suddenly you find yourself up $6 million and it's still only June!

To be 100% clear: this is not mindlessly doubling down at a casino because you have seventeen black chips in your pocket. This is increasing your bet size on high odds opportunities because you have the capital to do so. This is how you generate outsized returns without risk of ruin.

No matter what type of trader you are, there will not be an infinite number of years where you start the year very strong and the trading environment is favorable. When the stars align like this, be courageous. Go for it. If you draw down to your predetermined point, that's OK. Trading is about risk. Sometimes you'll be wrong and you will lose. That's trading. Then you hunker down and start building up the P&L again.

• Another thing to try if you are in the 5 to 7 range and have been doing OK: Increase all your risk parameters by a fairly small increment, say 20%. If you are normally trading 200 e-minis, go to 240. If you are a home trader risking 1% of capital as your daily stop loss, increase it to 1.2% of capital. If you are a bank trader who usually trades 20 million EURUSD, try 24 million. This is something you should do when you are confident and trading well. Incremental risk increases break you out of the habit of sizing your positions the same all the time.

Many traders establish a comfort level and standard position size and never move away from it. If you work at a hedge fund, you are often forced to change position size as your capital increases. But if you work at a bank or at home, you can feasibly trade the exact same position size for years at a time. To grow, you need to keep gradually increasing risk until you either hit capacity constraints (a significant problem when it happens, but not a concern for 95% of traders) or until you reach the maximum allowable position for your capital base. Position sizing is discussed in Chapter 11.

Depending on your capital base, you may already be running the largest possible positions given your risk framework. If you are a home-based trader with a $1m account and you've determined that 3% of capital is the right daily stop loss for you, and you're hitting your stop loss once a week, that's too much. If you hit it once per year, you are probably too risk averse. Your variance is probably too low and you can up your risk.

Trading is always a tension between taking the most possible risk to make the most possible money when you are right, and taking small enough risk that you don't blow yourself up when you hit a string of bad ideas. Think about where you are on this continuum. Most traders that I have seen could take more risk. Some (including myself) would do better if they took less. And that brings us to the other end of the risk appetite spectrum.

Risk appetite score: 8-9

Strong risk appetite

A trader with a risk appetite score of 8 or 9 has the most upside but also requires more supervision and has more downside risk than a trader with a lower score. I would say the sweet spot for risk appetite is somewhere in the 7.5 to 8.0 area, though traders with very high scores, when harnessed, can deliver blockbuster returns. Then again, they can be scary to watch sometimes.

A trader with strong risk appetite needs rules. If you are in this category, develop specific but simple rules to regulate your desire to take risk.

All of the following limits should be clearly defined and deemed to be unbreakable:

1. Maximum daily, monthly, and yearly loss. This can be a formula based on total capital and current P&L. Depending on trading style, the liquidity of products traded, and time horizon, daily stops are not appropriate for all traders. There is a full discussion of risk management in Chapter 11.

2. Permitted products and strategies. Can a hedge fund PM sell volatility with unlimited downside, for example? Can a home day trader short low-priced stocks? Can an FX trader take a position in a pegged or managed Asian currency?

   Depending on where you trade, this question may not be relevant. It is an esoteric question that does not come up all that often, but can be the difference between blowing up and not blowing up.

   Many of the blowups that I have witnessed first-hand have been the result of trades where the trader never should have been trading that product in the first place. Hedge fund managers risking 24 basis points to make 1 on Bank of Canada day. Retail day traders going short a thinly-traded biopharma stock. Option traders selling top-side USDCNH volatility. Retail FX punters going long EURCHF at 1.2010. These are all blowups caused by traders dealing in products that they never should have touched.

If you are day trading from home, what stocks are fair game? The way you answer this question might be the difference between long-term success and instant, nuclear devastation of your trading account. See GameStop shorts, for example.

3. Maximum position size by product.

4. Value at risk (VAR) or stress-test P&L. These are higher-level frameworks used at banks and hedge funds, but both methods have many issues when applied in real life. If you trade from home, don't worry about VAR, it's a tool used by institutions. Some problems with VAR and stress testing:

   » VAR often depends on historical volatility which is not always a good predictor of future volatility.

   » Stress tests can overweight rare events and ignore the fact that stop losses are effective loss control mechanisms in liquid markets. For example, stress-testing the P&L of 50 million USDJPY against five years of data might show a maximum possible loss of 500 pips or $2.5 million (approx.) but a stop loss will protect a disciplined trader from anywhere near that large of a loss.

   » VAR and stress testing often rely on historical correlation which is backward-looking and unstable.

   This book is for active, short-term traders attempting to generate alpha. It is not meant to address carry, short volatility, rolldown, basis, and other trading strategies that involve convex and non-linear payout structures.

5. Cooling off levels. If a trader draws down X from high water or over-earns by Y, she should enter a two or three day cooling off period. During cooling off periods, all risk is cut in half. This helps stabilize P&L after weak periods and avoids winner's tilt after strong periods.

If a trader has enough experience, P&L history, and self-awareness to know she does not suffer from winner's tilt or overconfidence after very strong periods, the topside cooling off levels can be excluded. Cooling off levels are different from stop losses on the downside as they relate more to bad streaks and drawdown from peak, not absolute levels of P&L.

Risk appetite score: 10

Too much risk appetite

If you gave yourself a score of 10 on risk appetite, you need to be careful. You are probably in the sensation-seeking, trading-for-excitement, or gambling category. Trading can be a lot like gambling (if you want it to be) and it has similar dopamine payoffs if you have an addictive personality. Along with the rules I listed above, traders with a risk appetite score of 10 need to honestly analyze their motivation for trading and be self-aware enough to know whether they are acting more like finance professionals or gambling addicts.

Traders on the extreme end of the risk-taking spectrum use trading as another method of sensation seeking. This is not good. We will talk much more about trading for fun (instead of profit) in Chapter 7. That ends this discussion on risk appetite. Now let's go back to the non-cognitive traits that define the Alpha Trader.

Decisiveness

Good traders are decisive. I want to acknowledge here I know there is overlap between many of the traits I describe in this section. In fact, as I stated much earlier, most of them fall under the Big Five psychological trait of *conscientiousness*. Risk appetite, courage and decisiveness are all similar personality facets. I could have lumped them all under risk appetite but I want to dig deeper and unpack some subtle distinctions.

So yes, decisiveness is like courage and risk appetite, but here I mean it more as the specific ability to press buttons once you have an idea. Trigger happy vs. gun shy. Do you find it easy to put on a trade once you have a good idea? Or do you hesitate? Does this hesitation lead to worse entry points and tactical weakness, or is it healthy calibration and impulse control? If you gave yourself a 10 out of 10 score on decisiveness, there is a good chance you are too impulsive, overconfident, or both.

Here is how I would describe the continuum from decisive (10) to hesitant (1):

9-10 **Probably trigger happy**. Risk of overconfident and impulsive trading. If it is too easy to decide and pull the trigger every time, perhaps you need to hesitate a bit more? Most likely you should filter out some trades and focus on your best ideas. Decisiveness is great but think about whether it is possible you are too decisive. Maybe you need to filter your ideas a bit more and either reduce your number of trades or at least be sure to size your best trades much larger than the others.

Traders with a score of 9 or 10 in decisiveness probably have a hard time ignoring random headlines and feel the urge to trade on every bit of news. "News" sounds a lot like "noise".

7-8 **The sweet spot**. Decisive but still cautious enough to understand that not every shiny object has value. Able to hit the buttons when a headline comes out but also able to not hit the buttons.

5-7 **Probably a bit too hesitant** but still nothing to worry about. Think about whether you are waffling on good ideas. What exactly do you need to get over the line and put on a trade? Are you waiting for confirmation from others? When you come up with a trade idea, do you feel better if you run it past a few other traders before executing? Try not to look for validation from others. Own your ideas and remember that if other people agree with your idea, that does not necessarily make it better. It may mean it's a popular idea with less upside than a unique or contrary idea that nobody likes.

1-4 **Too hesitant.** You are probably leaving good trades and good money on the table as you fail to pull the trigger. Force yourself to do a certain number of trades per day or per week as described in my quota system earlier. This takes away the should I / shouldn't I hesitation because knowing you have to do X trades this week, the decision has already been made. The question then just becomes which trades to do, not whether to trade.

Another exercise to help short-term traders get more comfortable hitting the buttons and trading more frequently (and with less hesitation) is to make markets. If you are a day trader at home, put a small bid and a small offer in the same stock, 3 cents apart. When both sides trade, do it again. Set a stop loss in case it blows through one side of your price and keep putting in two-way prices for an hour or so. This is also a good way to get quicker on the keys if that is relevant to your trading style (if you trade headlines, for example).

Finally, get a trading coach. This does not have to be a huge financial or time commitment. You can meet a trading coach once per month and communicate with him by email once a week. Talking out loud about trading-related issues can be valuable. Thoughts buzz around in your head and sometimes make sense and sometimes do not. A conversation can help you identify and unpack the issues that cause your hesitation.

While trading coaches often have a psychology background, the most important part of talking to a trading coach is the talking, not the psychology expertise. Putting your thoughts, concerns and weaknesses out in the open often clarifies them and will help you deal with them. A co-worker or experienced trader you know can most likely offer nearly as much help as a trained psychologist. That has been my experience anyway.

Self-awareness

Part of the intent of this book is to make you more self-aware and more honest about your strengths and weaknesses as a trader. There is no shame in having low scores on some dimensions. Nobody possesses all positive characteristics in abundance. Better to admit that you are risk averse and trade accordingly than pretend your name is Gordon Gekko or Dollar Bill.

The number one way to build and cultivate self-awareness is to maintain a trading journal.

This is such a cliché of trading advice. That's because it's true. You can journal individual trades or individual days or just sporadic thoughts. Keep a document or spreadsheet open in the background and note what you are doing.

I will tell you this up front: keeping a journal is a tough habit to maintain. It's a huge pain in the butt and two things tend to happen. Either:

A) You start trading really well and you get in the zone and you can't be both-ered updating your journal because you feel like a trading God or

B) You keep losing money and you get worn down and the last thing you want to do is spend 20 minutes journaling what happened because all you really want to do is bolt out of the office and go meet some friends for a G&T.

It is extremely difficult to maintain a trading journal habit but it is worth it. And just because it is difficult, that is no excuse not to do it. Very few highly-productive habits are easy to maintain. Remember that if trading was easy, it would not pay so well.

One trick that works for any difficult-to-maintain habit like lifting weights or not smoking or keeping a trading journal is to find a partner who wants to do the same thing. If you promise to exchange one paragraph a day with a friend, you are not just letting yourself down if you get lazy, you are letting down your friend as well.

If you think "I'm going to go lift weights today at 10 a.m.", that is much less powerful than setting an appointment to meet your friend and lift weights at 10 a.m. Most people find it easier to let themselves down and will work harder to do the right thing for a friend (or acquaintance for that matter).

This can also be handled with a professional trading coach. On the most basic level, a trading coach can simply be there to help enforce your daily reg-imen. Like a personal trainer, a coach can keep you on track and help you enforce the good habits that you don't quite have the willpower to enforce your-self. This section is about self-awareness: if you know you are not good at form-ing strong habits, find a way to get one paragraph of journaling out every day. Somehow. Some way.

A trading journal helps you keep track of emotions, bias, themes, and thoughts. There are many ways that a journal can help you. It can take two basic forms. One is a trade-by-trade journal. If you are new to trading, I recom-mend this approach. A free form approach is fine for more experienced traders but a more granular system will help new traders collect more data.

The more data you collect, the more likely you will learn something from your journal. Think about areas where you know you are weak and see if you can come up with data that might reveal your progress in that area.

Here's a sample trading journal in a spreadsheet:

Entry date and time	Exit date and time	Days held	Conviction (out of 5)	Long/ Short	Asset	Asset class	Position size
3/9/20 3:00 PM	3/10/20 3:00 PM	1	5	Long	USDCAD	FX	50,000,000

Entry	Stop loss	Take profit	Reward vs. risk at inception	$ at risk	Actual exit	P&L	Reward vs. risk actual
1.3460	1.3340	1.3950	4.08	445,765	1.3650	695,971	1.58

Rationale
Saudi Arabia / Russia start an oil price war and USDCAD has barely moved on the Sunday open.

Reassessment triggers
1. Saudi Arabia / Russia truce 2. NYMEX crude oil goes above $30

Notes after closing
Took profit way too early for no good reason. Got antsy seeing the big green P&L and did not have the courage to stay with it. Could have moved my stop up instead of taking profit so early. The trade hit the take profit two days later. **Grrrrrr.**

I have formatted the information to fit it on the page here but in real life I record each trade across a huge row in Excel. This makes it is easier to process the data later. For example, you can calculate the average length of time you are in a trade, or see whether you stick to your stop losses or not by creating simple formulas below the final row.

In this example, you see a frequent problem that many traders have: This trader put the trade on looking for USDCAD to go to 1.3950. But when it ripped higher from 1.3460 to 1.3650 in just one day, he took profit because it felt like "too much, too fast". He didn't stick to his plan. Instead he should have done one of the following:

a) Trailed his stop loss up. We will talk more about this in the chapter on risk management. It can be a good strategy, but it also has downside.

b) Stayed with his original plan. This is usually the best course of action. Before you put the trade on, you were a sober tactician. Once you have the risk and the market is flying higher, you are an emotional human being who does not want to give back a huge profit. If you always cut your winners prematurely, the risk/reward ratio you think you are using is inaccurate. If you risk 1 to make 2 at inception, but then cut half way to your take profit all the time, your real risk/reward is 1 : 1. That is why there are boxes for reward vs. risk at both inception and exit. You need to keep track of whether you are sticking with your ideas or jumping out of good trades too early.

c)   Sold one third or half of the position and let the rest ride. This can be a good way of dealing with your desire to cut. Can you reduce just 33% of the risk and at least make yourself feel better?

A trading journal is the most direct route to trading self-awareness. Ideas become concrete when you write them down. By recording each trade along with a rationale and thought process, you can pick up on recurring errors, problems, or leaks in your trading.

> **Thoughts are abstract and fuzzy.**
> **Writing is concrete and solid.**

Often, the process of writing things down will bring out new ideas and thoughts, and will lead to different results. As Daniel Boorstin once said: "I write to discover what I think." [57]

Sit down and do a deep dive into your trading journal every month or so. See if you can find meaningful takeaways. For example:

- Do you stick to your plan? Does your risk/reward at inception come close to your actual risk/reward. If not, why?

- Are there any consistent features of your good or bad trades?

  » Time horizon

  » Asset class

  » Conviction level

- Did you hit your stop loss more often than usual? This might be a sign that your positions are too big or the volatility regime has changed and you have not adapted.

---

57. He was Librarian of the United States Congress from 1975 to 1987. Don't feel bad that you've never heard of him.

Once you have your takeaways, set one goal (or two at most) to address a leak or issue you have discovered. I am a big believer in working on just one or two measurable and achievable goals at a time. Let me explain.

When I was a senior manager at a bank, we used a formal corporate goal-setting system and usually it allowed for somewhere between five and fifteen goals to be entered. I found that was just way too many goals for me to supervise or coach as a leader and way too many goals for an employee to manage as an individual.

I eventually instituted my own "One Goal" system. I told the people that worked for me that all those goals in the corporate system were great, but all I cared about was their one most important goal. I asked them to e-mail me that goal and explain why it was important and how they planned to achieve it. This was effective. I saw much more impact from this One Goal system than I ever saw from more formalized, multi-goal systems.

So… After reviewing your trading journal, come up with a goal. Something fairly short-term (a few months at most). Another feature of good goals is that they are specific, and not too long-term. If you can set a goal that covers the next month or two, that is much easier to achieve.

You are more likely to succeed with a goal like "I will not drink any soda for the next month" than with "I'm never going to drink soda again." Chunking into smaller, achievable, and short-term goals develops habits and process that will lead to achievement of bigger-picture, longer-term goals.

Here are a few hypothetical examples of useful takeaways or goals that might emerge after you analyze your trading journal:

- No S&P futures trades for 30 days. All the money I make in other assets, I give back with my irresistible urge to go short S&Ps!

- My trading journal entries are much more emotional than usual. Tighten daily stop loss to $15,000. My normal stop is $30,000 but I have been trading badly and I know I'm in a weird state of mind because my Dad is really sick.

- No trades between noon and 3 p.m. Those trades hit 35% of the time vs. 57% of all trades initiated outside that time frame.

One of the easiest ways to lose money in trading is by hitting buttons somewhat randomly in response to stimulation from noisy price movement. This sort of thing:

{TSLA RALLIES FROM $444 TO $449}

"Tesla's rallying! Something must be going on. Whoa, it's breaking $450! There must be news out."

{TRADER BUYS 300 SHARES AT $450.70. THE HIGH IS $450.85. THE STOCK FADES DOWN TO $450.10.}

"Hmmm. It's losing momentum."

{TRADER FRANTICALLY SCROLLS THROUGH TWITTER LOOK-ING FOR POSITIVE TESLA HEADLINES. TSLA DRIFTS BACK DOWN TO $449.00}

"Crap. That was dumb."

{TRADER SELLS AT $448.60 FOR A LOSS OF $2.10 PER SHARE}

If you update your trading journal with every trade in real-time, it is less likely you will put on pointless trades like the one above. First of all, as you fill in your trade journal in real-time you will realize you have nothing to put in the "Rationale" box. *Ummm… Because it was going up?? Because I thought there might be a headline? Because: FOMO?* Second, once you are in the habit of completing your trading journal, you will become rooted in a process where you already know you need a decent rationale before entering a trade.

When you know you need a decent rationale to enter in your trade journal, that tightens up your filter. You avoid dumb noise trades because you know as you move your hands toward the buttons that there is no good rationale. You don't hit BUY or SELL, because you have developed good discipline.

Knowing that you are going to record every trade in a trading journal makes you more selective and logical when trading. You are less likely to hit buttons for no good reason and get sucked in by the deafening noise. It also boosts your confidence once you are in the trade because you have clearly laid out your reasoning, and it is solid.

Everything in your head is abstract. There is a ton of noise in there. Multiple competing voices with logic, ego, mental shortcuts, bias, memory, and emotion, all competing for airtime. When you record a plan, you filter out the noise and distill the logical output.

The Alpha Trader always has a plan.

A trading journal is not the only way to build self-awareness. Here are some other methods:

1. Step outside yourself. This sounds a bit weird and self-helpy, but it can be a powerful way to up your self-awareness. Sit there, quiet your mind and imagine your rational self, standing right next you. What do they think of your trading right now? This is a way of shutting down System 1 (gut) and activating System 2 (logic). When you ask, "What would my rational self think?", you break through the storm and noise of swirling thoughts and focus on the logical. This is especially important for active traders, because rapid trading activity is more likely to be driven by quick decisions influenced by emotion and bias.

The key here is to slow things down and observe yourself and your actions rationally. If you identify a mistake, correct it as quickly as possible without much further thought. Seeing yourself making a mistake is step one, but then you need to take action and correct it. I have literally said out loud: "I know this is a mistake, but I'm doing it anyway," as I press buttons to enter a trade. I showed good self-awareness there, I guess, but it is clearly not good enough to simply identify a mistaken action. One needs to stop it before it happens.

You need to have the self-control and willpower to take over when you see your dumb brain doing something suboptimal. Your dumb brain is the one that wants to yell "squirrel!" when it sees a squirrel. Your smart brain is the one that resists impulses and takes control. Try to be aware of the different layers of thought that go on in your mind and notice repeating patterns such as the urge to:

- Buy something just because it's going up.
- Do a trade because you are bored.
- Exit a good position because it's not moving.
- Cut a position because you don't like the price action.

When you are self-aware, you understand the many pieces that make up the mental puzzle. You are part intelligent, rational thinker and part impulsive, jumpy, fight-or-flight lizard. Know when your smart brain is in control, and notice yourself acting irrational and dumb. Comment on it. Then grab the steering wheel. *Sorry dumb brain, you're not taking me where I want to go. Move over, I'm driving.*

2. Think about your motivations. This is another way of building self-aware-ness. Human beings are driven by incentives. What motivates you to succeed? The most reliable motivation is a strong internal desire to achieve. External motivations like money, proving yourself or outperforming the guy that sits next to you will not lead you to the promised land. This is well-known in edu-cation circles. Intrinsic motivation crushes extrinsic motivation.

In other words: are you trading because you enjoy it, you want to win, and/or it satisfies you intellectually? Or are you trading to get rich? This is a complex question given the instant feedback and direct monetary rewards of successful trading. Research shows that if you dream of being rich… No matter how rich you get, you will always wish you were richer. So, pursuing money for the sake of money is a pointless goal.

There is a concept known as the hedonic treadmill which states that as a human being earns more money, his desires and expectations rise in tandem so that no amount of wealth will lead to greater happiness. Research shows this to be generally true. Once someone makes enough money to comfortably acquire shelter, clothing, food, and health care (annual income somewhere around $75,000 to $125,000 per year in most parts of the United States), additional increases in income do not increase happiness much.

Harvard's Study of Adult Development followed the lives of hundreds of people over eight decades and found the happiest people were the ones that had the strongest and most durable relationships with community, family, and friends. Relationships predict longevity and happiness better than money, intel-ligence, or fame.

Making ten million dollars is not going to make you happy on its own. But if you truly love trading… It might! You should (generally) enjoy the process and act of trading. You should find it intellectually stimulating, exciting and (sometimes) fun. You should look forward to going to work most days. If you don't, you are doing it wrong. Here is a quote from one of the great books on self-awareness: Eckhart Tolle's *The Power of Now*.

> See if you can catch yourself complaining, in either speech or thought, about a situation you find yourself in, what other people do or say, your surroundings, your life situation, even the weather. To complain is always nonacceptance of what is. It invariably car-ries an unconscious negative charge. When you complain, you make yourself into a victim. When you speak out, you are in your

power. So change the situation by taking action or by speaking out
if necessary or possible; leave the situation or accept it. All else
is madness.

I highly recommend *The Power of Now*. The book is not directly related to trading, but it does offer insight on mental skills that help with good trading and good thinking. Specifically, the book (as you might guess from the title) is about a focus on the present, the *now*. Good traders don't get mired in what ifs. They trade the market one day at a time and do not waste finite mental energy on thoughts of past outcomes or fears of an uncertain future.

Trading is not life or death. If you fail, you will learn and the sun will rise tomorrow. This is not emergency heart surgery where failure is catastrophic. Maintain perspective. If you spend a stretch of more than 18 months of trading where you are mostly miserable, I would think about finding another role or another career. Trading is not just about P&L. It is also about learning, personal growth, self-discovery, and self-improvement. Focus as much as possible on self-improvement and process development—let the money take care of itself.

For the record, I have found myself miserable on several occasions and for me it has always been about the role, not the career. If you work in an unpleasant setting; if you work for a manager that does not respect you or does not know how to run a risk business; if you work for a firm that is extremely risk averse; or if you trade at home with insufficient capital or insufficient support from your family, the problem is probably the role, not the trading.

If you are in a good firm and you like your manager, or you are trading independently with plenty of capital, and you still dread sitting down in front of your computer in the morning: that is bad. Make a change.

If trading isn't fun most of the time, you need to figure out why.

3. Morning prep. Another way to build self-awareness is to do a quick morning prep and self-check-in. You can simply fill out a quick one pager when you first sit down at the desk. For a NASDAQ day trader, it might look something like this:

DAILY SHEET 4/20/2020					
One word to describe how I feel today	Pumped		TODAY'S STOP LOSS	$4,500	Maximum $5,000
My Mood (out of 10)	10		TARGET P&L	$9,000	
Quality of opportunities today (out of 10)	8				
Events today	Nothing really. China PMI tonight at 9PM				
My plan today	Trade news aggressively, risking $1,500 per news trade				
	Buy 300 NFLX at $418.01 with a stop at $410.97 (risking $2,100)				
Personal	*Call the irrigation guy to fix broken sprinkler (1PM)*				
Key levels	Support2	Support1	LAST	Resistance1	Resistance2
NFLX	412.70	417.70	422.96	439.17	449.52
TSLA	652.00	693.00	753.89	774.00	807.00
SPCE	14.81	17.66	18.90	21.06	25.15
STAY FLAT FROM NOON to 2:30 p.m.					

It takes about two minutes to complete; this is not a major task. It sets a professional and organized tone for the day and allows you to ask the key questions. This Daily Sheet as I call it, forces you to lock in on what is most important for the day; your mood, the market, and your plan. To steal a term from mindfulness and yoga, the Daily Sheet forces you to center yourself before you start trading.

Complete your daily sheet, then take a few breaths, clear your mind, and center yourself.

Then go.

A few comments on this trader's DAILY SHEET:

- The trader has a max daily risk of $5,000 and then reduces risk depending on mood and opportunity set. The formula is the average of the mood and opportunity scores divided by 10 times $5,000. In this case: ((8.5 / 10) * 5000). It makes sense to adjust your risk based on your perception of your own mood / confidence and your assessment of what the market might give you today. There's no point in allocating max risk to a quiet Monday. *We will talk about risk allocation later, but note that daily loss limits should be set as a percentage* *of free capital, not a raw $ number. In this case, I am using $5,000 to keep things simple.*

- This trader's target P&L is always 2X stop loss. That is reasonable but can vary by trader. The target can be important for traders who like to press and add risk when they are trading well. Hitting the day's P&L target alerts the trader that maybe it's time to reduce risk, not increase it.

- The plan does not have to be anything super-complicated. A general strategy and any specifics you know in advance will suffice. One or two sentences.

- Personal reminders can go at the bottom. Schedule all your personal and business meetings for the afternoon. **Never schedule meetings (business or personal) before noon. That is your time to trade. Keep it sacred and free of distractions.** Whether you are a home day trader or a Senior MD at an investment bank—if you want to trade successfully, do not schedule meetings that interfere with prime trading time. Your performance will suffer.

To reduce your morning workload, the technical levels section can be filled in the night before. The rest must be completed, in full, before you allow yourself to start trading. This is not difficult. Do it every day.

**Write a brief plan for the day
before you start pressing buttons.**

Trading is a journey that can bring you wisdom that will benefit your non-trading life. By the same token, self-improvement efforts outside of trading can make you a better trader. We have scratched the surface of self-awareness here, mostly as it pertains to trading. Pursue self-awareness as a trader, but also as a curious and growth-oriented human being.

Embrace meditation, yoga, exercise, and other paths to self-awareness and you will become a better trader. A healthy body and a healthy, self-aware mind will give you the endurance for long-run survival in the market.

Ability to handle stress

Whenever people ask me "Don't you find trading stressful?" I reply: "Yeah, but it's good stress." Like playing professional baseball is stressful. Or flying a fighter jet is stressful. And sure, the stakes are high but it's not life or death. It's important. But it's not life or death.

Good traders have the right perspective. They take the job seriously but do not allow it to consume them.

Trading is not who you are. It is what you do.

A fair bit of research has been done on the physiological impacts of trading. The book *The Hour Between Dog and Wolf* by John Coates covers the topic well. When a human senses danger, the brain releases adrenaline and cortisol. This boosts the person's blood pressure and heart rate and prepares them to fight the lion or run from it. In our case, the threat is market risk, so the problem is that the stress reaction is not temporary, it goes on and on.

The original purpose of our response to danger was to allow for fight or flight, either of which is meant to be a temporary burst of activity followed by recovery. In trading, we can stay stressed all day and eventually this puts strain on our digestive, immune and other systems because we are flooded with cortisol. Excessive cortisol can lead to poor memory, paranoia, anxiety, and all sorts of bad stuff. That is why traders burn out.

Nobody who is 24 years old believes they can ever burn out. People who have experienced almost exclusively success in their early life can't imagine ever being tired or burnt out or failing. But trading is exhausting. If you don't manage your stress level properly and stay somewhat healthy in your 20s and 30s, you probably won't be trading in your 40s or 50s.

One trader I work with had her Apple Watch monitoring her heart rate as the Fed announced its interest rate decision in August, 2019. She had a ton of orders to watch and was at significant risk through the meeting. Check out Figure 5.3 for a chart of her heart rate that day.

How good traders deal with stress:

- **Perspective.** Like I said earlier, we are not storming the beaches of Normandy here, we are buying and selling assets in an attempt to generate short-term profits. If you can take the job seriously and treat it as a profession, but still understand the sun will come up tomorrow no matter how well or how badly you trade… You can win.

- **Relax.** Learn to relax and breathe when you have big risk on. Don't white knuckle every trade and grind your teeth over every basis point jiggle. You need to get comfortable with being uncomfortable. This took me a long time, but it is a nice state of mind to have a ton of risk on and know that you can see the world clearly and breathe. This does not mean you don't care. It just means you have put on risk before, you will put on risk again and this is just a single trial in a process with thousands of trials. Each trade is a spoonful of water in an ocean. Don't get riled up.

Figure 5.3: Trader heart rate goes from 60bpm resting to 100bpm on Fed announcement

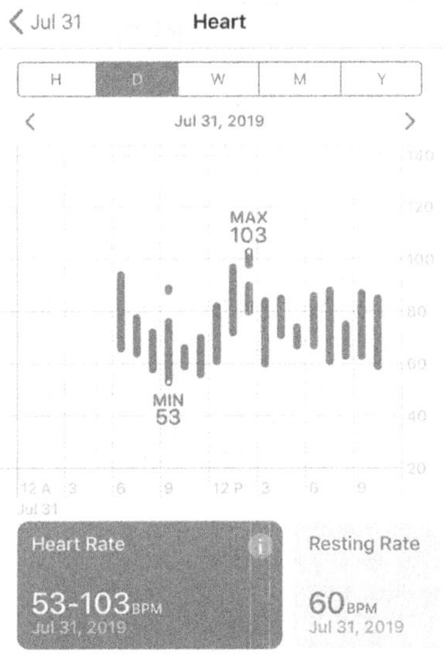

Source: Christina Fusilli's phone

- **Go off the desk**. Many traders hate to go off the desk because they are worried about missing something. In the long run, the benefits you gain from going off the desk exceed the risk you take of missing something. When you go off the desk, your heart rate goes down and you will often experience stunning moments of clarity. Every experienced trader knows the feeling of that super-clear market insight that pops into your head when you're off the desk.

The human brain produces new ideas by creating connections between disparate thoughts and stimuli and it does this best when it is at rest. To achieve clarity and produce a-ha moments of trading insight, sometimes you need to go off the desk and let your brain work. Much in the way sleep allows your brain to process everything you have experienced during the day, pulling yourself away from the screens allows your brain to cool off and run some different, less urgent subroutines.

Frequently heard on the trading floor: "Man, I just realized something really interesting on my way back from the bathroom…"

- **Turn off your phone at night.** Checking your phone four times a night makes you feel important and allows you to impress your friends with your aggressive commitment to capital markets. Checking your phone at night is more addiction than useful habit. Markets are always awake, but you need time to rest. They will be fine without you for a few hours.

> **Leave a stop loss and a take profit on every position you hold at night. Then turn off your phone and get some proper sleep.**

I used to leave call levels in various currencies and I would get the call from Hong Kong or Tokyo or London at 2:30 a.m. This would result in:

a. Wife, annoyed.

b. Young kids, awake.

c. No good trades since I had no idea what was going on in the market and was groggy and not in a strong position to make split-second decisions.

d. Much more tired the next day because of elevated heart rate in the middle of the night and 60 minutes of tossing and turning and half-awake dreams about USDJPY before finally falling asleep twenty minutes before my alarm went off in the morning.

Eventually, I left instructions with all the other centers. Do not call me at night. Still, even once I kicked the call level habit, if I woke up to the go to the bathroom in the middle of the night, I was always tempted to check the market[58]. Again, this is pointless. Do not do it.

---

58. Pro tip: Don't drink any liquids after 7 p.m. and you will sleep through the night.

Turn your phone off when you go to bed and turn it back on when you wake up. It took me many years to learn this and implement it and my health and sleep quality improved dramatically when I did.

Well-rested outperforms sleep-deprived.

It is common sense but research also shows conclusively that humans perform tasks at a substantially higher level when properly rested and we make persistent and frequent errors when sleep-deprived. And if you use your phone as your alarm: don't. Get a normal alarm clock or a Shake and Wake[59].

- **Breathe.** Learn how to focus on your breath through meditation, yoga, or other mindfulness practices. Also, read the book *Breath* by James Nestor.

The ability to deal with stress is somewhat innate, but you can learn stress management and be thoughtful about your own reaction to pressure. Again, try to step outside yourself at times and make observations. Hmm, I just smashed my fist on my keyboard, maybe I should take a little walk. Observe your own behavior and understand what it might mean. I have a huge lump in my throat and I want to yell. This trade is getting under my skin in a bad way. I need to square up and start fresh tomorrow.

The struggle for self-awareness is a timeless piece of the human condition. Greater self-awareness will help you in trading and will help you in real life. Now let's move on to the next non-cognitive trait on our list.

Focus

Alpha Traders maintain focus even when flaming arrows are raining down on the battlefield and everyone else is losing their mind. Trading floors are quieter than they used to be but there is still plenty of chaos when markets are on the move. There are moments when market makers need to watch multiple markets, yell out accurate and tight prices to multiple salespeople and execute

---

59. That's what I use—it's a wristband alarm that vibrates—it quietly buzzes you awake without bothering your spouse at 4 a.m. or whatever time you get up.

trades in more than one asset at the same time. This requires military-style concentration and focus.

The sample size is small, but two of the best traders that ever worked for me came from the military. There is some overlap in terms of level of focus between trading and military operations and anyone who has engaged in live gunfire is certainly not going to be scared off by a flash crash in GBPUSD or a 7 standard deviation move in US 10-year yields! Another bonus when hiring ex-military into trading is that they are usually older and more mature than standard graduates. Thus, they are better-prepared and more able to jump straight into a trading seat.

One obvious tell, when new analysts join us on the trading floor, is whether they can process various streams of information simultaneously. Some young recruits have this skill and some do not. There have been times when two salespeople were yelling at me for a price at the exact same time and a junior analyst came right up to me and said "I'm getting coffees. Do you want one?" without even realizing I was engaged in multiple transactions. This sort of market awareness is hard to teach. New kids on a trading floor either have it or they don't.

I would therefore say that focus is one of the skills that is most innate and toughest to teach or upgrade. That said, here are a few things you can do to improve your trading focus:

- **Schedule**. Schedule all non-trading tasks either outside of work hours or in narrow, uneventful windows like 1:30 to 3:30 p.m. for equities or after 2:30 p.m. if you trade commodities. I mentioned this earlier but it is a dumb mistake that even senior traders make. I often made this mistake myself when I was running a large FX business and had around 50 people working for me. Outlook meeting notifications popped up on my screen like fireflies all day when I first started in management, but I realized that the good trading hours need to be protected from outside distractions.

  Your boss wants you to succeed so don't be afraid to ask to reschedule a request you receive for an 8:00 a.m. meeting. Most meeting times are set somewhat arbitrarily. Explain to your manager or employees or wife or whoever needs to set up a meeting: *these hours are sacred and I need to be on the desk from X to Y. Any other time is fine.*

- **Focus**. Close your email during peak trading periods. If your main trading time is the equity open, close your email from 9 a.m. to

11:00 a.m. Answering emails one at a time as they come in distracts you. Over and over and over. And 99% of them are completely useless. Open emails and deal with them in batches every few hours. Your efficiency and focus will improve. Also: you should learn about Inbox Zero.

- **Exercise**. In some years I have exercised like an athlete and stayed in outstanding shape. On the other hand, I have had a few multi-year periods where I could not fit proper exercise into my schedule for whatever reason. The difference is glaring. After a year or so of no exercise, my brain gets dull and hazy. I have trouble waking up in the morning and I am dying for a nap around 3 p.m. every day. Optimal mental performance does not require you to be a ripped V with six-pack abs. But it does require a minimal amount of physical maintenance—a few workouts per week, ideally combining weights and cardio.

  If you think you don't have time to work out. Make time. I moved my wake-up time from 5 a.m. to 4 a.m. to allow time to work out and the extra energy I get from the exercise, and the psychological benefits of exercise more than outweigh the hour of sleep I give up. Get up one hour earlier three days a week. It's worth it. Unless you have a newborn baby or a sick relative or some truly extenuating situation… You need to make time to exercise. It's a big part of playing the long game successfully.

- **Stretch**. Stand up and walk around a bit. Take short breaks away from the desk. This gets the blood flowing, resets your mind, and forces you out of mental ruts. Change your perspective and breathe a bit. This can be a 3-minute stroll. It sounds so simple but many traders stay welded to their chair for hours when they should be standing to stretch every few minutes. You need to move around a bit to maintain physical energy and you need to get off the desk every now and then for a change of mental scenery.

- **Put your phone away**. Many trading floors prohibit mobile phones for compliance reasons, and one side benefit of this policy is that it removes the distraction. You can answer the text from your mom later.

Peak trading requires flow.

Flow happens when you are in the zone and you process all the incoming information in the most efficient way possible. Remove as many distractions as possible from your point of contact with the market and be particularly brutal about protecting the most sacred hours of your trading day. For many styles of trading, that can be just two to four hours per day. Don't clutter up those crucial hours. Close Facebook, put your phone in a drawer, shut Outlook, and focus.

Patience

Winning traders very often use a style that also performs well in poker. The style is called "tight/aggressive". The idea is you play as tight as possible (waiting for clear opportunities where you have a substantial edge) and then act aggressively when those opportunities arise.

In poker this means instead of limping into many pots, often with marginal hands, you wait for strong cards in strong position or large pots that will justify the risk of entering with medium cards or weaker position.

In trading this means instead of trading every chart pattern and support and resistance and up and down jiggle and random news headline, you wait for strong set ups where you have an edge and then you commit significant capital to the idea.

The path to success is to take massive, determined action.

TONY ROBBINS

This is easy to type out in a document but much harder to execute in real life. What happens in real life is either a) the trader is not disciplined enough to wait for high quality opportunities, she gets bored and puts too much money behind too many low-quality ideas or b) the trader is not courageous enough to commit to even the best ideas and so she puts on small bets even when there is a once-per-year type opportunity. Then, when the trade works exactly as expected, she whinges about how she is "way too small!" and "she knew this was going to happen!"

While I stated earlier that good trading requires courage; it all also requires patience. Most traders have a bias to action and this can lead to poor trade selection and bad capital allocation. If you put money behind every idea that pops into your head, the high-quality ideas will be diluted by the random dumb ideas.

When I am trading well, I am patient, I pick my spots and I do fewer trades. When I am trading poorly, I react to every headline and chart pattern and flicker of the numbers on the screen. The key for me is to wait and wait and wait as long as possible. Reject as many trade ideas as possible until finally there is a trade idea that is so juicy I cannot resist. Then *attack* it.

Wait until all the planets are aligned.

You want to participate in trades where the macro story, charts, positioning, sentiment, and cross-market indicators all point the same direction. If you use 10 criteria for trade selection, you don't want a trade that ticks two boxes. You want the one that ticks eight! But those trades don't come along every few hours. the way you wish they would. You need to wait. This is especially difficult in low volatility markets where frequency of opportunity is lower.

Patience, of course, should not be confused with a bias to inaction. This is where self-awareness is important. If you are biased to inaction, you need to be *less* patient! Since I am always biased to action and overtrading, I need to be *more* patient. Think about where you lie on that spectrum. An interesting (though not very surprising) pattern that emerges from my innate lack of patience is that my Sharpe ratio is higher when I am in the red vs. when I am deep in the black.

If I'm in the red for the year, or even for the month, my main goal is to avoid going deeper into the red. This is the zero bound effect I describe earlier, in the section on Courage. Everyone has a point of discomfort as they near their stop loss, and your goal is to stay away from that point of discomfort so that you are not weak when a huge opportunity or great trade idea emerges.

Therefore, I know that when I am below zero on the year, I need to be selective. I wait and wait and wait and then the "I'll know it when I see it" moment arrives and I pounce. Often when I'm doing very well, my patience slips and I feel like I can afford to swing at some bad pitches. I get a bit sloppy and drawdown before going back to basics and renewing my commitment to tight/aggressive. Even though I know my bias to action is a weakness, I still struggle with it. Some rough parts of your personality are easier to smooth out than others.

A good trader is like a leopard hiding in the tall grass. The cat will wait for long periods, sometimes hours, for the right opportunity to pounce. If he lunges too early or too late, he will miss the kill. He waits and waits, until the perfect moment—and then attacks with 100% commitment and force.

Locus of control

Locus of control is our next non-cognitive attribute. Broadly speaking, locus of control is a concept in psychology that explains how people see their own influence on the situations, outcomes, and experiences in their lives. In school, students with internal locus of control believe success or failure come from effort and hard work. Students with external locus of control believe success or failure come from luck, fate, unfair or bad teachers, bias, and so on. Students with internal locus of control might blame a C grade on their own poor preparation, while students with external locus of control would blame the teacher or the test.

How do you view the outcomes and experiences in your life? Do you take responsibility or blame external forces? In life outside of trading, internal locus of control tends to lead to better outcomes, because when people believe they can control their own life, they take ownership and do the necessary work to improve their situation. Those who believe they don't control their own life, don't bother to try.

In games and pursuits involving probability, successful participants understand what they control and what they do not. This is the entire message of a book like *Thinking in Bets* by Annie Duke: if you focus on results instead of process, you fail to understand which part of the system you control and which part you do not.

While strong internal locus of control generally correlates with positive life outcomes (because those who believe they influence outcomes in their life tend to have stronger motivation and make more effort), it can also lead to the illusion of control. Many think (either consciously or unconsciously) that they have control in areas where they cannot possibly influence the outcomes.

A remarkable experiment by Langer and Roth showed that students who had success predicting a coin toss early on tended to believe they had superior coin toss prediction skills to those that did not. If people can convince themselves they are superior forecasters of a coin toss, imagine how they might convince themselves of their ability to predict markets!

Langer and Roth reported their findings in "Heads I win, tails it's chance"[60]. I love the title because it captures the faulty thinking of many an overconfident trader. *If I make money on the trade, I'm smart. If I don't, it was just bad luck.* That's not rational thinking!

> **Example 1**: You are playing poker. You have two aces and your opponent has a junk hand like 9-5. The player with 9-5 is drunk and goes all in and you obviously call. The flop is 9-9-5 and you lose to the full house.

---

60. Langer, E. J., & Roth, J. Heads I win, tails it's chance: The illusion of control as a function of the sequence of outcomes in a purely chance task. *Journal of Personality and Social Psychology* (1975).

Example 2: A tennis player hits a perfect shot down the line and the umpire calls it out, even though it was clearly on the line.

Example 3: A baseball player hits a line drive that looks like a clear home run but the opposing center fielder climbs the wall and grabs it for a very loud out.

A professional poker, tennis or baseball player in these situations will tend to understand that they did everything they were supposed to do and ran into a very unfortunate bit of bad short-term luck. They understand that if you re-ran the same event 1,000,000 times, the result would be a success more than 99% of the time. They can shrug it off and understand that their process was good and while the outcome clearly stunk, they have nothing to feel bad about.

On the other hand, a weak player or someone who does not understand process vs. outcome or what they control vs. what they do not control will be enraged. "I can't believe that guy flopped a full house! I am the unluckiest person in the world!" etc. That is what Annie Duke calls "resulting". When you focus on results, you fail to understand what you control and what you do not control—this is a major fault. In life, trading, sports, and everywhere, you need to understand what you control and what you do not.

In trading, internal or external locus of control is not most important. What is most important is making the distinction between those things that we do and do not control. This is captured nicely in the Serenity Prayer, a mantra popularized by Alcoholics Anonymous but relevant to everyone:

> *God, grant me the serenity to accept the things*
> *I cannot change, courage to change the things*
> *I can, and the wisdom to know the difference.*

The last line is key. Think about what parts of the system you control. You control the inputs, not the outputs. In trading, this means focus on good thinking and rational decision-making, and don't get upset when you hit a bad run.

Understand that variance is part of the game and you cannot and will not ever control it. What you can control (and change if necessary) is your process and your attitude. Nick Jonas (the Aussie trader I work with, not the singer) has this on a Post-It stuck to his monitor at work: "The only things I control are my effort and my attitude."

People waste way too much time worrying about random stuff they can't control. This is often true in trading but it is true out there in the world, too. A big part of my personal philosophy is to not waste time on things I cannot control. For example, when I was younger, I would spend months obsessing about what my bonus was going to be in January. As discussions started in September and expectations management took hold into October and November, I listened to all the speculation about the bonus pool and tried to keep my ear to the ground to get a sense of what my bonus might be.

As years passed, I realized something. If I come into work and try my best and perform well and do a good job… The bonuses take care of themselves. There is no correlation between how much you worry about what your bonus is going to be and how much you get paid. There is, though, a strong correlation between your bonus and: how hard you work, how well you prepare, how disciplined you are and what kind of attitude you have.

> **Come in to work each day with a positive attitude.**
> **Do the work. Focus.**
> **Behave rationally. Go home.**
> **Do it again tomorrow.**

That is the 22-word recipe for trading success.

Don't obsess over your MTD or YTD P&L or the bonus pool or what kind of car you might buy if you finish strong. Don't waste time on what might happen if you flame out as a trader and spill your entire account. Don't wonder why that guy got paid more than you or that woman got promoted or that dummy gets invited to all the client dinners and you don't.

There is always someone doing better than you and someone doing worse than you. Focus on yourself. Run your own race and ignore the runners in front of and behind you. Be better today than you were yesterday.

A bad poker player constantly complains about bad cards or bad beats. A good poker player knows that in the long run her superior skill will deliver outsized returns and short-term variance means nothing. A good trader doesn't spend too much time upset when they get stopped out at the high or low. That is just something that happens sometimes.

The good trader knows there will be just as many times they survive by a hair. Good and bad luck even out and the result at the end of many years is not luck. Also note: good traders rarely use words like "should have" or "would have" or "could have". They focus on what is and what will be. The present and the future. Not the past.

Other traits

Like I mentioned in a footnote earlier, it is a tricky exercise to place traits into cognitive and non-cognitive buckets. In the end, I did my best but still I was left with a bunch of traits and factors that don't fall neatly into either category. These "other" traits and factors I will call Category 3 Factors. I will discuss them in this section. They are:

1. Raw trading instinct
2. Passion for trading
3. Experience
4. Luck
5. Appropriate capital
6. Healthy risk-taking environment

Raw trading instinct

Trading instinct is what I call the x-factor. The thing that separates good from great. When you watch American Idol, you can detect this x-factor right away. The singer's voice might not be the best you've ever heard, and they might not be the best-looking or best dancer, but there is some hard-to-define aspect that moves you. Most people will agree on who has this x-factor and who does not.

There is a similar x-factor in trading. It is not just about risk appetite or quant skill or patience or discipline or any of the traits I have mentioned. It's about instinct. When new traders come to the desk out of an analyst program, it's easy to see when they have this x-factor.

They intuitively get what is going on much more quickly than others. They don't ask questions 15 seconds after a huge market move because they understand when is the right time to converse and when is the right time to keep quiet. They input tickets the right way and can mentally calculate P&L on a trade quickly without making a series of tortured faces first. They understand the metagame and know that if ten separate banks recommend short oil on the same day, that is not bearish oil.

Innate trading skill varies dramatically from person to person and can be a huge head start for some and a hurdle that is too high to get over for many. I believe that some people are innately good or bad at trading and it is fairly easy to see this early on. If you are a manager, invest in the people that have the x-factor and help those that do not have it to pivot as quickly as possible.

One trader that worked for me who did not have the x-factor told me, 10 years after he pivoted to a job that fit him much better, that he wished someone had told him earlier that he wasn't suited to be a trader. He could have moved on to a new career that fit his personality and skills more quickly instead of wasting five years in a job that he and I probably both knew was not the best fit.

This is a useful insight. Not everyone was born to be a trader… Even if they successfully complete a sales and trading analyst program at a major bank.

Some of this x-factor is the difference between street smarts and book smarts. Investment banks emphasize book smarts because they are easy to quantify and there is much less risk in hiring someone with mega quant skills from an Ivy League school. Pre-2005 or so, many traders emerged out of the back office or even the mail rooms of Wall Street firms because managers weighed x-factor and personality higher than they do now. While those managers probably overweighted personality and "fit", the system now overweights academic credentials while failing to appreciate the street smarts needed to succeed in most trading roles.

You cannot hone x-factor but it is important to be aware of it. Were you born to be a trader? Or did you just kind of fall into it by accident or because you saw how much money traders make? *This matters.* Traders that feel they were born to trade have a better chance of surviving through the inevitable existential storms that blow into every trader's mind from time to time. If you believe you are doing what you are meant to do, you won't quit when it feels impossible.

This brings us to the next Category 3 trait: passion.

Passion for trading

The number one thing I care about when hiring traders is their passion for trading. This is usually easy to see because fake passion is easy to discern. I care that traders are passionate because I believe:

1. their chance of success is exponentially higher than that of a less passionate trader;

2. they are much more enjoyable to work with because they are not complaining about how the market sucks or the job sucks or the world sucks; and

3. they are more likely to find personal happiness as a trader.

People that enter trading by accident, or because they are not sure what they want to do and just kind of land there after a training program, are less likely to succeed than the myriad of kids who have had their eye on trading since sophomore year of college. Trading is tiring, frustrating, and often unrewarding. You have to love it to stick with it.

When I worked as a day trader there was a huge banner that read: THANK GOD IT'S MONDAY! That is exactly how I feel about trading, even after 25 years. When the FX market opens on Sunday afternoon and when S&Ps open at 6 p.m. on Sunday night… I am logged in and often trading right away. I am excited for the week to get started and to try to outtrade everyone else after analyzing all the weekend news. This is borderline obsessive behavior but for me it is a passion, not an obsession.

I know that the line between passion and obsession is *crazy* thin. That is why I take specific steps to ensure I do not lose perspective. I turn off my phone at night; I square up when I am on holiday; I go for walks without my phone so that I am not constantly checking the market, etc.

I am a big believer in doing something you love. It's the biggest cliché in the world but most clichés exist because they are true. Something that is universally true often becomes cliché but that does not make it any less true.

My desire to always be in a growth environment, where I can come in every day and do my best while feeling passionate about what I do, is part of the reason I have changed jobs many times over the course of my lifetime. Why settle for a decent job? Why work for someone you don't get along with or in a job that doesn't really fit? Do something you are passionate about. If you lose the passion or find the role or environment does not fit—make a change if you can.

If you don't love trading, find another job!

Since not everyone is cut out for trading, part of the decision-making process for many traders is figuring out when to quit. When you have invested significant time and money into your trading career, how do you know when enough is enough? This is a hard question to answer because success in trading only comes with extreme perseverance and experience. Therefore, by its very nature, trading rewards those who refuse to quit.

You have to recognize that for most people there will never be a clear sign from above that tells you exactly when enough is enough. If you have been trading for more than two years and you are not making significant progress, that is a bad sign. I would say that anyone who has been trading for more than three years and does not feel confident that they are on the right path, is probably on the wrong path.

Not everyone can succeed at trading. If things are not working out after two or three years of effort, think about what comes next. Can you parlay your trading experience into another job or pursuit? Investing, financial planning, research, etc.?

Experience

One Catch-22 of trading is that experience is one of the most important drivers of trading success but if you don't succeed fairly early on, you never have the chance to get the experience. Young traders should put themselves in a position to gain experience at as low a cost as possible. If you want to learn to trade and have $25,000 to your name… Don't open a trading account with $25,000 in it! Most traders lose money when they start out.

A good substitute for experience is a strong mentor. Traders that go from college into junior trading roles at banks or hedge funds have an enormous advantage over those who do not. They get experienced mentors, solid training, and the ability to learn using someone else's money. Traders of any age trying to learn to trade from home need to be aware of the huge disadvantage they are saddled with, and find a way to develop a network of peers and some sort of mentorship.

Luck

There is an ironic fact about most good traders. They simultaneously:

- Understand the difference between variance and luck;
- Know that luck is not a long-run factor in successful trading;
- Don't really believe in luck; and yet
- Consider themselves lucky.

We will get into the topic of luck much more in Chapter 11 but for now let me just tell you that most good traders I know think of themselves as lucky. I think deep down most of them believe in the saying "luck is when preparation meets opportunity" but at the same time they also believe themselves to be abnormally lucky. You don't hear successful traders saying stuff like:

"The market is out to get me!"

"I am cursed!"

"I am the unluckiest person in the world."

If you say stuff like that: STOP.

Those are things you hear bad traders blurt out on a trading floor. Is the world out to get you, or are you going to take over the world? Good traders understand that luck is purely a short-term phenomenon and it is evenly distributed over longer time frames. Luck should have no impact whatsoever on a trader's emotions. Good traders say things like:

"Wow, another disappointing day today. I have now lost money five days in a row. I need to stick to my process more than ever. I will stay unemotional and work as hard as possible tomorrow."

Or…

"My methodology is not working in this regime. I will cut my risk in half and think about why there seems to be a mismatch between my style and the market."

There are only three reasons you are losing money:

1. Your methodology is not producing edge.

2. Mental or behavioral issues are causing you to deviate from your methodology (i.e., you are not sticking to the plan).

3. Variance.

That's it. Again, we will talk about this later but variance is part of trading. There is no good and bad luck. Just variance which can be explained with statistics and probability. That is why there is no reason to pray for a market outcome or beg the trading gods for a rally. *Please, just this one time.* The only god of trading is probability. Even a forecaster who can predict the market accurately 90% of the time will still be wrong five times in a row every now and then.

Locus of control, grit, growth mindset and an individual's perception of her own luckiness all come down to the same core belief: I control my own fate. The harder I work, the better things will get for me in the long run, even if bad stuff will inevitably happen in the short term. All that matters is the long game. Daily returns mean nothing, monthly and yearly returns are what matter.

**You control your own fate. Never blame
external factors when you lose money.**

Healthy trading environment

While I just spent several paragraphs talking about the importance of internal locus of control and embracing the belief that you determine your trading outcomes, there is one extremely important external factor to consider. You cannot succeed in an unhealthy trading environment. You must have a risk-taking environment that is not hostile to risk, or thinly capitalized.

This point could have been at the top of this chapter because in the wrong environment, even the most rational, disciplined, skilled and self-aware trader will fail. There are many features of a trading environment that can be desirable but there are two that are absolutely necessary for survival and success:

1. Appropriate capital.

2. Healthy and supportive risk-taking environment.

Let's look at each feature separately.

Appropriate capital

In terms of external factors, sufficient capital is an absolute prerequisite for successful trading. Let's look at what this means for the three main types of trader.

Retail traders

No retail trader can succeed with a $1,000 trading account because the income generated from the most successful strategy will be too small to move the needle. Even a 300% return will not be enough to make a difference and so the trader is very likely to employ too much leverage and blow up the account via gambling.

A tiny trading account is OK for learning the markets and much better than paper trading. It might give you a sense of the emotional and psychological hurdles that come with live trading, but it will never give you a chance to really know what kind of trader you are.

In general, position sizing can account for most issues around insufficient capital. If your capital is small, you need to take smaller positions. We will discuss position sizing in Chapter 11. But there are thresholds below which you cannot hope to succeed. For a young retail trader with no family to support and low expenses, this amount could be as low as $25,000. For a dentist with three kids in private school looking to quit his job and trade full time, this number would be significantly higher.

Bank traders

If you work in a bank, you don't have a fixed amount of capital. Instead, you have risk limits. As such, your risk limits need to be properly aligned with your performance expectations or budget. If you have a $30,000 daily stop loss and a budget of $10,000,000, you will fail. It's impossible to make ten million dollars in a year with such a tight daily stop.

The easiest way to determine whether your risk limits are appropriate in a bank is to run simulations. You can set up simple simulations in a spreadsheet to look at a 252-day period[61] and spit out ranges of outcomes based on various inputs. Retail traders can do this as well to determine risk of ruin. The greater idea you have of your prior performance statistics, the more accurate the simulation will be. I will go into a deeper discussion of how to use simulations to understand performance and risk of ruin in Chapter 11.

Portfolio managers

Capital or assets under management is a critical variable for every hedge fund and real money portfolio manager (PM). Good PMs can scale their strategy substantially and tend to think of performance in terms of basis points, not dollars. Good PMs comfortably scale their risk up or down as necessary based on the capital they are managing. On the other hand, PMs that think about P&L in terms of dollars tend to have trouble sizing up (or sizing down) because they are anchored on various P&L thresholds. If you think of a good day as $1 million of P&L, you won't adjust very smoothly as your capital increases from $100 million to $1 billion. On the other hand, if you think of a good day as 100 basis points, you will.

Note that it is possible to have too much capital. In fact, a common issue with hedge fund portfolio managers is that they have *too much* capital, not too little. Many traders at hedge funds are pressured to take on more and more capital, regardless of the capacity of their trading strategy. And it takes a trader with courageous integrity to say "no" to more capital. It is a bit like refusing a promotion—quite often it could be the right decision, but it can feel strange and potentially risky to do so.

Every trader and every trading strategy has an optimal level of capital. The more capital you take on, the worse your returns will be after a certain point, because your best strategies will reach capacity and additional capital will need

---

61. There is an average of 252 trading days in each year.

to be allocated to inferior strategies. If you are a PM at a hedge fund, you should target your optimal level of capital, not just look to increase your capital year after year.

Capacity depends to a great extent on the products you trade. A boutique institutional trader specializing in microcap stocks will have much lower capacity than a hedge fund PM trading G10 currencies. Capacity is mostly determined by liquidity.

Research shows there is a sweet spot for hedge fund size in the $250 million to $1 billion assets-under-management range. Below $250m, costs are hard to cover and above $1 billion, returns and Sharpe ratios fall[62]. This is logically true for individual managers as well. This does not mean all increases in capital are bad. You need to think about what your optimal capitalization level looks like and aim for that, not higher. As your capital rises to higher than optimal levels, the opportunity set is diluted and transaction costs increase disproportionately. The high-alpha opportunities are slowly drowned out by inferior trades.

A healthy risk-taking environment

A healthy environment breeds successful risk takers. Even the best trader is unlikely to succeed in a toxic environment. A healthy risk-taking environment means different things for different types of trader.

Retail traders

For people trading their own money, a healthy environment means enough runway to learn, make mistakes, bounce back and eventually prosper. Capital is crucial, as mentioned in the last section, but so is support from family, financial flexibility, and the ability to focus and get in the zone all day.

If you want to be a trader, but your wife wants you to get a "real" job and you have twins screaming from the other room and no money to pay rent next month... Put down this book and come back when you have a more conducive environment. Trading is hard enough; anything that makes it harder usually makes it impossible.

You own your life, so if you want to be a trader, do it. But pick the right time and circumstances to do it so that you give yourself a proper shot at success. There is nothing worse than wondering what could have been. Quite often,

---

62. See for example: https://www.aurum.com/insight/elephant-in-the-room-size-and-hedge-fund-performance/ and https://docs.preqin.com/newsletters/hf/Preqin_HFSL_Mar_14_Fund_Size_Performance.pdf

you can work full time and find ways to trade on the side (and more importantly, study trading) so that as you gain experience and confidence in trading you are still earning a steady income. Then, once you have a decent amount of money in the bank, you have a bit of runway to trade full time and see if you have what it takes.

Bank traders

You would think that most or all bank traders would operate in a healthy risk-taking environment but this is absolutely not the case. Banks have different levels of risk appetite and managers within those banks can have dramatically different incentives.

Let's say you trade 10-year bonds at a large commercial bank. Imagine two environments:

A) The manager that hired you and mentored you got a job offer at an investment bank and just left under somewhat acrimonious circumstances. Instead of replacing the head of trading, the bank has given the current head of sales responsibility for your group. He never liked your old boss, he has never traded before, and he plans to retire in a few years. He just wants to survive the last few years of his career and pay for his kid's last few years of college. He is extremely risk averse. He views the business model as an agency where clients do trades, the bank goes to market and offloads the risk, and the bank earns a small, nearly risk-free commission.

Or…

B) Your manager is fired up and entrepreneurial and previously ran global macro at a big hedge fund. He wants that kind of ambitious risk culture at your bank because he believes a strong, healthy risk culture best serves the clients of the bank. By employing meaningful risk appetite, the bank can provide best-in-class pricing to clients, world class trade ideas and expert market intelligence. Customers get superior service from the bank and the bank makes more money than the competition in the process. Win/win.

It is obvious which trader is going to have a greater chance of success and most enjoy coming to work each day. If you work at a bank, you should regularly evaluate your environment and study where your incentives are aligned with the bank's and where they are not. To succeed, you need clear risk limits and rules of engagement so that no one is ever second-guessing your actions, and you don't have to second guess them yourself.

Portfolio managers

Portfolio managers are most likely to work in a healthy risk-taking environment. Since hedge funds and asset managers are often exclusively in the business of taking risk, they best understand the nature of risk and they are usually good at creating a clear set of rules and then letting traders trade.

Still, it's important to understand where your incentives align with those of the firm and where they do not, so that you don't misfire. The most important example of this is that many hedge fund risk managers focus as much or more on volatility of returns than on absolute returns. This is because the risk manager at a pod-based hedge fund sees each trader as part of a portfolio.

If the returns of each PM look approximately like those of a call option (small downside with unlimited upside), then the aggregate performance of all those traders at the end of the year is likely to look pretty good. If, on the other hand, most traders are targeting 6% volatility while two or three are realizing 25% volatility, the business model does not work as well.

While you are paid a percentage of your absolute returns, quite often your manager is almost as concerned about your volatility as she is about the headline returns number. This makes perfect sense, especially as risk managers are constantly trying to separate luck from skill. A trader that makes money consistently with low volatility is much more likely to be displaying skill than a PM that puts up three years like: +70%, -24%, + 35%. Furthermore, the risk of ruin of a *Steady Eddie* is significantly lower than the PM I just mentioned, and nobody wants to be the one managing a trader when he blows up.

This is not an argument for you to target a specific level of volatility and forget about returns. All I am saying is that you should be acutely aware of your manager's (and your investors') incentives, not just your own.

A related phenomenon you will see at many hedge funds is that while your contract may have a stop loss, your real stop loss might be much tighter. Contractual risk limits are often wider than reality, depending on the personality of the business and risk managers involved. If you are new at a hedge fund, make sure you fully understand all the written and unwritten rules the fund follows. Your official stop loss might be -15%, but if every other trader that ever went down 9% at the fund got a shoulder tap, you should probably calibrate to a 9% stop loss (or tighter!)

Think about your manager's (and investors') incentives. Does your strategy and behavior align?

This advice applies to traders at every type of institution. When you understand the incentives of management, you can make sure you are playing by the correct rules and that you will not put yourself or your manager in an unwanted or awkward position.

Other features of a healthy risk-taking environment:

- **Peers.** There are other good risk takers to talk with and bounce ideas off. Hopefully there is at least one trader that is more experienced and/or more skilled than you. Otherwise you are always the mentor and never the mentee. For retail traders, I believe there is a huge benefit to working in a trading office, not at home. You learn from others, have people to share ideas with and share the pain with when things go wrong. A robust network of peers gives you a chance to talk about specific trades, general risk management and other trading-related topics.

  Make a concerted effort to build a strong network of trading peers. This can be online or IRL. Learning takes longer if you have to figure everything out yourself.

- **Rule-based limits and risk-taking framework.** The clearer the rules of engagement, the easier it is to develop a clear process and proper risk management. You don't want an environment where a loss is fine one day, but the same loss two weeks later results in a bunch of emails flying around asking what happened. Ask for clear, numerical limits and goals.

- **Management risk appetite.** Management understands that if you take real risk, you will lose money sometimes. It is common to hear bank traders joke about the "Take risk, but don't lose money" business model. This is a model that works well for management as it essentially means they can sleep well at night knowing that traders are monetizing client flow but not taking any meaningful risk. It is less attractive for individual traders because their leeway to express views is severely limited. The only time traders can take "risk" in this model is when they are already profitable (usually from a client trade). This model allows traders to risk money earned but not take real financial risk that may result in losses.

- **A mentor** to teach you, support your risk taking and help you maintain confidence during the inevitable down times.

- **A clear connection between performance and pay.** Risk appetite fizzles when traders don't expect to get paid for alpha they generate. Taking real risk requires significant mental effort and endurance and traders will not give their all to a business they do not believe will compensate them for doing so.

There are so many characteristics that make a good trader. That just about concludes this chapter on winning traits. When you finish this chapter, put the book down and take a moment to think about one or two characteristics you want to work on. Go through my tips and write down a couple of specific actions you will take to improve in particular areas. Then come back to Chapter 6.

I strongly believe that improvement comes in small increments and by focusing on one or two specific goals. Achieve those goals, then set new goals. Don't try to do everything at once or monitor seventeen areas where you hope to improve. Drill down and pick one or two. Then do the work.

That is the end of Chapter 5. Those are the positive traits that will bring you success in trading. Now let's look at all the faulty thinking and ugly habits that lead you astray.

CHAPTER 6

KRYPTONITE

Bad habits, mistakes, sloppy thinking, and leaks

There are specific bad habits, mistakes, unhealthy mindsets and persistent errors that lead traders to fail. Most bad trading follows a few specific patterns. In this chapter, I will go into some of the most common sources of trader kryptonite, and outline strategies to reduce the impact of negative traits. Building strength is important but you must also minimize destructive and unprofitable behaviors.

The most damaging of all forms of trader kryptonite is biased or bad thinking and we will discuss bias in depth in Chapter 7. This chapter will focus on everything else that holds traders back, other than irrational and biased thinking.

When thinking about why traders lose money, the starting point is simple. Trading is not a zero-sum game; it is a negative sum game. There are external costs (technology, hardware, research, data, personnel, etc.) and transaction costs (commissions, bid/offer, slippage) that eat away at your performance, day after day. If you generate small gains, your alpha will leak away in a steady stream of payments to vendors and market makers.

When I traded the NASDAQ bubble from 1999 to 2002, my gross daily P&L was rarely negative, and I was gross positive every single month. But I went from wildly profitable in 1999 and 2000 to flat in 2001 and net negative in 2002, as I had to trade more and more shares to generate the same P&L after the absolute value of NASDAQ stocks collapsed following the bubble burst.

Instead of trying to make $3 on 1000 shares as Qualcomm jumped from $600 to $603, I had to make 30 cents on 10,000 shares as Qualcomm moved from $60.00 to $60.30. The simultaneous collapse of stock prices and the decimalization of equity trading meant the highly-profitable strategies I employed in 1999/2000 were no longer profitable in 2002. Transaction costs are a constant drag on performance so you need a big edge to succeed in trading.

Today, stock market trading is "free" in theory for many individuals. But you know the saying: if the product is free, then you are the product. In the past, you paid a transparent commission and the bid/offer spread. Now, you still pay the bid/offer spread and you pay a hidden transaction fee which is the profit earned by a high-frequency market maker which receives an ultra-short-term "free" option as it chooses how to execute your trade. Trading costs continue to trend lower but are more and more difficult to observe or measure. And they still matter.

Another reason that trading is negative-sum for individuals is information and technology asymmetry. Large institutions (banks, asset managers and central banks) have better access to information, and superior (faster) technology. A trader at home watching news headlines cannot compete with algorithmic headline reading software. When market moving news comes out, individual human traders are at a meaningful speed disadvantage.

A portfolio manager at a hedge fund or a trader at a bank has a team of analysts and quants working with them to extract signals from the noise. They have in-depth analysis of upcoming events and instant breakdowns of important news. The Twitter era has democratized this a fair bit and substantially decreased the advantage of the institutions over individuals. There is a ton of high-quality information and analysis on Twitter if you know where to look. Still, institutional information is generally higher quality and easier to access than the information available to those outside the industry.

Let's look at some of the most common reasons traders lose money.

1. Bad discipline

2. Not enough edge

3. Overreliance on simple indicators

4. Too much focus on trade ideas and not enough focus on risk management

5. Emotion

BAD DISCIPLINE

The number one reason that traders lose money is bad discipline. No amount of edge or skill matters if you cannot stick to the plan. The most amazing alpha-generating strategy is useless if you deviate from it. The most sophisticated, optimized and adaptive risk management system will fail if you selectively ignore some of its rules and procedures, depending on your mood or emotional state. Every time you deviate from your process or your plan because of bad discipline or emotion, you leak money.

Learning the rules is easy. Following them is hard.

I am highly qualified to talk about the importance of discipline in trading because my best and worst trading always depends on my level of discipline. The market is like a siren from Homer's Odyssey, always trying to get you to crash your boat into the rocks, constantly trying to make you break your own rules.

Overtrading is my kryptonite and I could write an entire book about my own battles with bad discipline. One of the great contradictions of trading is that conservative, disciplined people tend to be risk-averse while risk-loving people tend to be compulsive and undisciplined. This is not a truism, just a general relationship between overlapping character traits.

The great paradox of trading is that it demands you be both risk-loving and highly disciplined.

Most people are one or the other. You need to be both. This is the essence of the tight/aggressive philosophy described earlier. You follow the rules, you wait, you analyze, you stay patient, you ignore low-quality ideas and then (finally!) a juicy trade presents itself and you attack aggressively.

Bad discipline often reveals itself as overtrading, gambling, or trading for fun and stimulation. Another symptom of bad discipline is the inability to stick to the plan—moving your stop loss and take profit when they get close, for example. Often this is a simple emotional reaction to movements in price. When people own an asset that is going up, they have trouble selling it, even if their initial plan was to take profit at a particular level that has just been reached.

If discipline is an issue for you, spend most of your time trying to level up this characteristic. Automate your process as much as possible.

Bad discipline is the #1 source of trader kryptonite.

There is a demon voice in many people's heads. The voice that tells skinny women they are fat or convinces alcoholics to have "just one drink". That voice is there to sabotage you and your trading. It can make you do things that make no sense and often you will barely understand your own actions when you follow it.

Have you ever heard a voice in your head saying:

"Just hold on a bit longer, it'll bounce back. Get back to flat, then square up. No point taking the loss here. It'll definitely bounce."

Or:

"The stock is rallying, you can't miss this move! I know you stopped out at the low already… But you have to buy the high now; you're gonna miss a huge rally! The guy next to you is long at good levels and he's making so much more money than you!"

Do you control that voice? Or does it control you? This sort of stuff gets existential pretty fast and "the voice in your head" is the subject of many books and articles on psychology, mental health, self-help and philosophy. The duality or multiplicity of the human mind is an incredible and fascinating topic, and you should be aware of how and when these voices in your head sabotage you.

Understanding how your ego and the non-productive voices in your head manipulate your behavior and self-worth is a critical step towards self-awareness. You must recognize when the wrong voices tell you to press the BUY and SELL buttons.

Meditation and mindfulness training along with books like *The Power of Now* by Eckhart Tolle can help you quiet and control the non-productive, negative or disruptive voices in your head. A well-designed process and an automated risk management system also help, as they create fewer decision points where you have to intervene or actively make decisions under stress. The less you have to decide on the fly while in a position and the more your parameters are laid out beforehand and not subject to revision, the better. We will get more into risk management in Chapter 11.

While bad discipline often kills off otherwise good traders, bad traders usually lose money because they suffer from one or more of the following problems.

NOT ENOUGH EDGE

Whether you trade at the biggest asset management firm in Midtown Manhattan or out of a spare room in your parent's house in Wichita, Kansas… Trading is an impossibly complex game of imperfect information played by many thousands of technologically-sophisticated and highly-motivated opponents. What is your edge?

**Successful traders can clearly
and confidently explain their edge.**

Do you have enough edge to outperform the market and exceed transaction costs? This is the most important question in trading, especially if you do not work at a bank. Banks have some built-in edge (better information, market making revenue, best access to liquidity) but if you work at home or at a hedge fund or at an asset management firm… What is your edge? Don't lie to yourself. Think about it and be honest.

Detour: Sources of edge

Let's take a detour for a minute and look at some sources of edge over the years. There are many other sources of edge, especially at the micro level. This list is meant to get you thinking about your own edge. The point is not to go through the list and pick one. It's a starting point for thinking about and understanding your personal trading edge.

There is a cliché that if you are at a poker table and you don't know who the sucker is… You are the sucker. Similarly, if you are a trader and you do not know what your edge is, you probably don't have an edge. I will focus on sources of edge for human traders and the date ranges I provide are my best estimate of when that source of edge was most prevalent.

Most of these sources of edge still exist, but are greatly diminished from peak.

Trend Following

1984 to 2003

Trend following systems were the go-to source for human (and computer) alpha in the 1980s and 1990s. Many large trend-following commodity trading advisors (CTAs) extracted meaningful abnormal returns for more than two decades. Returns from trend following systems have steadily declined over the past 40 years. Many studies cover the slow decline of trend following performance. This table from the Winton study[63] shows the decline in trend following Sharpe ratios over time:

Performance of trend following strategies across 20 asset classes

	1984-1993	1994-2003	2004-2013
Fast	1.85	0.85	0.00
Medium	1.54	1.18	0.70
Slow	0.95	0.94	0.38

10-year gross Sharpe ratio. Fast: Weekly, Medium: 6-week, Slow: 13-week

This does not show there are now zero profitable trend following strategies, but clearly the edge has dropped over time. This is not a surprise given the proliferation of academic literature on the topic in the 1990s and 2000s. As a strategy becomes well known, its Sharpe ratio grinds towards zero.

Asymmetrical information and lack of transparency
1980 to 1996

Before the internet, markets were opaque and it was hard for those outside financial institutions to get an accurate view of prices. Traders at banks and large investment firms had a meaningful advantage given their knowledge of accurate price levels and because of wide bid/offer spreads.

Meanwhile, relatively few macro traders had big research budgets and access to policy makers. Those who did had a massive edge over less informed and less sophisticated corporations and speculators.

Instantaneous communication speeds, near-unlimited availability of information and rigorous compliance and monitoring of non-public information have dramatically flattened the landscape for both macro and bank traders.

Technical Analysis
1980 to 2006

The most common trading strategy on most trading desks I worked on before 2006 was technical analysis. Most techniques were fairly basic, while some of the smarter-sounding people might throw in some Elliott Wave or

---

63. Check out this, for example: https://www.winton.com/research/historical-performance-of-trend-following

more esoteric systems built in Lotus 1-2-3. Most of these strategies produced what amounted to trend following or breakout signals. Continuation patterns, breakouts, head and shoulders etc. were the favored setups and these piggy-backed on the underlying high Sharpe of trend following strategies in that era.

As algorithmic strategies became more common in the mid-2000s and trend following Sharpes fizzled, traders using simple technical analysis lost their edge because technical strategies are easy to replicate with a computer and computers are better than humans when it comes to risk management and unbiased trade selection. Now, I believe technical analysis has been reduced to a risk management tool and does not work effectively for trade selection or forecasting.

Analyzing Price action
1970s to 2015 (?)

It feels to me that price action in recent years has become increasingly meaningless. The idea that something "trades well" or "looks bid" pretty much just means it's at the highs these days, not that it's going higher. Price action has lost most of its forecasting value. I think very short-term, there is still meaning in Good News/Bad Price setups (i.e., when something can't rally on good news, that is temporarily bearish) but this effect has a short half-life.

Here is Stan Druckenmiller commenting on the decline of price action as a signal in 2018[64]:

> These algos have taken all the rhythm out of the market and have become extremely confusing to me. And when you take away price action versus news from someone who's used price action as their major disciplinary tool for 35 years, it's tough, and it's become very tough. I don't know where this is all going. If it continues, I'm not going to return to 30% a year any time soon, not that I think I might anyway, but one can always dream when the free money ends, we'll go back to a normal macro trading environment.

I think perhaps algorithms which are less emotional and react less predictably to news, are partly to blame for the decline in the importance of price action, but there could also be the simple fact that everyone knows about this style of analysis, so it has lost its edge. The current generation of 30- to 45-year-old traders were all brought up on *Reminiscences of a Stock Operator* and *Market Wizards* and thus we are always scouring the price action for a signal.

---

64. https://macro-ops.com/notes-druckenmiller-real-vision-interview/

Throw in the massive price distortions from non-price sensitive central bank buying of various assets and it's not hard to see how whatever signal price action might have carried in the past has been destroyed by central banks, and arbitraged away by speculators who all learned from the same books and interviews.

Global Macro
1970s to ???

Global macro is very crowded as the proliferation of pod-based hedge funds and internet macro strategists pushed global macro into the mainstream around 2005 and left too much capital chasing too little alpha. If you assume that any market strategy or inefficiency has X amount of alpha available, then the more actors trying to gobble up that alpha, the lower average returns and average Sharpes must fall over time. Too much competition and low interest rates are the top two challenges to global macro hedge fund returns since 2008.

Massive moves in asset prices driven by Fed QE, Abenomics and ECB QE delivered monster alpha to hedge funds at various points in the 2010s, but these epic events have been rare in recent years.

Correlation and intermarket analysis
2004 to 2014

This was my bread and butter back in the Lehman Brothers days but after the 2008 Global Financial Crisis, everyone became acutely aware of the importance of correlation and intermarket analysis for short-term trading.

Just about every global macro trader (and blogger) in the world is highly proficient in this style of analysis now. And there are many, many computerized systems using dynamic correlation to trade every asset class. Again: Too much money chasing too little alpha.

I still use correlation as an important input for my trade ideas but I think its usefulness has declined significantly over the past 20 years.

Data Trading
1990 to 2005

It's 1997. I expect a strong nonfarm payrolls (NFP) number and USDJPY is 118.80/85. As 8:30:00 a.m. approaches, I key up a bid for 100 million USD-JPY at 119.01. I stare intensely at the US economic release page on Bloomberg.

5, 4, 3, 2, 1…

If the number is significantly better than expectations, I hit send. If not, I do nothing. Often, pre-2005 or so, you could scoop all the lazy offers left by risk averse traders and make an instant $100k or $200k profit in the seconds after any major economic release. Now, there are hundreds of algos set up with a series of commands like: (If NFP beats by 1 standard deviation + Unemployment rate drops, buy 100 USDJPY, limit X). All available liquidity is sucked up in microseconds as an army of algos wipes the battlefield clean.

There are some second derivative ways to make money trading the economic data now, but 95% of the alpha is now owned by algorithms. This creates a form of singularity where price finds its new equilibrium point almost instantly after economic data hits the market. Instead of flailing all over the place as it tries to find the right price, USDJPY just ratchets to the new "correct" price in a few minutes as similarly-tuned programs react at faster than human speed.

Pattern Recognition
1980 to ???

There is a famous story of Paul Tudor Jones and Peter Borish using price and volume patterns to uncover an analogy between the price and volume pattern in the stock market in 1987 and price and volume in the stock market in 1929. Using this analogy, macro analysis, and his concerns about derivatives, portfolio insurance, and equity futures without price limits, Tudor predicted the Crash of '87 and returned 62% in October 1987![65]

In 2019, this type of analogy would be tweeted twenty-two times by day traders and online bloggers and would be revealed in the output of every machine learning, AI and pattern recognition machine at every hedge fund and bank in the world. Computers are significantly better than humans when it comes to unbiased pattern recognition.

I do believe, though, there is still an edge in pattern recognition. Experienced human traders can still combine complex pieces of information to form conclusions that would elude the best computers.

Leverage, carry and selling risk premium
Forever

Borrow at 2% and buy an asset that yields 7%. Carry and roll down. Sell insurance to hedgers. Sell SPX puts. These are the tried, tested and true ways

---

65. http://www.chartpattern.com/articles/40greatest-trades-article.pdf

to generate consistent returns. These strategies produce non-normal returns and lead to occasional blowups and meltdowns and are often more beta than alpha. Tactics like timing on entries and exits and superior risk management, though, can make simple levered carry and option selling strategies more like alpha than beta.

Quant / discretionary combo
2012 -

While quantitative analysis was once mostly the domain of systematic and algorithmic trading programs, human traders now use more sophisticated quantitative methods. Combining the best quantitative analysts, the best datasets and the best discretionary traders into one business pod looks to me like the ideal model for discretionary alpha capture in the current era. Quantitative analysis is greatly enhanced by experienced humans who can ask the right questions. Models are great for many types of trading, but are not as good at other tasks such as predicting or reacting to regime change or handling one-off events.

All these styles of trading still work, off and on. The challenge is to find a trading style that gives you an edge in the current market, and then stay clear-eyed, open-minded, and adaptable so you can transition or pivot as the market changes. Your edge this month might not be your edge next month, or next year.

• • •

Detour complete! I hope this brief roundup of historical sources of edge helps you think about and identify your current edge. Before we get back to our main discussion about why traders lose money, let's play a quick little game.

Take a look at Figure 6.1 and Figure 6.2. I pulled these from Bloomberg and took the name of the security off so that you won't be biased. See if you can predict the next move in the asset (or at least get a feeling for where it might go next). Think about what you see in terms of trend, support, resistance and any other tradeable patterns. What is your view on the future direction of these two assets? How strong is your view? If you were forced to trade these, would you go long or short?

Figure 6.1: Mystery Asset: Chart 1

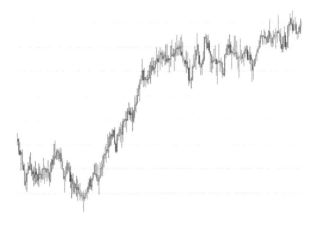

Figure 6.2 Mystery Asset: Chart 2

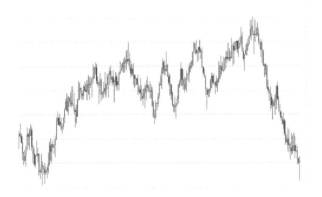

Did you take a view? Long or short?

I lied. These are not from Bloomberg. The two charts were generated using the =RAND() function in Excel. They are randomly-generated and have no connection to any security. If you had any view or guess as to where these charts are heading… That view has no basis. These are randomly-generated squiggles that might go up, down, or sideways.

This brings us to the next reason that traders lose money: They rely too much on simple indicators.

OVERRELIANCE ON SIMPLE INDICATORS

Many traders put way too much faith in simple indicators. While there is something to be said for simplicity, you also need to be realistic enough to grasp that drawing a trendline on a daily chart and buying the break of that line is probably not a strategy that will offer much edge in the long run. Anything a computer can easily do is unlikely to be a huge winner.

Many retail traders get sucked into seminars and trading courses that advertise simple breakout or similar technical strategies. Often the sellers of these strategies offer up impressive data showing that a particular strategy has generated outsized returns. Remember that this is all backward looking. Using any simple trading software, I can backtest a few thousand strategies and then cherry pick the ones that were incredibly profitable in hindsight. Then advertise those. The problem with this sort of analysis is that it does not work out of sample[66].

Do not believe the hype of online trading seminars that claim consistent profits from simple technical indicators. There is an entire industry built around the idea of easy profits and simple strategies and the sad fact is that these programs do not work. Instead of dumping $15,000 into a bogus training program, put $10,000 into a trading account and buy a huge pile of trading books and a bunch of meditation classes. Think of that $10,000 in a trading account as tuition and start trading. Very cautiously.

Reliance on simple indicators is not just a problem in retail trading. Very often, a bank trader will send out a trade rec featuring something like a trendline going back five years that just broke. They will advocate a trade based on the breakout. Personally, my philosophy is that simple is good in general but there is a point where analysis is too simple. Buying an asset because a line on a chart broke belongs in the "too simple" category for me.

Does it really pass the sniff test that you can draw a line on a chart and then wait for it to break and that will be a sustainable source of alpha or edge in a complex game played by the most expensive computers and some of the smartest human beings in the world? I doubt it. These sorts of basic trend following strategies were money in the 1980s and into the 1990s but not now. A computer

---

66. In-sample is data you analyze to come up with a strategy. Out-of-sample data is a separate set of data you use to test the strategy. This helps avoid datamining and snooping problems because almost any set of data will eventually yield what looks like a decent strategy if you torture it long enough. If you want to learn more about backtesting and the pitfalls of datamining, there is a lesser-known book called *Fooled by Technical Analysis: The perils of charting, back-testing and data mining* by Michael Harris. It is available online.

has better discipline than you and can execute a simple technical breakout strategy with less slippage and zero emotion.

Simple technical strategies, especially breakout strategies, are like dashboard indicators in your car. Yes, they are helpful, almost indispensable, really… But you would never drive a car just by staring at the speedometer, tachometer and GPS.

If you want to succeed in trading, you will need to find a more sophisticated source of edge than technical analysis. It is a part of the toolkit but it doesn't work by itself.

We'll talk more about the behavioral pitfalls of technical analysis when we discuss apophenia in Chapter 10, and I touch on the good, the bad and the ugly of technical analysis throughout this book. Now, let's move on to the next reason traders lose money:

TOO MUCH FOCUS ON TRADE IDEAS AND NOT ENOUGH FOCUS ON RISK MANAGEMENT

For every 100 trading books available on Amazon, I would estimate that one is about risk management, 29 are about trading psychology and the remaining 70 are mostly focused on trading systems or how to come up with trade ideas. And half of those "How to come up with trade ideas" books describe simple strategies that have no edge.

Finding good trade ideas is the start of the trading process, but risk management is the ultimate determinant of success or failure in trading. Even if you can properly forecast the direction of the market 65% of the time (a very high success rate), if you don't manage your risk properly, you will either slowly bleed out or quickly blow up. Risk management is so important that I have devoted all of Chapter 11 to the topic. For now, just know that bad risk management leads to failure mainly via three channels:

1. **Risk of ruin.** This is the big one. It doesn't matter how smart you are or how much edge you have, if you look into the abyss enough times, eventually you will fall in. Some trading styles and strategies are more prone to ruin than others.

2. **Slow bleed.** If you cut your winners too fast or regularly ignore or move your stop losses, trades where you were risking 1 to make 2 turn

into trades where you are risking, say, 1.3 to make 0.8. Your capital slowly leaks out, like air from a tire.

3. **Static position sizing.** Failure to understand how position sizing relates to volatility, capital levels and profit objectives can lead you to trade the wrong position size, especially when macro or volatility regimes change. This will lead to both suboptimal performance and increased risk of ruin.

I will save the rest of the risk management discussion for Chapter 11. Let's look at another reason traders lose money: emotion.

EMOTION

Emotions are not necessarily bad but they are detrimental when you do not recognize them and when you allow them to influence your thinking. Emotions can make you less rational.

When an attractive trade idea comes along and you have a solid process, it doesn't matter whether you have lost money five days in a row or just finished a record six week run. It does not matter if you woke up in a great mood or can barely get out of bed. Your process will determine when to take risk, what position size to set, and what reassessment triggers make sense. But emotions *can* trigger bad thinking and bad trading, if you let them.

Several studies confirm this including one by Lo, Repin and Steenbarger which says:

> Specifically, the survey data indicate that subjects whose emotional reactions to monetary gains and losses were more intense on both the positive and negative side exhibited significantly worse trading performance, implying a negative correlation between successful trading behavior and emotional reactivity[67].

Some emotions that cause trouble for traders:

Frustration

When you smash your fist repeatedly on a pinball machine, it eventually tilts and stops working. The human mind can be similar. When faced with a series

---

67. Lo, Repin and Steenbarger: Fear and Greed in Financial Markets: A Clinical Study of Day-Traders (2005)

of stressful losses, especially particularly hard to believe or unlucky losses, many traders will tilt. When on tilt, they will either shut down or take extra risk in order to get revenge on the market. Traders who attempt to get revenge on the market are more likely to face ruin, not find redemption.

The point is not to turn yourself into a robot and operate in an emotionless void, but to recognize your emotions via self-awareness, and develop strategies to deal with strong and harmful emotions before they jeopardize performance. Often, all it takes is a quick walk outside or across the trading floor to clear your flooded mind and return to emotional equilibrium. For more severe or prolonged negative emotional states, a few days off might be required.

Since I work at a bank and have client-facing responsibilities, it's not practical for me to take a day off when my frustration level is high. Instead, I still come in to work, but I don't trade. I write and research, or work on quantitative projects. The benefit of this approach is that I still stay in touch with the market but the drawback is that if you are in front of the screens, there is always going to be the temptation to trade.

If you are worried that you are not disciplined enough to keep your hands off the keys; find something else to do. Take a day with the kids or go watch a movie or spend a day reading at the library. Some traders prefer the mental clarity and cleansing that comes with getting away from the computer and truly disconnecting from the market. I can see that logic.

Whatever you need to do, do not sit there with an angry lump in your throat, pounding the BUY and SELL buttons out of frustration. This is like the poker player who loses eight hands in a row, turns red-faced and shoves all his chips into the pot without even looking at his cards. This is not good.

Euphoria

On trading's emotional spectrum, the opposite of frustration is euphoria. In my trading, I tend to have more of a performance issue around euphoria than frustration. When I am frustrated, I tighten up and wait for outstanding opportunities and that makes me better, not worse. On the other hand, when I am doing very well, I sometimes increase my risk more than is justified by the set of market opportunities. This is the "house money" effect I mentioned earlier.

Rarely will I see my P&L crash after a moderate or bad trading period. My biggest drawdowns almost always come after a sustained period of overearning.

I get overconfident. Cartoon dollar signs flash in my eyes. I double a position that is deep in the money when I should be taking profit.

There is a particular level of P&L where I know I tend to get sloppy so I use conditional formatting in my P&L spreadsheet to create an alert. The month-to-date cell turns orange as the "I'm doing too well" level gets close and then the cell turns red once the overearning threshold is crossed. For me, trading well seems to lead to more good trading up until a point and then eventually I hit a point of overconfidence/sloppy trading which sometimes leads to a big drawdown.

This phenomenon is also called "Winner's Tilt". Tilt is usually a condition associated with traders or poker players that are losing or on a run of bad luck. They go on "tilt" which means they start chasing with bad cards in bad situations because their minds are flooded or they are seeing red.

In contrast, Winner's Tilt is another way of describing the house money effect: temporary madness brought on by a series of winning trades or winning days. I can feel this coming on now as usually I feel a bit giddy when it's happening and might even find myself singing or joking around more than usual on the desk.

Thaler and Johnson find strong evidence of the House Money Effect in their 1990 paper: "Gambling with the house money and trying to break even: The effects of prior outcomes on risky choice". The gist of the paper is that when wagering with uncertainty, we should logically make decisions based on the probabilities associated with various outcomes and those decisions should be rational and independent of what happened beforehand.

Instead, we gamble more recklessly when our pockets are full of black chips. Meanwhile, when we are in a negative position, sitting on a loss, we find bets that offer the chance of break-even inordinately attractive. Anyone who has ever traded recognizes these two related forms of bias.

**Rational bettors evaluate current odds
and do not factor in prior outcomes.**

Be aware of your own emotions at all times and watch for the house money effect in your trading. Do you trade strong when you are up money? Or do you trade overaggressive and sloppy? If you are singing on the desk or yelling with excitement or pumping your fist... Achtung! You are about to get punched in the mouth.

Here's a short post I wrote on this topic in 2020.

Joyful yelling signals imminent P&L crash

One of the underappreciated features of working on a trading floor is that you are allowed to yell; pretty much whenever you want. In contrast, at other jobs I have held in the past (pizza maker guy at Little Caesar's, data entry clerk at Statistics Canada, gas pumper at Texaco)… It would be super weird to randomly yell out (for example) the number 32 at max volume. It would generally be frowned upon if I suddenly screamed: YOU'RE DONE!!! from a government office cubicle.

But on a trading floor, random yelling is perfectly fine!

As much as it is fun to yell on a trading floor, though, it can sometimes be a sign of euphoria and overconfidence. Overconfidence leads to overtrading, poor sizing, confirmation bias and a failure to see alternative hypotheses (because you know you're right, why bother thinking about how you could be wrong, right?) Overconfidence is also one of the main reasons men underperform women in trading.

Anyway, I am generally a fairly humble guy and I like to think about alternative hypotheses and all that… But one of my leaks is a particular type of momentary overconfidence. When I am doing abnormally well, I get excited; I want to add risk even though I should be reducing. I am momentarily swept up by a wave of irrational exuberance and should be thinking about reversion to the mean, not further upside momentum. Many traders commit this error.

Example: Last Thursday I could sense the market putting on a bit of a deflation trade (or, more accurately, taking off the popular reflation trade) and so I bought a USDMXN call to hedge a predicted flurry of coming risk aversion. Almost instantly, USDMXN ripped higher from 18.76 to 18.85 and our franchise lit up. All at once, a flood of client trades came through from sales.

Excited about my good timing and all the flow coming in, I yelled "FX IS BACK!" across the trading floor… A hopeful nod to the idea that the recent long and painful months of low FX volatility might be over. Then, I looked over to my chat log and saw one of my brokers had just typed "Hey Brent: NICE CALL MXN!". A trader on the options desk congratulated me a few seconds later. I glanced at my P&L and saw one of my best days in the past two months. And then...

You can probably guess what happened next. *Sad trombone.* It all went terribly wrong. Here is the chart:

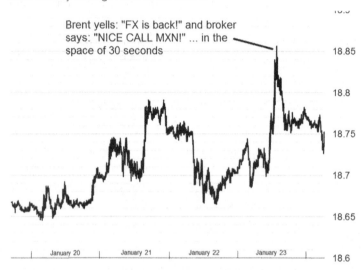

This is a phenomenon I call the Cheer Hedge. When you cheer for a position or yell or sing or fist bump on the trading floor—watch out. Your P&L is about to crash. The reason I call it the Cheer Hedge is that when I was a manager, whenever one of my traders started singing or cheering for a position, I always hedged the position in the management book right away. And the hedge always made money!

I wrote about this in THE ART OF CURRENCY TRADING and I now make this mistake less than I used to. But knowing the rules and following the rules is not always the same thing. That's one reason trading is so hard.

• • •

The takeaway here is that you need to be aware not just of your own general level of risk appetite but also of how your risk appetite changes under different conditions. I described the house money or "Winner's Tilt" effect in that story and you probably have similar personal experiences.

What makes your risk appetite go up and down? Catalog the factors and be aware when they kick in. Note that I have just described how euphoria can lead to overconfidence. I will dig much more deeply into the topic of overconfidence in the next chapter. Let's wrap things up with one more reason traders lose money and then we will move on to Chapter 7.

FAILURE TO ADAPT

Chapter 14 is all about adaptation so I don't want to front-run myself here. I just wanted to include "Failure to adapt" here because it is critical, but also different from the other reasons for failure I describe in this chapter. While the reasons I listed above are generally reasons traders fail in the first place, failure to adapt is the reason many good traders end up failing over time.

Some traders are really good at one type of trading. Maybe it's breakout trading, or trend following or mean reversion or cross-market or whatever. But a single style of trading does not work forever. Markets are by their nature highly adaptive and efficient. Almost by definition, whatever works best today is unlikely to work very well in the future. The whole process of price discovery is built to sniff out abnormal returns. The more people or algorithms discover a popular trading method, the less likely it is to work going forward.

Do not form a strong bias toward a particular trading style. Adapt to what the market is rewarding.

Markets are forever evolving and traders that cannot adapt are eventually pushed over the cliff by an invisible hand. Flexible, open-minded, creative and humble traders understand the fact that just because they are making money today, that does not entitle them to make money tomorrow.

They must earn tomorrow's money by thinking harder, working smarter and discovering new and untapped sources of inefficiency or low-hanging alpha in the market. Before we end this chapter on kryptonite and how to fail at trading, I am going to take a quick detour and talk about three moments in my career where I failed. Then, I extract the lessons.

THREE BIG MISTAKES AND
WHAT I LEARNED FROM THEM

While I have read most of the top trading books, the great lessons I have learned about trading have come from real life experience. In this section I go over a few specific trading experiences that went wrong for me. I hope that reading about my mistakes will help you avoid making similar errors in the future.

1. Thinking it would go on forever (2000)

When I was trading the NASDAQ bubble in the late 1990s, I was in my late 20's and appropriately immature. I took my trading account from $25,000 (the only money I had at the time) to more than $350,000 while simultaneously using the account to pay expenses including rent, travel, fun and a black M3. To give you a sense of my overconfidence at the time, another trader and I called the office we worked at "The Faucet". Because all you had to do was walk in and turn it on and… Out came the money. We were kind of joking, but not really.

Trading is never easy, but the market in 1999 was about as close to easy as trading could ever get. A simple, disciplined approach that followed momentum and headlines was fairly easy to monetize if you had confidence and some courage. The mistake I made was thinking it would go on forever. I did not have the experience or maturity to realize that any period where trading delivers outsized or easy returns is, by definition, unsustainable. Markets can be inefficient for short periods but not forever.

By the end of 2002, my edge was gone, my account was shrinking fast and I was out looking for a "real job".

Make hay when the sun is shining. If the market is paying a particular style of trading, lever up as much as you reasonably can and work as many hours as you possibly can. It will not last forever. Instead of working my butt off and squirreling away my gains, I worked when I felt like it because I thought I could come in and make money whenever I wanted. I had no sense of urgency.

The positive takeaway from my dumb approach in the late 1990s was that when a similar moment of outstanding trading opportunity appeared in 2008, I recognized it. I knew it was time to work as hard as humanly possible because the period of insane volatility and fat pitches was only temporary. The tuition I paid in 1999 paid off with my best year ever in 2008.

2. Failing to ride the Abenomics trend (2012)

In late 2012, USDJPY was trading near 80.00 while the Japanese stock market (Nikkei 225 Index) was languishing in the 8,500 area. Japan was in a deep economic funk. The country was on the wrong end of a multi-decade deflationary sucking machine that had sapped all confidence and left an overvalued currency and undervalued financial assets.

That all changed with the announcement of Abenomics, a major economic program spearheaded by prime minister Shinzo Abe. Abenomics was a series of initiatives that called for major structural reforms and massive monetary easing in Japan. Over the next three years, the Nikkei Index rallied 250% and USDJPY had an eye-popping rally from 80.00 to 125.00. I know three traders that pretty much made their careers on that move.

For whatever reason, I struggled to close my eyes and go with the move. Positioning became extreme very quickly (as one might imagine when a country's leader decides to devalue the currency and ramp the equity market higher). I knew very well by that point in my career (I started in 1995) that when there is a major economic or policy shift, positioning doesn't matter, but for some reason I had a mental block and struggled to go with the trend.

I had seen enough times where positioning didn't matter for extended periods, so I should have known better. For example, in 2008 (the global financial crisis, most people were short stocks most of the way down), 2010 (US quantitative easing, the market went short USD and cleaned up) and 2011 (the Eurozone crisis, the market was short EUR all the way down though punters did get badly rinsed when EURUSD finally bottomed).

Eventually, positioning always matters but in the early and middle stages of watershed economic and policy changes, the macro is much bigger than any concern about positions. Thing is, as USDJPY climbed from 80 to 90 to 100, I struggled massively to trade from the long side. Instead, I was playing retracements and "big levels" and trying to top tick one of the biggest economic stories of my lifetime.

I still don't have a good sense of why I could not get myself to trade the Abenomics trend successfully. I have various excuses but no good understanding of where the mental block came from. But when a similar trade showed up in 2015 (ECB quantitative easing, which drove EURUSD from 1.40 to 1.05 in pretty much a straight line) ... I was ready. I recognized the similarity of the setup and was strict about trading EUR only from the short side until after the pair had already dropped massively lower.

A hedge fund PM told me about how the founder of his fund (and the firm's biggest risk taker) put a Post-It note on his monitor in 2009 that said: LONG OR FLAT. At that time, the authorities had just changed all the rules (suspended mark-to-market, banned short selling, bailed out the banks, bailed out the car companies, announced quantitative easing, etc.) and he realized that it was going to be impossible for stocks to go down from that moment on.

I usually preach "nimble" as a key defining characteristic of successful short-term traders. There is, however, a time to have one core view and stick to it. Identifying these rare moments where the markets will be one-way for an extended period can be the difference between an uninspired trading career and a great one.

3. Sprinting out of the gates

One recent December, after a decent trading year, I decided I was going to try something different in the new year. I had been pretty consistent over the previous 5 or 6 years, putting up excellent but not amazing yearly P&L and I thought: "I have hit a plateau. I want to do something bigger. Trade bigger. Double last year's P&L." So instead of starting slowly and building a base of P&L before adding meaningful risk, I took a different approach.

It just so happened that I had a very strong view that the USD would sell off in the new year and so I decided to go all in right off the bat and take a ton of risk on January 1. Take a guess what happened. I got absolutely crushed, losing ½ of my prior year's P&L in the first four weeks. This put me in a devastating hole where I could barely trade for a while as I scraped back and precariously avoided getting to the point where I would need to worry about my YTD stop loss.

Sprinting out of the gates is a bad strategy!

No matter how strong your view at the start of the year, there is too much path dependence involved if you go hard on Day 1. Even if you are placing what you think is an 80/20 bet, if that 20% comes up, you are so hobbled that you threaten your entire year. It's not worth the risk. You are essentially betting your entire year on a small sample. This is not good!

I spent the next six months scratching back to flat and managed to finish up a tiny bit on the year. But those 11 months were a grueling and painful marathon. The following year, needless to say, I started with smaller risk and successfully built a base before taking on larger risk.

Sometimes you have to do the wrong thing to be reminded why you need to do the right thing. You cannot make your year in January, but you can lose it. Learn from my mistake. Start slow, build the base and be like a call option with limited downside and unlimited upside. We will dig into the concepts of path dependence and risk management in Chapter 11.

That's it for Chapter 6 and that ends our initial discussion of trader kryptonite. Now let's dig even deeper and talk about bias and irrational behavior, and how traders can recognize and avoid bad thinking and bad habits.

CHAPTER 7

SMART PEOPLE DO STUPID THINGS

Rational, unbiased trading

One of the great a-ha moments of my life was the realization, not so many years ago, that smart people still do stupid things. All the time. Once you recognize this, the world starts to make a lot more sense as you observe both your own actions (assuming you are smart), and the actions of others. In this chapter we will delve into some of the ways that even the smartest traders act irrationally, and then we will try to find remedies for these biased behaviors.

In Chapter 3 you learned that superior performance on the Cognitive Reflection Test (CRT) predicts trading success. In other words, traders that rely on System 1 and heuristics (thinking fast) will underperform traders that favor System 2 and logic (thinking slow). There is a conundrum here though: trading requires fast decision making!

The Alpha Trader needs to make quick decisions that are not contaminated by behavioral bias. There is an inherent conflict here, obviously, because fast thinking generally relies more on shortcuts while slower thinking relies more on rational logic. In this section, we will discuss a host of behavioral biases, and then think about how to counter them.

High-performing traders understand behavioral bias and are self-aware about how their own bias negatively impacts their decision-making. They know that even the best, most knowledgeable trader is subject to many types of behavioral bias.

The amazing thing about most behavioral bias is that it works on you, even if you know about it. This is similar to the way optical illusions work. Even if you have been told about the exact way your thoughts are malfunctioning, it doesn't matter. I can tell you there are no gray dots in the intersections in Figure 7.1, but you will see them anyway! You are a silly human just like the rest of us.

Figure 7.1: The Hermann Grid Illusion

Image: Donnelly

It's important for you to internalize the fact that mere awareness of a bias does not make you immune to it. So first we will examine the different types of trader bias, then discuss techniques to deal with each. This chapter will outline the types of bias that vex traders, and present specific methods you can use to avoid, or at least reduce, their potential damage.

Trader Bias #1: Overconfidence

> *The only thing I am 100% sure of is that anyone who*
> *is 100% sure of anything is not worth listening to.*
> **MATTHEW GITTINS** *(a well-known FX spirit guide), 2019*

As mentioned in Part 1, overconfidence is the most important and most devastating bias in trading. The line between confidence and overconfidence is wafer thin.

Confidence is critical but overconfidence is deadly.

If you think all your trades are 5-star home run/*amazeballs* ideas, your ability to determine the expected value of those trades is likely to be hampered by this overly rose-colored view of the trade's prospects. Overconfidence leads to overtrading, poor assessments of probability, and rigid, closed-minded assessments. Overconfident traders are also less likely to explore alternative hypotheses and will embrace confirmatory information much more openly than contradictory info.

Overconfident traders:

- take too much risk
- trade too frequently
- behave recklessly
- make poor assessments of probability
- do not keep an open mind
- overweight evidence that confirms their idea and ignore evidence that does not
- fail to consider alternative hypotheses
- refuse to admit when they are wrong

In the 2020 Super Bowl, the San Francisco 49ers were up 13-10 early in the fourth quarter. They intercepted a pass to take a commanding 20-10 lead and the entire 49ers defense ran into the end zone for a show-offy group celebration and team photograph.

Even if you are not an NFL football fan, you can probably guess what happened next. The opposing quarterback, Patrick Mahomes put up 21 straight points. The Kansas City Chiefs won 31-20 and Mahomes is now my favorite quarterback of all time. The San Francisco 49ers were reckless and loose. They failed to consider the alternative hypothesis (that they might lose).

A less cocky team in that spot would be thinking about finishing and winning the Super Bowl, not assembling like a group of clowns in the end zone while the opposing team game-plans the next possession.

There is nothing more dangerous than a team that celebrates as if they won the championship before the game's over. By the same token, there is no trader more likely to dump a huge wad of cash than the one who pumps his fist, celebrating a trade he hasn't squared up yet.

San Francisco celebrates prematurely; their overconfidence soon leads to ruin

Don't do this in the middle of a football game! Photo by Doug Benc (AP Images)

Perhaps surprisingly, research shows that the more difficult a task, the more overconfident people tend to be. This is obviously a problem when it comes to finance, given its extraordinary challenges. Research shows that training and experience can reduce miscalibration (of confidence), but only to a minor degree. You must appreciate and understand that we all tend toward overconfidence. Remain humble and do your best to consider what you don't know or might be missing in a given situation.

For a fascinating read on overconfidence and miscalibration, Google: "Calibration of Probabilities: The State of the Art to 1980" by Lichtenstein, Fischoff and Philips. Not only is the paper full of interesting insights, it was scanned from a typewritten document presented to the US Navy in 1981, so it has a cool retro vibe. And it's not boring.

There are three types of overconfidence:

1. **Overestimation**, where people tend to overestimate how well they will perform a task.

2. **Overplacement**, where people grossly overestimate their rank or placement among others. This is also known as the "better-than-average

effect". Most individuals think of themselves as better than average at most tasks, even though it is not mathematically possible for more than 50% of individuals to be better than average. There has been considerable research on this topic. One of the earliest studies showed that 93% people surveyed in the US and 69% of Swedes thought they were better than average drivers![68]

3. **Miscalibration.** This occurs when an individual believes his ability to estimate something (say, the price of a stock) is better than the reality. His confidence interval should be wide but it is narrow.

Research shows that overconfidence can have positive consequences in many aspects of life. Overconfidence helps with ambition, morale, persistence, and helps individuals signal a better-than-reality level of skill or knowledge to peers. Overconfident people are viewed by peers as more competent than properly calibrated people.

On the other hand, when it comes to trading (and investing): *overconfidence is unambiguously negative.*

There is so much research showing that overconfidence leads to negative outcomes in both trading and investing that it's hard to know where to begin. The first study I want to discuss[69] uses miscalibration to assess subjects' potential overconfidence and then compares that to their trading performance. A standard psychological questionnaire to measure calibration asks subjects to give a low and high estimate for difficult questions such as:

- Martin Luther King's age at death.
- Length of the Nile River (in miles).
- Number of countries that are members of OPEC.
- Number of books in the Old Testament.
- Weight of an empty Boeing 747 (in kilograms).

And so on. Properly calibrated individuals will write down low to high ranges that include the correct answer most of the time. Overconfident or

68. Svenson, O., "Are we all less risky and more skillful than our fellow drivers?" (1980).

69. Biais, B., et al. "Judgemental Overconfidence, Self-Monitoring, and Trading Performance in an Experimental Financial Market," *The Review of Economic Studies* (2005).

miscalibrated individuals will answer with ranges that are too tight and often do not include the correct answer.

In the Biais et al. study, subject miscalibration was measured and then subjects were grouped into quartiles from most to least miscalibrated. The subjects were then placed in an experimental asset trading market. At the end, trading profits were checked against miscalibration to check for a relationship. As you might guess, there was a strong relationship. Miscalibrated individuals performed worst and well-calibrated individuals *killed it* (see Figure 7.2).

Figure 7.2: Average trading profit by calibration quartile

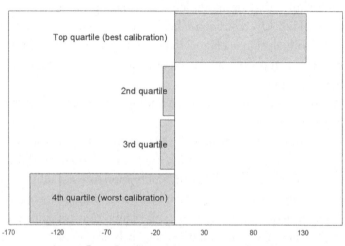

Image: Donnelly, with data from the paper cited above

This gets at the idea of knowing what you know and knowing what you don't know. If you have no idea about an answer, you should answer with an extremely wide range. People that don't have a good understanding of their own lack of knowledge perform poorly in this trading experiment and I believe these experimental results match real life outcomes. It is important to know what you know and also to be humble about what you don't know. As Mark Twain or Josh Billings once said:

> "It ain't what you don't know that gets you into trouble. It's what you know for sure that just ain't so."

Alpha traders have intellectual humility.

Prolonged time in the market inevitably beats the overconfidence out of you. Traders who have survived for many years understand that no matter how smooth the sailing is right now, there is always another storm just over the horizon; no matter how much you know, you barely know anything.

The study just referenced shows a direct connection between miscalibration and trading performance. There is often a more indirect connection too, as overconfidence leads to overtrading which reduces performance through higher commission or bid/offer spread paid plus reduced trade selectivity.

Patient, well-calibrated and aggressive traders will trade less often than impatient traders who always think the market is wrong and they are right. Properly-calibrated traders understand the public signal (the market price) is probably correct most of the time and they need a very strong reason before believing in the superiority of their own private signal (their alternative view of where the price should be or where it's going).

If the market was always right, you could never make money. On the other hand, markets are generally very efficient; they are usually right, or correct themselves quickly. You should always give the market the benefit of the doubt and think about what you might be missing before you decide to challenge the wisdom of the crowd (i.e., the current market price) by entering a trade.

Another excellent study conducted in 2001 looked at six years' worth of retail discount brokerage trading records for more than 35,000 households[70]. The study concluded that men executed 45% more trades than women and this overtrading was the primary reason women outperformed men by about 1% (net returns).

In another study[71], researchers measured subjects' confidence and then set up ten experimental asset markets. They constructed some markets of overconfident traders and some of people with a more rational view of their own abilities. Prices in the rational market tracked the fundamental asset value fairly accurately while the market of overconfident traders saw higher prices, greater volatility, higher trading volumes and more bubbles.

Anyone watching the NASDAQ in 1999 or bitcoin in 2017 (and 2021) can see how this experiment is an accurate reflection of reality. Overconfident traders think they are right and the market is wrong. They overvalue their own opinion (private signal) and underweight the market price (public signal).

---

70. Barber and Odean, "Boys will be boys: Gender, overconfidence and common stock investment" (2001).

71. Julia Michailova and Ulrich Schmidt, "Overconfidence and bubbles in experimental asset markets", Kiel Institute for the World Economy (2011).

The majority of the research shows that women are less overconfident than men and that they outperform men in trading and investing.

> ...girls are not necessarily less confident than boys, but rather they are less overconfident.[72]

> ...although both men and women were overconfident, undergraduate men were especially overconfident when incorrect.[73]

That last quote is from a paper called: "Highly confident but wrong." What a great title. It makes me smile. And here is the conclusion of an even more topical study:

> This paper studies performance predictions in the 7-item Cognitive Reflection Test (CRT) and whether they differ by gender. After participants completed the CRT, they predicted their own (i), the other participants' (ii), men's (iii), and women's (iv) number of correct answers. In keeping with existing literature, men scored higher on the CRT than women and both men and women were too optimistic about their own performance. When we compare gender-specific predictions, we observe that men think they perform significantly better than other men and do so significantly more than women.[74]

That quote is particularly relevant because it comes from a study of gender differences related to the Cognitive Reflection Test. Recall the CRT is the test we covered in Chapter 4. Performance on the CRT is evidence of rationality and predicts trading success. A well-calibrated estimate of CRT performance is also likely to predict trading success.

There is a strange irony that aggressive Type A males are often attracted to trading and this sub-category is (in general) most likely to be overconfident. Then again, it also makes sense. Risk-seeking behaviors and overconfidence tend to go together (if you think you're invincible, you take more risk) while less overconfident but risk-averse individuals are not interested in, or likely to be good at, trading.

---

72. Seo-Young Cho, "Explaining Gender Differences in Confidence and Overconfidence in Math" (2017).

73. Lundeberg, M. A., Fox, P. W., & Pun coha , J., "Highly confident but wrong: Gender differences and similarities in confidence judgments" (1994).

74. Patrick Ring, Levent Neyse, et al., "Gender Differences in Performance Predictions: Evidence from the Cognitive Reflection Test" (2016)

There is much more research I could present but I think you get the two main points:

1. Women outperform men in trading, mostly because they are less overconfident.

2. Overconfident traders trade too much and underperform those with well-calibrated confidence.

How to combat overconfidence

1. **Respect the market.** The market is not always right, but it is not often wrong.

2. **Do a pre-mortem** on your trades. Picture the trade going wrong and see if you can imagine what might have caused the failure. This puts you in the mindset opposite to overconfidence. Instead of assuming it's the best trade ever and you are smarter than the market, you assume it's a failure and ask yourself why.

3. **Be aggressively open-minded** and stay humble. No matter how confident you are, there's still a good chance you are wrong. Embrace the fact that part of being a good trader is accepting that you will frequently be wrong. Daniel Negreanu (one of the best poker players in the world) still loses countless hands.

4. **Bounce trade ideas off people** you respect. I send out my trade ideas every day and the feedback I get is tremendously useful on many levels. First, people that disagree with me will present reasons they disagree and I can assess these reasons and recalibrate my confidence level. If the reasons are strong enough, I might even change my mind or exit the trade. Second, I get a good sense of sentiment. If everyone agrees with me, the market is most likely positioned that way already. If everyone disagrees, I am probably in the minority position and if I can comfortably rebut the counterarguments, my idea is more powerful.

Trader bias #2: Overtrading

Trading can be incredibly fun. That's good. But that is also a problem! Enjoyment should always be a side benefit of trading and not the primary objective.

The first objective must always be profit. Very often, traders will get involved in the market out of boredom or out of a need for stimulation. This gets them into trades that have weak (or no) logic and low or negative expected value. Remember: tight / aggressive. Look for juicy, low hanging fruit and pluck it. Don't climb up into the treetops and risk a big fall. Be patient.

How powerful is trading as a stimulant? *Very*. This is from a 2001 study[75]:

> The psychological processes underlying the anticipation and experience of monetary prospects and outcomes would appear to play an important role in gambling and in other behaviors that entail decision making under uncertainty. In this regard, it is striking that the activations seen in the NAc, SLEA, VT, and GOb in response to monetary prospects and outcomes overlap those observed in response to cocaine infusions in subjects addicted to cocaine.

In case you are wondering: NAc (nucleus accumbens), SLEA, VT, and GOb are four reward-related brain regions. And the following is from Andrew Lo's testimony to Congress on Hedge Funds, Systemic Risk, and the Crisis of 2007-2008:

> ... the same neural circuitry that responds to cocaine, food, and sex—the mesolimbic dopamine reward system that releases dopamine in the nucleus accumbens—has been shown to be activated by monetary gain as well.

Both the anticipation and receipt of monetary gains trigger the reward circuitry of the brain. Human nature is to seek activation of this circuitry both consciously and unconsciously. You must come to grips with the fact that trading often involves sitting there doing nothing, just waiting for a great opportunity. Unfortunately, the numbers moving up and down on that screen are like squirrels, and you are a dog.

Various commentators, including Jean-Paul Sartre, have commented that war is "...hours of boredom interspersed with moments of terror". Trading can often be the same. There is a strange temporal rhythm to trading where time speeds up and slows down depending on what is going on.

I remember instances after a major economic announcement or market

---

75. Breiter, Aharon, Khaneman et al., "Functional Imaging of Neural Responses to Expectancy and Experience of Monetary Gains and Losses" (2001)

event where I did 5 or 6 big trades, got into a position and out of a position and made hundreds of thousands of dollars. The time elapsed felt like 15 minutes. Then, later in the day when things were quiet, I would go look at the 1-minute chart and could not see enough detail to capture what had happened. I would have to go to a 1-second chart to see the levels at which I did those 5 or 6 trades and I would realize that the entire sequence, which felt like 15 minutes, actually took more like 90 seconds.

This time dilation is a common feature in sports, military action, trading, and other fast-moving pursuits that require rapid-fire, high-stakes decision making. Of course, the stakes are much higher in the military but the mental effect where time slows down is similar.

Once you get that feeling of excitement, the *in the zone* moments where the P&L piles up so fast you can't believe your eyes—you want that feeling again. Problem is, you can't get that feeling by trading low probability set ups. Instead, those low EV trades give you that "why did I do that" feeling. You can't trade to chase a rush. Your only goal each day should be to maximize P&L.

In 2018, Stephen Brown of NYU et al. conducted a cool study where they dug through vehicle ownership records and found the make and model of car driven by more than 1,000 hedge fund managers[76]. Then, they compared fund performance to car type and found this intuitive result:

> Using a novel data set of automobile purchases by hedge fund managers, this paper exploits cross-sectional variation in vehicle attributes to investigate the effects of sensation seeking on investment behavior. We argue that the purchase of a powerful sports car signals the intent to drive in a spirited fashion and therefore conveys a propensity for sensation seeking. Our results empirically validate the advice given by some hedge fund allocators to avoid managers who drive fancy sports cars. We find that managers who own performance cars take on more investment risk than do other managers, without being compensated with higher returns. Therefore, performance car owners deliver lower Sharpe and information ratios than do non-performance car owners.
>
> The incremental risk-taking by sports car enthusiasts extends beyond financial markets to the fund operations arena. Sensation

---

76. Brown, Stephen and Lu, Yan and Ray, Sugata and Teo, Melvyn, "Sensation Seeking and Hedge Funds" (2016).

seekers are more likely to terminate their funds, disclose violations on their Form ADVs, and exhibit greater operational risk. Sensation seeking also shapes trading behavior. Managers who embrace powerful sports cars trade more frequently, actively, and unconventionally than do managers who eschew such cars. They also gravitate toward lottery-like stocks. Trading hurts the performance of sensation seekers more than it hurts the performance of sensation avoiders.

Here is another excerpt:

... sports car drivers underperform non-sports car drivers by 2.92% per year while minivan drivers outperform non-minivan drivers by 3.22% per year.

Jesse Livermore did not drive a mini-van! :] This is more evidence that you can be risk-averse and still succeed as a trader. The researchers also found that hedge fund managers who received more speeding tickets also underperformed, which is consistent with the idea of sensation-seeking leading to more risk but not better returns. Other studies also confirm: sensation-seeking traders overtrade, pay more commission, and perform worse than non-sensation-seeking traders[77].

You need to be honest with yourself. Just like it's OK to be risk averse, it is OK to be sensation-seeking or boredom-averse. You just need to be aware of it and institute a set of rules to control your behavior and manage your weaknesses. You also need to accept that this sensation-seeking or disinhibition is a weakness you will need to deal with throughout your career. Attitudes toward risk are highly innate and very difficult to modify even with the healthiest, most growth-oriented mindset.

Sensation-seeking and gambling often go hand in hand. To get a sense of whether you are trading to feed your desire for excitement (i.e., as a form of gambling) take a look at the following excerpt from the DSM-V. The DSM-V or DSM5 is the Diagnostic and Statistical Manual of Mental Disorders. It contains descriptions, symptoms, and other criteria for identifying mental disorders and it is the authoritative guide to mental illness throughout most of the world.

Here, I have taken the section on identifying gambling disorder (previously known as pathological gambling) and replaced the word "gambling" with "trading". Do any of these line items sound familiar to you?[78]

---

77. For example: Grinblatt and Keloharju, "Sensation seeking, overconfidence and trading activity," (2009).

78. https://www.psychiatry.org/patients-families/gambling-disorder/what-is-gambling-disorder

A diagnosis of ~~gambling~~ trading disorder requires at least four of the following during the past year:

1. Need to trade with increasing amount of money to achieve the desired excitement

2. Restless or irritable when trying to cut down or stop trading

3. Repeated unsuccessful efforts to control, cut back on or stop trading

4. Frequent thoughts about trading (such as reliving past trading experiences, planning the next trade, thinking of ways to get money to trade)

5. Often trading when feeling distressed

6. After losing money trading, often returning to get even (referred to as "chasing" one's losses)

7. Lying to conceal trading activity

8. Jeopardizing or losing a significant relationship, job, or educational/career opportunity because of trading

9. Relying on others to help with money problems caused by trading

Many traders would recognize their own thought patterns in that list. A trader who scores himself as 10 out of 10 for risk appetite might see himself in five or six of those behaviors. Think about these criteria for gambling disorder and be honest with yourself about how trading impacts your life. It should be an enjoyable, intellectually stimulating profession, not a way to achieve a gambler's high.

Jesse Livermore is celebrated as a trading hero but it is worth remembering that he took his own life after going bankrupt for a third time, after his second divorce. He is a trading hero and a cautionary tale wrapped into one.

The process and mechanics of trading and gambling overlap. Both involve risk management, probability, randomness, risk of ruin, emotion, bias, and irrational human beings. Bad trading can often be very much like casino gambling. It is impulsive, emotional and has a negative expected value.

Excellent trading deals with incomplete information and variance of a game like blackjack, but has a positive expected value, like a professional poker player at a table of weaker opponents.

One final note here: The term "gambling" usually describes a form of entertainment where the gambler's odds or expectation are negative. Some forms of gambling, like poker, can have a positive expectation if the player is highly skilled. I would say that when a highly-skilled and highly-disciplined poker player sits down at a table full of tourists or recreational poker players, that is not gambling.

The skilled player has a significant mathematical edge. Poker is much closer to trading than most forms of gambling because it offers a small group of highly-skilled players the ability to generate abnormal returns consistently. In other words, poker is skill, not luck. Research confirms this unequivocally.

I think it is interesting that research also shows that hedge fund managers who are skilled in Texas Hold 'em outperform those who are not. Here's the conclusion reached by Yan Lu, Sandra Mortal and Sugata Ray in a 2019 research paper[79]:

> We find that hedge fund managers who do well in poker tournaments have significantly better fund performance. This effect is stronger for tournaments with more entrants, larger buy-ins, larger cash prizes and for managers who win multiple tournaments, suggesting poker skills are correlated with fund management skills.

Like Taylor in Billions. This further solidifies the skill link between poker and trading and separates them from luck-based gambling such as roulette, craps and (mostly) blackjack[80]. Trading, like poker, involves significant variance and path dependence but long-run outcomes are primarily driven by skill. We will talk much more about skill, luck, and variance in Chapter 11. For now, remember:

If you want to gamble, go to a casino.

A substantial portion of investor underperformance can be explained simply by the fact that investors are active when they should be doing nothing. This is proven again and again by the consistent and sizeable outperformance of index funds vs. active managers and by the poor returns in retail accounts. Most of the time you should be doing nothing!

This is a simple concept but one that is extremely difficult to put into practice in real life.

---

79. Lu, Yan and Mortal, Sandra and Ray, Sugata, "Hedge Fund Hold 'em" (2019).

80. It is theoretically possible to play Blackjack with positive expectation but with 6-deck shoes and security cameras everywhere, not so much!

Your default mode should always be to do nothing.

Flat is the most powerful position in trading. When you have no position, you are unbiased, ready to pounce, and unconstrained by any prior view or notions. You are not anchored on any price or level. You are most open-minded and nimble when you have no position.

Yet people often feel bad when they are flat, especially if they remain flat for many days. "I'm not putting my capital to work", they might think. Or "My boss is gonna think I'm lazy." Human nature equates doing nothing with laziness, and in most jobs that's a pretty accurate assessment! An employee who sits there and does nothing over multiple days is probably not doing a great job in most roles. In trading, though, the opposite can be true. Quite often, the trader doing nothing is the wolf waiting silently in the long grass. Ready to pounce. An Alpha Trader.

Take pride and comfort in your ability to remain flat. The very nature of the tight/aggressive framework in trading is that you should be flat as often as possible and only engage when the expected value of a trade is high.

Flat is good. A trader with no position has no bias.

How to combat overtrading

1. **Think about your motivations for trading**. Do you overtrade? Why? Self-awareness is key before any action can be taken to fix the problem.

2. **Create speedbumps** that must be cleared before you can trade. Maybe that means filling in a quick pre-trade checklist. Maybe it means going through an execution desk instead of pressing the buttons yourself. If all you have to do is press a button to trade, you can easily become the lab rat pushing the little button for more cocaine. If your process includes a speedbump or two, it is harder to overtrade.

   The idea is to create friction around unwanted behaviors. For example, I find when I leave my orders with a broker, I am much less likely to cancel them than if I watch them myself. It can be rude or annoying to cancel a close order with a broker and so the bar to cancel is higher. This is good. You should not be cancelling your take profit sell order just because "it looks bid". It always looks bid at the high.

At one particular bank I worked at, we had the ability to trade at any time through an app on our phones. Most other banks did not have that functionality. As you might expect, the ability to trade on your phone was incredibly convenient but it also led to overtrading. It takes particularly high conviction for me to contact a trader in Hong Kong or London and put a trade on, but if all I need to do is open my phone and press a couple of buttons, I am much more likely to put on any trade idea that pops into my head at whatever time of night.

A good trading process usually involves some sort of written trade plan. It is not always practical to completely write up a trade before you put it on, given that short-term trading often requires quick thinking and rapid execution. That said, once you have the trade on, you usually have plenty of time to write it up afterwards. By doing so, you justify the trade, you game plan it and you may find out that the trade was a dumb idea before you get stopped out. Have the flexibility to get right back out of a trade if you realize as you write it up that the idea is weak.

3. **Create hurdles and barriers between you and the market.** If you can trade with a single click, you are going to trade more. If you can trade on your phone at 3 a.m. (and your phone is on), you will trade more. If you need to convene a 10-person investment committee to vote on a new investment, you are going to trade less. If you need to log into Bloomberg or call someone at 3 a.m. in order to execute, you will trade less.

   Obviously this is a continuum and there can be huge negatives to slowing down your process, too. But knowing that overtrading and too much activity is the biggest leak for many traders, what can you do to slow down your execution process? What is the right balance of speed/accessibility and restraint/selective trading? I would say it's too easy for most people to trade. Can you create a trading framework that allows you to express your views but that also constrains any impulsive urge to jump into new trades or out of existing ones?

4. **Stop staring at the screen**. Take a break from the screens once in a while. Staring at price action will lead to suboptimal decisions triggered by price action and random noise. Once you have a position

on, let it breathe. Price action is mostly meaningless. Staring at the screen ups the amount of stimulus you receive each day and may lead to excess action.

5. **Set a maximum number of trades per period**. This needs to be logical and based on your trading history. Answer this question: When I am trading well, how many trades do I execute per day or per week? Then set a maximum that you feel is close to optimal. A lower number forces you to be more selective (and tight/aggressive). On the other hand, your returns will suffer if you set the limit too low. Market conditions should be the primary determinant of when and how much you trade, but a maximum trades figure anchors you around the appropriate level of activity.

   My time horizon is short and my trades usually last one hour to three days. If I take more than two or three positions in a day, I am usually overtrading. As a market maker, I tend to trade much more than an average hedge fund PM and this has become a bad habit for me at times. Client trades provide a convenient excuse for a market maker to take on risk that makes no sense. Instead of covering a client trade for a small profit or loss, the temptation can be to justify the position and ride it. It's the endowment effect again… We overvalue trades we have on. It's dumb, but we all do it.

   A similar rule you can set for yourself (which is easier to follow if you are mostly a day trader) is to set a maximum number of line items. When I was day trading stocks, I never had more than three positions. There is a good reason for this. When things go wrong, it's hard to manage 14 line items in your book and anyway, most traders will find there is high correlation between their positions. Instead of spreading yourself thin, focus on one or two core positions and put all your risk where it belongs. Diversification has benefits in investing but **good trading is all about concentrated risk**.

6. **When you put on a trade, establish firm stop loss, take profit and reassessment triggers**. Then, do your very best not to take the trade off before one of them hits. Overtrading doesn't just mean putting on too many trades. Often it means taking off trades prematurely for no reason. It is hard to stick with a trade when nothing is going

on but remember that most of the movement in a security comes in short bursts of activity that take very little time. Most of the time is boring, random drift.

Let's say you spend an hour analyzing spreadsheets, thinking about positioning, planning out your trade, etc. Your idea is solid, all the planets are aligned and you decide it is time to go short Venn Corporation (VENN). Let's go.

You sell 1,000 shares of VENN, risking 1% to make 3%. Two hours later, the market is quiet. VENN has been stuck in a tiny range and you're bored. A random headline comes out that is vaguely bullish one of VENN's competitors and a flash of a thought crosses your mind that VENN might rally in sympathy. You press a few buttons and cut the trade.

The stock rallies 30 cents then drops a buck as the market decides the story is good for the competitor, but bad for VENN. Now your trade idea should have been 70 cents in the money and instead you cut for reasons you don't even really understand. You are now in a tricky position. Do you get back in at worse levels? Or just forget about it?

Man, if this thing drops 3% this afternoon …

(EVIL VOICE IN YOUR HEAD: And you know it's gonna drop… 'Cuz you cut like a chicken!)

If you had input your stop loss and your take profit in an automated system and controlled your impulsive desire to press buttons… Things would be so much better. Remember, once you have a position on, you are steaming hot bias stew. Your first assumption should always be: the original plan was the best.

Stick to the original plan unless material new information emerges. Or, better yet, just stick to your original parameters every time. Sure, new information might matter, but your interpretation of new information once you have a position on is often biased. Always err on the side of inaction. When you have a position on, you should almost always ride it out until the stop loss or take profit hits. Not always. But almost always.

7. **If you have a constant need for activity, find productive outlets.**
Every time you have an idea for a backtest, trading strategy or analysis, write it down so that you have a list of projects to pursue when you are bored. I am constantly jotting down stuff like "What hour of the day has the highest volume in USDJPY?" "Does bitcoin outperform on weekends?" etc. Then, when I'm bored, I can work on these questions instead of sitting there twitching as I try to keep my fingers off the BUY and SELL buttons.

When in doubt: Do nothing.

There is a fascinating 1975 essay by Charles Ellis called: "The Loser's Game". It is mostly fascinating because even back in 1975 it was obvious (and easily proven with data) that active management of investment portfolios consistently underperformed passive management. This is still true today but for some reason it took the world about 40 years to catch on and now money is finally flooding out of active funds and into passive indexes.

The essay is worth a read; there are some great analogies in it and it goes into some detail on why active will underperform passive by definition due to transaction costs. Later in this book, I show just how dramatic transaction costs are as a drag on your performance. The more you trade, the more money you leak. Remember this: All other things being equal it is a fundamental truth of trading and investing… The more you trade, the more you pay.

Make fewer, higher quality decisions.

This is the essence of the tight/aggressive way. This is a core behavior of the Alpha Trader.

Trader bias #3: Confirmation bias

Faced with the choice of changing one's mind or proving that there is no need to do so, almost everyone gets busy on the proof.
JOHN KENNETH GALBRAITH

There is a good chance you already know about confirmation bias. It is one of the best-known and most-discussed forms of bias out there. It is most-discussed because it is critically important and hard to fight, even when you understand it.

Confirmation bias is the tendency for humans to seek and incorporate information that supports their existing view, and ignore or reject new information that does not.

Instead of impartially evaluating new evidence in the search for unbiased conclusions about the market, people tend to stick to their current view and then look for evidence to support it, while ignoring evidence that does not.

While Kahneman and Tversky tend to be the names we most associate with behavioral bias, confirmation bias was discovered by British psychologist Peter Wason. His experiment was simple. He gave subjects the series: 2-4-6, then told them it satisfied his Pattern Rule. He then told subjects they could construct other sets of three numbers to test their assumptions about the Pattern Rule. Each time the subject showed the experimenter their three numbers, the experimenter would tell them whether or not it satisfied the Pattern Rule until the subject was confident they figured out the rule.

Subjects would test either a series like 8-10-12 (satisfies rule) and 22-24-26 (satisfies rule) or 3-6-9 (satisfies rule) and 5-10-15 (satisfies rule) or 4-8-12 (satisfies rule) and 10-20-30 (satisfies rule) until eventually most would answer that the Pattern Rule is either:

- Count up by 2's
- Count up by a multiple
- Some formula like add the first two numbers to get the third number.

But whatever answer people came to, they tended to get an idea and then test it over and over until they were certain it was right. What they did not do, generally, was try deliberately-wrong sequences to see if those might work.

The actual Pattern Rule was "any three numbers that increase in value". Anyone that tested 1-2-3, for example, would have instantly ruled out all three patterns listed above. But subjects were always busy testing patterns that fit their rule without ever thinking to test those that did not. Instead of looking for more and more evidence that their hypothesis was correct, they should have tried sequences that did not fit their hypothesis, in an attempt to invalidate it.

Look harder for evidence and arguments against your hypothesis.

Confirmation bias is one of the most harmful bugs in human reasoning. You see it everywhere in media and on Twitter as consumers of information ignore competing views and augment their existing opinions with more and more confirmatory evidence.

The concept is especially disruptive in trading and investing because it inhibits good thinking, locks us into a view, and blocks out useful non-confirmatory information. Also, other types of bias (such as the endowment effect) work together with confirmation bias and make it very difficult for investors to change their mind once they take a position in the market. You see confirmation bias in action almost every day on a trading floor.

Example: You have been following Zzap Corp. for months and you bought the stock at good levels. Everyone has been excitedly waiting for the hot new Zzap Flidget Fone to come out. A headline hits:

*ZZAP REPORTS 90-DAY FLIDGET FONE LAUNCH DELAY DUE TO SUPPLIER ISSUES.

An unbiased market watcher might think that is bearish. The stock drops 4%. But you are a fan of Zzap, you are long the stock and so you might think something more like: "Meh, this isn't big news, the phone's still coming out. It's not even Zzap's fault. This is an overreaction. The stock's gonna bounce."

Meanwhile, two analysts downgrade the stock. They say this is further evidence that Zzap's supply chain is overly reliant on a single chip supplier in Vietnam and that the supplier is severely mismanaged. The stock drops another 4%. You might think: "Man, I can't believe how much the market is overreacting here!"

On the other hand, bears are probably yelling: "I knew this was gonna happen!"

How to combat confirmation bias

1) Read about confirmation bias. It is one of the most catalogued psychological phenomena out there and the research is surprisingly interesting. Confirmation bias is powerful and kind of frightening because it severely compromises the human capacity for reason. For example, if you take two people who have opposite views on a divisive issue like capital punishment, and give them new information, here's what happens. *Excerpted from an excellent article on confirmation bias from the New Yorker*[81].

---

81. https://www.newyorker.com/magazine/2017/02/27/why-facts-dont-change-our-minds

> One of the most famous of these [confirmation bias experiments] was conducted, again, at Stanford. For this experiment, researchers rounded up a group of students who had opposing opinions about capital punishment. Half the students were in favor of it and thought that it deterred crime; the other half were against it and thought that it had no effect on crime.
>
> The students were asked to respond to two studies. One provided data in support of the deterrence argument, and the other provided data that called it into question. Both studies—you guessed it—were made up, and had been designed to present what were, objectively speaking, equally compelling statistics. The students who had originally supported capital punishment rated the pro-deterrence data highly credible and the anti-deterrence data unconvincing; the students who'd originally opposed capital punishment did the reverse. At the end of the experiment, the students were asked once again about their views. Those who'd started out pro-capital punishment were now even more in favor of it; those who'd opposed it were even more hostile.

I have found over the years that the more deeply I read about confirmation bias, the more easily I can see it happening to me in real time. I have realized mid-sentence sometimes that I am shooting down the importance of a headline simply because I am positioned the wrong way.

The longer you trade, the more you will notice that when news comes out and you are flat, you react quickly and without bias. When news comes out that goes against your view and position, you will often hesitate or freeze or explain away the news. Watching yourself make a decision influenced by confirmation bias in real time is the first step toward beating the problem. Until you see yourself doing it, you have not really recognized how confirmation bias negatively impacts your decision making.

2) Actively consider other hypotheses. We talked about this in Chapter 5. If you can spend two hours reading reports and studying charts and coming up with a thesis on why you want to buy PommeTech stock.... Can't you at least take 15 minutes to think about why NOT to buy it? Or, even better, think about the reasons you might want to go short PommeTech.

This intellectual exercise greatly strengthens your trade ideas because if you can come up with five good reasons to short PommeTech at this point, your bull case weakens. If you can only think of two, and have good rebuttals to both, that's more like it. And finally, if you can think of exactly zero reasons anyone would want to short PommeTech, your thinking is probably biased and you better ask around.

Step outside yourself and pretend you are an analyst forced to write a bearish piece about PommeTech. What might it say? While many smart individuals are happy to play Devil's advocate whenever they hear someone else's ideas, they are often unable to poke holes in their own logic.

Not only does actively considering other sides of the story help deal with confirmation bias, it can also help you later on. If the facts of the story start to change, you may recognize the competing hypothesis coming true and your hypothesis losing steam. Having explored the bearish case, you are more likely to recognize it when it comes along as opposed to remaining blind to it or shrugging it off.

Once you have a great trade idea: poke some holes in it for a few minutes.

3) Be a Bayesian. Think about the world now as your prior and commit to updating as new information comes in. If today you think the probability that Italy leaves the Eurozone in the next 12 months is only 10%, and that is a big reason you are bullish euro, adjust your probability honestly as new information comes in. Don't just scan the news for bullish stories about Italy and skip over the bad news. That sounds silly but it is *exactly what people do!*

Read both sides of the story and continuously adjust your worldview. When you have a solid grip on Bayesian thinking, you will suffer less from confirmation bias ("Bayesian thinking" is explained in Chapter 5).

4) Create a quick pros and cons sheet for any trade that involves meaningful risk. This is such a simple exercise and your mom probably told you about it when you were 11. Still, it's effective. When I am making a major decision (new job, new home, kids' school, etc.) I always create a list of pros and cons. Quite often, the decision becomes much easier afterward because the result of the pros/cons list is so clear. Research shows this simple procedure produces a marked improvement in the appropriateness of confidence judgments[82].

---

82. Koriat, A., Lichtenstein, S., & Fischhoff, B., "Reasons for confidence." (1980)

I do the same thing when I'm writing about trade ideas. Once I'm done writing my thesis or trade idea in AM/FX (pros), I spend a few minutes trying to take the other side (cons). This is important because I'm sending my ideas out to thousands of people and I don't want to look stupid, but it's also part of a strong intellectual process and sound trade idea development. Questions I ask:

- Why might this trade not work?
- What are the key assumptions I have made?
- What are the key risks to the idea? What might go wrong?
- Imagine the trade as it crashes and burns. What happened? Sometimes by imagining the adverse scenario, we can tease out risks we might have missed. This is the pre-mortem concept discussed in the section on overconfidence.

In the climactic rap battle in the movie *8 Mile*, Papa Doc wins the coin toss and elects to let B-Rabbit (Eminem) go first. Eminem uses the "Stealing Thunder" technique to bring up and tear down and run through every insult that his opponent might possibly use on him. By the time Papa Doc hits the stage, there is nothing left to say. Eminem refuted every possible argument Papa Doc could have made.

Your trade ideas should be like that. You know the contrary view so well, you can dissect and refute it better than anyone else.

5) If you have a particularly strong economic worldview, don't get sucked into the echo chambers that support specific narratives. Too often, the bears read only bearish material while the bulls are plugged only into cheerleading analysts. Gold and bitcoin bulls can spend the whole day reading bullish forecasts and stories on the internet but they will laugh off anything bearish with "Those guys don't get it." Don't be like that.

Give weight to, and spend time evaluating, credible opposing viewpoints. Don't lock into one view. It's intellectually lazy and can be hazardous to both your wealth and your credibility. Discount the views and analysis of anyone who always has the same view.

There is a reason I sign off AM/FX each day with: *Good luck, be nimble*. Intellectually nimble is the best mindset for successful trading.

It is important to know that confirmation bias is *not* strongly related to intelligence. This is consistent with the idea that rational thinking and intelligence are not the same thing[83]. That should be one of your main takeaways from this book.

Smart people do stupid things. All the time.

To succeed in trading, you can't just be smart. You also have to be rational. You have probably spent most of your life getting smarter. Now it's time to train yourself to be more rational. To quote from an article titled "Why Intelligent People do Foolish Things"[84]:

> The absence of knowledge in areas important to rational thought creates a mindware gap. These important areas are not adequately assessed by typical intelligence tests. Mindware necessary for rational thinking is often missing from the formal education curriculum. It is not unusual for individuals to graduate from college with minimal knowledge in areas that are crucial for the development of rational thinking.

Everyone, including you, suffers from confirmation bias.

Trader bias #4: Extrapolation

One thing you learn after five years or so of working on Wall Street is that most "forecasts" you read are simply extrapolations of the current trend. I will show you a few good examples, but I could literally make 100 of these charts and then 100 more if I had time.

Figure 7.3 shows EURUSD in black and the average FX strategist's EURUSD forecast in dotted gray. If you look closely, you can see that the forecast simply follows the trend and turns when the price of EURUSD turns. The forecast is useless. This is a concept you should get used to. If you piled up all the research showing humans cannot forecast accurately, it would stretch to the moon. I strongly recommend you read *Superforecasting* by Tetlock and Gardner to get a full grasp of the perils of forecasting.

---

83. Stanovich, K.E., West, R.F. and Topiak, M.E., "Myside Bias, Rational Thinking and Intelligence." (2013)

84. https://psychcentral.com/lib/why-intelligent-people-do-foolish-things/

Figure 7.3: EURUSD (solid black line, right y-axis) vs. average analyst EURUSD 12-month forecast (dotted line, left y-axis)

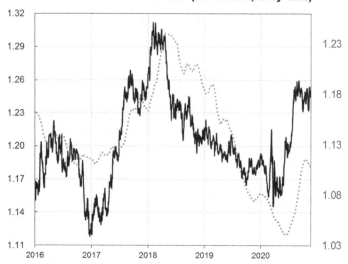

The chart is comical (to me at least!) but it's even funnier when you see it in real time. In 2017, Emmanuel Macron won the presidency in France and this was seen as a bullish development for the euro. EURUSD started trending higher and every analyst set a topside target of 1.15 or 1.20. When EURUSD rallied to 1.20 fairly quickly, forecasters did not say "mission accomplished" … They simply raised their forecast to 1.25. When it got to 1.25, they raised their forecast to 1.30.

Take a look near the middle of the chart where EURUSD peaked. You see the black line crash lower, then the "forecasts" follow a few months later. As EURUSD sold off hard from 1.25 to 1.18 in April 2018, analysts climbed over each other to lower their forecasts for months and months. This is not forecasting—it's extrapolation.

The default and easy view to take in the market is to assume that whatever is going on right now will continue. But that is often not how the world works. Periods of outperformance are very often followed by reversion to the mean.

This is the logical explanation for the "sophomore jinx", the Cheer Hedge, the Sports Illustrated jinx and the Magazine Cover Indicator. A theme or market move that has become such an important story that it landed on a magazine cover has probably outperformed in a major way and thus is more likely to revert to the mean than to further outperform its already stellar outperformance.

In markets, there is another reason why price reverts to the mean. Extremely low or high prices change the supply and demand profile for the asset. If oil goes to $100, new rigs come on board and increase supply and this pushes the price lower. If oil goes to $20, people buy more fuel-guzzling trucks because gas is cheaper. This increase in demand for gasoline pushes oil prices back up. If the price of corn triples, companies will substitute other commodities that are cheaper. And so on.

Watch for changes in supply and demand in your market after large price changes. Are medium or long-term sellers or buyers entering the market to take advantage of high or low prices? This change in participant behavior can mark the beginning of the end of a trend.

The number one input into almost every forecast is the current level and trend of the asset. There are notable exceptions, such as the fact that everyone has been (mostly) calling for higher US yields despite a 40-year trend lower, but generally you will see that when something is going up, it is forecast to go up more and when something is going down, forecasters expect it to keep going down.

Extrapolation bias is a form of recency bias. Humans tend to overweight more recent information in most analysis simply because that information is more available (i.e., top of mind). Events from years ago are harder to remember

Figure 7.4: Greek yields and two major rating agency announcements

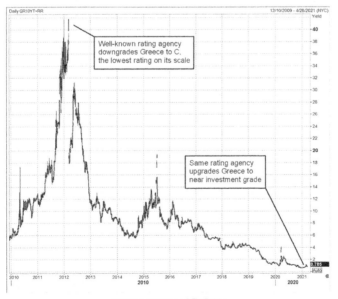

Chart courtesy of Refinitiv

and incorporate. This is why you see analysts put out bullish predictions for oil when it's trading at $100 and bearish predictions for oil when it's trading at $25.

Check out Figure 7.4. When Greek debt was the most attractive and yielded 35%, the ratings agencies downgraded it. As of December 2020, it is the least attractive it has ever been, with yields close to zero. And they upgraded it. Note that yield moves opposite to the price of the bond so the ratings agency downgraded the bond at the lows and upgraded it at the highs.

My point is not to troll the ratings agencies, and I know technically they are not forecasting, they are just nowcasting. The point is just that when an asset is in trouble, everyone hates it. When an asset is ripping, everybody loves it.

Now let's do oil (see Figure 7.5).

Again, note how the price moves first and the forecast follows and has no predictive value.

Extrapolation bias does not just impact economists and forecasters, it impacts traders (big time). Most traders are much more comfortable buying things that are going up and selling things that are going down. Sometimes this is an appropriate strategy, often it is not.

The bias manifests in another way besides the tendency to chase the market higher and lower. Many traders put on a trade, and when it hits their target, instead of taking profit, they raise their target. "It looks bid! I can't take profits here!" they will say.

Be aware of this bias. Notice it in your thought patterns. Be rational. As my friend The Gold Crow says:

**It always looks great on the highs
and terrible on the lows.**

When there is a strong trend and you have faith in it for multiple reasons, that's not extrapolation bias. That's a rational expectation that the thing will go up. When a stock rallies three bucks out of nowhere and your instinct is to buy it because "someone must know something" you are making an irrational extrapolation.

There are traders out there that have the opposite bias and tend to trade mean reversion all the time, even when things are trending. That's me. I am more biased towards mean reversion and this bias can be just as costly as extrapolation. Trading mean reversion all the time can be like trying to catch falling pianos.

Figure 7.5: Brent crude (black) vs. analyst year-end 2020 price forecast (gray)

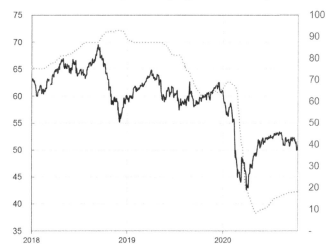

Strong trend = falling piano[85].

Do you like to catch falling pianos?

This is really important: good traders go with the trend, *or fade it*, depending on the regime, the setup, the fundamentals, the technicals and so on. They don't identify themselves as trend or mean reversion experts. Don't say "I'm a mean reversion guy" or "I'm a trend follower". Different styles work at different times.

You should identify and trade what works in the current market. Don't commit to one trading style and hope the market cooperates. It won't.

Negative extrapolation

While what we typically witness in financial markets is positive extrapolation (everyone assumes whatever is happening will keep happening), there can also be the problem of negative extrapolation. That is: it has never happened before so it can't happen now. This is a failure of imagination. The best outlook is to always consider almost any possibility, no matter how unlikely. This does not mean you need to position for extremely low probability outcomes; you just need to consider them.

---

85. Copyright 2021, Angus Greig.

A famous example of negative extrapolation is Ben Bernanke's infamous failure of imagination just before the 2008 Global Financial Crisis:

> INTERVIEWER: Tell me, what is the worst-case scenario? Sir, we have so many economists coming on our air and saying, "Oh, this is a bubble, and it's going to burst, and this is going to be a real issue for the economy." Some say it could even cause a recession at some point. What is the worst-case scenario, if in fact we were to see [housing] prices come down substantially across the country?
>
> BERNANKE: Well, I guess I don't buy your premise. It's a pretty unlikely possibility. We've never had a decline in house prices on a nationwide basis. So what I think is more likely is that house prices will slow, maybe stabilize: might slow consumption spending a bit. I don't think it's going to drive the economy too far from its full employment path, though.

In case you were born very recently: housing went down nationwide in 2008. It went down *a lot*. People used similar logic when assessing the SNB's EURCHF floor at 1.20 before it broke in 2015. The idea was: "They held it this long; there's no way they'll let it break!"

Annndddddd.... It's gone.

Another concept that long seemed ridiculous and unimaginable but then quickly became mainstream is the idea of negative interest rates. Most market pricing before 2012 or so always treated zero as the absolute lower bound for interest rates.

Therefore, punters made many bets in Swiss rates (for example) that went horribly wrong when the SNB cut rates below zero.

Always remember:
anything can happen.

Figure 7.6: Two unbelievable actions in one short statement
The SNB abandons the 1.20 EURCHF floor and cuts rates to minus 0.75!

Press release	SCHWEIZERISCHE NATIONALBANK BANQUE NATIONALE SUISSE BANCA NAZIONALE SVIZZERA BANCA NAZIUNALA SVIZRA SWISS NATIONAL BANK ✛

Communications

P.O. Box, CH-8022 Zurich
Telephone +41 44 631 31 11
communications@snb.ch

Zurich, 15 January 2015

Swiss National Bank discontinues minimum exchange rate and lowers interest rate to –0.75%

This does not mean you need to be wracked with fear, on high alert for extremely low probability events all the time. It means you need to be open minded to outliers and their possible impact. Consider low probability events and think about how they could influence your risk of ruin. No matter how unlikely an event might be, it's not worth taking the other side if it can blow you up. Many learned this the hard way after the SNB debacle in 2015.

Trader bias #5: Favorite vs. longshots

Human beings generally prefer to bet on longshots and avoid favorites, even though favorites almost always offer higher expected returns. Before we delve into why that might be and how it is relevant to trading, let's look at a bit of evidence from the world of horse racing. Here is the money quote and an accompanying chart from a 2010 paper by Erik Snowberg and Justin Wolfers[86]:

> The racetrack provides a natural laboratory for economists interested in understanding decision making under uncertainty. The

---

86. Erik Snowberg, E., and Wolfers, J. "Explaining the favorite-longshot bias: Is it risk-love or misperceptions?" (2010).

most discussed empirical regularity in racetrack gambling markets is the favorite-longshot bias: equilibrium market prices (betting odds) provide biased estimates of the probability of a horse winning. Specifically, bettors value longshots more than expected given how rarely they win, and they value favorites too little given how often they win. Figure 1 illustrates, showing that the rate of return to betting on horses with odds of 100/1 or greater is about -61%, betting randomly yields average returns of -23%, while betting the favorite in every race yields losses of only 5.5%.

Figure 1: The rate of return on win bets declines as risk increases.

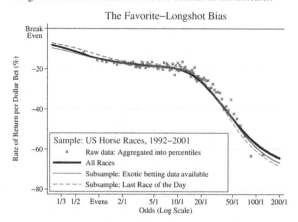

The chart clearly shows that betting on favorites is a better (err… less bad…) strategy than betting on longshots. Yet even though the effect is well-known, it has persisted over many decades. Favorite/longshot bias was initially discussed in 1949 and yet the effect still shows up in many (but not all) gambling and financial markets[87]. The more asymmetric (lotto-like) the payout, the more likely traders, investors, gamblers (and regular folk) will overbet the longshot.

There are three main reasons for the existence of favorite / longshot bias:

1. The marginal utility of a large win is often higher than the marginal utility of a small win, even if the odds of the small win are near 100%. With a fixed amount of capital at risk, small payoffs don't really "move the needle" financially or psychologically.

---

87. Baseball betting is an interesting exception. Despite some underdogs paying 2:1 or even 3:1, baseball bettors prefer to bet favorites.

Say you are a hedge fund manager who wants to generate a 10% return this year. You are offered two trades, both risking 5 bps if wrong: Trade 1 has an 80% chance of making 5 basis points (expected value = +3 bps) and Trade 2 has a 5% chance of making 80 basis points (expected value = -0.75 bps).

Even though Trade 1 is clearly more attractive mathematically, many traders (whether they will admit it or not) are more attracted to Trade 2 because it moves the needle for their YTD P&L while the first one does not, unless they place a huge bet.

2. Betting on favorites is not as fun as betting on longshots. Bettors and investors looking for excitement or stimulation prefer longshots.

3. Human beings tend to overestimate the likelihood of lower-probability events and underestimate those with higher probability (see Figure 7.7). Keep this in mind when assessing odds. If you think something is a 5% shot, you are probably too high. If you think something is an 85% shot, you are probably too low. In contrast, humans are good at evaluating probabilities in the middle of the spectrum (the 25% to 60% zone).

Figure 7.7 shows a stylized curve of how research shows humans typically estimate probability (solid black line), versus how probability looks in real life (dotted line).

Since estimating probability is a critical skill in trading, you must understand: It is more difficult to estimate high and low probabilities than those near the middle.

In trading, the longshot bias effect shows up in language like "levered bets", "outstanding risk/reward", and the ever-popular "asymmetric payout profile". Looking for asymmetric payouts makes sense in aggregate: if you are always betting $1.00 to win $0.50 in a game where the odds are not known beforehand (only estimated), it is hard to achieve persistent success. On the other hand, this preference for longshots can sometimes lead to bad trades with good optics (like those 5% one-touches that are always so hard to resist).

The longshot mentality is bolstered by financial media features that shower adulation on tail risk managers in the rare moments their highly-levered

Figure 7.7: Actual probability vs. human estimates of probability

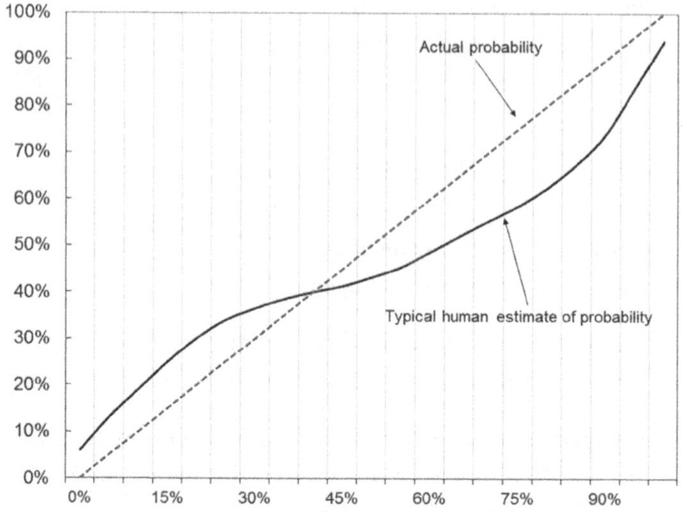

Various estimates put the cross-over point around 35%/40%

insurance bets pay off. There are no stories written about the tail risk fund that bleeds for four straight years while the VIX is pinned at 12! The takeaway here is: be aware of favorite/longshot bias. Don't get sucked in by bad trades with good optics.

An example of favorite longshot bias in action

You often see favorite-longshot bias over economic and central bank events. For example, when a central bank meeting is coming up, and there is a tiny (but not zero) chance of that central bank cutting rates, the market loves to go into the meeting short the currency. This often creates an imbalance where there are so many people betting on the longshot (a rate cut) that you get an outsized move when no cut is delivered.

Here is an example: in early February 2020, COVID-19 was popping up all over the world and had triggered the first wave of fear about the global economy. Given Australia's dependence on commodities and global growth, some observers thought the Reserve Bank of Australia might cut rates in response to the virus contagion.

Interest rate markets priced the probability of an interest rate cut as less than 10%, but if the cut was delivered, AUDUSD might drop 100 points. The simple longshot trade was to go short AUD and cover quickly if the RBA did not announce a rate cut. Traders in this set up thought they were risking a few pips for a chance to make 100 pips of profit. But Figure 7.8 shows what happened:

Figure 7.8: AUDUSD 5-minute chart around the February 2020 RBA meeting

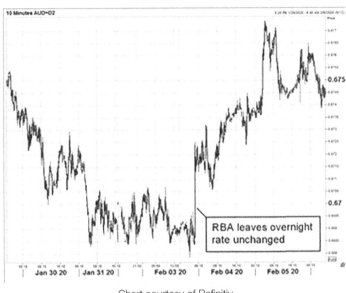

Chart courtesy of Refinitiv

There were so many traders caught short on the lotto ticket trade, the pair gapped 30 pips higher (from 0.6690 to 0.6720). Traders thought they were risking 5 pips to make 100, but were actually risking 30 to make 100. If you assigned a 10% chance to the RBA cut (which was probably generous), the expected value of the trade with 5 pips of downside risk was +5.5 as you can see in Table 1. But in real life, because the "no cut" cost you 30 pips, the expected value of the trade was actually -17 pips! See Table 2.

Analyzing Short AUDUSD into the RBA: February 2020

Table 1: ex-ante

An estimate of expected value, before the event

	Probability	profit/loss	
RBA Cut	10%	100	10
RBA No Cut	90%	-5	(4.5)
	Expected Value of the Trade		5.5

Table 2: ex-post

Same expected value calculation, but adjusted for new information after the event

	Probability	profit/loss	
RBA Cut	10%	100	10
RBA No Cut	90%	-30	(27)
	Expected Value of the Trade		(17)

Note that while we don't know for sure (because it didn't happen), a cut from the RBA might have yielded a drop of less than 100 points, because the position was so crowded. In other words, the expected value of the trade might have been even *worse* than -17bps.

Any time you hear people talking about a lotto ticket trade or a trade where there is very little risk, or where you win in almost every scenario: be cautious. This is probably a sign that traders are flocking to a trade that has great optics on paper but possibly bad mathematics in real life. Those trades get crowded. As a trade gets crowded, the risk/reward gets worse and your ability to get out quickly becomes impaired.

Favorite/longshot bias also shows up in option pricing. Speculators love to buy low-delta options (cheap options that pay out a huge windfall if something very unlikely happens) and market makers generally do not like selling them. Therefore, research shows that the lower the probability of an option paying off (and thus the more leverage is embedded in that option), the more overpriced it will tend to be.

Watch for favorite/longshot bias in your own trading and in setups that unfold in front of you.

Trader bias #6: Round numbers

When you fill your car with gas, do you sometimes have the urge to round it off to the nearest dollar, even though you are paying with a credit card? Do you get a tiny thrill watching a car's odometer roll over from 99,999 to 100,000? For many amateur marathon runners, a finishing time of 3:59:58 is a great success while 4:00:02 is a disappointment. These are examples of round number bias.

Human beings tend to pay attention to round numbers and treat them as special or more important than other numbers. *OK, sure Brent… Who cares?*

You should.

Round number bias appears in financial markets, and while this knowledge will not be life- or career-changing for you, it will save you from the occasional big disappointment. Due to round number bias, many market participants leave their orders on the round numbers. Many more than you would see if orders were randomly or evenly distributed. I will show you two examples from the world of equities, but these anomalies are present in every market I have studied.

Figures 7.9 and 7.10 show the distribution of the last two digits (the cents) of each daily high and low in TSLA and NFLX from 2015 to 2020. For example, $520.40 would be 40. $765.00 would be 00. $509.33 would be 33, etc. Note the huge overrepresentation of highs and lows at 00 and 50, exactly as round number bias would predict (00 is far, far left).

Figure 7.9: Distribution of daily highs and lows in TSLA (by the cents, or last two digits of the price)

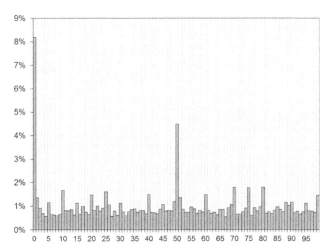

Therefore, if you leave an order to buy at, say $473.01, you are statistically more likely to get filled than the person with an order at $473.00 or $472.99 because the majority of buy orders will be on the round number at $473.00. Most days, you'll probably get filled at any one of those three levels, but the occasional time you get filled at 01 when you would not have got filled one cent lower can have a big impact on your performance.

On the flip side, if you are leaving stop loss orders, always leave them on the correct side of the round number. Sell stops should be below 00 and buy stops should be above. The day you leave a stop loss at $474.99 and the low is $475.00, you will feel like you got lucky, but these tiny alterations in behavior can sometimes be skill masquerading as good luck.

P.S. When that happens, you owe me a beer.

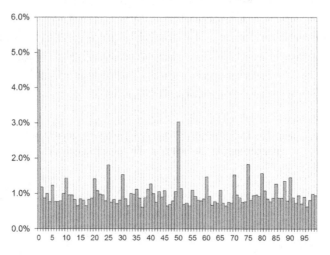

Figure 7.10: Distribution of daily highs and lows in NFLX (by the cents, or last two digits of the price)

Trader bias #7: Apophenia

Chaos is not dangerous until it begins to look orderly.

MAX GUNTHER, *The Zurich Axioms*

Great traders are masters of pattern recognition. They will see a setup and recognize it either consciously or unconsciously. I remember many times after great runs of trading that I felt like I knew what was going to happen before it happened. This ability comes from the incredible powers of human pattern recognition. The problem is:

Humans are built to see patterns, even when none exist.

Apophenia or patternicity are terms psychologists use to describe the human predisposition to see patterns or connections, even where none exist. Apophenia leads to many flaws in human thinking and explains why people see Jesus on toast, UFOs in the sky, bigfoot in the woods and so on. This human bias toward pattern recognition also leads gamblers who are on a winning streak to believe they will keep winning. Even smart, logical people often feel like they are "heating up" after a lucky series of hands at a poker table.

This is also known as clustering illusion. People have a hard time believing that streaks are the result of randomness, even though random data contains many streaks!

We are wired to find meaning and significance in random and meaningless data. Apophenia goes a long way toward explaining why humans believe conspiracy theories, suffer from paranoia, and embrace pseudoscience. When you see patterns everywhere, you see meaning and connections too. Understand that you are not immune! You are predisposed to see patterns, even where none exist.

The human ability to see patterns is a critical part of our evolution and allows us to understand the world without having to analyze every single new piece of information. If we have never seen a large black cat with large teeth on the savannah, a useful evolutionary trait was to assume that its behavior and risk profile is similar to other large animals with huge teeth we have encountered in the past.

We can correctly infer that the presence of dark clouds in the sky above us represents an increased probability of rain in the next few hours. We know a hissing sound nearby means snake bite risk is higher than normal and we dramatically increase our alert level.

Evolution favored false positives over false negatives because the cost of a false positive in the wild was much lower than a false negative. For example, there is a loud grumbly noise in the bush that Caveman Kror cannot clearly identify:

- False positive (Type 1 error): That sounded like a lion, I think?! I'm out of here!

  Cost: *Kror may have used some unnecessary energy avoiding what could have been just a random sound.*

- False negative (Type 2 error): Hmm, I wonder what that grumbly noise was. It didn't sound exactly like a lion. I guess I'm good. (42 seconds later) Oh, dang, it was a lion.

  Cost: *Kror is dead.*

Seeing patterns where there are none may be superior evolutionary behavior, but it's not helpful in trading. Given the very strong human instinct to see patterns, how useful do you think simple eyeballing of charts, basic trendlines and breakout patterns is likely to be? What are the odds that chart break is just a standard false positive—like the loud noise in the bush? Now add on human confirmation bias… Are you just seeing what you want to see? Probably.

This does not mean that there are no patterns in the world. If you run into heavy traffic four days in a row at a particular interchange, it makes sense to consider whether there is causation. Investigating further, or temporarily changing your route is likely to be optimal. But you need to be aware that the way humans see patterns is biased to Type 1 errors. You need to be discriminating and use a tight filter when looking for patterns. You need to consider that what you are looking at could be random.

How to combat apophenia

There are three ways to beat apophenia in trading. Awareness, skepticism, and analysis.

1. **Awareness.** Hopefully this section has you thinking about, and more aware of, apophenia and patternicity. It's a deeply engrained and basic part of human cognitive function. Once you appreciate that the human brain is biased toward pattern recognition, new patterns you detect are placed in the proper context.

2. **Skepticism.** Start from a place of skepticism. When you see a pattern or a correlation, assume it is bogus and try to work out why it might not be. Most people assume patterns are valid and then spend time further validating them with other analysis or information. You should start by assuming patterns are meaningless and work your way towards meaning via analysis.

3. **Analysis.** Let's say you see a headline on Bloomberg: "Death Cross in silver futures triggers bearish signal". You pull up the story and see a fugly chart where the 50-day moving average has just crossed below the 200-day. Is your first instinct to sell silver? Or to investigate more deeply? Patterns like this should not be taken at face value. Most of them are meaningless and have no empirical basis. Take half an hour to pull some data into Excel and backtest the pattern. Does it have any predictive value?

When I say "patterns" that does not just mean technical analysis. It is any cause-and-effect relationship that appears to exist in markets. Again, humans tend to ascribe causality to many things that are the result of pure chance.

On the other hand, patterns like the following examples could be meaningful, persistent, and predictive:

- gold tends to go lower from 9 a.m. to 10 a.m. (maybe gold producers sell at this time?)

- whenever US rates go lower, USDJPY goes lower (Japanese investors prefer higher rates?)

- AAPL tends to lead the QQQs (large caps lead indexes?)

And so on. Sophisticated pattern recognition can be a significant source of edge when it is free from bias.

I spend a good part of my time analyzing data in an attempt to determine whether patterns have predictive value or not. Most often, the answer is "not". Taking the time to analyze patterns and to determine whether or not they are useful for forecasting is a good way to overcome apophenia and discover useful tools for beating the market.

This is my simple four-step method for accepting or rejecting patterns:

1. Identify a pattern or relationship.

2. Generate a hypothesis.

   The best patterns have some sort of underlying logic. If gold goes down every day from 9 a.m. to 10 a.m., maybe that is the window when gold producers sell? If you can logically explain why a pattern works, it is much more likely to be non-random and persistent.

3. Analyze the data.

4. Accept or dismiss the pattern.

Anyone who took a science class as a kid should recognize this as a short-form version of the scientific method. Most patterns you analyze will be worthless. You will dismiss them and move on. On the other hand, the few patterns you find that are non-random can be incredibly valuable to your future trading.

Every time you notice a pattern, reduce it to something you can test and then get to work. You don't need sophisticated quantitative skills to do basic backtesting of simple theories. Once you backtest a pattern, you have a much deeper understanding of whether or not it is random, and you know whether to factor it into your trading decisions.

For example, I like to use moves in one market to predict moves in another market. Here is an example of how I will look at a pattern and try to determine whether or not it has meaning. This excerpt from AM/FX also gives you an idea of how I pull together multiple reasons for a particular trade idea. We will discuss how to build a trade idea in much more depth later on.

From July 1, 2020:

> We had a rare setup at the close yesterday as US rates have dropped 8 bps in the last five days while USDJPY was up 1.3%. There have been 2610 trading days in the last 10 years and just 49 of them have satisfied the condition: (USDJPY up >1% and US 10-year yields down more than 7bps). Here is how USDJPY performed after:

USDJPY performance after two conditions met (sample = 49)

	t+1	t+3	t+5	t+10	t+20
Average return	-0.1%	-0.3%	-0.6%	-0.9%	-0.5%
% of time USDJPY goes down	56%	55%	63%	63%	65%

Two conditions: Up >1% in past 5 days and
US 10-year yield down >7bps in past 5 days.

> And note that USDJPY rallied from 88 to 107 in the last 10 years, so if you took any random sample it would show USDJPY going up, not down. That makes this result even more interesting. The medians are similar to the averages, so there is not a small group of instances skewing the average.

> Overall, I think USDJPY is a sell based on yields, the move in gold, and USDJPY's consistent inability to take out 108.00. Also, there was a three-day run of buying madness in NY time from 7 a.m. to 11 a.m. and there is no evidence of that today. It was probably a major rebalance into month end. So that is over, which also helps.

> Note in Figure 7.11 how USDJPY bashed against 108.00 four times (four arrows) before a huge false break and then it retested the 108.00 level again afterwards (fifth arrow).

> I am therefore adding a short USDJPY recommendation. You could either sell here or leave an offer at 107.75 with a stop at 108.26.

With ISM and payrolls tomorrow, there is a decent chance you get done. And with Yield Curve Control on the horizon and the explosion of coronavirus cases in the US South, I doubt strong US data will impact yields much.

Note by leaving an order to sell above market at 107.75 through nonfarm payrolls, I attempt to take advantage of the noisy volatility created by an event I think is meaningless to get set at a good level on a trade I like for a bunch of reasons. See Figure 7.11.

Figure 7.11: USDJPY Hourly, April to July 2020

Chart courtesy of Refinitiv

I got set on the trade the day after payrolls (at 107.75) and USDJPY went pretty much straight down.

Backtesting is an entire field of quantitative research and there is considerable complexity involved. I am not a computational finance or applied math expert, so I like to keep things as simple as possible. I come up with a theory, and then I test it. I don't tweak the parameters or snoop around until I find something useful. I just go in, test, and get out. While a full course in backtesting is beyond the scope of this book, you don't need a degree in financial engineering to conduct basic backtests of patterns you identify and ideas you come up with.

When testing your hypothesis, be aware of a few things:

1. The law of small numbers. You need a decent sample of observations for your analysis to mean anything. If you see that TSLA stock went down the last four Aprils in a row, that's meaningless. If it went down 33 of the last 41 Fridays, that might mean something. While there is no hard rule for legit sample size, any study using less than 30 observations is risky and likely to be unreliable.

2. The harder you have to look, the more likely whatever you find is bogus or biased. Let's say you want to see how the stock market performs the Monday after a 3% drop on Friday. You find nothing interesting. So then you test how it performs after a 4% drop on Friday. Still nothing. Then, you up the threshold to 5% and find the subsequent Monday averages a 2% further fall. Then you test, "What if stocks fall 2% or more Thursday AND 5% or more Friday" … The more you mess around with your parameters, the more likely you are to find "interesting" results. This is called "p-hacking" in the research business. You keep tweaking the inputs until you get an interesting result. That is not good research.

   Don't torture your data in an effort to make it confess. Keep your analysis simple. For the best ever and super simple explanation of how p-hacking, snooping and data-mining work, Google "xkcd green jelly beans".

3. Be aware of the trend in your data. If you do any study of S&P 500 data since 1930, you will generally find that bullish strategies perform well and bearish strategies perform poorly! This makes sense since stocks have gone up a zillion percent in that time period. Similarly, you will find it easy to "discover" bullish NASDAQ or bearish oil company strategies. The secular trend in the data is an important driver of the output of any strategy you analyze.

4. No matter how well something worked in the past, there's no guarantee it will work in the future. In a world of infinite data, many relationships, and a huge number of sophisticated analysts, people are going to find strategies that worked in the past. If you have a strong opinion on why the strategy is likely to work in the future, the value of your analysis is higher.

   For example: Turnaround Tuesday (discussed in more detail below) is well known and has existed for many years. It is founded on a reliable and repeatable pattern of human behavior and a persistent fear and greed cycle that repeats around weekends, even if statistically savvy investors know about it. Also, as a short-term strategy, it is fairly expensive to execute (in terms of transaction costs) so large institutions are unlikely to quickly arbitrage it away.

5. Don't build regression models unless you know what you are doing. Regression models can be useful but often require sophisticated knowledge to avoid datamining, overfitting, and other errors.

Most patterns in finance are random. You need to find evidence and use logic before accepting a pattern as meaningful.

As a quick detour, here is a bit more info on Turnaround Tuesday, in case you are not familiar with its amazing power.

Turnaround Tuesday

During periods of market fear, there is a common intraweek pattern that stock markets often follow. This sequence is shown in Figure 7.12. Markets don't always follow this pattern but they do follow it a surprising proportion of the time.

Figure 7.12: Anatomy of a sell-off

Thursday	*Hmm, I'm getting a bit nervous here, maybe I should reduce a bit of my stock market exposure.*
Friday AM	*I need to hedge, this looks really bad*
Friday PM	*I better sell some S&P futures to hedge my weekend risk. Wow, what a brutal close.*
Saturday	Everyone reads the alarming media coverage of the scary thing(s) that knocked the market down Friday
Sunday Asia / Monday morning	Markets gap open lower and selling builds as Asia selling cascades into Europe. NY traders press their shorts.
Monday around 4PM	The low.
Tuesday	Turnaround Tuesday as shorts get squeezed.
Wednesday	See saw battle between bulls and bears.
Thursday	*Hmm, I'm getting a bit nervous here, maybe I should reduce a bit of my stock market exposure.*

The most reliable part of this pattern is "Turnaround Tuesday". This is the tendency for stocks to rip higher on Tuesday if they sold off the Friday and Monday before. It is a simple human pattern that occurs because when the news appears bad, traders get nervous into the weekend and sell some of their holdings on Friday. Then, they read all kinds of negative media reports about the big scary thing and that scares them into selling more on Monday.

Investor selling pulls in momentum traders who go short on Monday. This adds to the selling pressure. Then, Tuesday comes and there is nobody left to sell. Then the shorts get squeezed and that triggers Turnaround Tuesday.

In case you think this sounds silly, have a look at this evidence. First, here is how the S&P performs in the most extreme Turnaround Tuesday setup which is when it falls Thursday and Friday and then is down more than 5% on Monday. This is rare but check out the returns in Figure 7.13.

Figure 7.13: Tuesday 1-day S&P 500 return after
(down Thursday, down Friday, down >5% Monday)

9/13/1932	-4.3%
10/19/1937	3.2%
5/29/1962	4.6%
10/20/1987	5.3%
10/27/1987	2.4%
10/28/1997	5.1%
9/1/1998	3.9%
8/9/2011	4.7%
3/10/2020	4.9%
Average	**3.3%**

In contrast, if you study all days after a 5% one-day drop, the average return the next day is just +0.9%. Not terrible, but nothing amazing.

Second, to give you more evidence supporting Turnaround Tuesday, Figure 7.14 shows SPX performance for Tuesday vs. all other days in 2008. Note that 2008 was one of the worst bear markets in history so Turnaround Tuesday was a thing almost all year. If you traded in 2008, you probably find this chart pretty mind-blowing.

Figure 7.14: Total cumulative performance of Tuesdays (solid line) vs. rest of the week in 2008

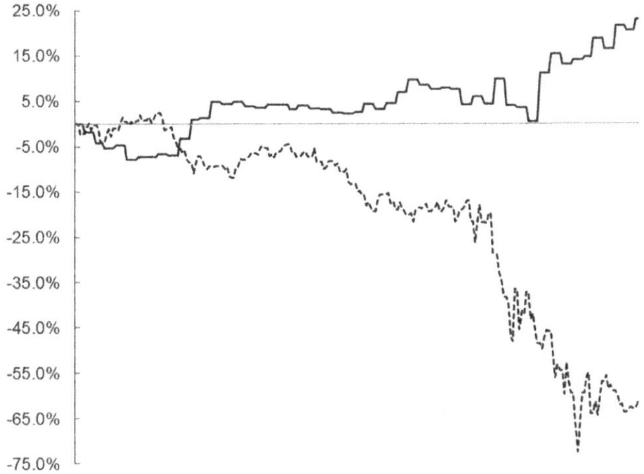

Image: Donnelly, with data from Refinitiv

Trader bias #8: Anchoring

I have always found anchoring bias to be one of the most interesting forms of trader bias. The basic idea of anchoring bias is that when we are asked to guess or predict something, we are biased toward the first reference point offered.

Outside of finance, this is most commonly seen in negotiations. If we are told the price of a car is $12,000, anything below that feels cheap and anything above that feels expensive. Even if we find out later that the car is only worth $10,000, we will still find ourselves anchored on the initial price. Heaps of research proves this. Weirdly, anchoring works even if the initial number is unrelated to the question at hand.

A simple anchoring experiment (which my son did for Science Fair once, and it worked) goes as follows: subjects first draw a random number from 1 to 100 out of a bag. Then, they are asked to guess (for example) how many African countries are in the United Nations. Those that drew low numbers from the bag answer consistently lower than those who drew higher numbers out of the bag.

Another famous example of anchoring is when you ask people to quickly estimate $1 \times 2 \times 3 \times 4 \times 5 \times 6 \times 7 \times 8$ you get a much lower answer than if you ask them to quickly estimate $8 \times 7 \times 6 \times 5 \times 4 \times 3 \times 2 \times 1$.

In negotiation, you often hear "never make the first offer" because you are giving up too much information and optionality. In contrast, an effective negotiation strategy can be for one side to make an outrageous first offer, thereby anchoring the negotiation on a figure that is hard to get away from.

Say you are negotiating with an employer: you want to get paid $500,000 and you believe you have decent power in the negotiation. You open by suggesting a salary of $650,000. Now, both sides are anchored so high that when you both finally settle on $550,000, everyone feels like a winner.

Once you know about anchoring, you see it all over the place, especially in how companies price their goods. Treadmill: Was $1299, now $999. That sounds like a good deal, but it could well be the company has never sold a single unit for $1299 and they are just trying to anchor you on that inflated price to make you feel good about paying $999.

In markets, anchoring bias manifests in four main ways.

1) We anchor on our entry point. This is the most common and powerful way you see anchoring bias in markets. If you buy a stock at $99.40, that specific level becomes very powerful in your mind. You will find it much easier, for example, to sell at $99.41 (a small profit) than $99.39 (a small loss) even though the economics of selling at these two different levels is practically identical.

Losing is painful and negative. Winning is pleasurable and positive. So even though two cents is meaningless to your P&L, the difference between selling below or above your cost is the difference between winning and losing. Human beings are hard-wired to avoid losses. As discussed earlier, research shows the pain we feel from losses is about double the pleasure we get from gains of equal size. This bias is called loss aversion.

A related bias is the disposition effect. This is the strong and consistent tendency for investors to prefer to sell assets that have increased in value while holding onto assets that show a loss. If it goes up, you sell it. If it goes down, you hold on to it and pray for a bounce. These related forms of bias all come down to the same thing: humans don't like to lose[88]. The remedy is simple:

You must learn to love small losses.

When you take a small loss, try to feel good about it. Say: "Taking small losses is the way to achieve trading success." Say it over and over.

Taking small losses is the way to achieve trading success.

---

88. Multiple investor biases are explained by Prospect Theory. To read more about this huge topic, just Google 'Prospect Theory Kahneman Tversky'.

Taking small losses is the way to achieve trading success.
Taking small losses is the way to achieve trading success.
Taking small losses is the way to achieve trading success.
Taking small losses is the way to achieve trading success.

Trading losses are an expense incurred by your trading business. Your goal is to minimize trading loss expense while maximizing trading revenue. You minimize trading loss expense by cutting bad trades quickly and by sticking to your plan. You increase trading loss expense with shoddy risk management, poor discipline, and sloppy trading.

As a beginning trader, you will no doubt hear yourself thinking "This trade feels wrong. As soon as I get to break even, I'm out." Two problems here:

Problem One: "This trade feels wrong" is not rational analysis. Unpack why it feels wrong. Is there something inherently wrong with the price action, or is the stock just not moving and you're bored? Those are two completely different things. Often your instincts are just your impatience and emotions trying to sabotage a perfectly good trade.

Problem Two: "As soon as I get to break even, I'm out" is not logical. Do you think the market cares where you got in? As if there is something magical about your entry point? If you have determined, via logic, that the trade is not worth holding onto, get out. If you have not determined you should get out of the trade, maintain your existing parameters.

Every trade you put on should have a stop loss and a take profit. After that, you need a solid reason to cut the trade. Otherwise, stick to your original plan. Don't keep recalibrating based on every emotion you feel. Emotions are fine but overreacting to them is not.

Just remember: Your entry point is meaningless.

2) We tend to anchor on price level highs and lows. The feeling you get from the market is often more about recent changes, not absolute moves. This is why if you buy gold at $1570 and it goes to $1670 you feel good but then when it drops to $1600, you feel more bad than good even though you are still $30 in the money. How we feel about a trade is often more influenced by recent changes in price than by aggregate moves.

Say you are long gold with a stop at $1540 and a take profit at $1680. It rallies to $1670, then pulls back to $1620. Quite often a trader will say: "If it just gets back to $1670, I'll get out." They are anchoring on the high because that was their moment of maximum pleasure. Sure, if $1670 is a major tech level now and you realize that $1680 was the wrong level to take profit… Be my guest and move your take profit lower. But don't just move it because you are anchored on that level now.

3) We also anchor on P&L highs. Have you ever been up $15,000 at midday then you give back half and you say: "OK, if I get back to +$15,000, I'll square up." That's not rational. When you hear your internal monologue saying something like this, recognize that you are not being rational. Trade the current setup, not the arbitrary P&L threshold you hit two hours ago.

One of the key overall lessons I hope you get from this book is this:

Recognize when you are thinking or behaving irrationally and *stop it.*

Even after 25 years of trading, I still think and say irrational things on the trading floor. The biggest difference now is that I hear myself saying these things and quietly laugh at myself. The ability to get outside yourself and see when you are not being rational is a necessary step towards becoming an Alpha Trader.

4) Economists anchor on prior economic data. If the nonfarm payrolls (NFP) number was +325,000 last month and all signs point to a much lower number this month, research shows that economists will tend to anchor on the prior number and their forecasts (on average) will be too high.

Say you are an economist and your extremely detailed and complex econometric model says that this month NFP should be +38,000. If last month's number was +325,000, that +38,000 number feels kinda low. You will be inclined to submit a number that sounds a bit less extreme or "more rational" like +100,000. In fact, that number is less rational and is influenced by anchoring bias.

If you trade the economic data, look for moments when this month's data is expected to be significantly different from last month's. Then, assume the actual outcome will show an EVEN LARGER discrepancy than economists' forecasts suggest.

If you are interested in the specific topic of how economists anchor, check out the research footnotes on this page[89]. Here is a quick excerpt from the Campbell and Sharpe paper[90]:

---

89. Tong, Sean, "The anchoring and adjustment bias in estimates of US employment" (2014).

90. Campbell and Sharpe, "Anchoring bias in consensus forecasts and its effect on market prices" (2007).

We examine whether expert consensus forecasts of monthly economic releases from 1990-2006 have a tendency to be systematically biased toward the value of previous months' data releases.
We find broad-based and significant evidence for the anchoring
hypothesis; consensus forecasts are biased towards the values of
previous months' data releases, which in some cases results in siz-
able predictable forecast errors.

Trader bias #9: Herding

One great paradox of markets is that they are mostly driven by the wisdom
of the crowd but occasionally by its madness. Separating the two is a key source
of alpha. Before we talk about herding and temporary madness in markets, let's
first discuss the wisdom of crowds.

Most of the time, the errors made by buyers and sellers cancel out and the
average of all the transactions is some approximation of a reasonable equilibrium price. This outcome is similar to the jelly bean experiment. In that experiment, a crowd of people are asked to guess how many jelly beans are in a jar.
The interesting result is that the crowd (the average of all guesses) is always very
accurate and often more accurate than ANY individual in the entire crowd.
This is astounding and suggests you should be humble when trying to beat
the market.

Instead of a bunch of undergrads guessing how many jelly beans are in the
jar, imagine 1,000 highly-trained quants who have millions of dollars to invest
in jelly bean estimation technology. Do you think you can beat them? That's a
more apt analogy for the markets.

The wisdom of crowds, though, relies on diverse and unbiased opinion.
And it relies on incentives. If there is no prize, estimates will be lazy and less
accurate. Or (for example) if the jar is extremely far away from the people trying to estimate the number of jelly beans (say at the very front of a huge lec-
ture hall), the crowdsourced conclusion might be too low because the jar looks
smaller from afar. If everyone is drunk or distracted, the estimate also might
not be as good.

In trading, if you can explain exactly why you think the crowd is wrong, you
are on the right track. Usually this will be either because the crowd is biased
or the crowd's incentives are not aligned with the goal of finding the equilibrium price. I will explain both in the section that follows. The main takeaway
for this section is:

**Assume the crowd is wise most of the time and look
for moments when you can explain exactly why
it is wrong or identify that it has gone mad.**

As the amount of quality data available to all investors approaches infinity,
it is more and more difficult to find an informational edge. Before 2000 or so,
economic and financial market data were expensive and difficult to acquire for
non-institutional investors. As recently as 2006 or 2007, a trader with live price
feeds and a solid understanding of correlation had an informational edge over
other short-term traders. Live news feeds were expensive and out of reach for
individual investors until recently.

Now, literally anyone can access reams of financial data, read dozens of well-
informed blogs doing sophisticated cross-market analysis, and get free real-time
news from Twitter. Informational edge is incredibly difficult to find. This puts a
premium on other types of market analysis and (I believe) potentially increases
the value of sentiment and positioning analysis.

By their nature, markets are prone to periods of herding. Narrative-driven
markets with many traders chasing the same themes and responding to the exact
same information and incentives can drive everyone toward the same cliff. If
you can identify the times when the entire market is running in the same direction, you can pivot and profit by going the other way.

There are a multiple reasons market participants herd to the same themes
and trends:

1. **Herding is human nature**. In Chapter 5, we talked about the Asch
   conformity experiments, where even when it was obvious that a line
   was the same size as other lines, many subjects would go with the crowd
   if the majority said one line was longer. Asch did another famous experiment to show how human beings prefer to conform with their peers.

   The experiment involved multiple actors who enter an elevator and
   face the back of the elevator, away from the door. Asch found that
   most random strangers who entered the elevator afterwards joined
   the crowd and faced away from the door. Conformity and herding are basic human instincts that help society function. If you see a
   group of people acting a certain way, it sends you a strong subconscious signal that the group behavior is appropriate and so it requires
   strong, conscious pushback for you to act independently.

2. **It is much easier to believe in and respond to a narrative than it is to value securities**. "The internet is going to be huge! You gotta buy Cisco!" is an easier story to understand than "Cisco is overvalued at 100X sales." Since human traders are more stimulated by stories than they are by data, the price level of an asset is often less important than the story being told. This is why good companies can be terrible investments.

While there is usually great uncertainty surrounding the appropriate value of a company's stock, there is frequently little disagreement over good stories. "Amazon is a revolutionary company that offers an unprecedented customer experience" is hard to debate and easy to invest in. Since most people are trading narratives (whether they want to admit it or not), and narratives are often pretty clear and one-sided, investors herd into the great stories. This is not just true with stocks, it is true with macroeconomic stories too.

3. **FOMO**. The *fear of missing out* pulls in those who have not yet bought into a narrative. As they see their peers making money on an investment (and hear the amazing stories of ginormous profits over IPAs at the bar), they do not want to miss out. This is especially powerful in the professional investment business where most managers are benchmarked to their peers and where portfolio managers fear looking stupid if they miss a big story.

When a powerful macro narrative appears, you see hedge fund money pouring into the story. Not just because it's a good story they believe in but also because managers are afraid their peers will make money on it and they won't. FOMO is a terrible yet common reason traders put on trades. You see this at a micro level on trading floors, too. When two or three traders on a desk have a profitable trade on, other traders get jealous and put the trade on to avoid looking bad in case the trade continues to perform.

I remember multiple FOMO periods during the 2012 to 2015 period, when Abenomics and Bank of Japan (BOJ) easing were driving USD-JPY higher. Portfolio managers knew their peers were killing it on the trade so even later on, when USDJPY had already gone from 80 to 120, traders "had to have it" because they felt stupid if they did not.

Before the BOJ meetings in 2015 and 2016, I often heard hedge fund PMs say something like "Well, I don't think the BOJ is going to do anything tonight but I'm going in long USDJPY anyway just in case." This is FOMO and favorite/longshot bias all wrapped into one negative EV trade idea. PMs were thinking more about the lotto ticket style payoff profile and how they might look bad for missing it instead of rationally sizing up the risk/reward of playing for a low probability event that was already heavily subscribed.

4. **As a rule, human beings are not very original** and this is true both inside and outside the investment industry. This is why independent thinkers are so highly valued in investment firms: there are not very many of them. Many traders on Wall Street are extremely book smart, gifted test-takers that made their way into trading by playing the Ivy League game to perfection. Get straight A's, crush the SATs, play a sport, network like crazy and voila. None of this requires much independent thinking.

This is not to say Wall Street is a particularly unoriginal environment, it is just to say that on average, most people follow the crowd and Wall Street is no exception. Original, creative thinking can be a huge source of edge in trading. If all you see is the same stuff everyone else sees, how can you find inefficiencies? How can you profit? You probably can't. You follow the crowd, stick to benchmark and hope nobody finds you out.

5. **Incentives**. Many traders and investors are incentivized to stick with the crowd. As an investment manager, if you hug your benchmark and own mostly technology stocks during a tech bull market, you are unlikely to get fired. On the other hand, if you think tech is overvalued and you stay underweight throughout the bull market, you are very likely to get fired! If tech crashes, and you were long with everyone else, your investors are likely to give you a pass.

"Everyone else got killed in the crash, too… Nobody could have seen it coming!"

Traders and investors who have mortgages and kids in private school often think more about keeping their job than they do about maximizing profits.

Let's go back to the jelly bean game again for a moment. Imagine a game where 400 students are asked to guess how many jelly beans are in a jar. But the five highest and five lowest guesses are expelled from school and the rest compete for a prize of $50. How would that change the distribution of the guesses? My bet is that particular set of incentives would herd everyone towards the average, and greatly reduce the number of extreme guesses.

Herding does not just happen in investing, it is a feature of trading too. Let's say you are a trader at a macro hedge fund and there is a huge macro theme (e.g., the ECB is doing QE). Most people in the business are doing the trade; in fact, you went to a macro round table dinner at Milo's last week and 12 out of 15 traders said long Italian bonds was their TOP TRADE.

Thing is, you don't like Italian bonds. You think they are priced for perfection. Then again, you know if Italian bonds rip and all your peers deliver returns of 10%+ while you drop 3%, it's going to look bad. Your wife just delivered your second child and you just upsized to a 5,700 square foot McMansion in Westchester. Maybe it would be better to just plug your nose and buy the stinking Italian bonds. If the bonds crash... You and all your peers end the year down and investors be like: "What are you gonna do! Bad year for macro!"

Quite often, herding is caused by career risk. It often feels riskier for a trader to go against the herd than it is for him to just follow along. Doing the opposite of what everyone else is doing is hard! It goes directly against human nature. Most people react strongly to incentives and so instead of solving for: "How can I make my investors the most *money?*" they solve for: "*What will give me the best chance of keeping my job?*" Even if they are not doing this consciously, there is a good chance their subconscious is busy doing it for them.

To recap: wisdom of the crowds works when the crowd is diverse, unbiased and motivated by aligned incentives. When you see a market where these conditions are not met, start to think about going the other way.

Herding is a tricky concept because being part of the herd is often profitable. In fact, the reflexive contrarian will lose more money than the sheep because major trends get very crowded for a long time before they blow up. Don't be the trader that is always trying to be smarter than everyone else and who is always going the other way. There is a time and a place to be contrarian. Alpha traders identify the time and place to be contrarian but are also perfectly comfortable riding with the herd (going with the trend) much of the time.

How to detect and combat herding:

1. **Embrace independent thinking.** Humans are built to conform: fight this instinct and make confident, independent judgments while staying humble at the same time. This is not easy!

2. **Get comfortable with feeling uncomfortable.** Humans are social animals that find comfort from doing what others do, and success in trading requires you to go against that instinct somewhat regularly, so successful traders are going to feel uncomfortable a fair amount of the time. Get used to feeling uncomfortable.

3. **Study and quantify sentiment.** Sentiment data is widely available and comes in all shapes and sizes. We'll talk sentiment in Chapter 10. Whatever asset you trade, investigate the best ways to collect and analyze sentiment data. While it's great to listen to the market noise and try to come up with your own view on sentiment, data usually beats anecdote. This is especially true in our current world where people on Twitter are constantly calling for the end of the world and bitcoin to one million. Data is much more useful than randomly-collected snippets.

4. **Use overbought and oversold indicators.** My experience with overbought and oversold indicators is that your threshold for putting on trades should be as extreme as possible. I like signals that come up a few times per year, such as Jake Bernstein's Daily Sentiment Index below 10 or above 90. The reason is that sentiment is not extreme most of the time. Sentiment that is *rather* bullish or *kinda* bearish means nothing. The market will spend most of its time in the space where sentiment has no predictive value. In fact, sentiment is a "go with" most of the time. The only time it's contrarian is at the mega-extremes. But if you can identify these mega-extremes, you can hit some huge winners.

5. **Always be on high alert for turns in sentiment.** If you ever notice bullish sentiment at the low or bearish sentiment at the high: pay

attention. Generally, sentiment almost always follows price. If something is going up, people will be bullish. If the price is falling, most people will be bearish. There are exceptions (many are always bearish the stock market, even when it's at the highs) but in general, that's how sentiment works. Very rarely, though, you will see the opposite and those moments are meaningful.

A prime example is the US dollar in March 2020. The COVID-19 pandemic triggered a liquidity crisis and there was a mad scramble for dollars. The Great Dollar Shortage drove EURUSD from 1.1300 to 1.0800 in very short order (stronger dollar, weaker euro). Then, the Fed went all-in, announcing a massive QE and dollar liquidity program. Due to ongoing pressures in emerging markets and equities, though, the USD remained in demand.

At that time, you could see a subtle but important change in sentiment happening. The market, which had been raging bullish USD, started to think about the future impact of all this new USD liquidity and sentiment slowly turned from bullish USD to modestly bearish USD. But the USD was still at the ding dong highs! This is a rare but extremely high EV setup. If you notice a subtle shift away from a popular narrative, but the price hasn't moved yet, get ready to go the other way. Often price will lag sentiment. A market that is bullish on the lows or bearish on the highs is getting ready to turn.

6. **Stay objective.** Understand the bias of the media you consume and look for unbiased sources of data. Twitter leans bearish stocks and bullish bitcoin and gold. CNBC is almost always bullish stocks. Zerohedge tends to be bearish Wall Street and bullish gold. Whatever you read, always consider which way it leans. I prefer to read analysts who are flexible because those who constantly stick to the same view tend to be locked in and plagued by confirmation bias.

One of the best financial-market-guru business models is to pick a view (hopefully a popular one) and pound the table on it year after year. You attract a following of like-minded people and you deliver the echo chamber that they need to reinforce their views. And they will pay you for it. This is not analysis or forecasting, it's marketing. Be aware when you receive information from people like this; they will never change their view and as such their view is probably not worth much. Good analysts will change their view (at least once every few years!) Good marketers will stick to one view and beat it until they have paid off the summer house in East Hampton.

Don't go on Twitter and see 400 bearish stock market posts and conclude that the market is short. It might be; it might not be. Collecting anecdotal information can be extremely useful but you need to know the bias of the source. Data is always better than anecdotes so look for objective sources of sentiment and positioning data and focus more on those than what you consume via traditional or new media.

A special comment on bubbles

Bubbles are the most spectacular of all financial herding events. Here is a commentary I wrote in June 2020 about the Davey Day Trader technology and retail stock trader bubble. It explains how I think about bubbles and how to trade them.

HERE'S THE THING ABOUT BUBBLES

I don't go around calling every bull market a bubble. In fact, when people do that, it bothers me. But this equity rally contains a bunch of micro bubbles. These sector and stock-specific retail bubbles are fueled by:

- People have extra savings and nothing to spend money on;

- People can't wager on or watch sports or go to bars;

- A new culture of day trading has emerged with Dave Portnoy as the supreme leader;

- People over consume free goods and retail stock trading is now "free"

There is no widely-accepted definition of a bubble but to me the evidence of a bubble is clear from people's behavior. They have an unwavering belief in the topside, completely ignore risk, use leverage to amplify gains and brag about how easy it is to make "free money".

The recent series of mini-bubbles has featured a rolling series of non-sensical moves.

Nonsensical moves

There are two kinds of nonsensical stock moves. One is where a bunch of people think a move is wrong because of valuations or whatever. Also known as sour grapes. Those "nonsensical" moves happen every day and are purely subjective and meaningless. The other kind of nonsensical move is when there is a move that represents a huge divergence from a mathematically known outcome that is on the foreseeable / tradable horizon. These are quantifiable or observable violations of efficient markets or the law of one price and are much less subjective.

There were multiple examples of this in 1999/2000. The most famous is when 3COM spun off 5% of PALM[91]. The hot thing at the time was hand-held gadgets so everyone wanted to own PALM and their awesome Palm Pilots. Nobody cared about poor old 3COM and their dial-up modems and PCMCIA cards.

The day of the PALM IPO, PALM closed at $95, giving it a market value of $54B. 3COM's closing price of $81 gave it a market value of $28B. So even though 3COM owned $50B worth of PALM stock, it was trading at a market value of $28B. The company had no debt and $1B in cash.

This (kind of) breaks the rule of one price and violates assumptions of market efficiency and arbitrage. One analyst asked: "Can the markets add and subtract?" You only get this stuff when the market is losing (or has lost) its mind[92]. Something similar happened in June 1999 when TD spun off its TD Waterhouse online brokerage division as discount brokerages were hot stocks at the time because the environment was just like it is today: retail gamblers galore.

Today, we have the curious cases of Chesapeake Energy and Hertz Rent-A-Car (aka Hertz Global Holdings). Chesapeake is on the verge of a potential bankruptcy filing and its bonds trade for less than 10 cents on the dollar. Hertz Global Holdings has already declared bankruptcy.

> 4:44PM yesterday: *CHESAPEAKE SAID TO PREPARE
> CH. 11 FILING, GIVE LENDERS CONTROL

---

91. For the record, Jared Dillian wrote a whole novel, *All the Evil of this World,* centered on the 3COM/PALM spinoff. I loved it, but apparently it was a love it/hate it type of book so it's a risky one to recommend. If you like dark stuff, and you want to know what 1999 felt like—go for it.

92. Generally, the main explanation for these illogical moves is that it's difficult or expensive to borrow a stock that is overpriced. Regardless, these large disconnects from basic math are usually a symptom of Bubbliciousness. See Cherkes, Jones and Spatt: "A solution to the PALM, 3COM spin off puzzles" (2013) for an academic paper that does a good job of explaining the PALM/3COM non-arbitrage.

It probably goes without saying, but shares of bankrupt companies should not be worth very much! They are almost always cancelled and end up being worth zero. They keep trading though, sometimes for years.

Usually they bounce along around $1 and eventually bleed to zero. At a low enough price point, even though the stock is worth $0, it's not worth it to go short and longs can't be bothered selling (or they already sold) so it never goes straight to zero right away. Figure 7.15 is the chart of a company that went bankrupt in 2014 but still trades. That is approximately what the stock of a bankrupt company should look like.

**Figure 7.15 The typical path followed by
the common stock of a bankrupt company**

Crumbs Bake Shop common stock: They were selling a million cupcakes a month in 2011

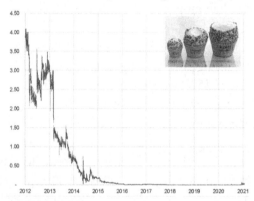

So what about Hertz and Chesapeake, then? Figure 7.16 and Figure 7.17 show their movement from from January 1 to mid-June 2020:

Figure 7.16: HTZ Common Stock   **Figure 7.17: CHK Common Stock**

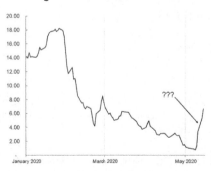 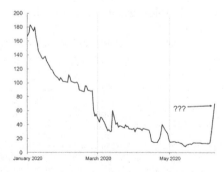

HTZ rallies from 41 cents to $6   CHK rallies from $7.77 to $77.50

I'm not a corporate finance guy and I have no opinion on the breakup value or recovery values of either of these companies. All I am saying is that in a normal market these two assets would be bouncing along between $0 and $1, not producing 1000% returns. Sure, there are squeezes in the stocks of bankrupt companies, but not like this. These moves are another sign of excess (especially relative to the HTZ and CHK bonds, which are priced around 35 cents and 6 cents, respectively).

Here's the thing about bubbles

Ok, sure, it's a bubble. Even if you agree with me, what do you do? First of all, let me clarify that I believe this is a retail bubble in a specific group of stories, not a broad market bubble. If you are a professional asset manager, you should know what stocks are being bid up by retail right now and think about your dream exit levels.

Here's the thing about bubbles. Just because you have identified one, that does not mean you should be short. Often the real money is made by identifying a bubble and jumping on for the bullish Wave 5 insanity.

For example, while it was obvious that bitcoin was a classic bubble by May/June 2017, it did not crash until seven months later after rallying another 500%. Correctly identifying bitcoin as a bubble in June 2017 would have cost you a ton of money.

Identifying something as a bubble just frames the volatility to expect (high) and lets you know you should use your imagination when setting upside and eventual downside targets. It also tells you that the endgame is a high-speed collapse of 75% to 90% off the ultimate high. It does not mean you just go short and collect the free money. In fact, it's often easier to make money long a bubble, not short. So what do we do?

Identify bubble assets that you own and find a moving average or other technical signal that will tell you when to get out. Bitcoin had already rallied from $300 to $3,000 when people called it a bubble. Then it went from $3,000 to $20,000. Missing the last leg of a bubble can be costly. Shorting the last leg of a bubble can be deadly. In the 2017 bitcoin rally, the 100-day moving average defined the trend the whole way up. Fit a moving average to the current price trend of whatever bubble assets you own and liquidate on a daily close below.

Remember that it's OK to be long during a bubble. It's also OK to be short! I worked at a day trading firm 1999/2001 and the people that went bust in that period mostly fell into two categories:

1. People that believed religiously in the future of the internet and the unlimited upside of the internet stocks and lost all their money trading from the long side.

2. People that believed it was a bubble and lost all their money trading from the short side.

3. I know I said two categories, but there was a very small third category: The gold bugs. There were two guys off in the corner that were like: "These sheep are stupid, we're long gold and PAAS (silver). This will all end in tears." They were right! But they couldn't hang on long enough and both had to liquidate and find "real" jobs in mid-2001.

The people that did well in 1999/2001 were the most flexible and open-minded. We never got married to a side. We didn't think the bull market was dumb and we didn't think the internet was a world changing miracle. We were not overly philosophical about anything; we just wanted to make money. Getting philosophical about markets (i.e., "The Fed is manipulating markets, this is dumb!") makes it way harder to win. Try not to do that.

Look for signs of blow off tops. One clue that it's over is when bubble stocks don't respond to good news. In 2000, many internet stocks topped out after failing to rally on blowout earnings reports.

When someone hears that a market is a bubble, they generally want to go short. Watch for the inevitable burst but don't get married to either side.

Detour complete! To sum up: When you see what looks to be a bubble, there are just two things to remember.

Be rational... And be flexible.

Before we wrap up this section on trader bias, let me first give you a few blurbs on other important forms of bias to watch out for.

Outcome bias

This is our tendency to evaluate a decision based on the outcome, instead of the process that was followed to reach that decision. I discuss process vs. outcome in Chapter 5 and it is extremely important to separate the two. If you do a ton of research, come up with a great trade idea and then a totally random news

event stops you out 10 minutes after you put on the trade… That's good decision / bad outcome. Don't worry about it. Annie Duke's book *Thinking in Bets*
spends a ton of time on outcome bias (she calls it "resulting"). It's a great book
if you want to learn more about thinking about thinking.

Squirrel-chasing bias

Human attention is drawn to shiny objects. Homer Simpson is often distracted by squirrels. Prices on the screen are stimulating and interesting and
human beings tend to confer much more meaning to price movement than it
generally deserves.

Chasing bias is the tendency to enter trades in a security simply because it is
moving. Something rallies, and you want to buy it. Something sells off and you
want to sell it. Rid yourself of this bias. It is a weakness that plagues many traders, even hedge fund professionals. It is essentially a combination of activity bias
(the need to be active even when doing nothing would be a better choice) and
extrapolation bias ("It went down so it's gonna keep going down!")

**Bad traders see price moving on the screen and
think somebody knows something. Good traders
know 97% of all price action is noise.**

"Apple's gapping lower! Somebody must know something!"
Nope. No. *No.* They probably don't. There is an endless series of buys and sells
going through the market and the overwhelming majority of those buys and sells
have no particular edge or informational advantage. It could be a guy selling to pay
for his divorce. It could be an asset manager reducing risk before she goes on vacation. It could be tax loss selling that has nothing to do with the company in question. Don't assume that someone knows something when you see price moving.

If you are bearish Apple for six different reasons, and you have been watching a key level all week, and Apple finally breaks down through that level, then
by all means, sell! But don't be the trader that just jumps on whatever is moving
just because it's moving. If you find yourself doing that… Stop. That is what
bad traders do. That is what traders with no plan do. It is the trading equivalent
of Homer Simpson chasing the squirrel.

Be aware of this leak and catch yourself chasing price. Step away from your
computer and give yourself a firm talking to. Chasing price without a plan is a
recipe for persistent losses and frustrating performance.

Hindsight bias

Humans tend to think they know more than they know and they tend to think that they knew things were going to happen even when they truly had no idea. My first boss was famous inside the bank for walking by, seeing what had moved up or down the most and then saying (for example): "I wanted to be long USDJPY! I knew it was going up!" Well, if you knew, why didn't you buy some?

After something has moved, you might remember some weak gut feeling you had or some random thought that flitted through your mind about buying that thing. It's meaningless! It is also annoying. Don't be one of those people that says woulda, coulda or shoulda on a trading floor. The only thing that matters are the decisions and actions you take in real-time.

Hindsight bias is also a constant feature of financial media. When you see a headline like "Stocks rally on higher oil price" remember that the journalist is writing with the benefit of hindsight. If you went back to the start of the day and asked people what stocks would do if oil prices went up, you might get 50% saying stocks would go down and 50% saying stocks would go up. Journalists are often storytellers, not traders or financial professionals. They are always trying to make up stories to explain moves that are often driven by non-macro factors like flow and positioning.

There are many excellent finance journalists but there is also the obligation for the financial media to tell a story based on fundamentals and macro when often that is not the driver of a market move.

You will never see a headline like "USDCAD rallies as macro portfolio manager stops out of huge short because he's going on vacation." If this is the reason USDCAD rallies, journalists will fabricate some sort of narrative that seems to fit in hindsight. That's their job! Overall, you should be extremely skeptical of most articles in the financial press. They are not intentionally false, but they are biased almost exclusively to trying to fit a macroeconomic explanation even when short-term moves in markets are often explained by other factors.

Don't talk about bad beats or ideas you never put on or the times you get stopped out at the high or low. That's all just part of trading and nobody will find you interesting if you tell them about these types of incidents. Always look forward.

Grizzly bias

Compulsive bearishness is a bias that has not received as much coverage as other forms of trader bias. The bearish bias in the market since 2008 is probably the costliest human bias in finance. Think of all the money lost on short ES futures in the past 10 years. All the "crash is imminent" blog posts. All the apocalyptic hedge fund bets. Crazy.

One way permabears justify imminently lower equity prices is by referencing the bond market. If yields are going up, that's bad for earnings, bad for margins, bad for borrowers, bad for severely indebted sovereigns, etc. If yields go down, it's "What do bonds know!?" or "The rates market don't lie!"

The relationship between stocks and bonds is fluid and for most of my lifetime, stocks have been going up and bonds have been going up. This is not to say it will go on forever, only to say that stock market bears need better reasons than "yields are going up" or "yields are going down". In times of plentiful liquidity, it is perfectly logical for both stocks and bonds to go up, up and away.

Bears sound smarter than bulls

Research shows conclusively that humans perceive people who present negative or pessimistic opinions as more intelligent than those who express positive or optimistic opinions. Bearish analysts are viewed as "cutting through the noise" while bulls are often viewed as naïve fanboys banging pompoms together on CNBC.

Strangely though, the path of human progress is an undeniable upward trend. As Deirdre McCloskey put it:

> … pessimism sells. For reasons I have never understood, people like to hear that the world is going to hell, and become huffy and scornful when some idiotic optimist intrudes on their pleasure. Yet pessimism has consistently been a poor guide to the modern economic world[93].

Similarly, stocks mostly go up, most of the time. Morgan Housel put it like this[94]:

In investing, a bull sounds like a reckless cheerleader, while a bear sounds like a sharp mind who has dug past the headlines – despite the record of the S&P 500 rising 18,000-fold over the last century.

Yet many of the best-known Wall Street pundits are persistently pessimistic and many of them have been around for decades. Think of all the famous bears

---

93. http://www.deirdremccloskey.org/docs/pdf/PikettyReviewEssay.pdf

94. https://www.fool.com/investing/general/2016/01/21/why-does-pessimism-sound-so-smart.aspx   I learned of the mcloskey quote (footnote 1) from this article, too.

in finance. I could make a list 20 names long without even Googling. Plenty of them have cool nicknames and there are even two different celebrity economists nicknamed Dr. Doom. I find that funny.

These are all incredibly smart guys who do amazing analysis that mostly points to an imminent large-scale bear market. And yet the evidence shows these forecasts are almost always wrong. Why do we keep reading their stuff? Because it sounds really smart! The forecasting business has very little accountability and is mostly about marketing and sounding smart, not accuracy.

These permabears are famous and they are highly paid. How is this possible when stocks have spent most of their time in a bull market since 1980? If you always call for a bear market, and then one happens, were you right? Answer: it doesn't matter. Pessimism sells, even if it's the wrong view most of the time. When you read a *"crash is imminent!"* piece ask yourself: is the author preying on my inherent negativity or is she actually providing useful and actionable analysis supported by a verifiable track record?

There is an entire industry of permabears because there is steady demand for them. Don't stoke that demand. Permabears sound smart, they are entertaining and they reassure us that our intelligent skepticism is not misguided despite mountains of evidence to the contrary. The funny thing is, if these permabears ever change their view, they lose followers and subscribers.

There is a tried and true strategy in the financial media: adopt one dramatic world view, stick to it no matter what happens, and sell sell SELL *SELL* it no matter what new information comes in to contradict your viewpoint. As the saying goes: never let the facts get in the way of a good story.

To be clear, I'm not advocating a permabull stance either. That would be equally bad. As a trader, you need to be flexible and open-minded, not perma-*anything*. This discussion is meant to make you think about how pessimism is like intellectual candy. It tastes delicious, but it's generally bad for your financial health.

Negativity outsells positivity everywhere you look. Cynics and critics sound smart. People love to read negative stories. Here's a short excerpt from a study of how people perceive writers of book reviews[95]:

> Negative reviewers were perceived as more intelligent, competent, and expert than positive reviewers, even when the content of the positive review was independently judged as being of higher quality and greater forcefulness.

---

95. Teresa Amabile, "Brilliant but Cruel: Perceptions of negative evaluators" (1983).

The same bias exists in non-financial news. Multiple experiments show that people claim to prefer positive news but actually prefer to consume negative news. This negativity bias is part of human nature. Even infants react to negative stimuli with more intensity than they do to positive stimuli. When people of any age are subjected to two stimuli of equal intensity, one positive and one negative, the negative stimulus has a greater psychological impact than the positive one. Negative impressions are more salient and more memorable.

Negativity is an attention magnet. Like McCloskey said: "Pessimism sells." Be a rational consumer of information and do not allow smart-sounding permabears to bias your process.

Ignore the permabears.

Stories of funds that set money on fire trying to short stocks are plentiful. One fund I know opened in 2012 and the first trade they did was go short S&P futures. The last trade they did before shutting down in 2016 (due to poor performance) was cover a short S&P futures position. Another fund made 22% on Abenomics in 2013 but lost 18% on bearish S&P bets that year and ended around flat overall. It is a costly bias. When you trade, you should always be equally able to go long or short risky assets. If you can't, it's a major leak you need to work on.

Warren Buffett said it best:

> *For 240 years it's been a terrible mistake to bet against America, and now is no time to start. America's golden goose of commerce and innovation will continue to lay more and larger eggs.*

The Gambler's Fallacy and the Hot Hand

The Gambler's Fallacy and the Hot Hand are two opposite but related forms of bias. Some people see a roulette wheel that comes up red eight times in a row and they think black is due. Some win a few rolls at the craps table and want to increase their bet size because they have the "hot hand". Thing is, in randomly generated data, there are many streaks. They don't mean anything; they're just how random sequences go. Seven heads in a row does not impact the eighth flip. The coin has no memory.

Probability has no memory.

There is no supernatural element to probability; it is a mathematical construct. The intuition people get at casino tables is nonsense. If you had a hunch you were going to win and then you won... It's a coincidence. Every spin of a roulette wheel is mutually exclusive and each roll of the dice in craps is independent of the last.

In finance, things are trickier. If TSLA is up 10 days in a row, is it wildly overbought and more likely to fall on day 11? Or is day 11 an independent event with no relationship to the prior 10? It can be hard to say.

The best starting point is to assume each financial minute, hour and day is independent from the last. Then be open to exceptions. A good example of this is seasonality. If GBPUSD is up 8 Aprils in a row, does that mean it is more likely to go up in April of Year 9? Probably not. There are 10 or 15 actively traded currency pairs and 12 months in every year, so odds are high that if you look hard enough you'll find some months that show a seasonal pattern. Especially if your sample size is just eight years. But this seasonal pattern is probably simply a random streak.

There are, however, many examples of persistent, non-random seasonality and price patterns. The Halloween Effect, more commonly known as "Sell in May and Go Away" has been in existence for more than 300 years and has worked out-of-sample for decades after it was discovered. It is almost impossible to dismiss this effect as an artifact of randomness. It is far too persistent.

If a pattern is persistent, then we try to explain it. In the case of "Sell in May and Go Away", the explanation could be a pattern of human optimism where we start the year optimistic, eventually overshoot, pull back from that bit of irrational exuberance, then rally into year end.

Similarly, there are micro patterns of seasonality and repetition that make sense and repeat for a reason. The first day of the month is a day when a big lump of automatic contributions go into US employee 401k retirement plans. A good proportion of these contributions end up in index funds and as such the first day of the month tends to be a bullish day for stocks. Same goes for the start of the year.

There are other seasonal patterns like this in various markets and ideally when you spot a pattern, you want to be able to ascribe some sort of logic to it. If you can't, assume it is random unless you are studying a large sample of data or have some other reason to think the streak is not just a product of chance.

The paper "The hot hand belief and the gambler's fallacy in investment decisions under risk"[96] is an excellent summary of two ways in which investors fail to understand that most events are independent. Here is the abstract:

We conduct experiments to analyze investment behavior in decisions under risk. Subjects can bet on the outcomes of a series of coin tosses themselves, rely on randomized 'experts', or choose a risk-free alternative. We observe that subjects who rely on the randomized experts pick those who were successful in the past, showing behavior consistent with the hot hand belief. Obviously the term 'expert' suffices to attract some subjects. For those who decided on their own, we find behavior consistent with the gambler's fallacy, as the frequency of betting on heads (tails) decreases after streaks of heads (tails).

Assume most events in financial markets are independent, but always look for ones that are not. When you find a pattern, dig deeper. Keep digging until you find patterns that might logically repeat in the future. Most streaks and patterns in finance are random. But not all of them.

●●●

There are literally 100s of ways behavioral bias influences traders and investors. I have gone through a short list of some types of bias that I believe are particularly important but there is an entire academic field (and a library-full of books) devoted to the topic. At some point, make sure you read *Thinking, Fast and Slow* (Kahneman), *Fooled by Randomness* (Taleb), and *Irrational Exuberance* (Shiller). Those are my three favorite books on behavioral finance.

Also, just Google "behavioral bias trading" occasionally and go down the rabbit hole of academic research and blog posts. It is such an interesting topic and there are many people writing about and researching it passionately. Humans are so silly, there will never be a shortage of foibles to unpack.

Before we complete this chapter on rational thinking, I want to venture into the weird and wonderful world of counterintuitive math facts. I want to open your eyes to just how counterintuitive mathematical reality can be. Your takeaway from this section should be that it is important to coldly examine your

96. Huber, J., Kirchler, M. & Stöckl, T. "The hot hand belief and the gambler's fallacy in investment decisions under risk" (2010).

assumptions and interpretations when looking at data because your intuition can often be wrong.

Also, math is fun.

COUNTERINTUITIVE MATH FACTS

Education has made all the difference for me. It builds software for your brain. Mathematics taught me to reason logically and understand numbers, tables, charts, and calculations. Even more valuable, I learned at an early age to teach myself.

EDWARD O. THORP, *A Man for All Markets*

One of the most fun parts of math is that even though it is 100% objective and rational, it can still surprise us and it can sometimes feel a little bit like magic. Part of acquiring a higher-level and rational understanding of math and probability is to simply understand that math, statistics, and probability are not always 100% intuitive. Many empirical and statistical outcomes can be surprising.

In this section I will take a look at a few instances, not so much because these specific examples are critical for trading but more so you can see that it is worth challenging your system 1 assumptions if you want to get to the right mathematical answers. Alpha Traders have a strong basic understanding of numbers and statistics. You should constantly be working to improve your numeracy.

The counterintuitive math facts that follow highlight just how wrong your gut can be when it jumps to conclusions and should reinforce that your slow rational mind is where it's at.

Example 1a and 1b: The bat and ball problem
Even simple problems can be counterintuitive

The classic counterintuitive math problem is the bat and ball problem. If you have not heard this before, take a quick second to answer. The question is:

> A baseball bat and a ball cost $1.10 total. The bat costs $1.00 more than the ball. How much does the ball cost?

Did you answer 10 cents?

That is the standard System 1 answer but if you stop to think for just a moment, you will see that the answer is 5 cents.

Let x represent the cost of the ball

$$x + (\$1.00 + x) = \$1.10$$

$$\$1.00 + 2x = \$1.10$$

$$2x = \$1.10 - \$1.00$$

$$2x = \$0.10$$

x = \$0.05

This is question one in the Cognitive Reflection Test discussed earlier. It shows how, if we listen to our gut, we get the wrong answer. Our brains can take data and jump to seemingly logical, but completely wrong conclusions. Slow down and use System 2 for mathematical analysis. Evaluate alternative hypotheses, even when the answer seems obvious.

When it comes to trading, the more obvious the conclusion, the more likely it is already priced into the market and thus the more likely the trade you enter based on the conclusion will lose money[97].

Another quick one: You have \$100,000 split evenly between ten stocks. They all drop one percent. What percentage of your portfolio did you just lose in total?

Most people get that one right (1%) but hear the wrong answer in their head first (10%).

Example 2: Up / down / up / down is actually... Down?
People don't always understand log returns

A \$100 stock goes down 10% one day then up 10% the next. What is the stock worth now?

If you answered \$100, you used System 1. And you are wrong.

If you answered \$99, you used System 2 and you are right.

This is another simple example of a mathematical result that is not always obvious on first inspection. If you ask someone what happens to a stock that goes down 20% one day then up 20% the next, their kneejerk or System 1 response would be that the stock is unchanged. But anyone that worked at Lehman Brothers in 2008 (to pick just one of many examples) knows that if something goes up and down 20% over and over, it will eventually end up much, much lower.

---

97. This is not always true! Sometimes the obvious trade is the right trade. But if it's obvious, spend even more time than usual thinking about what could go wrong because obvious trade usually means crowded trade.

Here's a chart:

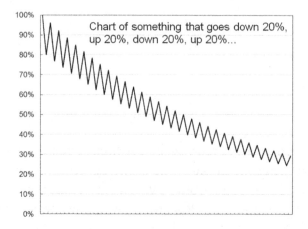

This truth can be painful in trading. If you lose 10% of your capital, you need to make 11.1% to get back to flat. If you drop 50% of your capital, you need to gain 100% to recover. If you lose your mind and drop 90% of your capital, you will need to make 1,000% just to get back to flat! The further you fall from your starting capital, the harder it will be to ever come back.

Example 3: NBA superstars[98]

People don't always understand averages

Take a look at the statistics from these two star basketball players and tell me who has the better career shooting percentage:

Per game statistics			
Michael Jordan			
	Field goals	Attempts	Shooting %
2-pointers	10.8	21.2	50.9%
3-pointers	0.5	1.7	29.4%
Reggie Miller			
	Field goals	Attempts	Shooting %
2-pointers	4.1	7.9	51.9%
3-pointers	1.8	4.7	38.3%

One would reasonably think that if Miller's shooting percentage is higher

---

98. This example is from a December 2, 2019 blog post by Noah Xiao on towardsdatascience.com.

from both 2-point and 3-point range, he must have the higher career shooting percentage, right? Wrong. Overall shooting percentage is weighted and Jordan took many more 2-point shots, so his lifetime shooting percentage was 49% while Miller's was 47%.

So the lesson again is: Don't just jump to a conclusion. Think.

A simple check you should always employ when analyzing data is to compare the average to the median. If they are similar, you are probably good but if there is a big difference, then something is up and you need to dig deeper.

A common source of discrepancy in my backtesting work is that when I include data from 2008, the moves that year can often swamp the average and distort the analysis. This will show up in the median vs. average validation check and then I can either cut the 2008 data from the series or use the median figures.

You should never overestimate the meaning of an average. If you put one foot in a bucket of boiling water and one foot in a bucket of ice water, are you feeling warm, on average? The more extreme the data points in your average, the less meaningful your median and average outputs will be.

The 1956 classic "How to Lie with Statistics" by Darrell Huff does a super job of explaining the basics of how to handle statistics like this. I think every human being should read that book, even if they don't care about statistics or finance.

Example 4: Arcsine Law
People don't always understand random walks

This example has a direct application to trading and finance. In fact, before I knew about Arcsine Law, I made a mistake that I now see others making from time to time. This one is *crazy* complicated, so if you don't understand the reasoning, just at least make sure you remember the conclusion. Arcsine Law is about as annoying and difficult to understand as the Monty Hall problem. But worth the effort to understand.

First, let me reprint some faulty analysis I did in 2017. If you know why it's wrong before you read the whole thing, you are either a genius or you already know about Arcsine Law. The following is an excerpt from a daily wrote toward the end of 2017.

> Have you ever noticed that the yearly highs and lows in G7 FX tend to happen more at the start and end of the year (and less in the middle)? It is true. We ran the numbers and they were so extreme that I did not believe them. So we ran them again and I manually checked

a bunch of it because again, I was shocked at the non-randomness of the distribution. Here is how annual highs and lows are distributed (by month) over the year for the G7 currencies:

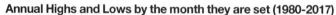

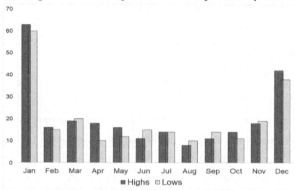

EURUSD USDJPY USDCAD NZDUSD AUDUSD USDCHF and GBPUSD
y-axis shows sum of how many times it happened

Now obviously there is a USD component to all these pairs so if one makes a high or low at a certain time, it is likely all the others probably will too. But the extremeness of the skew in the distribution is amazing. But wait! It gets crazier!

If you look at all the times a currency makes its year high or low in January, check out the day of January that it happens:

Y-axis is number of occurrences.
1980 to now. Synthetic EUR used for EUR pre-1999

Can you guess what December looks like?

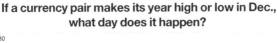

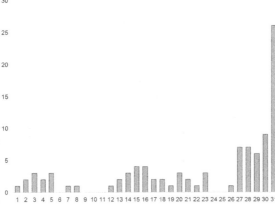

Insane, right? This is a massive anomaly in what should be close to randomly-distributed data. Clearly year end transactions (which are often not price sensitive and more timing-related), window dressing, positioning for the new year and reduced liquidity create enough distortions to make even the most unrepentant ivory tower academic question EMH. The front of the month sees NFP and back of the month sees month-end rebalancing so that is a partial explanation. Am I missing any other explanations?

I grind up the data like this all the time and rarely have I seen a more extreme result.

• • •

Pretty cool stuff, I thought. Until I learned… MY ANALYSIS WAS TOTALLY WRONG.

I have seen others make this same mistake since and you will occasionally see excited commentaries like mine remarking on the U-shaped pattern of highs and lows in a data set. This can relate to data on any time slice, monthly, daily or hourly. For example, I have seen blogs comment recently that stock market highs and lows are more likely to occur near the open and the close, vs. the middle of the day. It's the same fallacy.

In a random walk process, there is not a uniform distribution of highs and lows throughout the day, week, month or year. Instead, we see a U-shaped pattern with more highs and lows near the start and the end of the series. This fundamental property of random walks is described by a counterintuitive branch of probability known as Arcsine law.

If you spend a bit of time thinking about a random walk, it starts to make sense that the high or low is more likely to occur at the start or end of the year. Imagine a series of coin flips where you simply add 1 for heads or subtract 1 for tails. The longer you flip the coin, the farther the sum will move away from the starting point (zero) and thus the start and end point are more likely to be the extreme points relative to any point in between. Our intuition is that they would oscillate around zero, but this is not the case. They slowly move away.

Figure 7.18 demonstrates how random walks slowly make their away further and further from their starting point of zero. Therefore, the extreme low and high points appear more often near the start or the end of the series.

Figure 7.18: Cumulative sum of heads (+1) and tails (-1) over four simulations

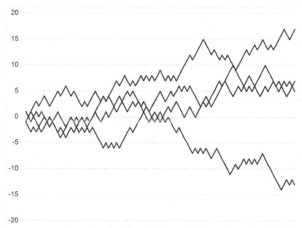

Example 5: The Birthday Paradox
People don't always understand probability

Here's a simpler one. There are 70 people in a room, what are the odds that two of them will have the same birthday?

If you don't know this problem, you might start with 70/365 and then realize it's much higher than that so maybe guess 50%? Or... 60%?

How about 99.9%? Most people's intuition is to start with one birthday and think through the odds of someone in the room having that birthday, but really all you need is one of any 70 birthdays to match any other birthday in the room. Figure 7.19 shows you the numbers.

You only need 23 people in a room to have a 50/50 shot of two matching birthdays. I learned this 20 years ago and it still gives me a mild case of vertigo when I think about it. It's weirdly counterintuitive.

When you analyze market data and come to conclusions, make sure you are confident that your conclusions are logical. Not just intuitive. Logical. Even if something seems obvious, check it. Think about it.

Figure 7.19: Probability of two matching birthdays vs. number of people in a room

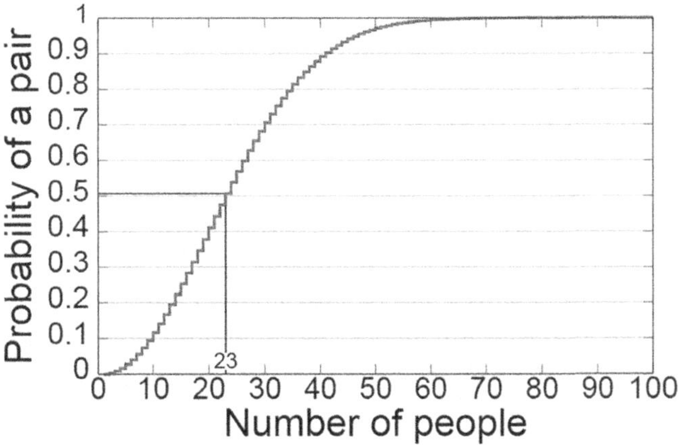

Image by Rajkiran g via Creative Commons 3.0 (Wikipedia)

Example 6: Non-linear craziness
People don't always understand non-linear relationships

When you go to a casino, you know you have a good chance of losing, but do you truly appreciate how your equity evolves over time in an environment with negative leakage? Think about this: If you start the night with $100 and play a fair game (50% chance of winning, bet $1 to win $1), what are the odds you will hit +$100 before you lose your $100?

Trick question! Because it's not a trick. 50%.

OK, now what are the odds you get to $100 before losing $100 in the same $1 game, but now the odds of winning each time are 49.5%? Answer 11.5%.

What about if the odds in the game are 49%? Answer 1.8%.

As you repeat a game with negative edge, the probability of loss is non-linear. This is why the only way to make money at a casino is with highly variable, or lumpy bets. If you want maximum odds to win in Vegas, go to the roulette table when you arrive and put your entire stake on black (or red). Another "strategy" is to place lumpy bets with your $100. Bet $50 then $2. $60, then $1, etc. At least this way you have a chance. Any methodical application of a strategy that has a sub-50% win rate will lead to almost guaranteed loss.

When I'm trading badly, my P&L kind of looks like the $1 bet with the 49% odds.

Note that this is just an example of how math can be counterintuitive. The takeaway should not be that you want to randomly make lumpy bets in in trading. In trading your bet-sizing should:

- Eliminate risk of ruin.

- Be proportionate to conviction level.

- Be large enough (even if it's a low conviction trade) to move the needle toward your goal.

Finally, note that if your capital is slowly bleeding lower over an extended period, it is a sign that you have negative edge. Figure 7.20 is the chart of 10 simulations of a 48%/52% game where you risk $1 to make $1. If your P&L chart has that steady top-left to bottom-right skew like these simulations, it is time to think about your edge. Has it disappeared? Have markets changed and you didn't adapt? Are you paying too much in transaction costs (a major source of negative edge)?

Figure 7.20: 10 simulations of a 48%/52% game where you win or lose $1

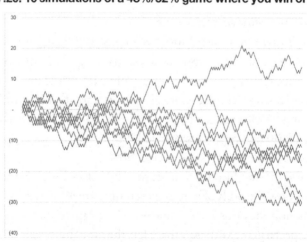

250 trials (that is, the game is played 250 times in each simulation)

Example 7: Survivors and incomplete samples

People don't always think about whether their sample
is complete or biased

In World War 2, the US Navy wanted to reduce the number of its fighter planes being shot down and wanted to add armor at various points to reinforce the fighters. Armor increases a plane's weight and makes it less efficient, so you need to be selective about where to put armor. The statisticians in the wartime Statistical Research Group received a diagram showing data something like this:

Figure 7.21: Distribution of bullet holes in damaged US fighter planes

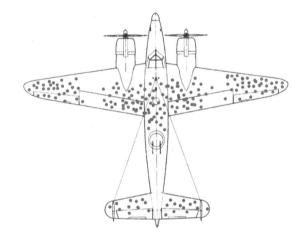

By McGeddon - Own work, CC BY-SA 4.0

The intuitive or obvious answer is to reinforce the areas that are getting hit by enemy fire. The wings, fuselage, and tail look like natural places to add armor since they get shot up the most.

But legendary mathematician Abraham Wald ignored the intuitive answer and thought more deeply. He thought to ask: "Why are there so many holes in the fuselage and wings, but no bullet holes in the engines?"

This is like asking: why are there so many ER patients with gunshot wounds to the arm but so few with gunshot wounds to the heart, even though both sections of the human body are in a similar area? The answer, of course, is that the planes that got shot in the engine went down and were destroyed, so they couldn't be examined. There are no bullet holes in the engines of the planes that return to base because the planes that are shot in the engine *don't make it back to base*. Victims shot in the heart don't make it to the ER.

Survivorship bias is the phenomenon where we evaluate a sample (say planes returning from battle or mutual funds) and then draw conclusions based on that sample without considering all the parts of the sample that did not survive. We look at planes that returned to base without considering the ones that got shot down. We look at performance of existing mutual funds without considering all the ones that went out of business. This is another way we misinterpret data.

Here's one way this applies to trading. A friend of yours shows you a specific strategy that earned 1105% returns last month. Your first reaction might be "Wow, tell me more!" When really your first reaction should be: "What other strategies did you test before coming up with this one?"

When analyzing data, look for missing evidence.

This is a common trick in the sports gambling industry. Say the Tigers are playing the Bears tonight. You send 10,000 e-mails out to new prospects. 5,000 of the e-mails read: "Attention subscribers: OUR GOLD STAR, GUARANTEED PICK TONIGHT IS: **TIGERS TO WIN!**" and 5000 say: "Attention subscribers: OUR GOLD STAR, GUARANTEED PICK TONIGHT IS: **BEARS TO WIN!**" Then, they wait to see who wins. Let's say it's the Tigers.

The next game is Lions vs. Panthers. The marketer now takes the list of 5,000 e-mails that received the correct Tigers pick e-mail and splits those into two groups of 2,500. Half the e-mails predict the Lions and half predict the Panthers. They do this twice more and now have a list of 625 people that just received FOUR STRAIGHT GOLD STAR PICK WINNERS! Then, they call up those 625 prospects (many of whom are suitably impressed—*nobody else had the Panthers to beat the Lions in that game!*) and try to close the deal on a $1,200/year subscription to the GOLD STAR PICK SHEET.

Those bettors that got the four accurate e-mails in a row have to be very smart to think of the hidden evidence they might be missing. More likely, their emotional desire to win overrides their logical or rational mind and they hand their credit card number over to the waiting operator.

• • •

Numbers on their own do not always tell the full story. You need to think more deeply about conclusions and treat even the most obvious answers with rational skepticism.

Remember, skepticism is not cynicism. It doesn't mean you assume everything is wrong and everyone is lying and nothing is true. Alpha Traders filter information with slow System 2 thinking, even if the conclusion drawn from that information seems simple or obvious at first.

Skepticism is a healthy state of mind that represents quality thinking. The healthy skeptic understands that most knowledge is uncertain to some degree and looks to support statements with evidence. She listens to experts but does not take their claims or forecasts at face value. She uses research and logic to see through false claims and avoid hasty, incorrect conclusions.

The goal of this section was not to provide examples of counterintuitive math that you could apply directly to your trading. The idea, instead, is to get you thinking on the next level. Don't just scan the surface of information you receive and let it make its way into your mind, unfiltered. Think deeply. Seek accuracy and truth, and identify and ignore bad thinking when you encounter it.

• • •

That concludes our discussion of counterintuitive math. I hope you found it interesting and fun and I hope that it shakes you up a bit and gets you thinking more actively about your own thinking. If you enjoyed this section, I highly recommend Darrell Huff's book *How to Lie with Statistics*. It is a classic that explains in clear language how innocent-looking data and statistics can often be devilishly deceptive.

Be curious. Be open-minded. Seek evidence.

That is the essence of high-quality thinking.

ALWAYS QUESTION COMMON KNOWLEDGE

This is also a useful rule when you run into "common knowledge" in markets. Don't just listen to pundits and take their word or accept their forecasts at face value. Quite often, even Wall Street professionals on Bloomberg or CNBC will spout non-truths as if they were fact. Be on the lookout for statements that are presented as fact but could be totally false.

When you hear forecasts, no matter how smart the person sounds, assume they are probably pretty random. Analyze declarations, verify them with data and come to your own conclusions.

Here are some examples of questionable "common knowledge" that you hear in markets all the time.

1. Higher interest rates are bad for stocks
FACT CHECK: Sometimes true

Very often, when interest rates are rising, it is in response to a strong economy. A strong economy can be good for stocks if the central bank is accommodative, and bad for stocks if it leads the central bank to hike into restrictive territory. Rising interest rates and falling bond prices can be good or bad for stocks. It depends on many factors, especially where the Fed is in the cycle. If the Fed has hiked seven times and the economy is still strong and yields are ripping higher, then sure, that kind of rising rate move is probably bad for stocks.

On the other hand, almost every time US interest rates went up in recent years, that was likely good news for stocks as it signaled reflation and momentum away from the dreaded deflationary secular stagnation environment. Any time someone posts or blogs or tweets that rising rates are bad for stocks, stop and think. What do higher rates represent? Why are rates rising? Where are we in the interest rate and economic cycles? Unless you're near the end of the cycle, rising rates are usually good news for stocks, not bad news.

2. Bonds are smarter than stocks
Or: "The bond market knows something."
Or: "The bond market smells a rat in the economy."
FACT CHECK: False

Bond traders sit only a few rows from equity traders in most banks. They have the same information as multi-asset macro PMs with billions of capital under management. Bond traders do not have access to secret information about the economy that is kept hidden from traders in every other asset class.

No, no, no, no… No.

Many permabear pundits feel nauseous when they see the stock market going up, so they will come up with any excuse for why the rally is "on thin ice" or "set to falter". If bonds happen to be rallying along with stocks, these fear-peddling pundits assume that the bond market has some sort of secret information that hasn't yet been disclosed to the stock market. They will say that the bond market knows something and stocks are going to crash any minute.

When people say any of the three clichés listed above, chuckle to yourself and hit ignore. Figure 7.22 is a chart of stocks and bonds for the last 10 years.

Figure 7.22: Total return of stocks (black) and bonds (gray), January 2010 to October 2020

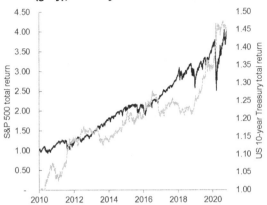

Does it look like bond rallies have been bad for stocks? Nope. It would be just as dangerous to say stocks and bonds always go up together. That's not true either. It's more complicated than a simple soundbite will allow. Quantitative easing creates long periods where stocks and bonds go up in tandem.

The relationship between stocks and bonds is complicated and varies considerably depending on the regime. It depends what part of the economic and Fed rate hike or rate cut cycle the world is in. Any simplistic comment formulated as: "Bonds are doing X so stocks should do Y" is a waste of time.

The stock vs. bond relationship is dynamic and unstable. Any statement about correlation or cross-market signal between stocks and bonds needs to be evaluated with a heavy dose of critical thinking and analysis. Mostly, your starting point should be: *bonds don't predict stocks*. Then work from there.

If you are astute, you might have noticed that these first two sections on "common knowledge" can be boiled down to:

1. Higher rates are bad for stocks

2. Lower rates are bad for stocks

The permabears leave many heaping piles of steaming hot brown nonsense in the financial forest every day. Learn to step over and around it and don't waste your time trying to convince the bears that their guano smells. Just slowly and quietly walk away.

3. Gold is a safe haven

FACT CHECK: Kinda. But not really.

A safe haven is an asset that goes up or at least holds its value during periods of risk aversion. Bonds typically perform this role, though with interest rates approaching zero in most countries by the year 2020, that role is likely to be questioned going forward.

The Japanese yen and Swiss franc are traditionally viewed as safe havens though their role as safe havens has diminished in recent years due to central bank and semi-official currency intervention (perceived or actual). Many prognosticators and journalists talk about gold as if it is a safe haven. When you see a headline like: "Gold rallies as US stock market sell-off accelerates", ignore it. Gold is just as likely to go down on days or during weeks that stocks go down.

Gold's behavior during periods of risk aversion depends mostly on positioning and overall financial market and USD liquidity. If stocks sell off because of economic worries, you might see gold rally. On the other hand, if stocks sell off because of liquidity fears (like in March 2020), expect gold to plummet right along with stocks.

The correlation between changes in the price of gold and changes in stock prices is usually mildly positive, meaning gold and stocks go up and down together, a tad. In Figure 7.23, I present a simple chart to quickly demonstrate.

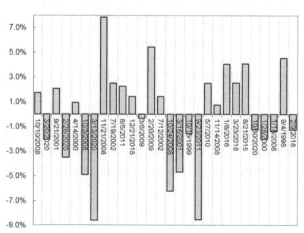

Figure 7.23: Weekly performance of gold in weeks where S&P 500 dropped 5% or more (since 1990)

I found the 25 worst weeks for the stock market (largest fall, in percentage terms) between 1980 and 2020 and then checked what gold did during those same weeks. If gold is a safe haven, it should reliably remain unchanged or go higher at these moments. The table shows the results, sorted by worst SPX performance, starting with the worst week in S&P 500 history.

The average move for gold in big down weeks for stocks is -0.4%. There are 13 down weeks vs. 15 up. The takeaway is that gold is not a reliable safe haven. If stocks collapse, gold might go up, or it might not.

4. Bad economic news is bad for stocks
FACT CHECK: Sometimes true.

The economy is one of many, many factors that influence stock prices. Analysts often overweight the importance of the economy when discussing stocks and giant question marks appear over their heads as they discuss the baffling divergence between equities and the economy.

Sometimes it's all about the economy; sometimes the economy has nothing to do with stocks.

2020 was the most glaring example in history of a feature of the stock market that really bothers some people (especially journalists, pundits, and noob traders): the stock market is not always a reflection of the economy, nor is it a reflection of social mood. It reflects *supply and demand for stocks.*

Often, nobody really understands what is driving the stock market (in either direction), and most of the "analysis" you see is simply ex-post rationalization for things that have already happened. If we really understood stocks, we could probably predict them better!

There are so many variables that can drive a wedge between stocks and the economy. For example:

- Excess liquidity provided by central banks.

- Expectations of future economic conditions are often more important that the current economic situation or economic numbers.

- Valuations can expand and contract in the same direction as the economy or in the opposite direction. This makes it hard to trace the direct connection between stocks and economic output. Multiple expansion and contraction (higher and lower price/earnings ratios) and many other factors unrelated to the economy can move stock prices.

- Supply and demand. If companies are buying back stock, other companies are going private, M&A activity is frenzied and retail traders are furiously opening new accounts, there can be a mismatch between supply and demand for stocks. These technical factors do not always correlate with economic growth.

- Sentiment. If everyone is raging bullish and caught in a speculative mania, economics don't matter much. Stocks are going higher.

5. The stock market is going to crash this week, this month, any day, etc.

FACT CHECK: Almost always false.

Fear sells. Dire predictions get clicks. Predicting crashes is a great media strategy. This is a fact and it has been confirmed by a huge pile of research. Human beings are attracted to dark narratives and scary headlines. As mentioned earlier, research shows that negative views on the stock market are perceived to be smarter while bullish views tend to be perceived as naïve, unrealistic, or rose-colored, despite the fact that empirical evidence strongly supports a bullish stance most of the time.

The fact that "the stock market is about to crash" is common knowledge on many websites and is a frequent theme on Twitter. People are always saying this; yet oddly enough, the stock market barely ever crashes! Take a look at history.

Figure 7.24: S&P 500 since World War II (log chart)

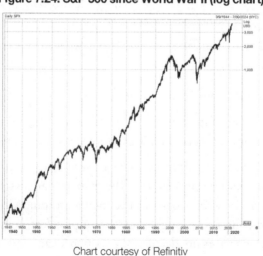

Chart courtesy of Refinitiv

Regularly predicting a crash is for people that want clicks and followers, not for people that want to make money.

When you see nonsense like "stocks can't fight gravity forever" remember Figure 7.24.

Prices operate in a vacuum; there is no gravity. Most people that "successfully" predicted a crash in the past (say 2008) just predict crashes all the time. A stopped clock is right twice a day.

Here are some statistics about the stock market that I hope will dissuade you from joining the permabear sloth.

Figure 7.25: Stocks go up more than they go down

	1946 to 2020			
	Any given...			
	Day	Week	Month	Year
Probability SPX goes up	53.4%	56.7%	60.1%	71.6%
Average return	0.0%	0.2%	0.7%	8.6%
Median return	0.0%	0.3%	0.9%	10.3%

It is true that stocks have a left tail, which means that the fastest, craziest moves in the stock market are down, not up. This is part of the reason it is more fun to be bearish than bullish. You are more likely to get instant gratification.

There is a crash (15% drop in one month) about once every five to eight years. Still, despite the four crashes between 2000 and 2020, the S&P went from 1,320 to 3,420 in that period (including four separate months when stocks ripped higher by more than 15%).

If your goal is to make money trading, you should be comfortable shifting between long or short risky assets depending on market conditions. You should trade without a directional bias. It's fine to be bearish, just don't let it become your religion.

Don't be a permabear. Don't be a permabull.

Keep an open mind and analyze the evidence, then make a rational and unbiased short-term forecast of market direction. That's the essence of good trading.

• • •

That concludes this chapter on rational, unbiased thinking. The biggest challenge with human bias is that studies show that even when we know about a bias, we can still fall victim to it. Therefore, it is important not just to know about various forms of bias and bad thinking, but to implement strategies and tactics to counteract bias in a rigorous and systematic way.

At this point, I hope you have a better understanding of the characteristics that make up an Alpha Trader and where you are strong, medium, and weak. I hope I have given you a few new ideas on how to improve your trading, tighten up your game, eliminate leaks and become more self-aware.

That's Part Two done. Now, it's time for some fun stuff. I've laid the groundwork and it's time to take action. You know what it means to be a rational thinking trader and you have learned many of the strengths and weaknesses that enhance or hamper trading success. Now, let's talk markets.

In Part Three, we look at how to become an expert in your market (Chapters 8 to 10) and then examine the topic of risk management in Chapter 11. Chapter 12 brings the entire book together as I explain exactly how I come up with, structure and execute trade ideas. Finally, I walk you through a detailed, real-life trade example in a way that I hope you will find both interesting and informative.

You are more than half-way through the book.

Let's move on to Part Three.

PART THREE

METHODOLOGY AND MATHEMATICS

"Nothing in the world is worth having or worth doing unless it means effort, pain, difficulty... I have never in my life envied a human being who led an easy life."

THEODORE ROOSEVELT

In Part Three I will outline the specific steps you must take to master your market. Your goal must be to become an expert in the product or markets that you trade. Stay narrow (focus on one or two markets) and go deep (learn as much as possible, right down to the nitty-grittiest details). This approach gives you the best shot at a sustainable edge. Wide and shallow can work, but has a much lower probability of success than narrow and deep.

Here is the abstract of an interesting study of Twitter sentiment that supports the idea that narrow focus yields higher returns[99].

Using tweets from StockTwits and machine-learning classification techniques, we find that social-media sentiment predicts positively and significantly future stock returns, and, importantly, such positive predictability decreases when the number of stocks users follow increases. The return predictability appears to stem from users' ability to forecast future earnings. Further tests reveal that reduced

---

99. Leung, Woon Sau and Wong, Gabriel and Wong, Woon K., "Social-Media Sentiment, Portfolio Complexity, and Stock Returns" (2019).

predictability due to stock coverage is significant only for firms that
are complex, opaque, and thus hard to analyze. The evidence suggests that stock analysis by users with a more complex portfolio is
inferior due to attention and time constraints.

Key words: "attention" and "time constraints". You have a limited supply of
attention and time and the more you spread it out, the less chance you have of
achieving mastery.

I can 100% confirm this from experience. Traders who master one area succeed much more often than traders that dabble in every market. That is why the
term "macro tourist" tends to be used in a derogatory way[100]. Locals have expert
knowledge and can find a great meal for a reasonable price. Tourists eat at the
overpriced restaurants and leave disappointed.

The next three chapters will outline the three steps you must take to become
an expert in your market. Step one: understand microstructure. Step two:
understand the narrative. Finally, step three: understand technicals, positioning and sentiment. Do the work to master these three areas and you are on the
way to trading success.

Think of the examples ahead as starting points for the deep dive you will
take into your own market. Each product and security trades differently and has
its own idiosyncrasies. I hope I give you enough detail here to both teach you
some aspects that I find important. I also want to open your eyes to the many
different ways one can think about, analyze and study markets. Ultimately you
should be able to analyze and dissect the market(s) you trade, using a framework *you've* created.

In other words, the examples and ideas I present in these chapters are not
exhaustive. Take my ideas and build on them. Come up with your own smarter,
better, more up-to-date ideas. Think about a long game where each day you
stack more and more expertise on top of your existing knowledge. Always maintain a philosophy of continuous improvement and lifelong learning.

The two greatest sources of edge in trading are expert-level knowledge of a
specific market, and a rigorous execution and risk management process. To succeed, you must know your product inside and out, and you must have a process
that maximizes leverage but also eliminates risk of ruin. Then you are smarter,

---

100. A Macro Tourist is a trader or investor who takes a position in a market they don't know very well, in an
     attempt to profit from a popular narrative. The appearance of macro tourists often makes the locals
     want to run for the hills.

more knowledgeable and more nimble than the competition and built to survive in the long run. Part Three is a study of the specific methodologies and mathematics you need to understand to achieve these goals.

Let's go to Chapter 8, where we will go into some depth on a topic I have always found supremely fascinating: *market microstructure*.

UNDERSTAND MICROSTRUCTURE

*Step one towards becoming
an expert in your market*

Excellent traders understand microstructure and have a deep knowledge of the products they trade. This chapter will explain how to become an expert in microstructure and how to use this deeper understanding to make more money trading.

You are playing in one of the most complex, competitive games in the world. You can't dabble in 14 products and expect to have an edge. Occasionally, traders can be experts in a particular strategy and apply that strategy across products, but in general most traders that succeed have knowledge that is narrow and deep, not shallow and wide. They are product experts. How do you become an expert?

Read. Observe. Study.

Let's say you have been trading for a while without much success and so you decide to day trade Tesla (TSLA) and focus all your energy there. You will trade nothing else. There are pros and cons to trading TSLA (like any stock).

Pros:

- it's liquid
- it's volatile

- there are opportunities in the stock every day
- many non-professionals trade it

Cons:

- there are 1000s of people trading it who probably know more than you do
- it's extremely volatile
- many traders are biased one way or the other when it comes to Tesla because of their love or hate for the product and/or its larger-than-life founder. Never trade the stock of a company you have an emotional connection to[101].

So how do you become an expert in TSLA? You start by studying its microstructure. Start by watching the price action for a few days. How does it trade on the open and close? Who are the players trading it and talking about it? What is the average daily range? Average hourly range? What is the average range on the day after earnings? How does liquidity vary by time of day? Does it trade differently around option expiries? How big are the close to open gaps after news comes out?

Those are sample questions you might ask about microstructure. Let me explain microstructure in detail so that you can ask the right questions in your market. A market's microstructure is determined by the following:

1. Types of participants
2. Liquidity
   a. Transaction costs and bid / offer spread
   b. Gap risk
3. Intraday activity patterns
4. Volatility

Let's start with a brief discussion of market participants then make our way through the list.

---

101. If you are a huge Elon Musk fan or if you really can't stand him for some reason, don't trade TSLA. You need to be equally prepared to trade a stock from the long or short side or you should not be participating. If you Stan for Elon, trading TSLA is like a Real Madrid fan betting on a Real Madrid / Barcelona game. Do you think he's going to make an unbiased bet on the team he thinks has the best chance of winning? Or is he going to bet on Real Madrid? Trade with your rational mind not your silly, silly heart.

1. Market participants

Who trades your product? Depending on your seat, you may have more or less visibility into who trades your product and who does not. If you trade futures you have very little insight, while if you are a market maker, you have a ton of insight. When I was day trading equities, I could often figure out by studying the Level 2 screen all day which market makers mattered and which did not. In general, there are six major market participants:

1. Retail. People sitting at home trading their own money or trading on their phones. The influence of retail varies from minimal (most of the time) to total dominance (Hertz stock in April 2020). Even in the largest market of all, foreign exchange, retail can matter. For example, Japanese retail investors can move the entire currency market sometimes with large mean reversion and stop loss activity.

2. Institutional. There are five main types of institutions:

   a. Banks. Commercial and investment banks are active players in most securities. They act as market makers, agents, principals and speculators.

   b. Real money. This is traditional investor capital, usually invested in stocks and bonds, but also other asset classes. It is pensions, mutual funds, 401k money etc.

   c. Hedge funds. These are pools of capital formed to invest and generate alpha. Hedge funds execute a wide range of strategies from trend following and systematic to discretionary macro. Hedge fund activity tends to be herd-like in aggregate, even though many individual portfolio managers run individual and unique strategies. Hedge funds generally employ more leverage than other institutional participants.

   d. Corporates. Corporations issue stock, buy back stock, hedge via futures, buy and sell currencies to hedge income and balance sheet exposure, etc. Their activity is hard to track unless you work at a bank. Decision making tends to be more timing or transaction-focused, not market or macro driven. That is, a company might have a large need to buy euros due to a cross-border acquisition. That does not necessarily mean they are bullish euro, they just need to buy the euros to complete their asset purchase.

e. Central banks. Central banks around the world hold huge reserves and manage those reserves by investing in countries and securities they expect to outperform. Second, central banks buy and (rarely) sell assets as a part of their monetary policy. The Federal Reserve bought a laundry list of assets in 2020 in response to the massive economic damage caused by COVID-19. Central bank participation in some asset markets is the primary determinant of price, while they are secondary actors in other markets.

Who are the players in your market? Can you identify any particular activity by specific participants? In some markets, this is impossible, but it is worth thinking about your market and whether or not you can monitor the activity of the largest players and use this as an input into your process.

Below are some examples of how to monitor these players. This is mostly expert-level stuff that you would not know when you are just starting out. As you spend more time studying your market, you will learn how to identify what the big players are up to. These are six real-world examples of how you can see the larger participants in action:

1. There is a well-known pattern where large real-money flows take place in currency markets on the last day of each month, peaking at 4 p.m. London time. I will give a short example later in the chapter.

2. If you are trading equities, study the supply and demand from institutions on the Level 2 screen. While the Level 2 info was much more useful and yielded much more edge in the late 1990s and early 2000s, there is still value in watching and studying it.

3. Track cross-border mergers and acquisitions to monitor possible currency flows.

4. Monitor equity moves around triple witching as market makers and real money hedgers trade actively.

5. Study a central bank's activities and operations and see if there is any pattern to trading activity when the central bank is active in the market vs. when it is not. Does it impact markets at a particular time of day or price level?

6. Learn how stocks trade on the day they are added to the S&P 500

index (as real money adds the stock to stay on benchmark) and trade that pattern.

Think about what you know about the various actors in your market and see if you can unpack any useful, predictive information about future moves by analyzing their actions. It sounds esoteric but in most markets there is some visibility into what people are doing, especially if you read like a fiend. Note that due to efficient markets, patterns that become well known tend to lose their predictability over time.

Assume markets are very, but not perfectly, efficient.

When you think you have found an inefficiency or exploitable pattern in the market, be skeptical but optimistic. Don't be so naïve as to think there are high-Sharpe pots of gold lying around all over the place but also don't fall into the negative trap of these two economists who believe that every good idea has already been found:

> Two economists are walking down the street when one points to the ground and says, "Look, a ten-dollar bill!"
>
> The second economist replies, "That's crazy. If that was a ten-dollar bill someone would have picked it up already."

This is a common trap in all areas of innovation. You have an idea for a novel and think "oh, I'm sure that's been done before" or you think of a product idea and imagine "Ah, someone must have thought of that already." That is a losing mentality. New ideas are the absolute lifeblood of capitalism and creativity. Never dismiss any idea on the assumption someone must have already thought of it.

2. Liquidity

Understand liquidity. Some products, like FX, are extremely liquid and trade continuously all day and all week. Some markets, like lumber and wheat, are much less liquid, trade short sessions with a defined open and close, and offer minimal price transparency and poor liquidity outside primary trading hours.

Some assets trade freely all the time while some futures contracts can hit limit up or limit down for multiple days in a row, leaving specs trapped on the wrong side. How does your product trade? Is there plenty of liquidity all the time, or do you need to consider liquidity when you execute? Let's drill into liquidity a bit so you can think about the specific features of your market.

Transaction costs and bid/ask spread

The difference between the bid and the ask in a market is called the spread.[102] Transaction costs are the amount of spread you pay when you trade.

(SPREAD) X (NUMBER OF UNITS) = TRANSACTION COST

If AAPL is trading 350.00 / 350.08, the spread is eight cents. This is often expressed either as a percentage of the mid-price[103] or in basis points:

= 0.08 / 350.04

= 0.029%

= 2.9bps[104]

2.9bps is one of the tightest bid/offer spreads you will see. Spreads vary dramatically by asset class and by product within an asset class. In FX, spreads in EURUSD (the most liquid pair) are often less than 1/10 of spreads in USDTRY (Turkish lira). The bid/ask in a small cap or microcap stock can be 50X the AAPL bid/ask. Gold trades way tighter than palladium. Spreads in credit are generally wider than spreads in fixed income. Spreads in agricultural commodities are generally wider than spreads in short-term interest rate futures. And so on.

Every market has a different texture and part of this texture comes from the bid/offer spread. Trading activity on each side of the spread is called bid/ask bounce.

Think about your average trade size and call that one unit. How much does it cost you to trade one unit in normal markets? For example: If your normal trade size is 10 million EURUSD and EURUSD trades 2 pips wide in 10 million (1 pip = 0.0001). Each round trip (buy and sell) costs:

= 10,000,000 * (0.0002)

= $2,000

---

102. I use bid/ask and bid/offer interchangeably in this book.

103. The mid (or mid-price, or mid-rate) is the center of the bid/ask spread. If gold's bid/ask is 2000.00 / 2000.20 then the mid-price is 2000.10.

104. Spreads are often expressed in basis points (bps). A basis point is $1/100^{th}$ of 1%. Therefore, for example, 1.00% is 100bps, 0.50% is 50bps and 0.02% is 2bps.

That is to say: if the market in EURUSD is 1.1000 bid / 1.1002 offer and you buy and sell without the market moving, you have paid 0.0002 in transaction costs which is $2,000 per 10 million transacted.

When you buy and sell stocks at zero commission, you are still paying a toll of somewhere between 0.02% and 0.50% (2bps to 50bps) due to the bid/ask spread. Some stocks are much wider than 0.50% but you probably should not be trading those. Spreads and commissions are the main reason trading is a negative-sum game, not a zero-sum game. Spread is the invisible enemy, like a slow leak in a tire. It costs you a ton of P&L but it can be very hard to observe or measure correctly.

Tiffany is an active day trader. She executes 15 round-trips per day (15 buys and 15 sells) and the stock she specializes in (Take Two Interactive, TTWO) has an average bid/ask of 38bps. That means if the stock is trading at $173, the average bid/ask is about 66 cents[105]. Her account size is $100,000 and her average trade size is 150 shares. So she is leaking:

150 shares X 15 round trips X $0.66 per round trip

= $1,485 per day

X 5 days

= $7,425 per week

X 48 weeks[106]

= $356,400 per year

Insane, right? These are realistic assumptions and they give you a good sense of just how expensive it can be to cross big spreads. She can reduce her transaction costs by using other execution strategies like limit orders, but we don't know if this will hurt her performance.

Obviously she can't keep doing this for very long unless her strategy has significant edge. If she used the same strategy but switched over to AAPL (and we assume 3bps bid/ask in AAPL), her transaction costs drop to:

$117 per day

$585 per week

$28,080 per year

---

105. $173 X 0.0038

106. She takes four weeks of holiday per year.

I am not saying you should only trade AAPL! What I am saying is that you should have a clear and thorough understanding of how much it costs you to transact. When you fully grok how expensive it is to transact, you will probably transact less. As we have discussed, transacting less is almost always a good thing.

Accurate data on bid/offer spreads can be hard to come by. In FX, the banks collect this data and some are willing to share it with clients while others view it as proprietary. In the stock market, the easiest thing to do is watch the stock you trade and take occasional snapshots of the spread.

Bid/offer spreads in an individual stock will vary substantially by time of day and around events. In times of stress, bid/offer spreads can widen dramatically but in normal markets, they are somewhat consistent. In other words, if AAPL trades 3bps wide today at 10 a.m., it will probably trade around 3bps wide tomorrow at 10 a.m. unless there is news, or a profound change in the markets.

In contrast, at the open (9:30 a.m.) it could be tighter or wider, and at times of higher volatility it will almost certainly trade wider. Your estimate of bid/offer spreads does not have to be perfect, just eyeball it and multiply by your estimated number of trades per day to get a rough sense of your transaction costs (TC). TC is a slow and steady leak that adds up substantially.

You need a significant edge to make money in any market because you don't just need to generate alpha, you need to generate alpha *net of transaction costs*. Figure 8.1 and Figure 8.2 show the theoretical P&L for two different traders. The thinner gray line shows the P&L before transaction costs (known as "gross") and the black line shows the P&L after TC (known as "net").

I used realistic bid/offer spreads to show the impact of trading costs on two realistic P&L streams so you can get a sense of the enormous strain TC exerts on performance.

You should not obsess over TC but you need to be smart about it. Most of all, you need to quantify and monitor it. TC is a serious and important leak that you need to reduce as much as possible.

At the same time, TC is a cost of doing business in trading and you don't want an unhealthy approach to reducing TC that could jeopardize your reputation or your future liquidity. Be smart, but not obsessive about reducing TC. We will discuss some ways to do this in the section on execution in Chapter 12.

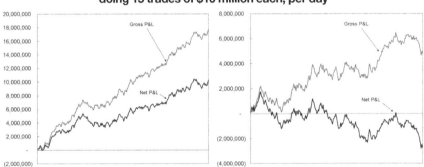

Figure 8.1: Two P&L simulations for a day trader who turns over 3,500 shares per day

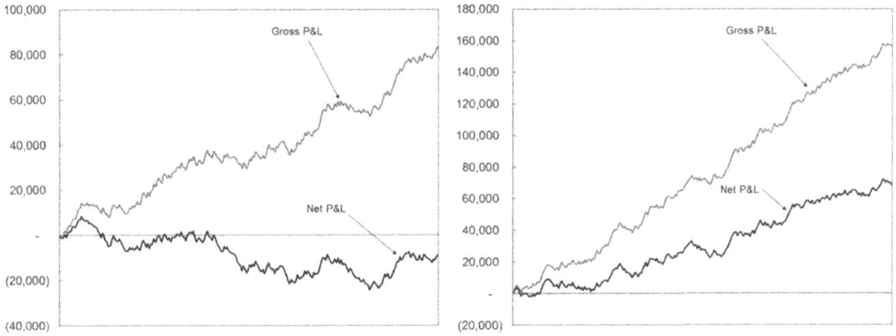

Average bid/offer spread is 10 cents. Zero commission. She trades 252 days per year.
Her average up day is +$3,000, her average down day is -$2,000 and her WIN% is 50%

Figure 8.2: Two P&L simulations for an FX trader doing 15 trades of $10 million each, per day

Assumes average bid/ask spread of 2 pips.
His average up day is +$800k, his average down day is -$350k and his WIN% is 50%

Gap risk

Another element of Liquidity is Gap risk. There are three types of gap risk. The first is when markets close and then reopen. A stock closes at $50 on Friday and then over the weekend their CFO quits and the company announces that they have fired their auditor. That doesn't sound good! The stock opens at $25 on Monday morning. Yikes. If you have a $50,000 account and you went home long at 2X margin, you're done. Ruined. That's gap risk number one.

Usually the timing of close-to-open gap risk can be predicted in advance since we know the trading hours of whatever securities we trade, but this is not 100% the case. Many futures have trading limits: if they move a certain amount, trading is halted[107]. Individual stocks are often halted for pending news or due to extreme volatility. You must have a complete understanding of how your market trades and avoid risk of ruin before everything else.

The second type of gap risk relates to events. When the US jobs report comes out the first Friday of each month at 8:30 a.m., you will often see S&P futures and USDJPY (and other markets) jump to a new level without trading continuously from A to B. For example, USDJPY might be 112.10/15 at 8:29:29 and then the jobs number comes in strong and the first trade after 8:30 could be 112.68. If you go into the number short and don't have a good understanding of the gap risk, you might get wrecked.

After economic releases and events, there is usually a fast market for 5 to 10 minutes as well, so not only do you need to worry about gap risk, but also liquidity risk. Even if you are trading small size, it can be difficult to get in and out in fast markets. You might deal on wrong prices or get error messages or, if you trade bigger size, simply find you cannot transact your full amount. Like I said earlier, unless you think you have a big edge on the number or event, go in flat and react.

The third type of gap risk comes from markets that are pegged, capped or floored by central banks or other entities. One famous example of this is the EURCHF floor at 1.2000. The Swiss National Bank tried to enforce an exchange rate and eventually, when they gave up, the largest one day move in the history of foreign exchange happened. In about two hours. EURCHF traded from 1.2000 to 0.8500 in a matter of minutes.

Pegs and caps and floors are most common in FX markets but also show up in equity markets in the days after an IPO. Market makers representing the investment bank(s) that underwrote the IPO are permitted to intervene in the market to stabilize the price of the stock if it starts to fall below the IPO price. This stabilization bid is not infinite. At some point, the underwriter will say enough is enough and pull away and the stock will usually gap aggressively lower.

There is a fantastic piece about the Facebook IPO stabilization effort on the Liberty Street Economics Blog[108]. Figure 8.3 shows how the number of shares on the bid (vertical bars) increased as Facebook's share price reached $38 (the IPO price) on its first day trading.

---

107. This information is usually easy to find on the interwebs. Or use DES {GO} for any future on Bloomberg.

108. Eisenbach, Lucca and Shen, "Evidence of underwriters' efforts to stabilize the share price in the Facebook IPO", Liberty Street Economics Blog, (2012).

**Figure 8.3: Facebook's order book depth
and share price on IPO day: May 12, 2012**

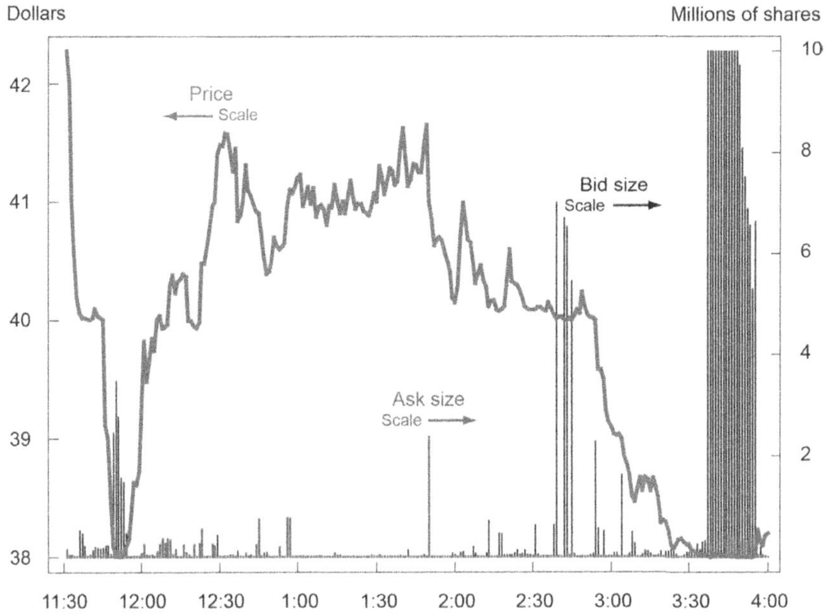

Source: Thomson Reuters Tick History.
Chart used with permission of Liberty Street Economics (NY Fed)

The huge bids that came in are from the underwriter of the Facebook IPO. The chart shows that the underwriter made a concerted effort to buy nearly limitless stock at $38. Traders might see this huge intervention and think it's smart to go long with a stop below $38. Generally that is not the right way to look at situations like this.

Instead, you should realize that the price is badly out of equilibrium. With one buyer and myriad sellers, the stock is out of line and the second the buyer disappears, it's going to be chaos as the price will gap lower in search of equilibrium. Figure 8.4 shows the first day of trading (same price pattern as above) plus the next five days.

When the stock opened the next day, the stabilization bid wasn't there and Facebook gapped lower. Longs were lucky if they got out at $34. The stock did not trade back above $38 again for more than a year.

While it's tempting to go with a market distortion like the FB stabilization bid or the SNB bid in EURCHF at 1.2000, counterintuitively the best move is often to go against it. When you follow an intervention bid, you are dead if that

Figure 8.4: Facebook stock price: May 12, 2012 and the five days after

bid disappears. If you go short against it and the price rallies, there will probably be a reasonable price where you can get out.

When an entity is supporting the price of a security or currency pair, it is usually reasonable to assume that the price is out of equilibrium and the entity supporting it is the only source of demand. Unless you have an edge in predicting what that entity is going to do, you should stay away. These setups present huge gap risk and can lead to risk of ruin.

Many retail investors and some large, well-known hedge funds were ruined by the SNB fail at 1.2000. Is it worth betting your job, your client's capital or your entire fund on a single trade? No. *Never.*

**When gap risk is extreme or hard to estimate,
avoid it. The risk is not worth the reward.**

Be thoughtful about major gap risks in your product and avoid them. This does not mean you can never carry a position through economic data. Gaps around economic data can be reasonably estimated. What it does mean is you should not go short a tech bubble stock into earnings. You should not go long USDHKD at the bottom of the band, and you should seriously consider your weekend positions and whether or not they are worth it. Oil can gap 10% over a weekend. USDJPY can gap 100 to 150 pips.

Avoid gap risk. Avoid gap risk. Avoid gap risk.

That concludes our discussion of gap risk. Now let's visit one of my favorite topics, an area where true experts shine. A field of study that can be an underappreciated source of edge: The idiosyncratic intraday trading patterns of each asset class.

3. Intraday activity patterns

Every market has a specific pattern that it follows (on average) during the day. Think about your favorite market. Are there specific times of day when volume and volatility spike? In currency markets, for example, there is a long list of key times that FX traders need to know including the US open, economic data, options expiry, WMR fix, Tokyo fix, etc.

Hedge fund portfolio managers and other large institutional traders need to know how liquidity ebbs and flows in their products over the course of the day. If you want to take a big position in USDJPY, for example, you should know that 10:57 a.m. NY time (3:57 p.m. LDN) is a much better time to put it on than 11:51 a.m. because FX is deepest from 7 a.m. to 11 a.m. Even small lot traders need to know these patterns because they affect not only liquidity but also volatility and volumes.

What are the key times of day for the products you trade? Let's take a look at a few major markets so you can get an idea of how time of day activity varies in different asset classes.

Volume by time of day for major markets

If you are an expert in the market or products you trade, you will know every important time of day and you will know the distribution of volume by time of day.

First, this is useful because it tells you when the "real moves" happen in your market. If there is very little volume going through, the probability of random, meaningless moves is higher. Second, if you need to transact meaningful size, volume by time of day is even more important as it tells you the trading time that minimizes your footprint. Third, intraday volume spikes often reveal important moments in the day like fixings and data releases.

Let's look at a few major markets. I will show you the volume by time of day in 5-minute increments and then give you a few short takeaways[109]. I wanted to include bitcoin but the volume data is too decentralized. Let's start with spooz.

---

109. Note regarding the charts that follow. All use four months of 5-minute data from January 6, 2020 to April 6, 2020. This subset works as a proxy for any period as intraday volume patterns are remarkably stable over time.

S&P futures (aka, e-minis, aka spooz)

Figure 8.5 shows volume by time of day for S&P futures. You can see the huge spikes on the open and close with dwindling volumes that trough at lunch time.

This chart explains why most day traders make most of their money from 9 a.m. to 11 a.m. and 3 p.m. to 4 p.m. This was 100% true for me when I was day trading the NASDAQ. If you trade stocks: Concentrate your efforts around the busy times and eat lunch, do research and lift weights from 11 a.m. to 2 p.m.

Figure 8.5: Volume by time of day - S&P 500 futures (ES)

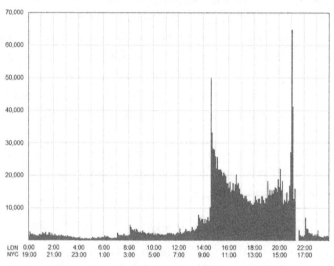

First row of x-axis label is GMT, second row is NYC time

10-year bonds

Figure 8.6 shows TY futures, which is the US 10-year note futures contract. The volume pattern for this one is not too surprising, though that huge burst at 3:00 p.m. is larger than I would have guessed before I made this chart. Otherwise, volumes are high in the NY morning with little spikes around the economic data. Volumes are super low until London comes in (7:00 a.m. GMT or 2:00 a.m. NY) and then pick up substantially when the US gets to work.

The 3:00 p.m. spike is the close of the Chicago Board of Trade (CBOT). Many strategies and funds mark to market against this closing price so there is a ton of activity at that time as these funds try to match the closing price. You often see buying of bond futures into 3:00 p.m. due to rebalancing and duration extension.

Figure 8.6: Volume by time of day – 10-year bond futures (TY)

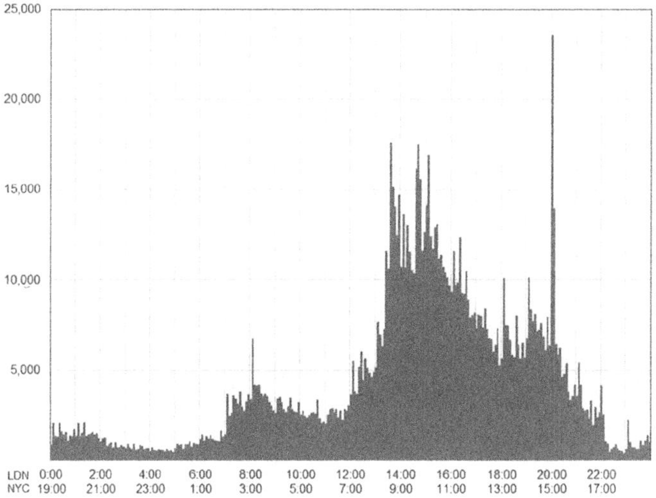

First row of x-axis label is GMT, second row is NYC time

Gold futures

Next, we look at gold futures (see Figure 8.7). Again, New York dominates but you can also see a big spike at 8:00 p.m. NY time when Shanghai opens. Shanghai gold markets have taken on increasing importance but remain less important than US and London markets. Again, you can see volumes pick up when London walks in and then huge spikes when data comes out and at the 10:00 a.m. gold fix.

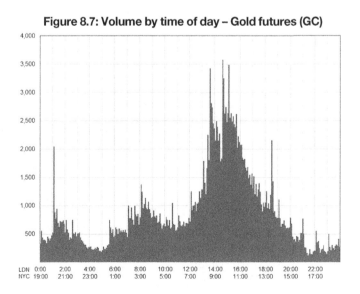

Figure 8.7: Volume by time of day – Gold futures (GC)

The COMEX close (1:30 p.m.) also sees a large spike in volume. Even though the gold futures trading pit is not a thing anymore, many systems still mark to the COMEX close and so activity jumps into 1:30 p.m. before fizzling into the end of the New York day.

EURUSD currency spot

Currency markets are most active in the London / NY overlap which runs from 7 a.m. to 11 a.m. NY (noon to 4 p.m. LDN). But even inside that 4-hour window, there are critical moments like the economic data at 8:30, options expiry at 10:00 and the WMR fix at 11:00 (all NY time). You can see this pattern in Figure 8.8.

Other currencies have important moments throughout the day, too, like USDJPY and the Tokyo fix (9:55 a.m. Tokyo time) which is the highest volume point of the entire 24-hour session for USDJPY. For a full and detailed look at critical times of day in FX markets, check out my first book: *The Art of Currency Trading*.

Figure 8.8: Volume by time of day – EURUSD currency spot

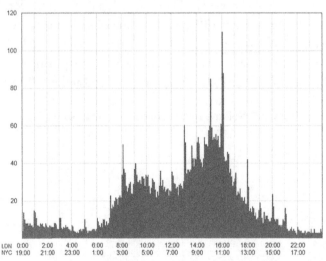

While volume and volatility do not always move together, it is generally true to say that volatility and volumes correspond. For example, Figure 8.9 shows average EURUSD volatility by hour of the day. You can see that this chart closely follows the intraday EURUSD volume pattern.

Figure 8.9: Volatility by time of day – EURUSD currency spot

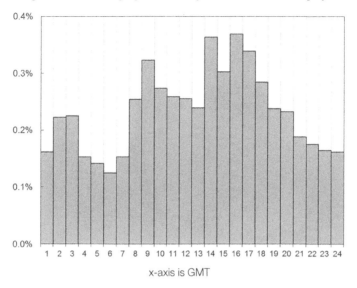

x-axis is GMT

NYMEX crude oil futures

Finally, Figure 8.10 shows how oil trades throughout the day.

If you are moving decent volume in US crude futures, you should be aware of when liquidity might be a problem. Selling 5,000 CL (NYMEX crude oil) futures at 2:25 p.m. will generally be easier than the same trade at 2:45 p.m. That insane volume spike at 2:30 p.m. is the NYMEX close.

Many participants use Trade at Settlement (TAS) orders to guarantee the closing price on their fill and the hedging of these TAS orders creates a monster volume spike in the minutes leading up to the close. If this volume is not balanced, you will sometimes see a huge move at that time. If someone yells "What's going on in crude!" right at 2:30 p.m., just shake your head and say "NYMEX close, dude. NYMEX close." :]

You need to understand whether liquidity is a possible constraint in the products you trade. If it is, track liquidity daily using a quantitative measure like bid/offer depth and ask traders or market makers for their opinion. Adapt your tactics and position sizes as necessary to avoid liquidity issues. If your products are deep and your volume is easily absorbed, life is good. If not, be thoughtful and strategic about what time of day you execute, and partner with a market maker you trust.

This concludes our discussion of liquidity and how activity varies by time of day. The last facet of market microstructure we will cover is volatility.

Figure 8.10: Volume by time of day – Crude oil futures (CL)

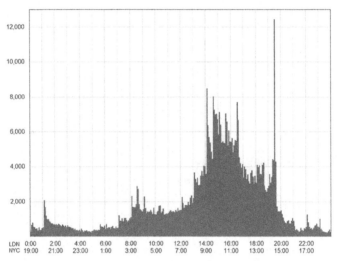

First row of x-axis label is GMT, second row is NYC time

4. Volatility

The next step in understanding how your market moves is to understand your product's volatility. Market professionals often call volatility "vol". Vol is a critical part of a market's microstructure. It is the dispersion of returns over time, usually measured as the standard deviation of logarithmic returns. In simple English: How much does the thing move?

Volatility is not constant or static. A currency pair like USDJPY might realize 6% volatility one year and 18% the next. Vol is a key concept to understand and you should always know your product's vol profile, how it has evolved over time, and how it might change in the future.

A few things you need to know about vol:

1. Markets tend to be more volatile around events because equilibrium is a function of all known information, and events introduce new information and upset the equilibrium. For example, overnight vol for AUDUSD might be 8% on a normal day and 20% on the day the Reserve Bank of Australia (RBA) meets. Facebook trades with higher vol on earnings day relative to other days.

2. Volatility within and across markets is correlated. If equity volatility is exploding higher, it is likely that FX, bond market and commodities

volatility will go up too. There is often a single factor driving volatility in capital markets. This can be economic uncertainty, geopolitical drama or something else. Volatility and uncertainty are usually associated.

3. It is hard to make money trading low vol markets. Most traders make more money when things are moving. One of the keys to success in trading is identifying the vol regime and adjusting your trading accordingly. You probably won't make money trading breakouts when the VIX is at 11[110]. You probably can't trade mean reversion when the VIX is at 80. My P&L is highly correlated to volatility. If you notice a meaningful drop in volatility in something you trade, consider trading something else or monitor the situation closely and see if your P&L is drifting lower along with vol.

To be 100% clear, when people talk about volatility, they usually mean *historical* volatility, but it is important to understand the two different types of volatility:

Historical volatility. This is the dispersion of returns in the past. You can measure it different ways but unless you are an options trader, I wouldn't worry about where the number comes from. Just know that when people say "volatility" they are mostly referring to daily historical or realized volatility. The amount the security has moved around in the past, based on daily data.

Implied volatility. This is the market price for volatility going forward. This measure is used in option pricing, and is a better proxy for future volatility than historical volatility. The distinction is not important here and for the purposes of an exercise like vol-adjusted position sizing, it rarely matters which data you use.

When it comes to the product you trade, what is the average daily range for your product? Daily average ranges are useful and it is also good to know the average hourly range and how that range varies by time of day. For example, Figure 8.11 shows how that looks for Apple stock (AAPL). I added SPY (the S&P 500 ETF) as well to give you some context.

Most stocks and equity futures have an intraday volatility profile similar to

---

110. VIX is the most popular measure of equity market volatility. 10 is very low. 80 is extremely high.

Figure 8.11: AAPL and SPY, intraday volatility pattern

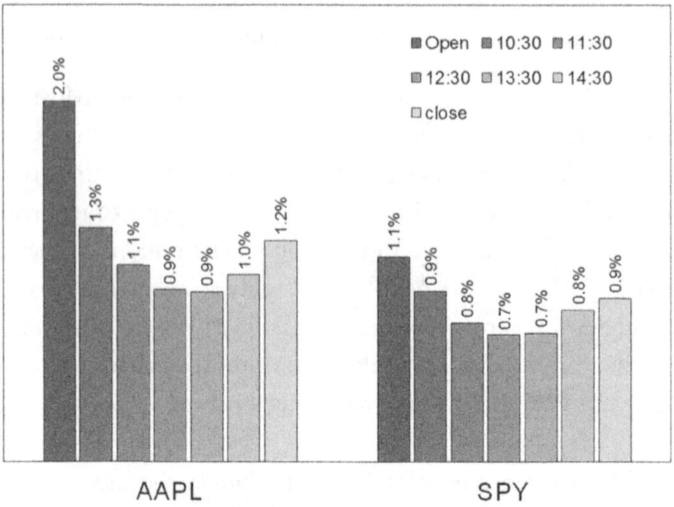

Using data from February, 2020 to August, 2020
First six bars are 60-minute average range.
Open (9:30 a.m.) to 10:30 a.m., 10:30 to 11:30, etc.
Final bar is the average range for 3:30 to 4:00 p.m.

the profiles shown above. Stock market activity is heavy at the open, heavy at the close and troughs around lunchtime.

When thinking about volatility, it's important to understand the current regime but you should also know how volatility has changed over time. You can get historical volatility for almost all financial time series on Bloomberg, Refinitiv or the internet. For example, if you want to know how vol is changing in Tesla stock, Just Google "TSLA historical volatility" and have a look. The absolute number is less important than the relative change.

Is the stock becoming more or less volatile? What are the most extreme periods of volatility, and what was going on then? The more you understand volatility and get comfortable with when it's likely to be high and low, the more likely you will avoid getting punched in the mouth.

If you have the skills and the data, you should study how your security trades on big event days. This information can be incredibly useful if you catch the right side of a move on event day because you can leave limit orders around the extremes and as the market extends or overshoots, you will take profit. It is nice to be the person selling the spike instead of the one buying it.

Here is a detailed example of what I mean.

Figure 8.12: AAPL common stock, distribution of 1-day returns, January 2010 to October 2020

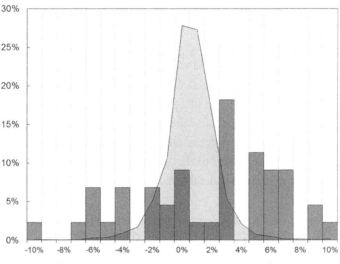

Curve shows normal days, bars show earnings days

You can see in Figure 8.12 that the normal curve for 1-day percentage returns in Apple shows most days are in the -2% to +4% range. On the other hand, earnings days show 1-day returns more like -6% to +7%. This is important information. If you are long on earnings day, you should modify your parameters relative to a normal day to account for the higher expected volatility. Most traders would know that a stock is more volatile on earnings day but when you crunch the data you get a deeper level of understanding.

If you catch a positive earnings move in Apple, it makes sense to leave a few limit orders around (yesterday's close + 7%) because that is about as big a move as you can expect based on historical data. As usual, this type of study gives you clues, not answers. There could be a day Apple rallies 20% in one day, but this analysis gives you one more piece of the puzzle and helps you understand what sort of volatility is likely and what is not. For one stock, 15% moves could be the norm on earnings day. For another, that figure could be 3%.

The best way to truly understand the volatility of a product or security is to watch it all day. The goal is to gain an intimate knowledge of how your market moves so that you get a feel for what is a big move, what is a logical stop loss, where you should take profit, and so on.

One way to enhance your feel for a specific market is to graph it by hand.

Maintain a simple point and figure chart for a few days and you will be surprised how much your market feel improves, especially if you are new to trading or have not traded the product all that much. Much like keeping score at a baseball game or taking notes in class forces you to pay keen attention, manually charting a market keeps you in the zone, engaged and connected.

You can also create point and figure charts in Excel if you are too embarrassed to whip out the graph paper and go old school. Point and figure is one of the original charting methods. It filters out noise and lets you focus on the meaningful changes in price. There is no time element in a point and figure chart, it simply measures price changes of a certain size (this is called the "price interval"). The x-axis is blank.

Figure 8.13 is a point and figure chart I made for TSLA on December 18, 2020 (the day TSLA was added to the S&P 500).

Here is how you create a chart like this:

Figure 8.13: TSLA point and figure chart for December 18, 2020 (the day it was added to the S&P 500)

Price														
698														
695			3:45PM to 4:00PM									X		X
692												X	O	X
689												X	O	X
686												X	O	X
683	X											X	O	X
680	X	O										X	O	X
677	X	O			X							X	O	X
674	X	O	X		X	O		X				X	O	X
671	X	O	X	O	X	O		X	O			X	O	X
668	X	O	X	O	X	O		X	O			X	O	X
665	X	O	X	O	X	O		X	O	X		X	O	X
662	X	O	X	O	X	O		X	O	X	O	X	O	X
659	X	O	X	O	X	O	X	X	O	X	O	X	O	
656	X	O		O	X	O	X	X	O	X	O	X		
653				O	X	O		X	O	X	O			
650				O	X			X	O	X				
647				O				X	O	X				
644								X	O					
641								X		X				
638								X	O	X				
635								X	O	X				
632		9:30AM to 3:45PM						X	O					
629														
626														

The black line separating the two parts of the day is just there for display purposes to show you how point and figure charts distort or eliminate the element of time

1. Get a piece of graph paper or create a grid of small squares in Excel.

2. Calculate the average daily range of your security and divide by 10. That is your price interval. I looked back two years to calculate that the average daily range for TSLA is 4.7%. The stock closed at $655.90 on December 17 and 4.7% of that is about $30. $30 divided by 10 means we will use $3 increments. Always round the number here to make the math easy.

3. Write the current price (rounded to the nearest price interval) in the middle of the y-axis. So using the previous day's close, I go half way up the y-axis and write $656. If you know where the stock is trading pre-market, that's even better.

4. Complete the y-axis by adding the interval as you go up and subtracting it as you go down. So you write 659, 662, 665, 668, etc. on the way up the y-axis and 653, 650, 647… on the way down.

5. When the stock opens, wait for $653 or $659 to trade. If $659 trades, draw an X in the box next to $656 and $659. X means the stock went up. If $653 trades, draw an O in the box next to $656 and $653. O means the stock went down.

As the stock continues in the same direction, keep marking the X's or O's. Or, if the stock reverses more than 3 intervals (in this case $9), switch to a new column and fill it in with the new X's or O's. You wait three intervals before reversing in order to cut out the noise, otherwise you would be switching columns too much and the chart would be wide and noisy. Point and figure charting is meant to cut out noise and capture meaningful reversals. You can mess around with the parameters but the choice of parameters is not important so I would not bother. Just use (daily range/10) for your intervals and 3 intervals as your reversal parameter.

The most interesting aspect of the chart is how the y-axis has no meaning and the chart is stripped of the time dimension. Instead, the chart shows any meaningful reversal, however long it lasts. Therefore, in this example, the violent final 15 minutes of TSLA trading takes up as much room as the calmer trading that took place throughout the prior 6+ hours. For context, Figure 8.14 shows a line chart of TSLA that day.

When you contrast the point and figure to the line chart, you see how time disappears and volatility is all that matters.

**Figure 8.14: TSLA bar chart for December 18, 2020
(the day it was added to the S&P 500)**

The insane closing rally is the demand from indexers at the close

If alternative charting techniques appeal to you, I suggest you investigate Market Profile too. It is more complicated, but can be another useful and intuitive way of charting and analyzing markets. There are some excellent resources online: see if you can find the CME Market Profile guide (300+ pages) in pdf form[111].

The book *Mind Over Markets* by Dalton, Jones and Dalton turned me on to Market Profile charting more than 10 years ago, and I continue to use some of the specific methods from that book to this day. You can play around with it using the MKTP function on Bloomberg (they call it "Market Picture").

Some people think it's stupid to create manual charts but this is not like some luddite clacking away on a manual typewriter just because he hates technology. There is a practical value to the tactile practice of closely tracking the market and recording its movements in a spreadsheet or on a piece of paper. I promise you will learn something from this process and if you don't, it hasn't cost you anything other than one or two pieces of graph paper. You were going to be watching the market anyway.

---

111. It used to be on the CME website but is harder to find these days.

As you gain experience in your market, your familiarity with its microstructure will improve your execution skills and it will give you the ability to recognize when the market is deviating from its normal behavior. This ability will prepare you for regime shifts or even allow you to recognize them at transition points when your market moves from rangebound to trending, or slow to fast. Expert traders have a detailed understanding of the microstructure of their market.

• • •

This concludes our discussion of microstructure. While microstructure is a topic that requires you to spend some time in the weeds, it is a critical area of study if you want to be a real expert in your market. You cannot expect your genius trade idea generation skills to carry you. You also need to be excellent when it comes to execution (and risk management).

A solid understanding of microstructure will improve your executions, increase the payout on your good ideas and reduce the cost of your bad ones. Even if you are confident in your knowledge of your market's microstructure, be on the lookout for changes and stay abreast of developments that might change how your market behaves. Simple changes to market microstructure can often lead to significant changes in your P&L and can turn profitable strategies into duds.

Now, let's move to the next step. In Chapter 9, I will tell you how I stay in touch with the narrative, and how that helps me forecast future moves and come up with trade ideas.

UNDERSTAND NARRATIVE

*Step two towards becoming
an expert in your market*

*In my whole life, I have known no wise people who didn't
read all the time – none, zero. I've gotten paid a lot over
the years for reading through the newspapers.*

CHARLIE MUNGER

This chapter will explain how to study narrative and fundamentals, and how to use this knowledge to better forecast short-term market direction. Excellent traders have an expert-level knowledge of the primary narrative and competing sub-narratives that drive their market. They understand the importance of the story the market is telling and can see, hear and feel when that story is changing. They know what is common knowledge, and what is not.

Once you understand the microstructure of your market and the basics of who moves the market, and how and when it moves, you should work on your understanding of what moves it, and why. The *what* and the *why* of market movements are never simple and as you gain experience, you will realize more and more that many explanations in the financial press are way off base.

The narrative is the story the market tells itself to explain movements in price. Like any good story, there is usually the main plot and then a few sub-plots. The main arc is the most important to understand because markets tend to focus on one thing at a time. But you also need to be ready for the next story as it elbows today's narrative out of the way. Here's how Bruce Kovner explains it in Market Wizards[112]:

> One of the jobs of a good trader is to imagine alternative scenarios. I try to form many different mental pictures of what the world should be like and wait for one of them to be confirmed. You keep trying them on one at a time. Inevitably, most of these pictures will turn out to be wrong — that is, only a few elements of the picture may prove correct. But then, all of a sudden, you will find that in one picture, nine out of ten elements click. That scenario then becomes your image of the world reality.

Understanding narrative is what most people used to call fundamental analysis but there is an important nuance. Narrative analysis is about studying not just what *you* think is the story, but (more importantly) what story market players are telling and what story the market itself is trying to tell. When it is done well, narrative analysis is a coherent and fluid combination of ever-changing macroeconomic fundamentals and behavioral factors. It is often about nailing down the one, most important story the market wants to trade.

For example, 2010 to 2012 was a remarkable period in FX markets as the market watched the near implosion of the eurozone at the same time as the US Federal Reserve enacted a series of quantitative easing (QE) programs. The eurozone crisis was bearish EUR and US QE was bearish USD. During this period, EURUSD was known as "two garbage trucks colliding" because both currencies had huge issues.

The interesting thing about trading that period, though, was that one story or the other clearly dominated most of the time. The market was either freaking out about the eurozone or going bananas over US QE but it was usually clear which theme was in the driver's seat. This is typical. It is very difficult for markets to hold two competing themes in its collective hivemind at once, and so the focus oscillates back and forth instead of going in two directions at once.

Understanding the narrative cycle is important because when you are good at it, it is a critical tool that helps you identify turning points and trends. You see the psychology and storytelling at work in the market and you can predict

112. Jack Schwager, Market Wizards (1989).

where price is going to go. Surprisingly, the **narrative often turns before price** because price has momentum of its own and a propensity to overshoot.

Speculators invested in a trend have confirmation bias and will ignore the changing narrative until the turn in price forces them to pay attention. Those turning points when the narrative has changed but price remains in the old trend can be some of the most exciting and profitable moments in trading.

Figure 9.1 shows the general narrative cycle:

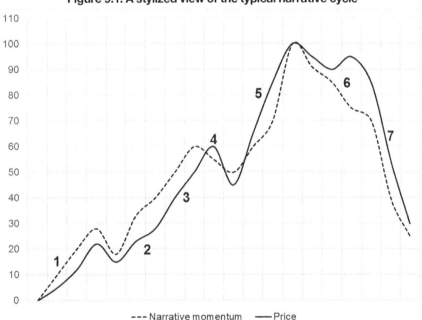

Figure 9.1: A stylized view of the typical narrative cycle

The numbers in figure 9.1 refer to the following section in which I will briefly describe each phase of the narrative cycle. You might recognize this as similar to other cycle analysis like the panic/euphoria model or the famous SELL? SELL? SELL? BUY! BUY! comic by Kal. It also rhymes a fair bit with Elliott Wave analysis[113].

---

113. Elliott Wave is an esoteric form of technical analysis. I studied it for a while and found its general approach useful but its specifics too subjective, arbitrary and confirmation bias-y. If you're bullish: There's a wave count for that! If you're bearish: There's a wave count for that too.

UNDERSTAND THE NARRATIVE CYCLE

It is important to note when reading this that the narrative cycle operates on many time fractals. There are the big macroeconomic narratives but there are also sometimes much shorter narrative cycles that can last as little as 24 hours. Often news or economic data will appear to be important but then run out of steam very swiftly as the market pivots back to the main story.

Picture a web of interconnected narratives with one or two dominating and the rest all swirling around and vying for attention. The goal is to determine what stories are driving your market now and what stories will jockey for position and come out ahead in the future. Traders with more experience will recognize the stage of the narrative intuitively and will often have a strong sense of when a story is running out of gas as the signposts are often similar at various stages of the narrative cycle. Ben Hunt (*Epsilon Theory*) is one of the kings of understanding, parsing and forecasting the narrative (or zeitgeist). I strongly recommend you check out his material if you want to excel in narrative analysis.

Each stage of every narrative cycle will look and feel familiar in many ways, even when the stories themselves will be radically different each time. Kind of like a Hollywood movie that follows a standard three act arc but with different characters, setting and plot. Let's go through the seven stages of the narrative cycle described by Figure 9.1.

Stage 1: Under the radar. At this point, there is a new narrative forming, but very few traders have heard about it. Some smart, independent thinkers and research-oriented people are talking about it and a few contrarians are putting on the position. There are usually a few pullbacks as initial believers have low confidence. Traders testing the waters tend to get bored or jiggled out because the price is not moving their way or they just figure they're too early and don't want to waste time on a narrative that is not valid.

The Holy Grail of trading, of course, is to identify below-the-radar stories that will eventually become important market narratives. You want to be early to the good stories but if you are too early, you need to make sure you don't get bored and give up before the market catches on to the theme.

Stage 2: Momentum Builds. At this point, the narrative goes a bit viral (at least among professionals or experts) and price jumps or falls to reflect the new zeitgeist. My narrative cycle chart shows a bullish story driving the price of an asset upward but you can flip the whole thing for a bad news narrative. As the price jumps (often on a particular piece of news that suddenly clarifies what was previously still a foggy narrative), people take notice.

Remember that at every stage of the narrative cycle, there is a dynamic interplay between price and narrative. The story drives the price and the price drives the story and often it is hard to tell which one is causing the movement. For example, say a stock has a good story but it's still in Stage 1 of the narrative cycle. Nobody is paying attention. A fund manager reads some three-week old research and decides he loves the story. He starts buying stock and liquidity is poor. The price rallies 4%. Some stale shorts stop out and the fund manager keeps buying and soon the stock is up 11% over the course of two days.

Because the stock rallied, it appears on a few radars (many firms and individuals run scans for stocks with unusual volatility) and this generates some new interest. Traders and investors look it up and some of them like what they see (great story!) and that triggers more buying. In this little description, the price is now feeding the narrative, not the other way around. The narrative already existed three weeks ago.

As momentum builds and the stock hits (for example) a 60-day high, trend followers and CTAs will start to buy. This feedback loop where changes in price influence investor expectations, which influence the narrative, which influences the price, is a form of reflexivity. Reflexivity is a concept from sociology that was transferred over to finance by George Soros. It is a fancier way of saying "circularity" or "feedback loops".

As momentum buying feeds the narrative and feeds on itself, we enter Stage 3.

Stage 3: The Primary Trend. This phase is where the narrative drumbeat takes hold and there are more and more converts lined up behind the apostles from Stage 1. Pullbacks are bought and the news reinforces the price which reinforces the trend which reinforces the buying. This stage is often the most profitable in a strong narrative because Stage 3 can last a surprisingly long time. Just because a narrative is well-known, that does not mean it's exhausted.

Stage 3 involves a lot of hype, usually from financial media and tourists who have joined the party fairly early. Again, just because there is hype, don't think the story is over. The hype phase can accompany dramatic price moves as demand outstrips supply for an extended period and the market ignores bad news and doubles down on good news.

Stage 4: First cracks. At this stage, some cracks appear. Bad news hits that threatens the narrative. The story is crowded and early entrants think maybe the story is over so they take some profits. There is a meaningful pullback in price. This pullback shakes off the weaker and more recent buyers but those that believe in the narrative appear on the bid and the price stabilizes. Slowly, the importance of the bad news dissipates and price climbs back towards the highs.

Stage 5: The final hype wave. As price breaks through and makes new highs, the narrative often goes into overdrive. Longs are emboldened by the price action and a strong feeling of FOMO comes over anyone that is not participating. Depending on the story, you will often see the narrative cross over from financial media to the mainstream media at this point if the narrative is interesting and important enough.

Non-experts will join the party (retail and macro tourists) and this will push price aggressively higher. Stage 5 is usually the most surprising and volatile part of the narrative cycle as sellers step away and buyers get desperate. In Elliott Wave, this is also Wave 5 and Elliott Wave Theory warns that Wave 5 can often be the most impulsive part of a move. This stage is often characterized by choppy, jumpy, volatile moves, euphoria and overshooting. Trend following systems add all the way up.

Stage 6: The Peak and the Turn. The top in the narrative and price can be a long drawn-out process or an impulsive overshoot and collapse. Often, it's like the climax in a movie with a huge flashy rip higher followed by a rapid reversal that catches everyone on the wrong side.

Excellent traders will realize there has been a meaningful turn in the narrative here, even when price continues to make new highs. Bad traders hate to give up on winning trades and great stories and will fall victim to powerful confirmation bias. As long as price continues to rise, most traders will ignore information that goes against the narrative. It is a skill to filter out what matters and what does not, of course, because powerful bull markets often climb a wall of bad news.

Eventually, price will start to turn and suddenly bad news from four hours or four weeks ago pops back into the mind of the market and everyone is like: "What the hell am I doing still long up here! Things have changed." Then everyone reaches for the SELL button at once and BOOM. It gaps lower and the top is in.

Quite often, the price rise itself will also change the supply and demand dynamic at this stage. There is a saying that "the best cure for high prices is high prices", which means that higher prices ultimately reduce demand and increase supply and that eventually leads to lower prices.

For example, when the price of oil rises or falls gradually, consumer and producer behavior does not change much. On the other hand, when the price of oil explodes higher from $50 to $120 (like it did in 2008), producers rush to bring on new supply and consumers simultaneously cut their demand because they can't afford to fill up their SUVs. They drive less. These shifts in supply and demand are not instantaneous, so price can continue to rise even as new supply works its way into the system and demand disappears. Then, suddenly, the new supply runs into falling demand and prices whoosh lower.

Furthermore, depending on the market, the higher price can also have other macroeconomic impacts that will lead to lower prices in the future. For example, a rise in the euro might lead to more accommodative ECB policy or a huge ramp up in Tesla stock might spur Elon Musk to sell stock in a secondary offering. Be sure to understand what price levels in your market might lead to major or non-linear changes in supply or demand.

If you are expert in your market and keenly attuned to its driving narrative, you will recognize moments when the story has changed but price is not yet paying attention. Those can be some of the juiciest setups in finance.

These tops can be false break spike highs that happen in a flash, or drawn out periods of distribution that trace out triple, quintuple or even septuple tops before finally capitulating lower. When you see a turn in the narrative you can use your knowledge of technical reversal patterns to help you align your strategy (turning bearish near the highs due to a change in the narrative) with your tactics (finding high-leverage setups that allow you to test your theory that the narrative has turned without risking a ton if you are wrong).

Stage 7: The End. As a narrative expires, people lose interest and only those with bad discipline hang on. Shorts hammer the price down and longs slowly but surely get out. Market themes are like fashion trends. The market's interest is fickle and limited. People get bored of a theme, and they move on. Sometimes this will be justified by fundamentals and sometimes it will simply be that a sexier, more interesting theme came along.

That is the narrative cycle. I am describing something clean and visible but the tricky part is that these cycles are anything but clean and are only easy to see in hindsight. As you gain experience, though, you will start to see these cycles play out in real time and will learn to anticipate and act before the cycle moves to its next stage.

Remember, this section is not about long-term investing. It is about understanding the current equilibrium so that as new information arrives, you can capitalize. If you know where you are in the story and understand current positioning, you will have an edge as the cycle moves from stage to stage. These narrative cycles can last hours, days or weeks.

> **Understand the stories the market is telling**
> **itself and learn to identify when the market is**
> **falling in or out of love with a narrative.**

• • •

Let's look at a very simple example of how understanding the narrative can help you when news comes out. You have been trading the stock of a hydrogen-powered truck manufacturer for a while and it has been in a steady up trend. The market has attached a huge premium to electric and autonomous vehicle stocks and the stock you trade benefits from the halo effect of TSLA. The main narrative is that autonomous vehicles have massive upside and almost any market cap can be justified.

With this stock, there is a bearish counternarrative humming in the background. That story is that the company has not yet delivered a single working truck to any customer and behind the scenes there is strife inside the company as the founder is viewed by some as a classic visionary entrepreneur and by others as a marketing genius with no technical skill. In contrast to TSLA, which has produced thousands of working automobiles, the narrative of the off-the-rails visionary founder has more potential weight because the company has yet to prove itself capable.

A famous short seller comes out with a detailed description of exactly how the founder of the company has used marketing and outright deception to convince people of the company's future success despite repeated product failures behind the scenes.

Short sellers come out with reports like this all the time. Some are credible, some are not. Some hit the stock on the open and it rallies back by the end of the day. Some are the start of a long slow march to zero. How do you decide what to do?

Obviously, the first thing you do is read the report. You are already an expert on the stock and the narratives that drive it. In this case, you know the worries about the founder have been whispered for a while and therefore this short seller's report will have more force than if a comparable report was issued on TSLA. You sell the stock short on the open and as fears mount, the stock (which opened down 7%) closes down 20%.

You are expert in this stock so you know the market's prior short position has been nearly eliminated over the course of the recent violent up trend. You know from all your reading that the high-profile bears mostly gave up a few months ago. The chart is a perfect island reversal day as the stock gapped up to make a new all-time high the day before the short seller's report came out. Your stop loss is clear: If the stock goes back above today's open, something is wrong with the idea, and you're out.

The first price a security trades after news comes out is called the NewsPivot. These are critical price points going forward. NewsPivots become significant reference points in the mind of the market and if price subsequently recaptures the NewsPivot, it often means that either a) the news wasn't all that important or b) larger medium and long-term players are using the news as a liquidity event to go the other way. If bad news comes out and your stock goes back above the NewsPivot: *watch out!* We will talk more about NewsPivots in Chapter 10.

So now you have:

- Abrupt flip from bullish narrative to bearish narrative
- Large long position and almost no shorts
- Textbook island reversal
- NewsPivot held and stock closed on the lows

Given all this, you figure this is a multi-day trade. Today is Tuesday. Knowing that historically the big, impulsive moves in the stock last an average of three days, and considering you don't like to take positions over the weekend, you set your stop loss at the NewsPivot + 1% and plan to take back the short either Friday morning or after another 15% drop. Naturally, you closely follow the narrative from here too and try to assess whether the company's responses to the short seller's report are credible or maybe just make things worse.

• • •

Whether it's a single stock or a macroeconomic narrative you follow, the idea is the same. You must understand the current equilibrium as well as anyone else does, and then when new information comes in or the narrative starts to turn, you are on it.

Here's how to be an expert on narrative.

1. **Read like a fiend with a focus on quality.** Seek out analysis, thought processes, trade ideas, event previews and unique insights. Avoid long-term forecasts, market summaries and recaps. You need to find forward-looking analysis that contains useful, non-duplicative information and ideas and incorporate that information and analysis into your own process.

   There is so much information available now, filtering has become an important skill. You can waste your whole day reading bearish NAS-DAQ tweets and pointless market recaps if you are not selective. It's important to curate a good list of reading and news sources. Then keep refining it and improving it over time. Learn who is good in your market and get your hands on their write-ups.

   As you gain experience as a trader, learn which names are worth reading and which ones are not. Do not simply take everything you read at face value. You can find the most intelligent permabear analysis from various funds but what value does that analysis have if the writer has been bearish for 10 years and never changes his view? Consider what you are reading, but also who wrote it.

   Reading obviously teaches you different thought processes and directly yields new information. It also gives you a sense of the zeitgeist. What narratives are dominant right now? Understanding the dominant narrative, and where your market stands in the narrative cycle are two important skills.

2. **Develop a network.** To form a strong network, you need to both give and receive information and ideas. Try to find peers and mentors either within your organization or online. No human being can scour all the information available. The better your network, the less likely you will miss key information.

   The way to form a strong network is by giving, not by asking for information. Post interesting comments in a message board. If you work at a bank, blast your best ideas to clients. If you trade from home, post your trades on a bulletin board or on Twitter.

To build a network, be authentic and give more than you take.

Building a network takes a long time. You will not get much traction at first because nobody knows you and nobody cares what the new guy has to say. Once in a while, an idea you send out into the universe might get some feedback. Over time, you will connect to a few people, then a few more. But it's exponential. If you work hard at it and find a way to authentically connect to people, after maybe 10 years you will have a huge network of followers or contacts.

To build a network, play the long game. It can't be done overnight.

Building a network is hard, frustrating work. Gains are tiny at first. But network effects scale geometrically. The eventual benefits are tremendous.

3. **Study the central banks.** If you are a macro trader, this is obviously key, but even if you trade single name stocks you should still understand what is going on with the major central banks (Fed, ECB and PBoC). Overall global liquidity is the number one factor driving all global asset prices much of the time and you need to have a decent sense of what is happening on that front. Central bank speeches are boring but necessary material for good traders.

   If you trade interest rates or FX, you should read every central bank speech for the countries you trade. A huge part of the narrative in rates and FX is driven by the central banks and you should know which central bankers matter, what their bias is, how their views have evolved and what they think right now.

   You don't need to forecast what the central banks are going to do. But you have to understand the current environment and what any future actions mean. Some of the best trades come from simply preparing for a central bank meeting by reading all the available materials and then going into the event with zero position.

   Then, you react to the news with a solid and complete understanding of what the new information means and how it will affect prices.

The only way you can do this is by reading and studying beforehand. If you trade macro, each FOMC and ECB meeting is a major exam. Are you going to study for a few days in advance? Or just cram a few bank previews the morning of, and hope for the best?

Even if you specialize in TSLA or crude oil, you still need to understand the Fed because its actions and statements are a major input into the price of those assets.

4. **Find the subject matter experts.** Who is the best analyst in your market? Can you get your hands on their writing? Much of the best Wall Street analysis can be found online and you can follow some of the best minds in finance on Twitter.

   As you read more and more about your domain, you will start to pick up on who is smart, who is biased, who is useless, and who to follow. This takes time. Also: talk to people! Go online and ask people on Reddit or on Twitter (for example): "Who is the best FX analyst out there? Who is a must-follow?" etc.

   As I mentioned earlier, building a curated list of experts to read and follow is an important part of your effort in understanding the narrative.

"How to understand the narrative" is fairly easy for me to explain but requires significant time and effort from you. You will notice over time that your ability to read the story the market is telling gets better and better. Soon, you will start to get a sense of what is about to happen, before it happens.

The narrative is the internal story of your market. But outside your market, there are hundreds of other stories being told in other markets, and each of those stories has some loose (or possibly tight) connection to your market. Global growth expectations, for example, will impact Canadian growth expectations and that will impact Bank of Canada policy and the narrative around Canadian interest rates and the Canadian dollar. At the same time, global growth expectations will influence demand forecasts for copper and the price of copper itself. Therefore, one might expect there to be a correlation between copper and the Canadian dollar (CAD), both driven by a third variable: Global growth expectations.

There are literally 100s of these connections all permeating the impossibly complex system that is the global economy and global markets. These connections create a huge matrix of correlations between markets and fortunately for traders, many of the correlations operate with various leads and lags. So copper might move right now and then CAD moves two hours later. When lead/lag trading works, it can feel like you have been given the answers to the test.

DRIVERS AND CATALYSTS

What drives the product or security you trade? What drivers matter for your particular strategy? This question can be fairly easy to answer for some traders and extremely difficult for others. For example, if you think of yourself as a global macro trader and your focus is on interest rate products, the answer is fairly easy. Growth, inflation and global monetary policy are the main drivers you need to worry about.

When you know the drivers, the catalysts are pretty obvious. For the trader concerned with growth, inflation and monetary policy, the catalysts are usually economic data and central bank meetings.

This is all theory, of course, and is easy on paper but hard in real life. While a strong US economic data point should be a catalyst for a higher dollar, for example, there are plenty of days when data comes in strong and the USD goes down.

There are many types of market catalyst. Here is a list of some biggies, working from most macro to least.

Market catalysts

1. International geopolitics (e.g., trade war, G20 Summit, global pandemic, OPEC meeting, military conflict)
2. Domestic politics (elections, coups, scandals, passage of new laws, court decisions)
3. Central bank action or speeches
4. Economic data
5. Company news
   a. Earnings
   b. Analyst up/downgrades
   c. Personnel changes (especially CEO or CFO)
   d. Capital structure (dividends, buybacks, secondary issuance)

6. Catalyst in a correlated market

7. Technical breakout

8. Time of day, week or month

The first five are easy to understand. If you are an expert in your market, you will know upcoming events in each of those five categories that might impact your trading.

The bare minimum for every professional trader is to know all the economic and market events that could impact the securities they trade. When an economic number is coming out, you should know in advance and you should be ready. If your stock reports earnings tomorrow morning, you should know that. You should be prepared with a list of scenarios so that the second the news hits, you can react intelligently.

> **If you are the person on a trading floor yelling "Is this bullish or bearish?!" when news comes out… You are not an Alpha Trader.**

You must be properly prepared, have an expert level of knowledge, and understand the narrative. Then, when important news comes out, you can react quickly and take massive, determined action.

Worse than the trader that does not know if news is bullish or bearish for a particular market is the trader that is not even aware of a scheduled release. I have heard traders yell: "Whoa, what just happened to USDJPY!?" after it jumped 15 points higher on an economic release like Consumer Confidence. They didn't even know the number was coming out. *That's not good!*

While macro traders have the luxury of at least knowing what the catalysts are (even if it's not always obvious what impact they will have), in other products, the drivers and catalysts are not as clear. Crypto is the most extreme example. The market is so new and has few fundamental anchors, so the drivers are mostly sentiment and technicals (charts). This is not true all the time as new adopters (corporations or financial institutions adding crypto to their balance sheet or approved products), forking and other events can be fundamental catalysts.

Because the short-term drivers in crypto are poorly understood, and regularly-scheduled events like economic data and central bank meetings don't matter much, catalysts often feel random. There is the occasional scheduled halving or obvious fundamental catalyst visible in advance, but mostly crypto is driven by sentiment shifts and randomly-timed news. That said, you could also argue that the same is true with most stocks, most of the time. For every move that is logically driven by a fundamental driver or catalyst like earnings, there are ten that are impossible to explain with any kind of macro or microeconomic logic.

Take time to understand the fundamental and technical drivers of your particular security.

Item 6 in the list above, "Catalyst in a correlated market" relates to the idea of lead/lag and correlation. For example, if you are long USDCAD and the pair has been trading with an 80% negative correlation to crude oil over the past 12 months, you should be aware if there is an OPEC meeting coming up. OPEC meetings often lead to large changes in the price of oil and as such can lead to large changes in USDCAD. If you want to be an expert in USDCAD, you should read everything you can about the upcoming OPEC meeting.

If you are long Citibank stock (C) and J.P. Morgan (JPM) reports tonight, you should be ready and know what to expect. You should know not just market expectation for JPM's numbers but also whether or not C tends to move in sympathy with JPM, on JPM earnings day. Understanding these ins and outs of how things trade and move are key. I will discuss this in more detail shortly in the section "Cross-market correlation".

Item 7 on the list, "Technical breakout", is important, but don't overestimate the importance of every tech level that you see. There is always another level nearby and not every break of a 10-day high or low or trendline or Fibonacci level has meaning. If you read about your market and talk to and follow other traders, you will start to get a sense for the big levels.

A big level isn't a level that is important to you, it is a level that is important to the market. This is a big distinction. You need to have your own views and thoughts but Alpha traders are also inside the mind of the market and know what matters most to the market as a whole.

This concept is best captured by Keynes' beauty contest analogy from *The General Theory of Employment, Interest and Money* (1936). Keynes asks us to imagine a newspaper which holds a contest where readers are rewarded for choosing which contestant will be chosen by the most other readers. The task is not to choose the most beautiful woman, but instead to choose the woman *others* will think is most beautiful. Sometimes that's the same woman, but not always!

Participants in complex, multiplayer games with incomplete information (like trading, poker, and bridge) play a superior metagame where they understand not just their own strategy and preferences but also the strategy and preferences of the other players. If everyone you talk to is talking about the 122^00 level in 10-year bond futures, you should have that level marked on your charts and you should closely observe how the contract trades around there. The market converging to the opinion that a particular level is important does not happen all that often but when it does you should pay attention.

If that level breaks, the price action afterwards has important implications for the future. A key level that breaks and follows through is indicative of a trending market, while a false break of a level everyone is watching (aka, a Slingshot Reversal[114]) is one of the best indicators for trend reversal.

**Strong up trends hold above major support,
and they break through major resistance.**

Always monitor how your market behaves at important levels. If a market has been trending and everyone is focused on a particular pullback level, that level should hold. If it does not, this may signal the trend is out of gas.

The final catalyst in that list earlier was Item 8, "Time of day, week or month". Often you will notice that trends exhaust themselves and turn around at the end of the day, week or month. For example, in months where the US stock market is up 3% or more, GBPUSD frequently rallies into month end and then sells off in the first week of the new month[115]. Figure 9.2 is a chart of how GBPUSD trades around the turn of the month, at the end of months where US stocks rallied 3% or more:

The point of this little section is not to tell you how FX trades on the last day of the month—though if you trade FX, you definitely should know this!—it is to show you a good example of how time of day, week or month can impact price. In this case, the month end effect determines the direction of the USD into month end and then the effect unwinds (mean reversion) in the first week of the following month.

The reason price very often turns at the end of a day, week or month is that many orders in the market are timed that way. A large CTA that needs to buy 1,000,000 shares of a company will start its VWAP at the open and end it at

---

114. Google "Brent Donnelly Slingshot Reversal" for a full definition and explanation.

115. This is caused by large hedging by foreign asset managers at month end which climaxes at 4 p.m. London time on the last day of the month. More detail on this in Chapter 12.

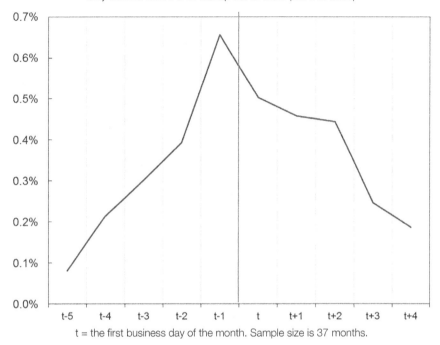

Figure 9.2: Average performance of GBPUSD in the 10 days around the turn of the month

Only months where SPX was up 3% or more (2010 to 2020)

t = the first business day of the month. Sample size is 37 months.

the close. A large corporation that needs to buy 1 billion USDCAD will tell the bank doing the trade to get it done by the end of the day. Month-end is a time when many real money investors rebalance so they will complete all their activity by the end of the day on the last day of the month, etc.

Very large orders can often dominate the supply/demand profile of an asset for a short period. Most large order executions take place during the most liquid period of the day. When that period draws to a close, it is reasonable to assume the supply/demand profile for the asset might change. Mean reversion kicks in as the large order is done and the market drifts back toward equilibrium. In other words, with the big buyer out of the way, the price can drift lower.

In stocks, there are patterns around the start and end of the month and around options expiry (triple witching, etc.) The takeaway here is that trends often mean revert at the turn of the week, the turn of the month or another key time such as options expiry. If you are looking to fade a strong trend, these are often good moments to take a shot. This is an example of something I think it's important to remember:

**There does not have to be an obvious exogenous catalyst
for every market move, reversal, peak, or bottom.**

When you discuss a trade idea with someone and they say "OK, sure, but what's the catalyst?" ... It is OK to say, "I don't know." Not every move has a logical macro catalyst. Market catalysts are often endogenous as supply and demand change for reasons unrelated to macro or fundamentals[116]. A market high can happen simply because the last buyer bought and the market has run out of buyers. Or because a single huge buyer is done buying (as in the GBPUSD example above).

When there are suddenly no buyers in the market, this is called a buyer's strike. A market that was grinding higher for days can often plummet suddenly. The catalyst for a sell-off after an aggressive up trend or ramp higher can sometimes simply be: no more buyers.

CROSS-MARKET CORRELATION

An important driver or catalyst for your market can be activity and moves in another security or asset class. Try to identify how price action in other markets may send clues about your market. To take an obvious example, if gold spikes $25 in three minutes and silver is unchanged, would you rather be long or short silver? Probably long.

While correlated products tend to move in sympathy with one other, there are usually leads and lags. If AAPL rips higher on good product launch news, can you find the sympathy plays before other traders do? Display makers and semiconductor stocks might benefit too.

This style of trading, where you follow many markets and try to determine which ones are potentially leading or lagging is called intermarket, cross-market or lead/lag analysis. This type of analysis can give you a significant edge, though it has become mainstream in recent years and does not have the edge it once did.

I use cross-market analysis all day, every day; it is a central pillar of my trading process. If I am trading USDCAD, I know all the products that are correlated with USDCAD (e.g., oil, US/Canada interest rate differential, Canadian equities, copper, gold, etc.) and I watch them all closely. I do this by setting up

---

116. Endogenous: having an internal cause or origin. Not attributable to any external factor. The opposite of exogenous.

a series of separate charts which overlay the main asset (USDCAD) with the correlated variables on top like you see in Figure 9.3.

Figure 9.3: Canadian dollar (solid line) vs. S&P futures (lighter, dotted line)
Daily, January to early September 2020

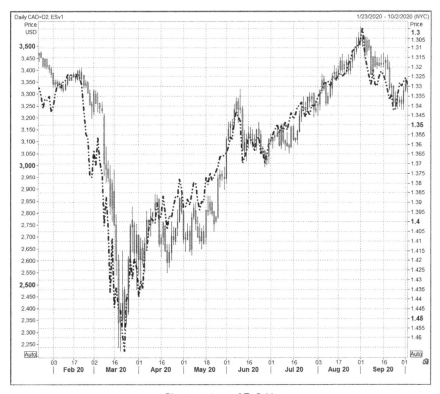

Chart courtesy of Refinitiv

You can see in Figure 9.3 the remarkable and steady relationship between US stocks and the Canadian dollar in 2020. Often, especially in periods of high volatility and uncertainty, correlations rise and everything seems to depend on risk appetite and not much else. With COVID-19 raging for most of 2020, this was one of those periods. Note that S&P futures often moved before CAD, providing some excellent signals for FX traders.

Australia is heavily reliant on Chinese growth and commodity prices because a significant portion of its GDP comes from commodity production and export. Therefore, there is a strong connection between the price of copper and the Australian dollar (AUD). Notice in Figure 9.4 that in July 2020 you can see how copper moved before AUD, providing an excellent bullish signal for the currency.

Figure 9.4: Australian dollar (solid line) vs. copper futures (dotted line)
Hourly, June to early September 2020

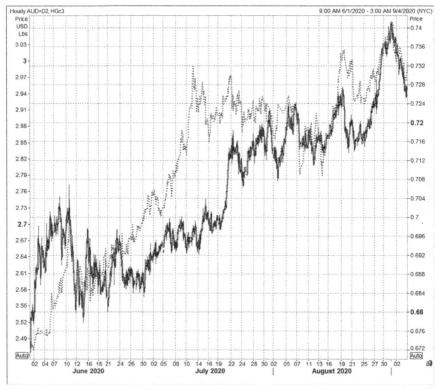

Chart courtesy of Refinitiv

Let's look at one more example. In Figure 9.5, we look at S&P 500 futures (the US stock market) against the equity volatility index (VIX). I inverted the VIX for this overlay because the standard relationship is that when stocks go down, volatility and the VIX go up (and vice versa).

Generally, when stocks rise, volatility falls and when stocks fall, volatility rises. This is true almost all the time because investors buy puts to protect themselves as markets fall. In a normal rising market, investors sell calls to take profit, earn income and monetize gains. When vol rises as stocks rise, it can be a warning sign… Something weird is going on.

Any strange behavior in markets or change in reaction function should always pique your interest. Whenever something weird happens in the market, go on high alert and investigate. Try to find out why. In Figure 9.6, volatility was rising, even as stocks rose in September 2020, because a large institutional

**Figure 9.5: S&P 500 futures (candles, right y-axis)
vs. VIX inverted (dotted line left y-axis)**
June 15 to September 1, 2020

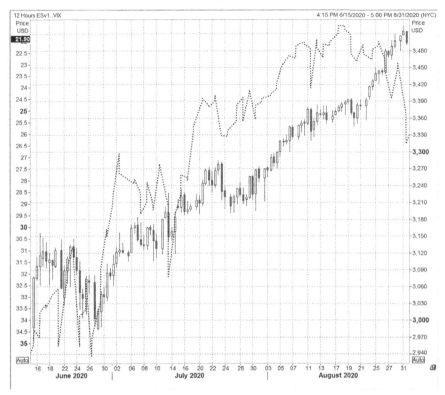

Chart courtesy of Refinitiv

player and a herd of retail investors were going nuts buying calls. This is behavior you see in bubbly and overhyped environments. Can you guess what stocks did next?

See Figure 9.6.

This is a textbook case of lead/lag trading. The rise in the VIX sent a clear and strong signal that something strange was going on and the rally in the stock market was highly suspect. This is not hindsight, I wrote about it at the time, before stocks dumped.

Here is my complete analysis of that moment (published in my daily on September 2, 2020) so you can see what other factors I incorporated into my thinking.

Figure 9.6: S&P 500 futures (solid line, right y-axis) vs. VIX inverted (dotted line left y-axis)
June 15 to September 30, 2020

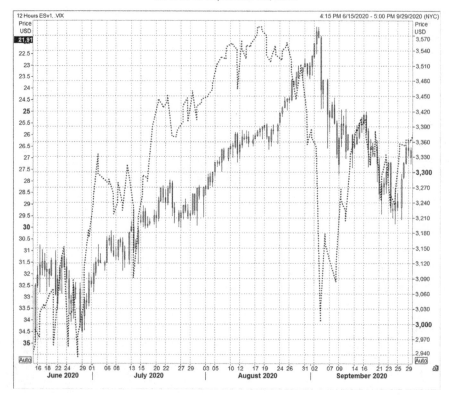

Chart courtesy of Refinitiv

I feel that today or tomorrow will be a short-term peak for this mega reflation trade. If I am correct, it would mean NASDAQ, lumber, gold, EURUSD and USD in general will start a meaningful correction in the next 48 hours. A few reasons:

1. Fed doesn't sound as dovish as I thought they would. Yesterday, Clarida had the opportunity to tee up September and did not.

2. **Vol rising along with stocks can be a sign of danger.**

3. Breadth in equity markets has been horrendous.

4. Real rates not making new lows.

5. Gold not making new highs. Actually, it's making lower highs. Gold has been trading like a risky asset.

6. 1.2000 target reached in EURUSD. EURUSD has been moving up and down with stocks.

7. September is historically the worst month for risk assets (weak seasonality).

8. USDCAD at key levels after doing a full round trip. USDCAD has also been highly correlated with the S&P 500.

You can see that the VIX UP / Stocks UP was one of many factors that went into my decision to turn bearish stocks on September 1. Each bit of information adds to the last and eventually (sometimes) you have enough building blocks stacked up that it results in a solid trade idea.

The more you understand your market, the better feel you will get over time as to what it means when divergences build between primary and correlated markets. I always feel more confident putting on a trade if the most important correlated variables are stable or moving in my direction.

For example, if I have a strong view that the Canadian dollar is set to rally based on my economic and technical analysis, but then I see oil has just dropped $2 in the past 30 minutes, I will probably wait on my CAD execution. In contrast, if I am bullish CAD and planning to get long and then notice crude rallying hard, I will hurry up and buy the CAD ASAP. If I am about to go short NFLX but then see DIS and GOOG rip higher, I will hold off and wait for DIS and GOOG to stabilize or for NFLX to catch up before I go short. And so on.

Correlated variables give you a hint as to where your product is going. But not the answer.

As discussed earlier, these cross-market relationships often exist because there is a third variable driving two correlated products. For example, gold and the US dollar have a common driver: US real interest rates. If the world thinks the Fed is going to do more QE and push real rates lower, you might see that reflected in higher gold first and then a lower USD shortly after.

All other things being equal, lower real rates mean stronger gold and a weaker dollar. But these markets will not all move in perfect sync. Rates and gold might be on the move but a big buyer of US dollars may be in the market, so the USD doesn't move. Then, when the buyer of US dollars is done, the USD will catch up.

Lead/lag traders look at the entire board and hunt for an overall pattern.

Then, they find particular asset prices that don't make sense, and try to position before those out-of-line assets move back into line.

Think of the markets as one huge, interconnected organism where information influences many assets at once, but not all at the exact same time. If a market moves and that market is correlated to yours, pay attention. What does it mean?

You can use common sense to come up with a list of correlated markets fairly easily. When you read articles about your market, do they mention other assets? You will often see a headline like: "Australian dollar rallies on China growth optimism". This tells you someone out there is equating AUD with Chinese growth. What are some other proxies for Chinese growth? Iron ore, the Shanghai Composite Index, FXI (the China A Shares ETF, which trades in NY time), copper, BHP and FCX (mining stocks), etc.

Every individual security or market is part of a universe of other securities and markets and they all orbit and influence one another. Figure 9.7 is a grid of examples to get you started.

Figure 9.7: Examples of correlated variables in different asset classes

Asset class	Asset	Variable 1	Variable 2	Variable 3
Equities	S&P 500	VIX	Dow Transports	AAPL
	PENN	DKNG	CHDN	IGT
	FCX	BHP	TCK	SCCO
	XLF	AMP	WFC	MET
Currencies	EURUSD	Germany/US rate diff.	Gold	Italian bonds
	USDJPY	US 10-year rates	Gold	Nikkei
	AUDUSD	Copper	Australia/US rate diff.	Shanghai Composite Index
	USDCAD	Crude oil	Copper	Canada/US rate diff.
Commodities	Gold	US real rates	Silver	GG
	NYMEX crude	Brent crude	XLE	COP

If you have Bloomberg, you can play around with the CORR and CFND functions to find things that are correlated to your market, but it is more useful to use logic rather than data mining tools. Start with things that should logically be correlated to your market, then calculate the correlation to see if your guesses are correct[117]. You can also go to websites like: market-topology.com and mess around with their correlation tools. Just remember to use a logic filter because you can data mine all kinds of nonsensical correlations if you try hard enough!

Eventually, as you approach expert level in your product, slowly branch out from your market and learn more about a small list of correlated markets. For example, over many years of trading currencies, I have accumulated a ton of knowledge about markets outside of, but correlated to FX. This knowledge helps me better understand and trade the currency market.

For example, if you trade USDCAD, it's good to know what the TAS order type is in the oil market because oil is correlated to USDCAD. It's good to know how volumes and volatility are distributed throughout the day in the oil market, too. It's helpful to know when NYMEX crude closes. And so on. But if you are going to trade USDCAD, first you need to be a USDCAD expert. Later in your career, go learn the markets that orbit your main area of expertise.

Seek to understand any market that is correlated to yours. Search for the most stable and logical correlations and ignore transitory or nonsensical correlations, even if they look statistically strong.

A full discussion of lead/lag trading could fill an entire book. Study the behavior of correlated markets and watch how correlations change over time. Correlations are not static. Sometimes stocks and bonds go up and down together. Sometimes they are inversely correlated. Sometimes stocks go up and down with the dollar. Sometimes they are inversely correlated.

Closely follow a small list of markets correlated to your primary market and you will slowly get a feel for how markets move together, even as they do not move in perfect sync. Lead/lag is part art and part science, so you should expect that it will take a few years to get a feel for it. Once you do, you will sometimes feel like you can tell what is going to happen before it happens as you pick up on a strongly correlated, leading variable that drives your market for a while. Regimes where lead/lag works well can be highly satisfying and profitable trading periods.

---

117. Use correlation of daily changes, not correlation of levels, when calculating correlation. If you want to know more on this topic, just Google "levels vs. changes correlation". It's a big topic, beyond the scope of this book.

Lead/lag and correlation trading is not the holy grail. It is a popular systematic strategy, therefore much of the edge is now captured by computers. It is an input into a good discretionary trading process, not an entire discretionary trading process. When you understand the story that drives your market and you understand the catalysts and drivers that move prices, you are ready to start trading.

But where do trade ideas come from? That is probably the number one question I am asked by new traders. How do you come up with ideas? Where do you start? What is the process? Chapter 12 is called "Bringing it all together" and that's where I will take you from start to finish; from trade idea to execution to take profit to post-trade analysis.

But before we can bring it all together, we need to cover a few more topics. Next up: The importance of technical analysis, sentiment and positioning.

CHAPTER 10

UNDERSTAND TECHNICALS, SENTIMENT AND POSITIONING

*Step three towards becoming
an expert in your market*

S uccess in any complex game, puzzle, or battle relies on both intelligent strategy and effective tactics. Tactics are just as important as strategy yet are often overlooked. This chapter explains technical analysis, sentiment and positioning and shows how a superior understanding of these subjects will give you a significant tactical edge. To be clear, when it comes to trading, strategy means coming up with trade ideas and tactics means how you execute and implement those ideas.

Nearly all my trade ideas start from either microstructure or narrative. They never come from looking at a chart or from any form of technical analysis. And I never put on a trade purely because of sentiment or positioning. My highest conviction trades generally have multiple inputs, but they always start with fundamentals or microstructure and then get refined, streamlined (or filtered out) by other factors.

I use technical analysis, sentiment and positioning as timing tools, but not as trade selection tools. My thinking on this has evolved over the years partly because markets have evolved, but also because I have seen enough evidence to conclude that technical analysis is not a source of alpha or edge.

Charts are not a good forecasting tool.

There is a pretty tall pile of research to back this up. I'll give you a quick run-down of one paper called: "Are Random Strategies More Successful Than Technical Ones?"[118] They analyzed four popular technical strategies: RSI, MACD, mean reversion and momentum. They ran them against four major stock markets (USA, Germany, Italy and the UK) and compared the results to a strategy that chose entry and exit levels 100% randomly. Here is their conclusion:

> Our main result, which is independent of the market considered, is that standard trading strategies and their algorithms, based on the past history of the time series, although have occasionally the chance to be successful inside small temporal windows, on a large temporal scale perform on average not better than the purely random strategy, which, on the other hand, is also much less volatile. In this respect, for the individual trader, a purely random strategy represents a costless alternative to expensive professional financial consulting, being at the same time also much less risky, if compared to the other trading strategies.

There are entire books that go through all the major technical patterns and backtest them and come to the same result: technical analysis is not a good forecasting tool. I explained my philosophy on technical analysis when I discussed overreliance on simple indicators and apophenia. I want to make it clear though: I use technical analysis in my trading every day. I just don't use it to predict markets.

Technical analysis gives you an important set of tactical execution and risk management tools. It does not help you forecast market direction.

Good traders are quick to admit when they are wrong. They make leveraged, asymmetric bets. Technical analysis can help you do these things better and provide strong and clear signals of when it's time to give up on a bad idea or take profit on a good one.

---

118. Biondo, Pluchino, Rapisarda and Helbing. "Are Random Trading Strategies More Successful than Technical Ones?" (2013)

Believe it or not, the exact technical indicators you choose are not all that important. The mathematics and concept behind most technical indicators are similar. RSI, MACD, and oscillators all give you a similar feel for trend and momentum. Simple trendlines plus support and resistance work just as well as more complicated or convoluted methods. The more esoteric you get with your technical analysis, the more likely you are to find yourself wasting time in the weeds. Keep it simple!

Remember: alpha traders do not use technical analysis to predict the market, they use it to optimize execution and risk management.

Here are some of the techs I look at:

SIGNIFICANT REFERENCE POINTS

Significant reference points (SRPs) are levels that are likely to feature prominently in the mind of the market. These are levels a majority of market players view as important. As is the case in Keynes' beauty contest analogy, it is important to know not just what *you* think is important but what *others* think is important. Here are some standard SRPs.

NewsPivots

A NewsPivot is the last trade in a market before important, market moving news comes out. I find that NewsPivots are the most powerful reference points in trading. You should be aware of all NewsPivots in your markets. If AAPL is at $100 when good news comes out and the first trade after the news is $103, the gap is $100/$103 with the NewsPivot ($100) marking the bottom of the gap.

Remember that price is a momentary equilibrium determined by the sum of all known information in the universe. When new information appears, the market frantically tries to find the corresponding new equilibrium. If the market believes the news to be meaningful, it should abandon the old equilibrium from before the news came out (aka, the NewsPivot) and find a new one.

A return to, or through the NewsPivot is important information. It tells you: the market has rejected the news and the attempt to find a new equilibrium, and reverted back to its old happy place.

When news comes out, the market fumbles around in the dark as it tries to find a new balance between supply and demand. Buyers and sellers of various time frames jostle for position. The first price that trades *after* news comes out is also a significant reference point going forward. Figure 10.1 is an example of a NewsPivot and price gap:

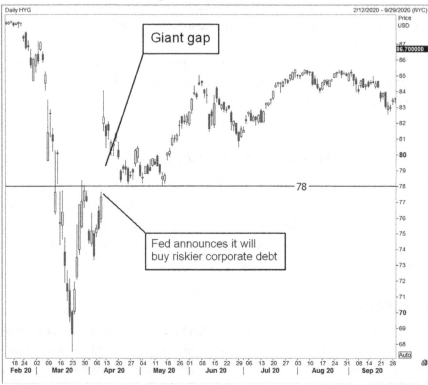

Figure 10.1: HYG gaps higher on news then successfully tests and holds the NewsPivot

Chart courtesy of Refinitiv

In the chart of HYG (Figure 10.1, the high-yield corporate bond ETF), you can see that on the day the Fed announced their intention to buy high-yield bonds, HYG gapped massively higher. It closed just below $78 the day before then opened at $82 the day of the announcement. Therefore, the NewsPivot (price before the news) is $78 and the other side of the gap is $82. These are both significant reference points going forward.

In the weeks that followed, HYG closed the gap and retested the NewsPivot. The NewsPivot held perfectly and HYG never fell back below $78 despite four separate tests.

Astute traders of HYG would be aware of the closing level before the Fed's announcement and would also be aware that that level is likely to be massive support. A simple strategy of buying just above the NewsPivot with a stop below the NewsPivot would have worked perfectly.

Always take note of the level of any market you trade going into a major event. This level is likely to be a significant reference point going forward.

Support and resistance

The next type of significant reference point to identify is simple support and resistance. If a stock is in a downtrend, but it starts to build a base and bounces off $80 three times, you should take note of this. The beauty of support and resistance are their simplicity. They are easy to identify, and their existence is logical because often they are a simple reflection of supply or demand at a particular level. A patient medium-term buyer in a market might decide to work a massive bid at $80 in a stock. That massive bid will be visible as the price repeatedly trades at $80, but fails to break through that level.

Support and resistance in your market can be identified simply by eyeballing both an hourly and then a daily chart. Here's what to look for:

1. Any topside or downside level that held more than once. This can often be a band, not an exact level. For example, you might see a series of lows in gold at $1914, $1908 and $1904. Don't use false precision when you determine significant reference points. A band of support often makes more sense than trying to identify an exact level.

2. Any level that represents a major high or low for your product (60-day low, one year low, etc.)

3. Broken resistance or support. When a major support breaks, expect that level to become important resistance in future.

4. Major round numbers. These do not always matter, but remember how humans love round numbers!

In the GBPUSD chart in Figure 10.2, you can see strong support formed at 1.3000/25 (marked with **1**'s), and the important swing high just below 1.3500 (**2**). Then, note how the old support (1.3000/25) became resistance once it broke (**3**). Also note that a round number (1.3000) is the critical pivot on this chart.

If your market has been in a nice up trend for a few weeks and pulls back to major support, bounces weakly off it, then breaks through the support... That is a warning sign. The trend has lost its power as it fails to hold above the levels that matter.

Figure 10.2: GBPUSD hourly chart July 16 to September 15, 2020

Chart courtesy of Refinitiv

Strong up trends hold major support.
Strong down trends stay below major resistance.

In Figure 10.3, which shows the price of gold in the Summer of 2020, there is major support at $1910. Before and after the "1" on the chart, there are five separate tests and holds of $1910. In this chart, I also show volume bars below the price. Volume can add an additional layer of useful information.

You can see the huge volume spike when gold tested the key $1910 support level in late August (the price and volume points marked as "1"). This tells you that aggressive selling was absorbed and therefore demand was significant at $1910. Successful holds of major support on high volume are super bullish.

High volumes reinforce the importance of a support or resistance level or can signal that it has been decisively broken. At the points marked "2" you can see another huge volume surge but this time, gold slices through the bottom of an important triangle and through the critical $1910 level all at once.

Figure 10.3: Gold hourly chart July 16 to September 26, 2020

Chart courtesy of Refinitiv

High volumes provide signal confirmation for technical patterns.

Figure 10.4 shows another example of a massive volume spike at a turning point. This chart of EURNOK shows a monster volume spike on the very last day of August 2020. That marked the ding dong low in the pair. Most likely, this was a huge rebalancing flow; many FX rebalancing flows coincide with 4 p.m. London time on the last day of the month and that's the timing of that big volume bar. If you squint, you can also see the second largest volume bar coincides with an important low in mid-June.

Remember that because support and resistance are simple and not subject to much interpretation, most people in the market will be monitoring roughly the same support and resistance levels. Therefore, you need to think about the metagame and leave your stops far enough below support (or above resistance) that you are not dinged by a weak stop loss run that takes out an obvious level.

Figure 10.4: EURNOK hourly, April 2020 to September 2020
Bottom pane shows EURNOK volume

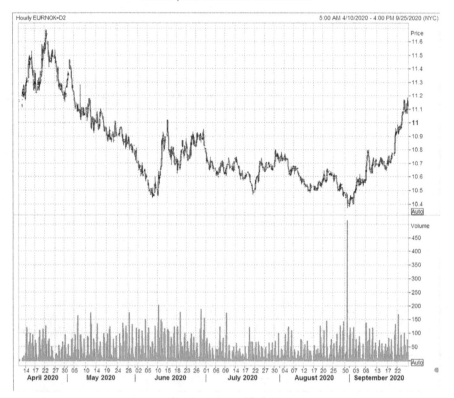

Chart courtesy of Refinitiv

It is often best to place your stop loss about a half-day's range below a major level to avoid any noisy whipsaws around that point[119].

If all you know about technical analysis is NewsPivots, support and resistance, you know enough to function as a competent trader. I will now go through a few more indicators that I use, but like I said: indicator selection is somewhat arbitrary and not especially important. If RSIs make sense to you, use them. If you prefer MACD, great. Your success or failure in trading will not be determined by the technical indicators you choose, and it will most certainly not be determined by which parameters you choose for those indicators.

If you have never read any technical analysis books or websites, my suggestion

---

119. Reminder: As discussed in the chapter on microstructure… You should know what one day's range is in your product, on average and at the extremes. This is the most important measure of volatility for short-term traders.

is that you either take 10 or 15 hours to read a bunch of technical analysis websites and watch YouTube videos about techs… Or read two or three good books on technical analysis (e.g., John Murphy's or Steve Nison's book[120]). Another great resource is the 6-part Market Profile Study Guide from the CME. You can Google it and find the PDF free online. Market Profile is a bit esoteric but I find it logical and easy to understand.

Your intention while reading about technical analysis is to find 2 to 5 simple indicators or patterns that you like. Use these as your primary risk management and market screening tools. Then, you can add a few more over time. You don't need 74 different technical indicators when you use techs to manage risk and improve execution tactics. Running 14 spreadsheets screening for every technical indicator ever invented is a waste of time. Keep it simple.

Make sure you allocate enough time to strategy (coming up with trade ideas) and tactics (entry point, stop loss, etc.) Many traders find it is more fun to come up with trade ideas and do not allocate enough resources to the tactics of extracting as much money as possible from the ideas.

You cannot win without good strategy and solid tactics.

SYMMETRY

Another setup I look for in financial markets is symmetry. It is logical that a quasi-natural system like financial markets would often produce symmetrical patterns. Furthermore, since volatility tends to be steady in many markets for much of the time, it makes sense that moves (whether they be up or down) would tend to be of approximately the same size. If something just rallied 5% in three months, it is intuitive and logical that it could fall 5% in three months, but less intuitive or logical that it might fall 12% in 1 month[121].

Let me show you two examples of symmetry that I found useful in September 2020. The first was USDCAD. The COVID-19 crisis triggered a massive shortage of USD as the market scrambled for liquidity and freaked out about the dramatic drop in the stock market. This pushed USDCAD from 1.2952 to 1.4669 in just two months. Then, the Fed launched an epic QE bazooka and stocks quickly stabilized. This helped USDCAD form a top and eventually the

---

120. John J. Murphy: *Technical Analysis of Financial Markets* (1999) and Steve Nison: *Japanese Candlestick Charting Techniques* (2001).

121. But still possible!

pair dropped all the way back down to within 30 pips of where it started (1.2952). See Figure 10.5.

Figure 10.5: USDCAD Daily October 2019 to September 2020

Chart courtesy of Refinitiv

See how USDCAD rallied 17.17 big figures then sold off 16.72? Just about perfect symmetry. Pretty amazing. Once it completed that symmetrical round trip, USDCAD held in the mid-1.29s and that was an excellent buying opportunity. This is not hindsight, I used this symmetry as one of several reasons to recommend a USDCAD long at the time.

Figure 10.6 is a thing of absolute beauty. It shows USDCNH as it followed a perfect M-shaped pattern and respected both price and time symmetry.

Each leg of the M was about 95 days with the first two exactly 99 days and the last two 92 and 97 days. The first rally matched the ultimate selloff just about perfectly and the V in the middle displayed just about perfect symmetry too. When an asset is completing a symmetrical pattern, you should be on high alert for a reversal.

Furthermore, when trading options, you should start with the assumption of price symmetry when choosing targets and strike prices. If you are buying USDCNH puts on the second run to 7.1965, it makes sense to start with 6.68 as your price target and then adjust for any other information you have on direction and expected volatility.

If you were short USDCNH at the point this chart ends, and you feel like the trade is losing its luster, this would be another input and possible reason to think it might be time to cut. If you are bullish USDCNH but want a reason to get long, this gives you one.

Figure 10.6: USDCNH Daily January 2019 to September 2020

Chart courtesy of Refinitiv

Note that one reason (especially a chart-based reason) is never good enough for a trade idea. More appropriate would be that you already have three or four reasons derived from fundamental, positioning or cross-market analysis and the chart symmetry gives you a nice entry point with a cheap stop loss.

REVERSAL PATTERNS

When you decide that you want to take the other side of a trend, it is helpful to have specific indicators and patterns that will give you a signal that the time is right. Copious cash has been set on fire by traders blindly fading strong trends for no reason, or using weak logic like "this is a big level" or "it's come too far too fast".

When I have a strong countertrend view, I don't execute right away. Instead, I go on high alert and wait for a sign that it's time to jump in. I would never enter a trade simply because of a reversal pattern or signal. But when I have a countertrend view already, for reasons unrelated to technical analysis, here are three reversal patterns I watch for.

1. Ending diagonal or rising wedge

This pattern works at the lows, too, but here I describe how it works at the highs.

An ending diagonal occurs when price rises in a slowly narrowing wedge as volatility contracts even as the price continues to make new highs. Figure 10.7 is a nice example using NYMEX crude oil in 2018.

An interesting feature of the rising wedge formation is that as the triangle narrows, the triangle must eventually close and the pattern must conclude. Therefore, you get a sense of when the turn might come, if it's going to happen, as the apex of the triangle is a timing tool.

My approach to trading wedges is simple. When I have a countertrend view, I wait for price to close below the wedge (under the bottom line, in the example above) and then I go short with a stop loss above the high. In the example above, I would sell crude at $70.80 on the day it dropped out of the wedge on the big down day. My stop loss is $72.85 (above the highest high).

2. Dojis

A doji is a candlestick that forms when the opening and closing price of a security are the same. The daily silver chart in Figure 10.8 has two dojis in a row after a 30% rally. The dojis are marked with large arrows.

A doji is a sign of indecision. Price went up and down and closed unchanged. When you see a doji or two dojis in a row, it is a sign that momentum has waned. The prior trend is losing steam. If you were bearish silver in the case of Figure 10.8, but wanted a sign that it was safe to get in the water, the doji is a good signal. Again, my methodology is simple. When I am bearish a market that is in a strong trend higher, and I see a doji, I sell on the close that day. I also use dojis on hourly charts.

Figure 10.7: Crude oil breaks down out of rising wedge

Chart courtesy of Refinitiv

If I had no other information here, I would put my stop 1.5 average day ranges away. 1.5 times the average daily range is my baseline starting point when picking a stop loss for a normal trade. Note that I also look for major levels to consider before determining my stop loss level. In this case, using one year of data as the lookback, the average daily range in silver was 36 cents. Therefore, the stop loss is placed at the entry ($12.91) plus (0.36 daily range X 1.5) = $13.45. There was another doji the next day (the high traded was $13.22 that day) and then silver cratered, reversing the entire July/August rally in 5 days. Dojis are simple and powerful warning signs of trend exhaustion.

3. Hammers

A hammer is a reversal candle where price makes a hard push in one direction and closes at the opposite extreme. These are especially powerful if they come as a failed attempt at a major new high or low. Figure 10.9 is an example of a bull hammer candle.

Figure 10.8: Two dojis in silver signal a major top

Chart courtesy of Refinitiv

If you were bullish bitcoin in early 2018 but wanted a signal to buy, you got a nice one in early February as the market made a bull hammer after the 50%+ decline. The bull hammer is marked with a large arrow. The strategy is to wait for the hammer, buy at the close, and put your stop loss below the low. Of course, the same setup (in reverse) at the highs is called a bear hammer and it is bearish.

Note these patterns don't work every time! There is also a bull hammer on that same chart in January and that candle gave a bullish signal that only worked for 3 days. No technical signal or setup is going to be anywhere close to perfect. These reversal indicators are extremely useful, though, as they help you enter countertrend trades with a set of logical risk management parameters that allow you to put on your reversal trade with meaningful leverage.

Develop a short list of reversal indicators that you like and use them as triggers when you have a strong countertrend view. Be patient, then strike with maximum force.

Figure 10.9: Bull hammer signals the bottom in bitcoin

Chart courtesy of Refinitiv

I have now outlined a few ways to identify important levels and turning points. You should also have one or two indicators in your toolbox that help you identify the trend, and if that trend is overbought or oversold. Here are two indicator sets I use for trend and overbought/oversold.

TREND AND OVERBOUGHT/OVERSOLD INDICATORS

Moving averages

To measure the strength, slope and direction of trend, moving averages are the simplest, most effective indicator. I use 55, 100 and 200-hour moving averages on all my charts. I almost always use hourly charts for technical analysis, though I sometimes zoom in with 10-minute charts or zoom out to the daily for a different perspective. When I zoom in or out, I still use 55, 100 and 200-period MAs.

Here are three ways I look at moving averages:

1. The 200-hour is a great trend indicator and I use it on its own for trend direction and also as support and resistance. If I am bearish crude oil futures and the price has been repeatedly capped by the 200-hour, I will use the next approach to the MA to get short. Many traders use the 55-day in the NASDAQ as a trend indicator. If the market is above the moving average and holding above it on pullbacks, that is a nice uptrend. And vice versa. One of the most basic and effective strategies in trading is to play the pullbacks in a primary trend using a moving average. This strategy is simple and effective.

2. Watch for crossovers. When the 55-hour crosses up through the 200-hour, that is a bullish signal. At that point, buying a pullback to the 55-hour could be attractive if you have other good reasons to be bullish.

3. Check the slope of the moving averages. If all three MAs are flat, that's a choppy rangebound market. If all three are sloping upwards, that's a strong bull trend.

Here is a variation of a simple and effective (bullish) tactical approach many use once they have a strong bullish view in a market: wait for a fast MA to cross above a slower MA, which signals that an uptrend has formed. Wait for the price of the asset to retrace back to the fast MA. Buy with a stop loss at least 1.5 day's ranges away and below the 200-hour MA. Simple and effective.

The selection of period for moving averages (55 vs. 50 vs. 20) is somewhat arbitrary and not super-important. Just pick two or three moving averages of different lengths and put them on all your charts. You can also fit a moving average to the current trend much in the way you would draw a trendline. Then, if price breaks through that MA, you know the trend has lost its mojo.

Relative strength indicator (RSI)

Every trader should have one or two indicators that tell them when their market is extremely oversold or overbought on the time horizon they trade. The big three are RSI, stochastics and deviation from a moving average.

RSI is the standard that everyone uses, and the textbook strategy is that if it goes above 70, wait for it to fall back below 70 and then sell. I use it differently. I take as much data as possible (using hourly data because that suits my trading time horizon) and find the extremes in the RSI going back as far as possible. I then calculate the top and bottom 5% most extreme and use these levels as "get out no matter what" levels. That is, if I'm long, and the RSI gets into the top 5% of the series, I cut. I find that at the mega RSI extremes, the risk of a reversal is too high so the risk reward on staying in the trend is poor. If I am trying to trade against the trend, I will also use these mega extremes as an entry point.

Here's a super short excerpt from one of my dailies (December 2, 2020) where I use an extreme in the RSI to get short NZDUSD:

> The textbook approach to trading RSI is to wait for it to rise above 70 and then fall back below 70 and then go short. I prefer to isolate the most extreme levels and use those as reversal points right away. While RSI is a trend indicator, generally, it can be an amazing reversal indicator at the MEGA extremes.
>
> I sorted all the daily NZDUSD RSI data from 2010 to now and the most extreme readings occur when the RSI breaks above 75. That happened this week. With the dramatic repricing in NZ rates and the non-stop flood of good vaccine news, much goodness is in the price of NZDUSD now. The table below shows how the pair performed in the twelve instances where the RSI went above 75 (since 2010).

Date	x+1	x+3	x+5	x+10	x+20	x+30	x+60
average	-0.0%	-0.4%	-0.8%	-0.7%	-0.7%	-2.0%	-2.7%
median	-0.1%	-0.0%	-0.4%	-0.3%	0.1%	-1.1%	-1.2%
% of time it goes up	50%	50%	42%	42%	50%	33%	25%

x+1 means performance one day after the first RSI reading above 75,
x+3 means three days later, x+5 means 5-day performance, etc.

You can see in this short example that if you isolate the times when the RSI is historically extreme, you can find points where you have high confidence to go the other way. When the NZD RSI is above 75, future performance is raging bearish as NZD averages a drop of 2.7% over the next 60 trading days and goes up only 25% of the time.

In this case, I was already bearish risky assets (NZD is a risky asset) so this just added to my thesis and gave me a way to play it. I went short NZDUSD at 0.7040 with a stop at 0.7111 and a take profit at 0.6911. A high RSI on its own would not be enough to get me involved but it's a nice seed that might grow into a full trade idea.

The Deviation

The other overbought and oversold signal that I use is the deviation of price from a moving average or what I simply call "The Deviation". My technique is pretty simple, as usual. I take the price of the asset I'm trading and check how far it is from the 100-hour moving average. Then, I look as far back as possible and see if The Deviation tends to oscillate in a steady range or if it looks unreliable or random. For many markets, you will see that The Deviation tends to peak and trough around the same levels over and over when volatility is fairly stable.

Figure 10.10 shows an example using S&P minis.

Figure 10.10: TOP: S&P 500 futures with 100-hour MA, MIDDLE: Deviation from the 100-hour MA, BOTTOM: Buy / sell signal triggers if S&P is more than 3.5% above or below 100-hour MA

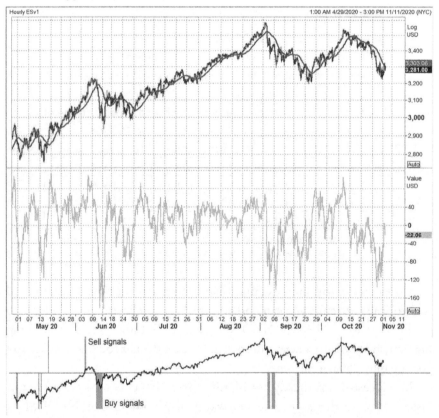

This is easy to set up on your trading system or in a spreadsheet. Use historical data to determine what the extremes are in The Deviation and then use those extremes going forward as reversal signals. In this case, I filtered for the 5% of most extreme values in the deviation and this represents a move in the S&P 500 of about 3.5%.

When using The Deviation, it is important to understand the skew of your market. Skew is the direction of the market that tends to happen faster and be more volatile. For example, stocks tend to sell off much more quickly than they rally, so you might want to use a more conservative entry point for your deviation signal on the downside or scale in gradually knowing that sell-offs can overshoot and are harder and more violent to fade.

● ● ●

An important note about using overbought and oversold signals: *think think think*. If the Fed just announced a massive QE program and stocks rip higher to extreme overbought… That is probably not a signal that it is time to go short. Things that are overbought can become more overbought and then more overbought again. Overbought on its own is not a reason to sell an asset. It's a warning sign that the future distribution of returns might be skewed lower and that's all.

An elevated RSI reading or a sexy stochastic are not reason enough to do a trade. Incorporate overbought and oversold indicators into your process and use them to fine tune entries and exits, but don't be the trader who fades a move solely because "It's come too far, too fast." That is not a valid trading strategy. Remember we are using these technicals as guidance and tactical inputs and not as a systematic quantitative trading framework.

MORNING QUICK TECHS

Most trading jobs are busiest in the morning. Markets are already moving when you sit down but still, you need to prepare for the day. By 7 a.m. each day, I am fielding client queries, producing content, planning my day and going through 100s of e-mails. I need to keep my morning process as simple as possible. I like to create a quick sheet of techs that looks like Figure 10.11.

Figure 10.11: QUICK TECHS

	EURUSD		USDCAD	
R3	**1.2014**	Post Jackson Hole high	**1.3400**	Early August double top
R2	**1.1917/1.1930**	Lagarde high + Philip Lane breakdown level	**1.3315/30**	Key pivot both ways (June 2020 low+++)
R1	**1.1855**	Post-FOMC high	**1.3250**	17SEP high
Spot	1.1785		1.3170	
S1	**1.1737**	Post-FOMC low	**1.3050**	Two shoulders of inverted H&S
S2	**1.1700**	Critical range bottom	**1.2950**	Symmetry target and late 2019 low
S3	**1.1600**	Election night low	**1.2783**	H2 2018 low

100H	1.1847	1.3170	
200H	1.1832	1.3152	Moving averages
100D	1.1446	1.3491	
200D	1.1225	1.3520	

Average daily range	0.0075	0.0077

Note that R1, R2, and R3 refer to the first three resistance levels while S1, S2, and S3 refer to the first three support levels. The grid does not take long to update each morning because many of yesterday's levels remain valid today and all the stuff on the bottom updates automatically using a data feed from Bloomberg. Good traders have an established morning process to prepare for the day and part of that process should be to identify significant reference points for the day ahead. You know the old saying about luck and preparation.

• • •

That concludes this section on technical analysis. I strongly advise you to keep things simple and stick with just a few indicators and techniques that make sense to you. Remember that techs are just the frosting on the trade idea cake. Don't try to make an entire cake out of frosting!

SENTIMENT AND POSITIONING

The market cycle is always a complex dance featuring narrative and sentiment. Sometimes the news drives the price but quite often, the price drives the news. In other words, sometimes a strong trend takes on a life of its own and unfolds faster than the story on the ground, which follows behind.

While I believe sentiment and positioning are important variables to consider in every trade, and can sometimes be the main driver of a trade idea, I also believe they are overrated as indicators by many traders. We discussed sentiment a fair bit in the section on herding bias but there are some other important points to cover.

Here are the key points on sentiment and positioning:

1. Sentiment and positioning matter sometimes, but not most of the time.

2. 80-90% of the time, sentiment just follows price so if you trade against sentiment and positioning you are often just fighting the trend.

3. At inflection points, a tuned-in feel for positioning and sentiment can be a huge source of edge.

Positioning is packed with potential energy, like fuel for a future fire. Positioning unwinds are like fires. They need heat (a spark or catalyst), fuel (large positions) and oxygen (more bad news, or mark-to-market losses that trigger feedback loops that lead to more position unwinds).

Image: Gustavb - Own work, CC BY-SA 3.0, https://commons.wikimedia.org/

You need large positions, a catalyst, and mark-to-market losses all at once and then you get a chain reaction that continues until it finally burns itself out (or is put out by a central bank). When I was in grade school, they taught us this process with the fire triangle.

Large positions are like piles of dry tinder that can potentially burst into flame at any moment, but probably won't. Remember, just because you have a large stack of dry wood next to an open can of gasoline… That does not mean there will be a fire.

Figure 10.12 is the simple positioning and sentiment framework I use.

Figure 10.12: The six sentiment vs. market price regimes

Sentiment	Bull Market	Bear Market
Bullish and increasing	Very Bullish	
Bullish and stable	Bullish	
Bullish but falling	BEARISH	
Bearish and stable		Bearish
Bearish and getting more bearish		Very bearish
Bearish but getting less bearish		BULLISH

In other words, going against sentiment works at the turning points but not during the trend. If you can identify a palpable turn in sentiment via observation of behavior or via data analysis, you can position ahead of the crowd.

Sources of sentiment and positioning data

The best source of sentiment and positioning information is knowledgeable observation of how people discuss a market. This is easier if you have been trading for a few years and talk to many people in the market, but you can also get a sense of this from reading news and social media. Just remember that many channels are biased.

In terms of data, the most commonly-used positioning data comes from the CFTC. This data shows the positioning of non-commercial speculators, and while it is closely followed and can be interesting information, it has no predictive power on its own. If you see "Copper longs on CFTC hit all-time high" your instinct is probably to go short copper but the inconvenient truth is that a setup like that is actually modestly bullish on all time horizons.

The CFTC data is slow-moving and trend-following and is directional, not contrarian. Do not use CFTC data by itself as a contrarian indicator.

A source of sentiment data that *is* contrarian is the Daily Sentiment Index, produced by Jake Bernstein since the 1980s. That data is the output from a survey of retail traders that simply asks: "Are you bullish or bearish on X?" It shows what percentage of survey respondents are bulls. When bulls get below 10 or above 90, that is a good indicator of a near-term extreme. DSI data is available only via subscription.

Options markets often contain important positioning information. For example, when stocks rise and VIX rises at the same time, you know that something unusual is going on because the correlation is almost always inverted between those two. Stocks up / VIX up is a sign that the market is so bullish it is adding to upside with calls, instead of hedging the downside with puts. You can also look at the put/call ratio for a read on equity sentiment.

In currency markets, people look at the risk reversal to see if traders have a strong preference for puts or calls, and how that preference is changing. As with most sentiment data, the risk reversal mostly follows price but when there is a divergence (USDJPY going up even as the risk reversal is more bid for USD puts) that can be a signal that something is amiss.

Positioning surveys can be a useful source of information. They are timely and fast moving. People change their minds quickly, as opposed to trend following systems which move much more slowly as they wait for price confirmation. Again, with surveys, most of the time they are directional and the only time they are contrarian is when they hit an extreme. In the positioning surveys I have done when working at banks, I found that when sentiment made a record high or low for the past year, that could often be a good sign of a turn.

In the stock market there are many sentiment surveys and indicators available. I like the AAII survey (bulls vs. bears). CNN's Fear and Greed indicator is a nice simple snapshot of equity sentiment.

Many banks publish sentiment and positioning data. In FX there is the Citi Pain Index and the HSBC Positioning Indicators. In broad macro, the Bank of America Global Fund Manager Survey gets a lot of attention and highlights crowded positions and tail risks. Retail brokers like Oanda, Dukascopy and DailyFX publish detailed positioning data. Each market has its important sentiment and positioning data, and this is generally easy to find simply by Googling.

As you become expert in your market, you will learn the best sentiment and positioning indicators to follow.

Finally, magazine covers can be the ultimate contrarian indicator. When a financial theme hits the cover of a mainstream magazine, always take note. By the time journalists believe a theme is worthy of a cover story, that theme is (by definition) well-known. That means the theme is probably also crowded. For more on the Magazine Cover Indicator, Google "Brent Donnelly magazine cover indicator".

How to use sentiment and positioning data

Sentiment and positioning data can help you significantly at turning points. The number one takeaway on sentiment and positioning, whether you are using surveys, options markets, or other sources of information, is that only the super-mega-extremes are times when you should consider fading. Otherwise, positioning and sentiment are mostly just trend indicators and they move up and down with the price.

In Chapter 9 we discussed how sentiment and positioning evolve as a market moves through its narrative cycle. I want to mention here that when sentiment is at an extreme and the narrative starts to turn, this is a situation where good sentiment and positioning analysis can make you money.

Extreme bearish sentiment usually reflects that the price has been going down and there is a strong and compelling bearish story that explains the sell-off. The interesting moment comes when the narrative starts to turn, good news starts to emerge, but price does not turn higher right away. Confirmation bias hampers the judgment of the individual and it also impacts the judgment of the crowd in aggregate. You will often see the news flow turn against a major trend but no reaction in the price at first.

Often, traders with lower confidence will defer to the market (they might say "Oh, I guess the news isn't that bullish after all, since the market keeps going lower") while expert traders with a strong understanding of the narrative and of positioning will see an opportunity in the mismatch between price and narrative. They will say something more like: "The news flow has clearly turned bullish here but the market is clinging to the old bearish narrative. Short positioning is in the 97% percentile and I bet there is going to be a huge reversal soon."

Then, that expert trader will go on high alert for signals that price has bottomed. This could be as simple as waiting for a moving average to break or waiting for a bullish reversal pattern like a hammer, ending diagonal or key reversal day. The savvy trader sees that the sell-off is set to reverse but waits. She looks for evidence that a reversal in price is happening and finds setups that allow for a reasonable stop loss. She knows better than to simply buy over and over as the price continues to plummet. Try not to catch falling knives. Remember what they say about bottom pickers.

Wait for an indication that things have turned before you trade against a powerful trend. In Chapter 12, I will go through a specific example of how I used a divergence between sentiment and narrative to get set on a countertrend trade.

Alpha Traders use multiple approaches to find high confidence trades. They wait for multiple indicators to line up. They use fundamentals, narrative analysis, positioning and sentiment, and other factors to get a reading on the market. Then, they use technical analysis to fine tune timing, entry and exit. They structure trades in a way that acknowledges that many ideas will be wrong so that when they are inevitably wrong, the cost is small. When they are right, the payoff is large.

**Excellent traders are confident in their views
but also know they are frequently wrong.**

Some hedge funds make all their trading decisions using macro analysis but then simply filter every idea with one or two simple technical indicators. Trade ideas remain in the OFF state until the technical indicator puts them in the ON position.

For example, let's say a fund has a pod comprised of three genius analysts and two senior portfolio managers. They currently hold five core views: Bullish USDJPY, AAPL and gold, and bearish bonds and AMZN.

The fund will then systematically apply a simple filter to the ideas, let's say a 55-day moving average. The pod will only put on the trades that are on the correct side of the 55-day moving average. For example, they will only go short AMZN if it's below the 55-day.

This avoids extended periods of wrongness because if AMZN enters a prolonged uptrend, the fund will stay flat the whole time as the stock trends higher and remains above its 55-day MA. When price breaks below the 55-day, the fund will put on their AMZN short. If AMZN closes back above the 55-day, they're out.

This approach of trading macro with a technical filter is an excellent model.

It allows you to find your edge on the analysis side but then forces you to admit you are wrong when price goes against you[122].

• • •

I hope this chapter has given you a sense of how I use technical analysis, sentiment and positioning in my trading process. There are no correct answers when it comes to trading, so take what resonates with you in this chapter and throw out what does not. You should develop a process that fits your personality and suits your objectives. Never strictly follow someone else's advice.

Now it's time to move on to the most important topic in trading: risk management. You can do everything else right but if you fail at risk management, you automatically fail at trading. No matter how good a chef you are, you will never succeed in the restaurant business if you keep blowing up your kitchen.

---

122. No approach is perfect. In choppy markets the trend signal will generate a ton of noise and that can be costly. But overall, the multi-factor fundamental approach with a technical filter is a strong, logical approach to trading.

CHAPTER 11

YOU FEELING
LUCKY, PUNK?

Data collection, risk management and variance

> *Most of what I have learned from gambling is also true for*
> *investing. People mostly don't understand risk, reward and*
> *uncertainty. Their investment results would be better if they did.*
>
> **EDWARD O. THORP,** *A Man for All Markets*

In this chapter, we will discuss risk management. If you are new to trading, this chapter will help you build and implement a robust risk management framework. If you are an experienced professional, I hope you will extract a few nuggets of wisdom and alternative viewpoints and use these observations to make incremental improvements to your current framework.

Risk management is the most important skill in trading. Everything else is a distant second. You can have the best ideas, the greatest algorithms, the best instinctive pattern recognition and the fastest execution systems but if your risk management system is not adequate... You will fail. I could write an entire book about risk management but a) that would be boring to write so I'm not going to do that and b) the real essentials of risk management are fairly simple and can be boiled down into one chapter.

The big challenges in risk management come from trading businesses that employ complex strategies, huge portfolios, correlated assets, illiquid markets, and non-linear derivative products. For short-term directional traders in liquid markets, it's pretty easy to establish an appropriate set of risk management rules. The hard part is following them.

COLLECT AND ANALYZE P&L DATA

Before you develop a risk management system, you need to build a solid data collection system. Collecting and analyzing P&L data is one of the most important and powerful activities in trading. Much in the way a trading journal provides qualitative feedback, P&L analysis provides quantitative feedback. This does not need to be complicated. If you don't already have one, create a spreadsheet to track your daily P&L.

Columns should include: DATE, STOP LOSS, OPEN, HIGH, LOW, CLOSE.

DATE is today's date. STOP LOSS is your daily stop loss today (if you have one). OPEN is how much you made overnight. That is, your P&L when you start trading in the morning. This is useful to track because it's a different type of trading than what you do during the day. HIGH and LOW give you a sense of your daily P&L volatility over time and also what the extremes tend to be.

After collecting a year or so of data, you might notice that you tend to top out at the same level all the time and then close lower. If you always peak around the same HIGH and then close lower, consider setting a take profit target for the day. Many traders will consistently have a tough time breaking through a specific level of P&L in a given day. This tendency to peak at a specific P&L level is not random. It reflects a combination of your position size and the volatility of your market.

If you trade $100 million positions in a product that tends to move no more than 1% per day, you are going to notice your P&L tops out around $1 million quite often. To break to a higher plateau, you first need to know the level of your current plateau and then you need to calculate how you can move to a higher level.

The next step to building a quality P&L tracking spreadsheet is to set up individual P&L columns for each major product and sub-product you trade. FX, BONDS, STOCKS if you're macro, for example, or individual stocks if you are an equity day trader that trades particular names.

This is highly individual and depends on what you think is worth tracking. A note of caution here: keep it high level. If you trade 50 stocks, there is not much point maintaining a column for each stock. There is a point at which your spreadsheet has so much data that it yields mostly noise and little actionable information. Note that if you are a day trader, you can't be an expert in 50 different stocks and you shouldn't be trading that many anyway.

Another idea is to set up columns for each strategy you run. If you have one strategy to trade the market open, another strategy that trades during the day and a third strategy that trades on news, you can create one column for each strategy to track how they are doing over time. The idea here is to have data that will help you answer: "What is working and what isn't?" and then you can do more of what is working and less of what is not.

This spreadsheet should not be more than 12 to 15 columns wide, including MTD and YTD columns on the far right. If you have more than 15 columns, aggregate or combine some of them until you can see the whole thing on one screen. There is a point where too much information is bad. Be thoughtful about what data might be useful and collect that data. You can always add new columns later. Keep it fairly basic for now.

Once you have about six months of data, calculate the following:

- **WIN%** (number of winning days / total number of trading days)

- **Average winning day** ($ or bps)

- **Average losing day** ($ or bps)

- **WIN/LOSE $ or bps ratio.** This is simply your average winning day ($) divided by your average losing day ($). This is the most important statistic for most short-term traders. Your P&L is simply:

$$(\# \text{ winning days} * \text{average winning day}) -$$
$$(\# \text{ losing days} * \text{average losing day})$$

There are just two numbers you need to control. Your WIN% and the ratio of the size of your winning days to the size of your losing days. That's it!

There is no right answer for how these two stats should combine, but WIN% is much more difficult to influence than the relationship between your winning and losing days. Your WIN% is usually determined more by your trading style and the seat you are in whereas the ratio of your winning day P&L to your losing day P&L is influenced by your discipline, patience, and ability to cut losses and ride winners. That ratio tends to be the best reflection of trading skill, in my opinion.

I have been keeping these trading stats since 2006 and it is surprising how consistently my WIN% hovers around 50%. All my success (or failure) is determined by the size of my winning days vs. the size of my losing days. And more precisely, if I can keep the losers under control, the winners tend to take care of themselves. I have no trouble making money, but I often have trouble keeping it. This is the profile of the active, risk-seeking trader.

On the other hand, a skilled but more risk averse trader might have a higher WIN%, say 60%. The idea here is to collect enough data and then start to think about changes you can make to either increase your WIN% or increase the size of your up days relative to the size of your down days. Like I said earlier, for most traders the up vs. down day ratio is easier to influence than the WIN%.

- **What stocks (or currencies or commodities…) you made money in.** Also which ones cost you money. Important note here: don't overestimate the importance of this information. Good products and good markets come and go. I have heard people say stuff like: "I keep losing money in EURUSD, it's just stuck in this stupid range! I really need to take it off my screen."

  In that scenario, the problem is not EURUSD, the problem is that it is in a range and it sounds like the trader isn't very good at trading ranges. If she takes EURUSD off her screen and then it trends higher for 10 straight days, she's probably going to miss a huge opportunity. Collect data on specific assets and asset classes, not so you can put them in the penalty box, but so that you can isolate what is working and what isn't. *And why.*

- **How many times did you breach your stop loss?** What were the causes, on each of those days? Any time your LOW or your CLOSE is lower than your stop loss, that is a red flag. Something is wrong with your process. Your positions are too big; you are too slow to stop out; you are out of control in some way. If you are a manager, take stop losses seriously. Don't increase a trader's stop when it hits; shut her down.

- **Performance by day of the week and on event days.** Are you making all your money on Fed days and month end and losing money every Monday? Look for patterns that make sense but be careful not to be fooled by randomness here. If you can explain why a pattern exists, it is much less likely that it's an artifact of randomness.

- **What time of day do you make and lose money, on average?** This is a bit more work and involves a separate spreadsheet where you take a snapshot of your P&L every 30 minutes. After a few months you will have an interesting P&L curve that will show you how your profitability evolves throughout the day.

  Are you making all your money on the open then leaking half of it back out over the course of the day? Do you lose money consistently from 11 a.m. to 3 p.m. every day? Many day traders make all their money in the morning and then spend the rest of the day trying not to give it back. This is dumb. If you make all your money in the morning, shut down at noon and find other ways to be productive. Do research, read, work out, etc. Even if you work at a bank, nobody is going to force you to trade in the afternoon.

  Try to get a strong sense of how time of day influences your performance. Personally, I make most of my money overnight and from 7 a.m. to 11 a.m. and the period from 11 a.m. to 5 p.m. NY is a P&L graveyard. Identify the juicy times to trade and act with focused aggression during these times. For the lackluster parts of your trading day, find replacement activities to keep you occupied so that you do not press buttons out of boredom.

You should also look at monthly and yearly data as time goes on. Ideally, your P&L should skew to the right on every time frame. In other words, your biggest days should be up days, not down days. Your biggest months should be positive, not negative. You should rarely lose money in a year and never two years in a row. The more edge you have, the more this paragraph will be true of your trading statistics.

DEVELOP A RISK MANAGEMENT SYSTEM

You have your data collection system. Now you need a risk management system.

This section is about risk management for short-term traders who trade liquid products and take mostly directional risk. If you sell low-delta options or run a 78-line portfolio or buy and sell frontier market bonds, this section does not apply to you.

I think the most useful way to explain my risk management thought process is to start with longer time horizons then gradually zoom in to smaller and smaller increments. I will start with one trading year, then discuss monthly risk management, then move all the way down to daily risk management and individual trades.

> **There is no single correct answer**
> **when it comes to managing risk.**

Your risk management system has to match your personality, your time horizon, your trading style, your capital, your access to leverage and the liquidity profile of the products you trade. I am going to outline how I think about risk management and give you some of the details of my risk management system. Take what makes sense to you. Discard what does not.

YEARLY RISK MANAGEMENT

In most trading jobs, one year is the most important unit of trading performance. Almost all bank and real money traders are paid based on annual performance and most hedge funds also use the calendar year as their main unit of time for evaluation and compensation. Sure, some hedge funds pay out more than once per year, and retail traders don't think as much about yearly increments, but all traders should think about, monitor, analyze and target yearly performance.

In order to survive in the long run, you want your yearly performance to look like that of a call option. This means flat or perhaps small losses in the bad years and medium-sized to huge gains in the good years. Twenty years of performance for a skilled, adaptable trader using the risk management style I will describe in the pages to follow, might look something like Figure 11.1.

To achieve this sort of distribution of P&L, you need to do three things.

1. Start slow and increase risk as YTD P&L builds

You cannot have the same risk appetite on January 1 with zero P&L in the coffers as you can have on August 15 when you are up 15 million dollars. This

Figure 11.1: Twenty years of trading for a skilled trader who behaves like a call option

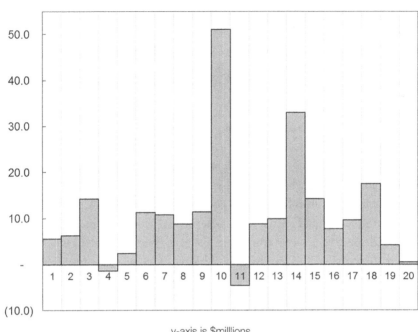

y-axis is $milllions

means there must be an arbitrary change in your risk appetite each January, but that's just the way things go. In an ideal world, you should always be varying your risk appetite based on conviction and market opportunity, but we live in the real world. As such, you need to start slow and build risk over time.

There is something special and scary about the zero bound in P&L. Let's say a hypothetical trader named Steven Kirk wants to make $10 million this year and his stop loss is $4 million. He will find that going from +$2 million to +$1 million feels significantly less bad than going from +$500k to -$500k, even though both are P&L declines of $1 million. Any red number next to your name feels bad. This is consistent with theory which tells us that if a gain gives us x pleasure, a loss of the same magnitude gives us $2x$ pain.

This is not all just psychological, though. As Steve's P&L falls below zero, his ability to take risk (his leverage) decreases. There is a non-linear real-world impact of losses as he moves below zero and closer to his stop loss. When you are below zero P&L, you wear a straitjacket.

Let's say it's February 15. How is Steve's psychology at YTD P&L of $750,000? He is not ecstatic, because he's a bit behind plan, but not too bad.

How about at YTD P&L of zero? Still OK, probably. At minus $1 million? He's getting a bit nervous now. At minus $2 million, Steve is halfway to his stop loss after only six weeks. At that point, he is going to need to reduce his risk in order to avoid hitting the disaster zone which is around $3 million. Remember: even if your stop loss is $4 million, you are in big trouble trading-wise much before then, because you will need to reduce your position size in order to avoid getting the shoulder tap.

You need to start the year slow and build up.

The year has a great deal of path dependence which means that how you start has a big influence on where you end up. If Steve loses $2 million in January, the odds that he will hit his $10 million goal are almost zero. If he makes $400k in January and $600k in February, he's behind budget but still in an OK position.

The idea is to get safely away from the zero bound and then when a mega-opportunity arrives and you have a cushion… Go for it. If Steve is +$1.5 million on February 25 and there is a fantastic opportunity, he is in a position to risk a bigger chunk of cash, say $500k, on the idea without worrying about putting himself underwater.

Remember that Rule #1 of trading is: *don't blow up*. Always give yourself a chance to play tomorrow. It is tricky to give precise mathematical formulas for risk management because this implies there is a correct answer. There is no precise answer in risk management. Every trader, every bank and every hedge fund must manage risk differently. What I can tell you is how I think about risk in different scenarios. You can either mirror parts of this framework if it makes sense to you, or you can transform it to fit your needs.

Before I can establish my basic yearly framework, I need to know my free capital. Free capital is the amount of money you can afford to lose. For retail traders, that's the portion of your account you feel you can lose in a year and still come back. For bank, real money and hedge fund traders, it's your annual stop loss.

My strategy is to start slow and build up capital, then get as aggressive as possible (if there are juicy market opportunities) by June or July at the latest. Hopefully earlier. Budgets vary over the years, but I will again use the $10 million goal and $4 million stop loss because that is a realistic ratio and the absolute numbers don't matter as much as the relative figures.

Using the same 2.5 : 1 ratio, a retail trader might be risking a maximum loss of $40,000 for the year with the goal of making $100,000. A hedge fund trader might have a stop loss of $40 million and a target of $100 million. This 2.5 : 1 ratio is not a rule, it's just a realistic ratio that's in the ballpark. Some bank traders might have a tighter stop loss of $2 million and be looking to make $20 million if they have a great market making seat. A retail trader might be risking $20,000 but hope to make $200,000.

Again, the numbers I am presenting in this chapter are not meant to be immutable laws of finance. They are realistic parameters that work in my world but may need to be adjusted in yours.

A trader with a maximum loss of $4 million and a target of $10 million can allow more risk taking when he is doing well and should take less risk when he is struggling. Based on year-to-date (YTD) P&L, a good system is to allocate a new monthly stop loss on the first day of the month and determine that stop loss using the YTD P&L. The better you are doing, the more leverage you use in the next month if good opportunities arise. For example, this is a reasonable scale for the $4 million stop loss trader who wants to make $10 million.

YTD P&L ($millions)	Maximum monthly loss ($)
Worse than negative 2	300,000
Negative 2 to zero	400,000
Zero to +1	500,000
+1 to +2	750,000
+2 to +4	1,000,000
+4 to +6	1,200,000
Above +6	1,500,000

The objective is never to get to your YTD goal and then put your feet up. The objective is to get stronger and stronger over the course of the year so that you can take maximum risk when rare opportunities appear. Under this sort of framework, you might find yourself up $6 million in June and able to spend $1 million on a strong trade idea that makes you $4 million. Then, you're up $10 million in July and you can sit on your hands until the next huge opportunity comes. If your goal for the year was $10 million and you are there in July, you have put yourself in a position to make $20 million or maybe more. Those chances don't come along every year. Keep trading.

Often the P&L chart of an alpha macro trader in a good year will look like a series of steps with interval periods where the P&L flatlines. This is the P&L trajectory of a trader that waits for the big opportunities and then puts on meaningful risk at the right times. This is not the trajectory for every alpha trader.

A good retail scalper or news trader, for example, will have a P&L chart that looks more like a 45-degree angle. But even a trader that is consistent should be taking more risk and making more money when they are strongly positive for the year and taking less risk when they are close to zero or negative YTD.

2. Understand the metagame

Trading successfully and moving the risk lever up and down throughout the year requires a good understanding of the specific metagame you are playing. You need to understand the internal rules, incentives, politics, and risk management framework where you work and incorporate these into your risk management decisions as well.

For example, does your boss freak out when you lose more than $X? If so, you know that is the internal no-go line, even if there has never been a rule set. Does your contract say you will be fired if you lose more than 9% while history shows that traders at your firm tend to get derisked or fired when they lose 5%? Forget the number in the contract, the metagame rules say your stop loss should be 5%.

If you work at a bank, does your compensation flatline once your P&L hits a certain threshold? If yes, then keep in mind that if you hit that threshold, losses will cost you more in compensation than gains will help you. Adjust your risk accordingly.

There are so many different metagames, depending on where you work. Take a few minutes to think about the metagame in your seat. Even if you are a retail trader, there is probably a metagame. For example, if you don't earn a certain amount of money in your first two years, will your spouse get antsy and ask you to get a "real" job? If so, then you need to set your target above that level!

You need your family on board or you will find life difficult. Trading is incredibly hard. It will inevitably test your belief in yourself. If those around you (management, family, the person who provided your trading capital…) don't believe in you, it will be impossible.

3. Don't blow up

This one is so simple and yet traders blow up all the time. Trade liquid products. If you are a retail equity trader, don't short the biotech stock that just tripled from $1.50 to $4.50. If you are a currency trader, don't take positions in pegged currencies. Manage your overnight and weekend risk tightly. The smaller your account size or free capital, the more careful you need to be. If you sell options, think about ridiculous worst-case scenarios and avoid them.

The universe of trades is so large in every asset class that there is no excuse for putting on trades that have unlimited downside. You should be confident about your ability to stop out of any trade or you should keep it small enough it's not going to kill you if it goes pear-shaped. If a trade you have on has a low probability of a huge tail risk, cover it and find something better to trade.

Understand path dependence

Path dependence is an important concept for every professional trader to understand. It comes into play in different ways. Path dependence means future steps of a process depend on its history. A series of coin flips is not path dependent. If you flip 10 tails, the coin has no memory and the 11th flip is fair and 50/50.

On the other hand, each month in a trading year is path dependent. Your performance in January will determine your free capital and your state of mind for February. The most important thing to remember is to never take actions in one period that could be overly detrimental to future periods.

For example: you work at a bank where P&L resets every January 1. There is a perfect, 5-star set up in S&P futures and you have never been so confident that they are about to (finally!) crash. Your approach to this trade, the sizing you choose and the amount of capital you will risk should be different in January than in August.

While this is irrational from a theoretical point of view, in real life there is too much path dependence in January for you to go all-in; you must act conservatively knowing that your performance in January will influence your performance in the following 11 months. On the other hand, if your annual target was $5 million, you are now up $7 million and it's September, you know that even if you lose $2 million on this trade idea, it won't have much negative impact on your trading for the final three months of the year. I know this might not seem rational to you, but believe me, it is. Playing the multi-period metagame correctly is just as important as maximizing P&L for a given period.

Another way path dependence matters is when you start a new job in trading. A trader that has made money 8 straight years doesn't attract much attention if she loses money in Year 9. On the other hand, a new hire that loses money in his first four months of trading might make a manager question why they hired him.

Financial firms are generally not very good at separating luck from skill or at comparing market regimes to trader performance. The absolute number next to your name matters much more than any context surrounding it. Therefore, when you start a new trading job, it is crucial that you understand how much runway you have.

As ridiculous as it sounds, your ultimate success or failure at a hedge fund is usually determined within the first 18 months. Your entire career (or lack of career) at the fund will be rooted in that initial performance. The trader that comes out hot and shoots the lights out will be given plenty of slack going forward and can probably draw down in future without too much hassle.

The equally-skilled trader that comes in and loses money for the first five months will be under heightened scrutiny, even if those five months were the lowest volatility period in the history of his asset class and he is known to be a trader that performs well in high-vol markets.

The way to protect against this path dependence when switching firms is to ensure you have at least one (and hopefully two or three) strong supporters within the organization. And make sure that the strong supporter who brought you in is planning to stay! Once your sponsor leaves, your life or death in that firm becomes even more path dependent. Try to avoid relying on luck by ensuring that you have sufficient runway when you go to a new firm.

Jerry, the greatest trader who never was

Jerry was one of the best pure traders I have ever seen. But he drove so fast we all knew that eventually he would slam into the wall…

Jerry was a 21-year-old college dropout who worked in the same day trading office as I did in the late 1990s. He had no financial markets background. He was a pure gambler who found his way onto the trading floor because of a few lucky coincidences. He loved to go out clubbing until 3 a.m. and then come in and trade the pre-open at 8 a.m. He was hilarious and immature and knew very little about markets.

Despite all this, he had incredible instincts. He had a professional gambler's eye for risk/reward and opportunity. He was like a modern-day Jesse Livermore who could read the tape and sentiment and price action and make money in ways that were incredibly skillful and fun to watch. Jerry could feel what was going to happen before it happened. He was so obviously good at trading that the 40-year-old trader that was randomly seated next to him decided to close his own account and back Jerry instead.

But Jerry couldn't stay away from the thinly-traded names. He would yell out "Look at -*insert ticker symbol of a thinly-traded stock nobody has ever heard of here-*. It's exploding!" We would bring up the chart and see some random micro-cap trading at $5.25, up 361% on the day. Instead of trading one cent wide in 500 or more shares like most stocks, these stocks jumped around in $1 increments, trading 30 cents wide in 100 shares. Jerry would sell 3,000 shares, taking it down from $5.25 to $4.25 and this would often trigger a waterfall move that let him quickly take profit at, say, $3.10.

There was yelling involved and it was incredibly fun to watch. He would then go back to trading normal stocks and making money and someone would say to him: "Jerry, you can't trade those microcaps. One day, one of them will just keep going up and you will get carted out of here."

He would listen closely and nod his head and say: "Yeah dude. You're right. I'll stop doing that. For sure."

Then three days later Jerry's yelling across the floor: "Oh boy! I'm short a lot of this one! This is not good!"

A stock went from $2 to $4, and he got short 14,000 shares. A few minutes later it was $6, then $8. His $50,000 account was suddenly worth minus $6,000. The manager of the trading floor issued a margin call and forced Jerry to buy back all the shares at an average of $8.20. The stock closed the day at $3.45.

Jerry was such an obviously talented kid that even after that incident, a different trader seeded him another $50,000. Four months later, guess what… The same thing happened. Jerry had amazing natural skill as a trader but it didn't matter. He blew up.

This is an extreme case, but a true story of how risk of ruin is the first and most important risk to manage. Never enter a trade unless you know you can get out. One of my previous bosses once said:

Trading is like driving a race car. You want to drive as fast as possible, but you can never lose control or crash into the wall.

Don't be like Jerry. Don't crash into the wall.

Astute readers might notice that Jerry's story sounds a bit like the story of the hedge funds that were mega-short low-priced, illiquid stocks in January 2021. Those funds, like Jerry, broke the first rule of trading: Don't blow up. The

GameStop episode was a friendly reminder that no amount of upside justifies putting on positions that you cannot properly risk manage. It was also a friendly reminder that short positions in cheap stocks have limited profit potential and unlimited risk. Stay away from trades with that payoff profile.

MONTHLY RISK MANAGEMENT

At the start of each month, you should take stock of your YTD performance and decide on a reasonable goal and stop loss for the month ahead. As the year progresses, you have more ammunition to take more risk so if you have been doing well, increase your monthly allocation. If you are struggling, keep it flat or cut it.

Keep in mind that increasing your risk allocation does not mean you have to start taking bigger positions on the first day of the month. What it means is that when a juicy opportunity arrives in the new month, you allocate more to it than you would have in the prior month.

Just before the start of a new month you should determine:

- Monthly stop loss
- Monthly profit goal
- $ at risk for Type I, Type II and Type III trades
  (I will define these trade types soon)
- One personal goal (fitness, sleep, eating, etc.)

As we move down the fractals from yearly to monthly to daily to single trades, there is an important concept you should always have in your mind: **variance**. Let's talk about variance for a few pages because it is a crucial concept in trading. First, here's a quote that sums it up nicely:

> *The laws of probability, so true in general,*
> *so fallacious in particular.*
> **EDWARD GIBBON,** *1774*

In statistics and probability, variance is the concept that in a series of numbers with a given average, individual data points will be spread out away from the average. So even if your average daily P&L over the last 10 years is +$23,000, you might still lose $25,000 five days in a row sometimes. This may not mean you did anything wrong. It's just variance.

Variance is a prominent feature in poker. A well-rested professional poker player will inevitably beat a drunk amateur over a long period, say 12 hours. But over any 10-minute or even 30-minute period, the drunk amateur might prevail. The key to understanding variance is that it is most visible in short samples. The larger the sample, the closer the aggregate data will approach the true average.

Luck is a short-term thing. In the long run, skill prevails.

Then again, as Keynes famously said… "In the long run, we are all dead." A very solid trading strategy with significant edge generates substantial variance, even year to year. This is why it is incredibly difficult to evaluate traders, portfolio managers and hedge funds. Was it luck or was it skill? Michael Mauboussin's book: *The Luck Equation: Untangling Skill and Luck in Business* is the go-to book on this topic.

To give you a sense of how variance impacts a year of performance in trading, let's run a few simulations. For simplicity, we'll use a static risk management approach where the trader does not change their risk appetite during the year, regardless of performance. That said, I strongly advocate increasing your risk as your P&L rises.

I include these simulations because I think very few people, even expert traders, truly appreciate just how dramatic the impact of variance can be on performance. It is probably a defense mechanism. If we truly appreciated how important variance was, we would feel like we barely control our own fate. And humans love to believe they are in control.

The first simulation (Figure 11.2) approximates the performance of a retail trader. She makes money 50% of days and loses money 50% of days. Her average winning day (net P&L) is +$2,000 and her average losing day is minus $1,200. Based on these figures, she will expect to make $100,800 in an average year. Here is her cumulative YTD P&L simulated 100 times.

The same trader using the same strategy in a world with the same probabilities might make $50,000 one year and $150,000 the next, with variance—and literally nothing else—to blame.

The second simulation (Figure 11.3) represents a bank trader. He makes money 55% of days and loses money 45% of days. His average winning day (net P&L) is +$150,000 and his average losing day is minus $120,000. Based on these figures, his expected value is +$7.2 million. But you see in Figure 11.3 how he fares in 100 simulations.

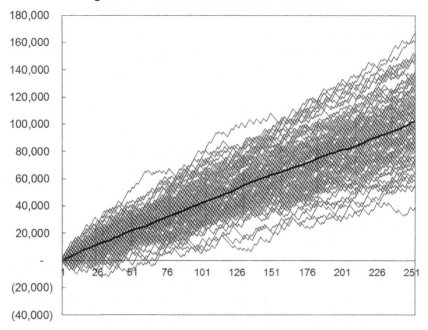

Figure 11.2: Variance simulation for a retail trader

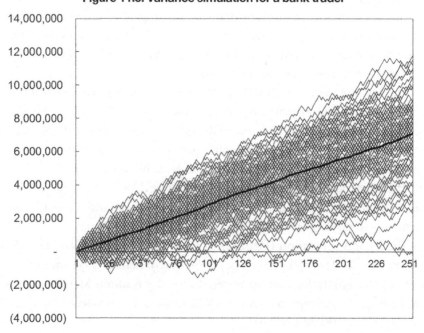

Figure 11.3: Variance simulation for a bank trader

You can see that despite employing a process with substantial edge and positive EV, a trader's annual performance is all over the place simply due to variance. This is a big reason why it is so *flipping* difficult for management to properly assess traders and for traders to evaluate themselves. It's easy to be fooled by randomness!

One of the most difficult and most important skills in trading is the ability to distinguish between variance and bad decision making. If you are losing money right now, is it because your process has broken down, your discipline sucks and the market has completely changed? Or is it because of the inevitable variance within the P&L distribution?

When you are on a bad streak, you need to ask yourself this. The longer you have been trading, the easier this is to answer (usually). For me, I can usually look back on a losing streak and determine with a fair amount of confidence whether it was variance. When you are starting out, it's almost impossible to tell.

Here are some examples of how I look at a losing streak and determine whether it's a product of variance or bad process.

Variance

1. I was wrong a lot. Being wrong is part of trading. It's OK to be wrong!

2. I got unlucky. I was long and some bad news came out yesterday. Today, I got stopped out at the highs.

When I am wrong and I lose money, I barely care. That's trading. As long as I have been sticking to my risk management system, I shrug and move on. Being wrong is where variance comes from in trading. Don't worry about it. On the other hand, some things can't be attributed to variance.

Not Variance

1. I have been right, and I am reading the market pretty well, but I am losing money. This is a strong indicator that there is something wrong with my process or risk management. For much of 2020, I was in synch with the market and my percentage of accurate calls was very high. But my performance was disappointing because of multiple breakdowns in discipline and process. I was wrong-sizing my trades and bleeding on random, low conviction ideas. **If you are reading the market well and losing money, that's a red flag**: something is wrong with your process and it's not just variance.

2. I traded with no plan. I walked in each day and started hitting buttons without a good sense of what I was trying to do. I cut out of good ideas early because I was bored.

3. I am overtrading. I should be tight/aggressive but instead I'm making a series of small bets on random, dumb ideas and leaking money every day.

4. I left a stale order in the system overnight and it triggered a loss. Poor attention to detail is not bad luck.

5. My discipline is poor. I broke my risk management rules. My positions were way too big. I kept moving my stop lower instead of cutting. I doubled a losing position.

6. The market regime has changed and I have not adapted.

7. My boss is giving me a hard time and making me nervous.

8. If I keep losing money, I am going to lose my job.

9. I am tired. I am arguing with my spouse or children. I think I might get a divorce. I am drinking too much. I feel depressed. I don't want to do this anymore.

If losses stem from any of 1 to 9 above; that's not variance. That is bad trading, bad process or bad mindset. Cut all your risk and figure out how to get things back on track. When you trust yourself to do the right thing, you are trading well. It should not matter all that much whether you make or lose money on any given day.

When you are trading with a good mindset, you see each trade and each day as a series of independent events with a probabilistic nature and you understand that some trades and some days you will lose money. Each day, you come in and do your best without getting too high or too low. You invest most of your energy in the process and very little in the outcome. Each trade, you go through a thoughtful process and execute in a rational and systematic way.

If you trade sloppy, don't say "I suck" or "I traded SO bad today". Instead ask: "Why was I so sloppy today? Am I burnt out? Discouraged? Disengaged?" Robotic application of a process keeps you sane and lets you know you can trust yourself. If you break your stop loss repeatedly, you should quickly figure out why. Bad discipline? No automation of stop loss? Don't care anymore?

If you go through the above lists (variance vs. not variance) and are still not sure whether a recent losing streak is caused by variance or bad trading, take a step back. The more experience you have, the easier it is to make this determination but if you are new, it can be very difficult, especially if you tend to be critical of yourself.

Traders with a healthy mindset who are confident in their process have a much easier time dealing with losing streaks because they can confidently identify the cause as variance and move on. Traders with a less healthy mindset or less confidence will tend to assume that a losing streak is the result of bad decisions and a lack of trading skill.

Alpha traders with a solid process and excellent risk management still hit losing streaks. In the long run, a solid process will win but in the short run, there are always going to be ups and downs due to variance. If you make money 50% of days, you can expect to lose money 6 or 7 days in a row once in a while. That is fine! When you lose money six days in a row and determine that it is simply because of variance, you need to double down on your process and believe in what you are doing more than ever. Variance can be managed, but never controlled.

Get comfortable with variance.

If you understand your edge and can confidently explain it, you will be much more comfortable with variance. Furthermore, if you continually spend time thinking about the current regime and how to adapt to present market conditions, you will reduce your variance and maintain steadier performance over time. No matter how good you are, though, you still need to understand that variance is a thing.

DAILY RISK MANAGEMENT

Daily stop losses can be good for some styles of trading and counterproductive for others. Daily stops work best for very short-term day traders. If your time horizon is generally two minutes to two hours and you square up your risk at the end of each day, a daily stop loss is probably right for you. If you trade a 1-week time horizon and often buy short-dated options, a daily stop loss makes no sense.

For retail traders, one of the simplest risk management systems is to simply multiply your free capital by 1% every morning and risk that much and no more. Then start fresh and do the same thing tomorrow. This increases your risk as you make money, decreases it as you lose money and keeps you in the game. If you are new to trading and plan to trade short-term views only, I highly recommend this approach. It is conservative but not ridiculously conservative. It will keep you safe but give you plenty of opportunity to succeed.

Daily stop losses are best for retail traders, day traders and junior institutional traders but less useful for most institutional or macro traders. Daily stop losses create a timing mismatch for traders whose time horizon spans beyond one day. They make it difficult to ride impulsive multi-day moves.

Say you are a bank trader with a $250,000 daily stop loss, a $1 million monthly stop loss and a $10 million budget. Some huge news comes out and it looks like a game changer for euro. You buy 50 million euros at 1.1800 with a 50 pip stop loss, risking $250,000. EURUSD rips 50 pips higher in 15 minutes and ends the day 100 pips higher at 1.1900. You are up $500,000 on the day and think the move will continue.

You believe the logical stop loss is your original entry minus 10 pips (1.1790) because you are a big fan of NewsPivots and feel if EURUSD goes back below the NewsPivot (1.1800) the news has been rejected.

If you go home long EURUSD with a stop at 1.1790, your total risk on the trade is just $50,000. But if you get stopped out your daily P&L tomorrow will be the $500,000 you made today plus the $50,000 loss = $550,000. That is way more than your daily stop of $250,000 so you either need to cut your risk by more than half or you need to move your stop closer. This is the tricky part of marking to market each day.

Very often in a case like this, you will see the trader simply put their stop 50 points (or less) away in order to stay below their daily limit. Instead of trading the market, they are trading their P&L. Inevitably, there is a 60-point dip overnight and the trader gets stopped out before EURUSD goes on a 400-point topside rampage.

On the other hand, if the trader's limits match their time horizon, there will be no such problem. If this trader is running with a $1 million monthly stop, they can trade the market the way they believe it is meant to be traded knowing that if it all goes horribly wrong, all they lost was $50,000. They can get back on their horse and keep riding the next day.

The key with any risk management system is that it needs to match your free capital, your trading style and your time horizon. Daily stops don't work with week-long ideas. Monthly stops don't make much sense for day traders, other than as a backup or overlay to a daily stop loss system.

INDIVIDUAL TRADE RISK MANAGEMENT

Managing the risk of an individual trade starts with understanding what kind of trade it is. Is this a standard day trade, i.e., the type of trade you do almost every day? Or is this a super rare opportunity that comes around a few times per year? Clearly those two scenarios require a different position size and risk management approach. Before I go through exactly how I choose position sizes, let's talk about conviction first.

Thoughts on conviction

Conviction level is one of the critical inputs into sizing your position. Good traders vary their bet size based on conviction. That said, if your conviction on a trade idea is not somewhere between "high" and "very high" … You probably should not do the trade.

Once you find a trade you like, and determine that your conviction is high, can you really extract a deeper level of granularity and determine what trades are "somewhat high", "high" or "very high" conviction? My experience suggests that most of the time, you can't.

You are unlikely to be able to judge, ex-ante, which routine day trades or short-term swing trades have a higher probability of success. On the other hand, there are some outlier trades that are clearly different from the norm and will come with a higher level of conviction.

Most good traders use some sort of tiered risk management system and the most common system involves three levels. A, B and C trades or 3-star, 4-star and 5-star trades are common ways of labelling conviction. These systems are simple, and they work, but there is a fundamental error in most of these systems: the increase in risk as you move up the scale is way too linear. I believe risk should increase exponentially on super high conviction trades.

The reason is that almost all trades have similar conviction. When you do a day trade or trade some lead/lag relationship, or execute against a pattern you see at the equity open… Those are the bread and butter trades you do all day, every day.

My view is that attaching a finer, granular determination of conviction or confidence level on those trades is kind of pointless. There is, however, an important exception. Once every three to six months, an unbelievably attractive trade comes along and you should allocate much more capital than usual to those trades.

I'm talking about those rare opportunities where the timing, risk/reward and probability of success all come together in a highly unusual and attractive way. The clearest examples of this can happen at a watershed moment for your asset market. For example: long hedged Nikkei futures in 2012 for Abenomics. The day they add your favorite stock to the S&P 500. Short the bitcoin bubble on the day futures started trading in 2017. Short Hertz and Chesapeake stock when the market bid them up even though they were bankrupt. These moments that are nearly once-in-a-lifetime require a different approach.

There can also be these super-high-probability trades that are less epic in terms of news flow but where all the planets align.

For me, there are three levels of conviction[123]:

TYPE I

Run of the mill trade you would do on any given day. Your conviction is high or you do not do the trade. This is not a rare opportunity, it is part of your regular process. Allocate 1% to 3% of your free capital, depending on your edge, experience level and historical performance. If you are new, keep to the 1% area, newish, stick to 2% or below and if you are comfortable with your process and know your success rate and statistics well enough, venture up to 3% max.

TYPE II

High conviction: This is a trade where something unique is going on, but not a watershed moment or extremely rare event. Maybe the Fed has turned hawkish after a period of dovishness. Or a stock you are expert in has a meaningful change of narrative. A 3-year trend in oil looks ready to reverse as Saudi Arabia has said "no mas" to production cuts.

Type II trades almost always involve a big narrative shift or some sort of significant dislocation. These are not routine trades. Allocate a meaningful chunk of capital to the idea based on your predetermined parameters. 3% to 5% of free capital generally makes sense but if you are having an excellent year, you may want to add 10% of your YTD profits on top.

The way you get outsized upside with limited downside is you reinvest profits when excellent opportunities arise. A TYPE II opportunity at the start of the year is a bummer because you cannot invest beyond 3% (or maybe 5% max)

---

123. FYI, in The Art of Currency Trading I used the terms 3-star, 4-star and 5-star. Upon further review, I feel a) Why have a system that starts at 3? Doesn't make a ton of sense, and b) calling each trade "TYPE" helps clarify that the system is not linear or incremental. TYPE I trades and TYPE III trades are completely different animals and should be handled with a totally different approach.

of free capital. On the other hand, if you are having a great year and it's only June… You can overbet the TYPE II opportunity knowing if you're wrong, it's completely fine.

Let's say a high net worth individual has given you $100 million of capital to trade with instructions to shoot for 15% returns and a $5 million stop loss (i.e., stop trading if you drop to $95 million). On January 1, your free capital is $5 million and your target is $15 million. Your compensation is simple. You get paid 20% of your P&L in cash, once per year. Now it's June, your P&L is +$11 million and a TYPE II opportunity presents itself.

Remember free capital is your stop loss ($5 million) + your YTD P&L ($11 million) so free capital in this situation is $16 million.

Scenario

The USD has ripped higher over the past six months as the Fed hikes rates. Money is piling into the USA because of the attractive yield and you think the USD is overvalued. The long USD position is crowded; all your metrics (and anecdotal evidence) suggest the market is max long USD. You want to sell the USD, but you are waiting for some sort of fundamental or at least technical catalyst. Hopefully both.

Today could be the day. The USD rips higher all morning, rallying to a new YTD high in the hours before the Fed meets. Everyone has added to their dollar longs as consensus calls for a hawkish meeting. The Fed is likely to ratify market expectations of at least two more rate hikes this year. You are ready for anything that sounds a bit dovish because that might be a catalyst for your reversal trade (short USD).

2:29:45 p.m. Fifteen seconds to the Fed announcement. Your palms are sweaty. Knees weak. Hands are heavy. You feel nervous but on the surface, you look calm and you're ready to sell dollars if the Fed moves to a more dovish setting.

2:30:00 p.m. BOOM! The red headline hits Bloomberg:

*FEDERAL RESERVE SAYS CURRENT LEVEL OF RATES IS APPROPRIATE AND FURTHER TIGHTENING UNLIKELY TO BE WARRANTED.

Whoa. This is a major change in the narrative and you want to get short USD. The USD gaps hard lower, you get short some USD and by the end of the day the chart shows a massive key reversal day off the new yearly high and the fundamental story has completely changed. You plan to hold this position for a multi-day drop of around 4% in the dollar.

Now, you need to determine how much capital to risk on the idea. It's not a once-in-a-lifetime trade but it's also clearly not a TYPE I. How do you decide how much to risk?

As a baseline, start with a simple high-end TYPE I or low-end TYPE II risk calculation. That would be around 3% of free capital. Free capital is the original $5m you are allowed to lose + the $11m year-to-date P&L which = $16m.

$16 million X 3% = $480,000

OK so that is the bare minimum, but that's high-end TYPE I risk sizing, not TYPE II.

**You get outsized returns (right tail) by making
big bets when you are in a strong capital position.**

You are more than 2/3 of the way to your yearly goal and it's only June. TYPE II opportunities are rare. In this situation, a simple formula for TYPE II is:

TYPE II RISK = 3% of free capital plus 10% of YTD P&L

In this case that would be $480,000 + $1,100,000 = $1,580,000

I like this formula. It's simple, and effective. But you don't have to stick to it religiously. Think about how you will feel if you drawdown that much. Is it going to kill you psychologically? $11m minus $1.58m will take you to around $9.5m YTD. That's still not too shabby and in my opinion, that would be perfectly manageable.

This is a good starting point and you can always scale up or down from there depending on other factors such as how strongly you feel about the trade and how sensitive your manager is to large drawdowns. This also depends somewhat on how loose or tight you are with defining trades as TYPE I and TYPE II. If you're finding yourself thinking two trades per month are TYPE II trades, you need to be more conservative. If you only find 4 or 5 TYPE II trades per year, 3% of free capital + 10% of YTD is probably about right.

Remember: Understand the Metagame

If you plan to take abnormally large risk on a trade, it never hurts to over-communicate with your manager. If management is used to seeing your daily P&L fluctuate +/- $300k and then you drop $1.5 million in two days... That will generate some discomfort. The best strategy is to fire off a quick email saying you have a high conviction trade idea and plan to risk more capital than usual on it given your strong YTD and elevated confidence in the set up. Managers hate surprises. Whether you work at a bank, hedge fund or other institution, my experience is that all managers prefer a trader that overcommunicates.

TYPE III

Outlier opportunity: This is a dislocation, policy change, historic moment or economic event so large it demands a huge bet—but only if you are in a strong position to make that outsized bet. If you are down on the year or near your monthly stop loss or near bossman shoulder tap level… Unfortunately, you just have to keep it small. Allocate TYPE I or TYPE II money and hope you are in a stronger position next time.

But… If you are in a strong capital position, you should rationally assess what is the most you can invest in this idea. Keep in mind that no matter how good the opportunity might seem—you could still be wrong! You could still lose money.

No matter how great the opportunity, you must remember that a) your assessment of the probabilities may not be accurate and b) you only get to run the experiment once. You never bet more than you can afford to lose. A roulette wheel will sometimes come up green and you will occasionally roll a "1" on a 20-sided die.

The point with these TYPE III opportunities is that they can make your year. They can make your career. And I think, in general, good traders know them when they see them. If a TYPE III opportunity presents itself, think long and hard about the optimal bet size. Have courage. Go big.

Here's a short excerpt from Stan Druckenmiller's famous Lost Tree Club speech:

> The only way to make long-term returns in our business that are superior is by being a pig. The first thing I heard when I got in the business, not from my mentor, was "bulls make money, bears make money, and pigs get slaughtered."
>
> I'm here to tell you I was a pig. And strongly believe the only way to make long-term returns in our business that are superior is by being a pig. I think diversification and all the stuff they're teaching at business school today is probably the most misguided concept everywhere.

Bulls, bears, pigs, sharks, snakes, hedgehogs, foxes, hawks, doves and owls. There are plenty of animals on Wall Street.

When a Type III trade comes along and you are in a strong position, you need to take the most possible risk. That could mean as much as 50% of your YTD P&L, depending on your risk management framework and your role. I cannot tell you an exact formula because it depends too much on where you work and how you manage your risk. But start with the TYPE II formula and then increase as much as possible without introducing any major path dependence problems. In other words, risk as much as you possibly can knowing that you still might be wrong and don't want to ruin the rest of your year by destroying your momentum. Yes, you want to be a pig in situations like this but you also need to consider you could be wrong.

Be like a call option

I have created a simple graphic (Figure 11.4) to show you why it is important to structure your process so that you take more risk when you are doing well and less when you are not. The chart shows is a P&L simulation for three traders who start out with $100,000, risk 3% of capital each day, make money 50% of days and whose average P&L on winning days is 1.5X the P&L on an average losing day.

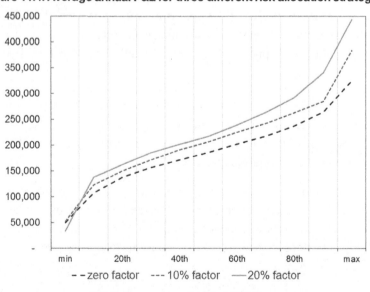

Figure 11.4: Average annual P&L for three different risk allocation strategies

250 trades per year, simulated 1000 times

The factors represent how much of YTD P&L each trader risks on each trade. The "zero factor" trader risks 3% each day, the "10% factor" trader risks 3% of free capital plus 10% of YTD P&L and the "20% factor" trader risks 3% of free capital plus 20% of YTD. You can see that the downside is similar for all three traders: A bad year is around +$50,000. This is because if the trader is struggling, they reduce risk and all three methodologies would take similar risk.

On the other hand, a great year for the "20% factor" trader is closer to $450,000 while a great year for the "zero factor" trader is more like $300,000. More upside without more downside! Nice.

Why not go to 50% or 100% of YTD then? In an experiment with unlimited time and infinite trials, higher percentages are best, but in real life, where you only get to live each year once, lower numbers are preferable. Higher numbers introduce unacceptable levels of variance. Even 20% is very high; I am just using it to make the point and show you how the average annual returns vary as you tweak your risk factor higher.

This is a toned-down version of the Kelly criterion at work[124]. As you make money, you take more risk and as you lose, you take less. This is the core of how you behave like a call option over the years. A hedge fund or trading business with a bunch of traders all behaving this way will have low downside volatility with a ton of upside.

When I suggest you allocate 1% to 3% of your free capital to TYPE I trades, this assumes you have only one trade on at a time. If you have more than one trade on, you need to very carefully assess the correlation of the trades and the probability that they could all go wrong at the same time.

Fewer trades = better trading = lower transaction costs = easier risk management

Generally, when I have more than one TYPE I trade on at the same time, I just treat them all as one trade for risk management purposes. In other words, I size my positions so that if every single one gets stopped out, I will not lose

---

124. The Kelly Criterion is a formula used by gamblers to calculate optimal bet size. Using the Kelly Criterion leads to higher wealth compared to any other bet-sizing strategy (in the long run). The Kelly Criterion relies on known odds and so it is not directly applicable to trading because the probability of winning or losing in trading can only be loosely estimated, it is not directly observable. Still, the concept behind the Kelly Criterion is directly applicable to trading and risk management, even if the precise mathematics are not. For an entertaining book that includes plenty of information about the Kelly Criterion, check out Fortune's Formula by William Poundstone.

more than 3% of my free capital. Life is much easier if you trade one position at a time or treat all your positions as one risk management blob. If you try to take on more risk and start assuming correlation between different trades, you might suddenly wake up one morning down 8% of free capital because the correlations didn't work out the way you thought they would.

Furthermore, are you an investor or a trader? If you have 14 line items, you are a portfolio manager or an investor, but not really a trader. Do you have 14 good ideas at one time? Probably not. Do you have 7 good ideas at one time? Again, probably not. Focus on one or two strong ideas and monetize them. Concentrate your bets in the places you think you have the most edge and the highest conviction. Spreading bets around is a recipe for higher transaction costs, lazy risk management, diluted returns and correlation confusion.

The big takeaway from this section is that when an epic, watershed trade comes along and you are in a strong capital position, it is time to go all-in. All-in does not mean risk your job or risk your fund. It means risk the maximum possible within the parameters you have set. Play tight when you're weak. Play extremely aggressively when you're strong and the opportunity is exceptional. Huge opportunities do not come along all that often. Jump on them.

Good trading takes courage.

Position sizing

One of the most common questions I get from new traders is: How do you size your positions? For me, the answer is pretty simple. Here are the five steps:

1. **You have a trade idea.** Let's say you think bonds are going to sell off in the days leading up to non-farm payrolls (aka The US Jobs Report) because the market is massively long, everyone has been super bullish for months and the whisper number for the jobs number is creeping higher and higher in recent days. This is a classic run-up trade as I will describe in Chapter 12. You have decided the best way to trade this is to buy TBT, the ultrashort bond ETF. While TBT is not a good way to short the bond market for more than a day or two, your time horizon is just two days so you have decided this will be the easiest, most liquid and levered way to execute the trade.

2. **Determine your conviction level.** You think this is a classic run-up trade and you love a good run-up trade. You decide this is a Type II

trade, which this month means $250,000 of risk would normally be allocated to this idea.

3. **Decide how much to risk.** You are up $1.0 million this year and have a particularly strong feeling about this trade. The chart set up is great, too, so you can take a big position. Since you plan to cover the trade BEFORE the non-farm payrolls release, you don't have to worry about gap risk through the number. You decide to risk the standard $250,000, plus 10% of your YTD P&L ($1 million X 10% = $100,000) so you are risking $350,000 on the trade.

4. **Determine the stop loss.** Use technical analysis and other inputs (average daily range, expected volatility, an understanding of round number bias, etc.) to determine the stop loss on the trade. You have a rule that you always place your stop loss at least one average day's range away from your entry point. This is a good rule of thumb for new traders. If I know absolutely nothing about a security, the first thing I do when looking to put in a stop loss is calculate the security's average daily range. Any stop loss closer than 1-day's range away is at high risk of getting dinged by short-term noise.

5. **Determine the position size.** To make the math easy, let's say TBT is trading at $100.00 and you have determined, after looking at the charts and studying the volatility of TBT, that the appropriate stop loss is $102.02. Liquidity is excellent and slippage is not an issue. You estimate 3 cents of slippage on your stop. So you are risking $2.05 / share and you decided in step 3 to risk $350,000. Here is how you calculate the correct sizing:

Position size

= $ at risk / (entry point - stop loss level)

= $350,000 / (102.05 - 100.00)

= 170,731

Therefore, the trader in this example should buy 170,731 shares of TBT. The formula for determining position size is always the same:

position size = $ at risk / (entry point - stop loss level)

Let's do one more just to make sure it's clear.

I am a retail trader and I want to sell AUDUSD because: reasons. The currency pair is trading at 0.7500 right now and after studying the pair's volatility and doing 20 minutes of technical analysis, I have determined that 0.7572 is the correct stop loss. My trading account balance is currently $165,000 and I always risk 2% of capital on every trade. I never run more than one trade at a time so this is a safe way to run my account. I will add 3 pips to my stop loss level to allow for slippage on execution.

2% of 165,000 is $3,300.

Position size

= $ at risk / (entry point - stop loss level)

= $3,300 / (0.7500 - 0.7575)

= $3,300 / -0.0075

= - 440,000

So our short position in AUDUSD should be 440,000 AUD. If we get stopped out, we will lose $3,300, which is 2% of capital.

Bad traders work in the opposite direction. They say: I'm short 2 million AUDUSD at 0.7500 but I can't afford to lose more than $10,000 so my stop loss will be 0.7550. This makes no sense because 0.7550 is a totally arbitrary level that does not take market factors like volatility or technical analysis into consideration. Always start with $ at risk, then determine your stop loss by analyzing the market. The position size is the output, not the input.

To summarize the five steps explained above:

1. You have a trade idea.

2. Determine your conviction level (TYPE I, II or III).

3. Decide how much to risk. This amount to risk can be in USD or in basis points, depending where you work. This amount is determined by your conviction level, YTD P&L and your risk management system.

4. Determine your stop loss using technical analysis and other inputs.

5. Do the math to back out the correct position size.

Using this methodology, your position size can vary substantially. A low conviction position with a wide stop loss for a good hedge fund trade might be 20 million AUDUSD while a high conviction trade with a tighter stop loss for the same trader could be 200 million AUDUSD.

Good traders vary bet size.
Good traders vary bet size.
Good traders vary bet size.

Whenever you see a trader that always trades in 1,000 share lots or $10 million USD FX positions, there is a good chance they don't know what they are doing. Alternatively, some traders are able to vary their position size to a point but then hit a plateau. Above a certain amount of risk, they feel uncomfortable and dial it back, even if that is not the optimal sizing. Keep an eye out for plateaus like this in your trading. If you tend to top out at a specific risk level, even when you know your capital and risk management system allow you to take more, figure out why.

The best traders have the largest variation in bet size. A great trader might trade lower conviction size of 1,000 shares of AAPL early in the year and then 15,000 shares of AAPL by summer when she has high conviction and a big chunk of P&L to work with.

Let me clarify something important here. When I talk about increasing risk as your P&L grows, I am not saying you keep doubling down until you bust. There is a bias known as the house money effect in which studies show that traders and gamblers treat money they have won differently from money they started out with. If you start the night at a casino with $100 and now have $500, the incremental $400 feels different than the initial $100. It's free money. Studies show that gamblers treat house money with less respect and are more likely to gamble it away recklessly. Don't do that! That is not what I am recommending.

What I am talking about is a methodical increase in risk appetite as your bankroll grows. This is like the Kelly Criterion in sports gambling. As your bankroll and your edge grow, you should take more risk. As your bankroll and edge fall, you should take less risk.

Note: Be on the lookout for the house money effect. When you are up huge on the day, do you trade sloppier? Many people do. I do. Remember the story from earlier, "Joyful yelling signals imminent P&L crash?" Systematic increases in risk appetite as capital increases are completely different from winner's tilt and the house money effect. Make sure you understand the difference.

THE EVOLUTION OF EXPECTED
VALUE OVER THE LIFE OF A TRADE

There is a particularly tricky concept in the mathematics of trading which is that the risk/reward of a given trade changes as prices move. An example is if you have a trade where you were risking 1% to make 2% and then it quickly moves 1.5% in your favor. At that point the question is, are you now risking 2.5% to make 0.5% (unattractive!) or do you ignore the mark to market and stick with your original plan. The answer is not obvious.

Most people respond that you should mark to market because the current market price is the only thing that matters. The problem with this approach is that you will never let your trades run to the take profit because the risk/reward is so bad once the trade moves more than halfway towards the take profit level. If you are risking 1 to make 2, but then you always take profit when it moves 1.5... Your risk/reward ratio was never 1 to 2, it was 1 to 1.5. Even worse, if you get nervous when it has moved just 1% ... You take profit and then your trading system is just risking 1 to make 1. Decide where the finish line is before you start the race.

One way to deal with this is to move your stop loss higher as the trade moves deeper in the money. This is generally logical, but introduces more noise risk as a random pullback might knock you out when the trade would have been safe under the original parameters. The most effective way to trail your stop is to use a moving average that matches the trend and update your stop loss once every 12 or every 24 hours.

There is no correct answer here, but my general feeling is that if you put a trade on risking 1 to make 2, you cannot take profit all the time once you make 1.4 because that means your original plan was not really true and your risk/reward on every trade is much worse than you think it is on inception. You are putting on a trade with a certain plan in mind and then moving the goalposts once the trade moves in the money.

Either trail your stop loss higher in a systematic way while still giving the trade plenty of room to breathe, or take partial profits at predetermined levels.

Trailing the stop systematically breaks the rule of setting stops based on technical analysis and market logic, which is not ideal. But you can always fine tune whatever stop loss the system spits out by looking at a few charts. What you should not do is cut every trade early because "the risk/reward sucks now".

That is a logical fallacy that ignores the original structure of the trade and ignores the fact that a core skill in successful trading is the ability to find trades that offer substantially more reward than risk. Don't truncate your right tail all the time. Trying to extract the last 20% of a trade may cause you to give back all your gains. That's just the way it is. That's just trading.

As an FYI, this discrepancy between actual payout on trades and forecast payout happens all the time and it's something you need to monitor. If you are structuring all your trades risking 1 to make 3 but then you cut everything early because you get antsy or bored or are risk averse and looking for excuses to reduce... Your risk/reward is not 1 to 3. It might be 1 to 2, or worse. Monitor this.

This is frequently an issue in options trading too. Often you will see an exotic option like a reverse knock-out that pays something like 8 : 1. But the only way for it to pay off that way is if the option expires exactly one basis point away from the barrier. That is a totally unrealistic assumption. If you are buying low-delta digital options at 8% because they look like juicy leverage but then you sell them every time they double to 16%... You might have been better off trading a simpler, more liquid structure.

**If you are structuring trades for maximum leverage,
make sure you get the leverage you thought you were getting.**

STICKING TO THE PLAN

There is always a tension between sticking to the plan and adjusting to new information. The problem with adjusting to new information is that a substantial percentage of the information you receive in a given trading day is noise. Some days are 100% noise. Your predisposition, once you have a trade on, should always be to do nothing. Leave it alone and follow your original plan. Plans are generally made in a rational state of mind. Adjustments on the fly are often emotional and biased reactions to the non-stop onslaught of stimulus.

Prices are almost always changing. New information is arriving constantly. Most of it is meaningless.

**If you have a trade on, stick to the original plan until
there is new information you cannot possibly ignore.**

That is, assume new information is mostly noise and react only when there is an unambiguous signal. Some traders impose a restrictive rule to avoid overtrading. For example, "Once I put on a trade, I will re-evaluate it once per day at 11 a.m. and otherwise leave it until the stop loss or take profit trigger." This avoids the problem of sitting there, staring at the screen as the dumb voices in your head say stuff like:

> *It's trading heavy… Maybe I should get out.*
>
> *That headline is making me nervous.*
>
> *If this trade goes south, I'll be down on the month.*
>
> *Look, a squirrel!*

KNOW YOUR DEFAULT MODE

Part of this calculus is knowing your own default mode network. The default mode network (DMN) is a cognitive science concept. Research shows that there is a particular part of your brain that becomes active when you are not busy thinking about anything in particular (wakeful rest). This area tends to have the same thoughts over and over. These are the thoughts you circle back to when you are not thinking about anything.

Mendel Kaelen suggests we think of the mind like a hill covered in fresh snow. Each thought is a sled that slides down that hill, leaving a trail. The more sleds that slide down those same trails, the deeper those trails become and the more difficult it becomes to avoid sliding into the same repetitive thought patterns.

What are your default modes?

When there is a trading lull, how do you typically think? What is the action you default to? When you have a trade on, and you're sitting in front of the screen, what is your default mode? Do you generally want to add to the position? Or cut it? Or are you fine to wait patiently and let it simmer until it's ready? Become familiar with your default thought and action patterns and think about whether they are destructive, whether they add to or subtract from your process, and whether they lead to productive or suboptimal actions.

When you're not busy at work, where does your mind go? Is it a positive or negative place? Are your typical thoughts constructive or self-critical? Do they encourage action or inaction? Does your DMN help you or hurt you? How do you break the bad habits?

One part of my default mode is to scan through charts and think about random market-related ideas. That's a positive and productive DMN. I default to thinking things like: "Hmm, VIX has dropped three days in a row, is that bullish for stocks?" or "I wonder what lumber and soybeans are doing; I haven't checked the soft commodities in a while" or "When's the next RBNZ meeting?" I also default to tossing around ideas for upcoming editions of AM/FX, my daily macro newsletter. I add them to a Word doc of future ideas.

The negative part of my default mode is a strong and steady urge to press the BUY and SELL buttons. I always want to put on or add to positions. Whenever markets slow down and enter a quieter intraday phase, I find myself tempted to increase my position size. I should be doing nothing, because unnecessary increases in position size often lead to suboptimal risk management scenarios, if price goes the wrong way.

This default mode is such a known part of who I am that my manager Pete once wrote "REDUCE" on a sticky note and stuck it to the bottom right corner of one of my monitors. Anyone who knows me as a trader knows my positions are either the right size or too big. Almost never too small. This is not good.

The "REDUCE" sign helped me maintain awareness of my default mode, which is a subconscious desire to increase risk even when there is no reason to do so. It helps me keep my hands off the BUY and SELL buttons when there is no logical action to be taken. Alpha traders hold two contradictory skills at once: they can sit there and do nothing for long periods, and they can act aggressively, without hesitation. Most people can do one but struggle with the other. I'm great at acting without hesitation, but I will always be working on my patience.

Listen to your default thoughts when your mind is quiet and determine if they are beneficial or toxic. For what it's worth, this is a useful exercise to run outside of trading too. Do the default voices in your head criticize or motivate you? Do they spur you toward action or convince you to procrastinate?

I believe that navigating the cacophony of competing voices in your head and choosing which ones to ignore and which ones to listen to is one of the most important determinants of survival and success in both trading and in life. Shutting out the toxic voices and following the beneficial ones is the definition of conscientiousness, willpower, and discipline. It also the primary purpose of meditation and mindfulness exercises.

When you have a choice to either watch TV or go lift weights, there are two competing voices that go something like this:

VOICE 1
You will feel great if you go work out.
All you need to do is get up off the couch and—

VOICE 2
(INTERRUPTING)
South Park is on! The really funny one from 2006! There's
Sour Cream and Onion Ruffles in the cupboard!

Your health and fitness will be determined by which voice you listen to. Same thing in trading. The voices are there too. For example, you slowly piece together a strong trade idea, execute, and write down your planned stop loss and take profit level. You like the trade idea and you have a clear plan. Then half an hour later, the voices start:

VOICE 1
Why hasn't it moved by now? This idea must be wrong. You
should get out. Last thing we want to do is lose money on a--

VOICE 2
(INTERRUPTING)
You are so cold right now. Like... Arctic cold.
Cucumber cold. You should just--

VOICE 1
(INTERRUPTING)
Wait! It's rallying now! Double your position!

It is remarkable that even the smartest people in the world have these dumb voices in their head. It's all part of the fun of being a human being. Ignore the negative voices and slowly tune your default mode network to think: *stick to the plan*. Stick to the plan. Stick to the plan. Treat it like a mantra. Stick to the plan. Stick to the plan. When that dumb voice in your head tries to steer you towards the rocks, throw it off the boat. *Stick to the plan. Stick to the plan.*

YOU CAN'T ALWAYS STICK TO THE PLAN!

Of course, there are times when you should abandon your plan and get out of Dodge. Like a commercial pilot, stick with the flight plan as long as humanly possible, but change course in the face of major new information.

A good example of when it makes sense to deviate from plan is if a trade has moved substantially in your favor just before a market-moving event (economic data, central bank meeting, etc.) You don't want to risk a major portion of your capital on a coin toss especially when you know there is gap and liquidity risk around big events. Unless you have a strong view on the outcome of a particular economic event, it usually makes sense to lighten up on risk beforehand.

That said, if your trade plan was solid, you probably saw that event coming and considered it in your trade plan. Upcoming catalysts should always be reassessment triggers.

• • •

That concludes Chapter 11. I hope you now have a solid understanding of how I think about risk. I hope you can use some of these tactics and fold some of my ideas into your process. I could say this 100 times and it would not be enough:

The number one rule of trading is: *avoid ruin.*

Before we hit Chapter 12, let's take a little detour here to talk about Jesse Livermore and the book *Reminiscences of a Stock Operator*.

• • •

END OF CHAPTER DETOUR:
A QUICK BOOK REVIEW KINDA THING

Reminiscences of a Stock Operator is a quintessential (and slightly misunderstood) piece of trading literature. This 1923 classic is a slightly fictionalized biography of Jesse Livermore written by Edwin Lefèvre. Livermore was a famous speculator and Bobby-Axelrod-style celebrity-rich-guy. The book is epic entertainment and full of all kinds of cool trading wisdom and nifty old timey Wall Street jargon like "tape reading" and "bucket shops". It is also a cautionary tale and a case study in overtrading, bad discipline, poor money management, and the dark side of trading.

Livermore, oft celebrated as a genius and as one of the greatest speculators of all time, went bankrupt three times and eventually committed suicide in the cloak room of the Sherry Netherland Hotel in New York City. By all accounts, he was an incredible trader—with fatal flaws.

An interesting fact that tells me he was a classy guy: each time he declared bankruptcy, he would borrow a small stake from a friend so he could start trading again. Then, he would build it up substantially, eventually making himself rich again. Once he was fully liquid, he would pay back all the creditors he owed from before he declared bankruptcy. He did this even though he was clear of the debts and was not legally required to repay, thanks to the bankruptcy proceeding. He just paid people back because it was the right thing to do.

Here are some of my favorite quotes from the book, with a bit of my own commentary sprinkled in.

> Fear and hope remain the same; therefore the study of the psychology of speculators is as valuable as it ever was. Weapons change, but strategy remains strategy, on the New York Stock Exchange as on the battlefield. I think the clearest summing up of the whole thing was expressed by Thomas F. Woodlock when he declared: "The principles of successful stock speculation are based on the supposition that people will continue in the future to make the mistakes that they have made in the past.

In other words, *this time is not different.*

> A stock operator has to fight a lot of expensive enemies within himself.

Learning the rules is easy. Following them is hard. Self-awareness is key.

> One of the most helpful things that anybody can learn is to give up trying to catch the last eighth—or the first. These two are the most expensive eighths in the world.

It feels SO GOOD when you sell the ding dong highs or buy the ding dong lows but it's not something that can be done on a regular basis. Don't bother trying.

> It takes a man a long time to learn all the lessons of all his mistakes. They say there are two sides to everything. But there is only one

side to the stock market; and it is not the bull side or the bear side, but the right side. It took me longer to get that general principle fixed firmly in my mind.

I also was better equipped than the average customer of Harding Brothers in that I was utterly free from speculative prejudices. The bear side doesn't appeal any more than the bull side, or vice versa. My one steadfast prejudice is against being wrong.

In other words: *be nimble*. Good traders are flexible and are not biased toward a particular direction in any market. I often ask people who work for some of the legends of trading, "What qualities make that trader so successful?" Just about every time, the answer includes something like: "He is happy to change his mind very quickly" or "He can be max short one day and max long the next". Bad traders are perma-something. Good traders are intellectually flexible. *Strong opinions, weakly held.*

Another lesson I learned early is that there is nothing new in Wall Street. There can't be because speculation is as old as the hills. Whatever happens in the stock market to-day has happened before and will happen again.

The thing that hath been, it is that which shall be; and that which is done is that which shall be done: and there is no new thing under the sun. Ecclesiastes 1:9

What beat me was not having brains enough to stick to my own game – that is, to play the market only when I was satisfied that precedents favoured my play. There is the plain fool, who does the wrong thing at all times everywhere, but there is also the Wall Street fool, who thinks he must trade all the time. No man can have adequate reasons for buying or selling stocks daily – or sufficient knowledge to make his play an intelligent play.

#overtrading

No, sir, nobody can make big money on what someone else tells him to do.

Trade your own view.

If you do not know who you are, the stock market is an expensive place to find out.

I love this one. It reminds me of a famous Ed Seykota quote: "Win or lose, everybody gets what they want out of the market."

> I was nearly twenty-seven years old. I had been at the game twelve years. But the first time I traded because of a crisis that was still to come I found that I had been using a telescope. Between my first glimpse of the storm cloud and the time for cashing in on the big break the stretch was evidently so much greater than I had thought that I began to wonder whether I really saw what I thought I saw so clearly. We had had many warnings and sensational ascensions in call-money rates. Still some of the great financiers talked hope-fully at least to newspaper reporters and the ensuing rallies in the stock market gave the lie to the calamity howlers. Was I fundamen-tally wrong in being bearish or merely temporarily wrong in having begun to sell short too soon?

This quote rang particularly true in 2007 when the market sniffed out a financial calamity very early on but many traders were too early to the trade and got shoulder-tapped before they could capitalize. For every legend of The Big Short winners, there were two or three bears who committed too big, too early and lost as they were forced to stop out near the highs. You only hear the stories of those who survive.

> I did precisely the wrong thing. The cotton showed me a loss and I kept it. The wheat showed me a profit and I sold it out. Of all the speculative blunders there are few greater than trying to average a losing game. Always sell what shows you a loss and keep what shows you a profit.

Cut your losses, run your winners.

> The game taught me the game. And it didn't spare the rod while teaching.

The best way to learn about the psychology of trading is to experience mind-numbing losses. As my boss once told me after a particularly bad day of trading: you don't learn anything when you win.

You are now around 79% of the way through this book. I hope you feel most of what you have read so far makes sense, and you see how you can incorporate some of my techniques into your process. In the next chapter, I will go step by step through my process, using many of the concepts and tactics described to this point. I hope to take all this disparate information and bring it together so you can see the entire trade selection and execution process from start to finish.

CHAPTER 12

BRINGING IT ALL TOGETHER

The lifecycle of a trade, from idea to execution to exit

The preceding chapters have covered a wide range of topics. In this chapter, I will bring it all together as I walk you through my real-world thought process and detail the lifecycle of a trade from start to finish.

Chapter 9 introduced some questions people frequently ask me, like: "Where do trade ideas come from?" "How do you come up with ideas?" "Where do you start?" "What is the process?" My philosophy has always been about combining as many disciplines as possible in an effort to narrow down and filter out ideas, with the hope of discovering the rare trade where all the planets are aligned. Many factors contribute to good trade ideas; they are not born from a simple chart pattern or single bit of fundamental analysis.

As mentioned earlier, I use fundamentals and microstructure to come up with most of my ideas. Then, I use other disciplines like technical analysis, sentiment, and cross-market analysis to filter and enhance the idea, and optimize execution.

Below, I present a visual that details the essentials of my process from start to finish. I will use this visual to walk you through how I come up with, execute, risk manage and analyze my trades. We'll start with generic explanations of each step (each box in the table) and then I will walk through a real-life trade I did recently to show you how it all works in real life.

Generally, the process flows through the table from left to right and top to bottom. Keep in mind that this table and the explanations that follow are a general framework. There are times when you may be doing this in a different order, or in your head, or in a less formal way.

For example, while this grid is laid out as a "Ready, Aim, Shoot" type of process, when it comes to headlines, my framework is more like "Ready, Shoot, Aim" (see Chapter 4). There is not enough time to think everything through when a headline comes out, so I allow myself to react as quickly as possible and execute the trade right away. Then, once I have the trade on, I go back through the remaining steps in the grid to make sure that my logic and risk management are sound. If they are not, then I quickly exit the trade or recalibrate my plan.

This is less risky if you are experienced and deeply engaged in the markets (i.e., have a strong knowledge of the narrative and an intuitive feel for volatility and weak side/strong side of the market without having to think about it much). "Ready, Shoot, Aim" is not recommended for noobs. Figure 12.1 is the table; we will go through it step by step.

Figure 12.1: The lifecycle of a trade

1 Idea generation	New narrative identified or existing narrative is stale or nearing exhaustion		Economic event or news changes outlook	Deviation from fair value	Pattern recognition and indicator scanning
2 Filtering	Where are we in the narrative cycle?	Positioning and sentiment	Events and catalysts	Correlated markets	Technical analysis (charts)
	Do these factors all support your idea? Or are there too many crosswinds?				
	Last step: Consider alternative hypotheses. Why and how might I be wrong?				
3 Tactics	What is the best product / market to express this view?	Determine entry, stop loss and take profit		List re-assessment triggers (where or when am I wrong?)	
4 Position sizing	Determine conviction level (TYPE I, TYPE II or TYPE III)		Determine risk capital to allocate to the idea ($ at risk)	Solve for position size using stop loss and $ at risk	Consider market liquidity and capacity
5 Execution	Execute trade		Automate / outsource stop loss		Enter trade in journal
6 Tracking	Did the thesis or facts change?	Stick to the original plan unless something major changes	How is risk-reward evolving?	Caution!!! Noise vs. signal	
7 Performance analysis	Post-mortem on the trade. Extract any useful lessons, then move on		Record results in detail	*Monthly analytics. What's working and what isn't?*	

1. IDEA GENERATION

The number one way I come up with trade ideas is by surfing the narrative. I explained this fully in Chapter 9 and I hope you have a sense of what I mean by now.

Surfing the narrative

Before you can come up with a trade idea in your market, you need to be an expert on the narrative that drives it. This narrative is an evolving story that drives price over time and can often be comprised of one major narrative along with multiple smaller narratives vying for attention. Rarely will the market embrace two major narratives at once. That is too complicated. Usually, one narrative dominates and the remaining narratives hum in the background, waiting to potentially emerge as important drivers.

When you understand the narrative in your market, you have taken the first and most important step toward becoming an expert trader. The evolution of the narrative is one of the major sources of trade ideas and can be a tremendous help even if you are a very short-term trader.

For example, if you are a short-term trader, you cannot possibly trade a news headline unless you fully understand what it means. Let's say your main market is gold. It's the Summer of 2020. You are short a decent-sized position in gold futures, risking 3% of your capital. A red headline hits Bloomberg:

*GOLD IMPORTS BY INDIA MORE THAN DOUBLE TO 35.5 TONS
IN AUGUST

What does that mean? Is it bullish? Or bearish? Or meaningless? If you are an expert in gold, you know whether the market cares about physical demand out of India right now and you know what was expected and what is normal for Indian Gold Imports in August. Often, the answer may be: nobody cares, that headline is irrelevant.

On the other hand, the market might be worried about Indian demand because so many weddings have been cancelled due to COVID-19. If speculators were worried that the only demand was institutional and ETF demand, this number might be highly reassuring and could trigger a $10 rally in gold. You need to know. If you are an expert in your market, you know what matters and what doesn't. You know what your market is trading off and what it is not. And then, as the narrative changes and new information comes in… You can react faster and smarter than others, ride the price to the new equilibrium, and get off as it overshoots.

Over time, this knowledge of the narrative will inevitably lead you to trade ideas. You will feel the winds change direction before others and you will jump on the turn before prices move. You may identify a new narrative before others, catch the impulsive middle part of a strong trend, or smell that an existing narrative is stale, crowded and ready to turn.

If you are still struggling to see how you can follow the narrative and come up with trade ideas, the walkthrough later in this chapter should help. For now, just remember that as you continuously study the narrative in your market and rise to expert level, you gain valuable intuition and insight into what matters and what doesn't. You get a feel for what is in the price, and what is not. You understand which catalysts will move the market and which will not.

Beyond understanding the narrative as described in Chapter 9, there are three other primary ways I come up with trade ideas. Note that generally I have more than one reason for a trade. Part of the filtering process is to make sure that wherever your idea comes from originally, it is supported by the narrative, sentiment, positioning, technicals, correlated markets and seasonals. We want ideas that are supported by multiple types of analysis, but also please remember:

There is no such thing as a perfect trade.

In trading, and in life, the quest for perfection is commendable but the expectation that the world, any situation, or any trade will be perfect is flawed. You need to know when you have reached "good enough" or you will wait forever for the perfect trade, perfect spouse, or perfect job. This doesn't mean you settle for a crappy relationship or put on sub-par trades, it means you must have the wisdom to understand that life is not meant to be perfect. Perfection is rare and fleeting and anything perfect should come as a positive surprise, not as an expectation.

As the Italian proverb made famous by Voltaire says:

Perfect is the enemy of good.

This applies to self-evaluation too. Many traders spend way too much time beating themselves up. Unless you finish the day at the ding dong highs, you will always wish you took profit earlier or had a bigger position or did something a little different. Assess your performance rationally. Set high standards but do not expect perfection from yourself, or every day will be a disappointment. When you do a good job: *be proud*. Don't niggle away at small performance glitches when you have generally run well. This is draining and pointless.

Once you understand the narrative, you are in a strong position to trade news and events as you will understand their meaning and how they might disrupt or transform the prevailing story.

News and events

News and events can be a tremendous source of edge and trade ideas. If you understand the current equilibrium and are familiar with the mind of the market and what information and events led to the current pricing, then when new info arrives, you are a ninja. Events like company earnings, FOMC meetings, other central bank meetings, product announcements, economic data and unexpected headlines are opportunities for the fastest, most informed traders to capitalize on mispricing.

Prices do not find their happy place right away. When new info arrives, there is a period of fast market action as hundreds of humans and algorithms disagree on fair market value and trade aggressively against each other until a few winners emerge and trading eventually settles at a new price. Often, these waves of intense trading are when you can enter a state of flow and capture outsized gains. These moments of in-the-zone trading sometimes last just 10 or 15 minutes but can account for an entire week of P&L.

Identify events in your market, educate yourself, read every preview and every word of pre-game analysis. Create a clear plan. When the news, event or announcement happens: *attack*.

Into events: Flat = strong

I don't always have the discipline to do this, but I try to go into major economic and central bank events as close to flat as possible. If you are a short-term news trader, this should be your approach. Here are some reasons it is suboptimal to hold positions into events.

1. Gap risk. Quite often you won't get out as fast as you want, and you will lose more money than you thought you would. You can't properly control risk in a gapping market.

2. You are biased. If you go into a Fed meeting short USD because you think they are going to be dovish, your interpretation of the news release and press conference are likely to be biased. You will be looking for headlines that confirm your prior dovish view instead of looking at the outcome through clear eyes. Flat is the most powerful position in trading because it is the only time you are fully and completely unbiased.

3. It is hard to flip if you're wrong. If you are positioned for a dovish outcome and the result is hawkish, you want to flip from short dollars to long dollars. This is difficult because 1) You will react slower when you are biased and leaning the wrong way and 2) liquidity is not unlimited. If you have a decent-sized short USD position, you may have trouble buying enough USD to flip long at a reasonable rate.

It is easier to react to events than predict them.

As a rule, if you are fast and well-prepared, the Sharpe ratio of reacting to events is higher than the Sharpe of trying to predict them. As we discussed last chapter: a big part of successful trading is to understand the current equilibrium and then when new information appears, react smarter and faster than your competitors, before the market finds the new equilibrium. If you are flat when new information comes out, you are stronger, faster, and unbiased. You don't always need to have a position. Good traders know when to be flat.

Although predicting the outcome of an event often has very little edge, predicting what the market will do in the days *leading up to the event* can be a good source of trade ideas. Instead of trying to predict what everyone else is predicting (the event itself), smart traders can often more easily forecast what the crowd will do *into* the event, and position ahead of the crowd before it starts to move.

The run-up trade

The run-up trade is a phenomenon where prices move in a logical and predictable direction in the days leading up to a major event. These run-up trades are often easier to predict and monetize than the events that follow.

The idea behind the run-up trade is to identify an upcoming market event and then estimate what traders will do before the event. If AAPL earnings are coming up this week, which way are traders likely to play it? If non-farm payrolls are a few days from now, what might the market do in the days leading up to the release? The run-up trade is usually a function of three things:

1. Positioning: Medium-term traders, investors and systematic strategies tend to reduce risk into major events. They do this because volatility tends to be higher and more difficult to predict through events. If they are sizing their bets using forecast volatility (which most do, because that makes sense), they need to reduce their exposure as high-vol events near. If everyone is long, expect prices to fall in the run-up to the day of the event.

2. What is the obvious trade? Quite often, the obvious trade works! Plus, traders feel stupid missing obvious macro catalysts so they will tend to position for them in advance then take them off quickly if they do not materialize. If the US economy has been hot, the Fed is thinking about hiking rates, and most indicators point to strong job growth… Expect bonds to sell off in the days leading up to the jobs report as traders get set for a blockbuster figure.

3. What is the lotto ticket trade? If a biotech company is announcing Phase 1 results on Friday morning and it looks like a good result could cause the stock to triple while a bad result will cause it to drop 20%… Expect the stock to rally into the news, even if the probability of a positive outcome does not justify the trade from an expected value point of view. Asymmetrical bets will always attract speculators, even if they are bad trades with good optics. So the run-up trade ahead of an event will often be driven by speculators putting on lotto tickets beforehand.

Sometimes, all three factors above will apply: that's a top-quality run-up trade. When you catch a run-up trade, you will be tempted to keep it through the event because you have a nice cushion by that point. Resist that temptation! It is often easier to forecast the madness of crowds going into an event than it is to forecast the outcome of the event itself. Furthermore, the very fact that you caught the run-up trade means the security has moved a fair bit already into the event and thus it is probably getting crowded in that direction and offers asymmetric risk/reward (in a bad way).

Everybody's bearish and nobody's short

Sticking with the topic of events, there is a subtler way that upcoming events can influence markets. Often, when a major risk event is coming up, risk managers and traders lean on the conservative side until it is out of the way (due to gap risk and concerns about extreme volatility). They reduce their risk as the event nears, regardless of their view.

Once the event passes (regardless of the result), risk appetite returns to normal and a move that probably should have happened before the event happens afterwards. Speculators put on the trade they wanted to have before, because now that the event (and associated gap risk) is out of the way, it's safe to do so.

This is one of my favorite setups. When there is a strong consensus view but no positioning to match the view, you often see highly impulsive moves. Once the event passes, the consensus move is free to unfold at high speed. Often the event itself contains no new information, it is simply the passing of the event (and thus the elimination of gap risk) that allows the move that should have happened earlier to happen now. This setup is powerful and has a high expected value, so watch for it.

Deviation from fair value

Another important source of trade ideas is scanning for moments when your market deviates from fair value. Fair value is a slippery concept and is almost impossible to measure with certainty so when I say "fair value" I mean "loose or best estimate of fair value". You never know what the *real* fair value of a market is, but you know that if oil drops $2 and copper drops 5% at the same time, fair value for the Canadian dollar has probably just gone down, not up.

I tend to think of fair value more in terms of direction and not level. That is, I might say: "Today's economic data was bad and oil is down 4% today, yields look way too high." But I would never say: "Given these numbers and the move in oil, I think 10-year yields should be 1.10 not 1.20."

One way to measure deviations from fair value is to use cross-market correlation. This is explained in Chapter 9. Start by identifying one or two markets that should logically be correlated to the market you trade. Follow them. You don't need to create a sophisticated regression model to track deviations and movements. Just track momentum in the correlated markets and get a feel for what it means for the market you trade. Over time, you will slowly learn to watch other markets for clues and you will experience how lead/lag trading can give you a forecasting edge.

Lead/lag or cross-market trading is not just about watching one market move higher then buying the other market. It is about putting together a coherent story using fundamental narratives plus moves in correlated markets. Let's look at an example of how deviation from fair value might lead me not to put on a trade.

Let's say I am an expert in trading FCX and BHP, two of the world's largest mining stocks. I am flat and US markets are closed, but since I'm a highly-motivated and curious guy, at 9 p.m. I flick on Bloomberg TV to check out the Chinese Export and New Loans data. There is a high degree of uncertainty about the direction of the Chinese economy right now so everyone is watching the release. The data comes out super-weak, much worse than expected.

Since China is a huge consumer of commodities, this weak economic data should be bad news for FCX and BHP. The market has been trading mining stocks from the long side for months on the back of a popular narrative that China stimulus and strong Chinese growth should boost earnings. The trade is crowded and the narrative looks stale. My metrics show there is a massive long position in copper so I expect it to get hit hard. I care about markets, but I also care about health and sleep so I go to bed at 10 p.m.

I spend the night dreaming about how much FCX and BHP I will go short in the morning and hope that the stocks have not sold off too much in Asia/London time. This seems like a solid multi-day trade idea with good risk/reward but I don't like trading on my phone when US markets are closed.

When I wake up, I'm surprised to see FCX and BHP are unchanged. Awesome! My entry point will be amazing here. Then, I flick to copper, expecting it to be down between 2% and 3%. It's up 1.4%. *Huh, that's weird.* The market has had seven hours to digest the bad China news, I thought the market was mega-long and yet copper is up 1.4%?

At this point, my interest in shorting FCX and BHP would fizzle fast. My thesis was that the market was long the whole China narrative but if that were true, copper should be down on the bad news, not up. By monitoring other, correlated markets, I can get clues about my thesis and filter out bad trade ideas while homing in on good ones.

The better you understand a suite of related securities and the underlying fundamental drivers of those securities, the more trade ideas you will come up with, and the more likely you are to weed out bad ideas before they cost you.

Here, I used deviation from fair value (copper rallying and BHP and FCX unchanged = BHP and FCX look low) to avoid a bad short. Let's look at a simple example where deviation from fair value helps get me into a trade.

I am bearish the US dollar as it has recently rolled over after a multi-year rally. I believe we are entering a new down trend and I am looking for opportunities but haven't pulled the trigger yet. The dollar had a huge interest rate advantage for the past few years, but the Fed recently cut rates all the way to near zero while the rest of the world kept rates on hold. The dollar is overvalued, the market is max long, the narrative is turning, and I want to find a USD pair to get short.

Today is the last day of the month and I know from my research that in months when stocks have gone up significantly, real money hedgers tend to buy USDJPY as 4 p.m. London time approaches. I also know that the most correlated market to USDJPY is US 10-year rates, which are still hovering around 1.20% despite many interest rate cuts by the Fed. Big moves in US rates almost always coincide with big moves in USDJPY.

USDJPY rallies from 107.00 to 107.60 as 4 p.m. London approaches. I check to see if interest rates are moving higher (which would justify the USDJPY rally). They are not. In fact, US yields are dribbling a bit lower. The USDJPY rally is probably just flow—it makes zero macro sense.

Meanwhile, significant resistance I identified on my techs sheet this morning lurks just above at 107.80. There is one more push up in USDJPY right at 4 p.m. London and I sell at 107.74. Again, I check the US rates market and see 10-year yields continue to trade lower. US stocks are also lurching a bit lower. This is a great setup. Working in my favor are:

1. Bigger-picture bearish USD view as narrative turns.

2. Time of day effect in USDJPY signals my timing is likely decent.

3. US rates and US stock market both say USDJPY should be going lower, not higher (cross-market supports the idea) and I can explain why USDJPY is rallying (non-price-sensitive rebalancing flow) and when the rally is likely to end (4 p.m. London).

4. Major resistance very close means I can put on a big trade with a tight stop (high leverage situation).

A trade like this is not unrealistic. For most good trades, I will have 3 to 5 decent reasons and very few arguments the other way. This trade is a good example of how cross-market analysis gives me greater confidence to take the other side of a flow-driven move that is not supported by fundamentals or by action in other markets.

Pattern recognition and indicator scanning

The final major source of trade ideas (after narrative, news, and dislocations from fair value) is pattern recognition and indicator scanning. This can mean many things and depends greatly on what products you trade. Good traders recognize patterns in their market and understand which patterns are the result of randomness and which are sending a persistent signal. In the section above, I talked about the fact that USDJPY rallies into month end when stocks have done well that month, and we discussed other patterns of activity in various parts of this book.

When I say patterns here, I am not talking about technical analysis. I am talking about recurring price patterns. The more you read and study your market, the more you will learn about, identify and backtest these types of patterns. Here are a few examples:

Stocks trade poorly from September 16 to October 9 then rip higher into year end

This seasonal is well-known and persistent. The worst week of the year for stocks has been the week after options expire in September (the week after the 3rd Friday of September). September 21-25 is the 5-day window in which you had the least chance of making money long US stocks from 1990 to 2020. Figure 12.2 shows the chart.

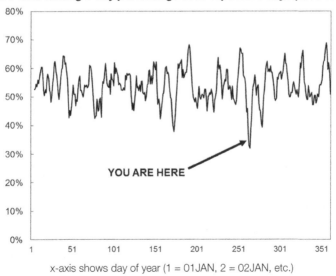

Figure 12.2: Rolling 5-day percentage of SPX positive days (1990 to now)

x-axis shows day of year (1 = 01JAN, 2 = 02JAN, etc.)

And Figure 12.3 shows the average path of equities over the course of the year, again going back to 1990.

Figure 12.3: The average path of equities since 1990

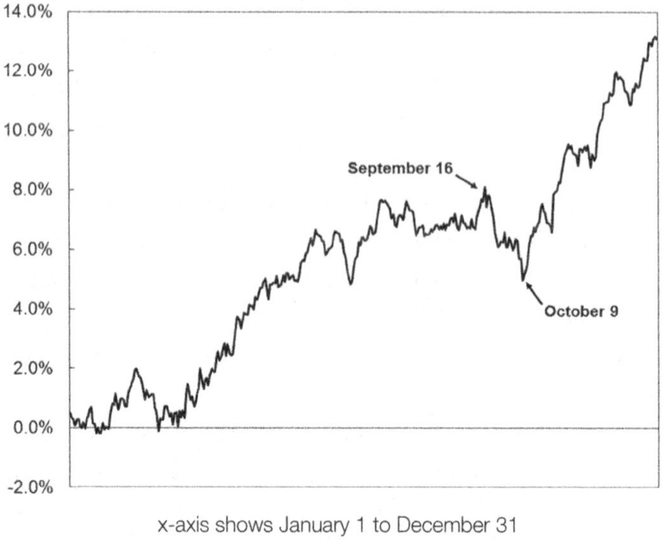
14.0%
12.0%
10.0%
8.0%
6.0%
4.0%
2.0%
0.0%
-2.0%
September 16
October 9
x-axis shows January 1 to December 31

There are all sorts of seasonal patterns like this in many markets. You need to be very careful with seasonality, as much of it is random. Experience and statistical acumen can help you sort through what is random and what is persistent.

Analogs

When you have a few years of market experience, you will start to see trades and narratives evolving in ways that you recognize from the past. **History doesn't repeat but it rhymes.** When you can compare the current period to some period in the past, that analog can help you predict what might happen next. For example, the EURUSD rally in 2017 and 2020 were both incredibly similar:

- Started with a relief rally after a euro-positive political event. In 2017 it was the election of Macron and in 2020 it was the agreement on a European Economic Recovery Plan.
- First wave of the rally went from 1.08 to 1.20.
- Both times, the ECB eventually pushed back as EURUSD neared 1.2000.
- Very few pullbacks in the first wave higher.

Here is a write-up I did on this topic in June 2020:

Going into round one of the French presidential election on April 23, 2017, Emmanuel Macron held a narrow lead over Marine Le Pen. Markets viewed Le Pen as a danger to the euro because (despite softening at the last minute) she spoke frequently of euro exit, arguing it would allow France to gain from competitive devaluation. Here are two representative Le Pen quotes:

> "The euro is not a currency. It is a political weapon to force countries to implement the policies decided by the EU and keep them on a leash."

> "(The end of the euro) would be an unbelievable opportunity. If we don't all leave the euro behind, it will explode. Either there will be a popular revolt because the people no longer want to be bled out. Or the Germans will say: Stop, we can't pay for the poor anymore."

So far, so wrong. Anyway, when Macron's round one win all but assured him a second-round victory, EURUSD gapped and trended higher. The current rally has a similar feel as the market has been waiting years for the EU to loosen the purse strings and take

**Figure 12.4: EURUSD after Macron round 1
and EURUSD after Merkel-Macron proposal**
Normalized to 60 days before the event date
Vertical line marks event date

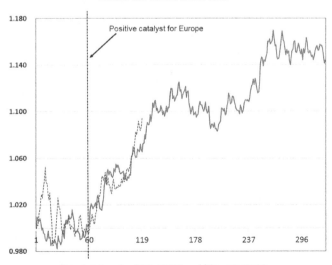

Event dates: April 23, 2017 and May 18, 2020

some baby steps toward fiscal union. The Macron-Merkel agreement on May 18, 2020 got the ball rolling.

Comparing the 2017 rally with the current move, you get a chart that looks like Figure 12.4.

The first takeaway is that this move in EURUSD matches the 2017 move pretty well. The second takeaway is that around this point in the 2017 rally, there was a 5-week consolidation. The third takeaway is that most dips were small on the way up. You didn't get more than a 1.5% retracement until the 4% correction in October 2017. Next, Figure 12.5 shows the rolling 40-day drawdown in EURUSD starting (once again) 60 days before the event date.

So if you believe in this EURUSD rally, and think it should follow a similar path to the 2017 move, scale in from 1% to 1.5% off the rolling high. Note that 1-month vol was in a 6%-8% range after Macron won in 2017 and is currently around 7%; so using the analog makes sense from a volatility perspective.

We touched a high of 1.1384 on Friday, so the 2017 playbook would put the current buy zone at 1.1213/1.1270.

Figure 12.5: EURUSD rolling 40-day peak to trough drawdown after Macron won Round One

Vertical line marks April 23, 2017 (Round One)

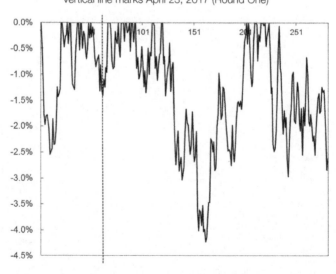

The analog was pretty good! It worked for months and correctly called the approximate path of the euro for the next 1000 points.

Analogs are never going to be perfect but they are excellent tools that will help you contextualize market action and set reasonable targets when you catch a move. If the EUR rally in 2017 was 1.08 to 1.25 and the rally looks similar in 2020 (and also started around 1.08)… You could do worse than to guess the 2020 rally might target 1.2500 too.

Analogs bolster your understanding of narratives and volatility.

Month-end dollar effect

On the morning of the last trading day of the month, European pension funds execute massive rebalancing trades. Any month that saw significant moves higher in US equities will see large USD selling by pension funds as 4 p.m. approaches while any month where US equities tumbled will see large USD buying. This pattern has existed since at least 2005. It does not work every time (nothing works every time) but it is about as reliable as patterns get.

This hedging goes the opposite direction of stocks and only matters when US equities have moved meaningfully during the month. Here is why it happens: imagine a foreign holder of US stocks who owns a billion USD of S&Ps and is short one billion USD to hedge the position. If stocks rally 10%, he now has 1.1 billion of stocks and 1.0 billion of USD hedges. So he needs to sell 0.1 billion ($100 million) USD to rebalance his hedges.

These asset managers are benchmarked to 4 p.m. London on the last day of the month so activity peaks at that time as managers attempt to match the benchmark rate. The huge volumes going through on the last day of the month create some large and often illogical moves and these dislocations can create significant patterns and opportunities for astute traders.

Bubbles tend to deflate by about 85% before rebounding

Looking at the major bubbles in recent history, here is how much price sold off from high to low before making the ultimate bottom:

Bitcoin	2017/2018	84.2%
XLF (financial stocks ETF)	2007/2008	84.6%
US homebuilder stocks	2005/2008	84.6%
NASDAQ bubble	2000/2002	83.6%
Japan's Nikkei bubble	1989/2008	82.0%
USA Crash of 1929	1929/1932	86.2%

If you are looking to buy a deflated bubble asset, look for the 80%/85% discount area. It is remarkably common for burst bubbles to bottom around there.

Highs and lows are more likely on round numbers than on other numbers

I explained this in the section on Round Number Bias. If you are looking for an optimal entry point and there is a major round number nearby, that's helpful.

Bankrupt stocks usually rally on the open

When stocks re-open after being halted for a bankruptcy announcement, that is often the ideal time for shorts to take profit. This is because once a stock trades sub-$1.00 after beginning bankruptcy proceedings, it can take months or even years before the stock is zeroed out. It is not worth it for speculators to stay short all that time where the is so little juice left in the trade.

This is kind of a ridiculous trade given you are buying the shares of a bankrupt company but it doesn't always have to make sense. Often, buying the shares of a bankrupt company when the stock reopens after the halt for the bankruptcy announcement can be highly profitable as a short-term (1 day to 1 week) trade.

The patterns I have described are just the tip of the iceberg. As you gain expertise in your market and watch markets in general over the years, you will discover more and more patterns. Remember that if you can explain a pattern, and why it should continue to repeat, there is a much higher likelihood that pattern will be useful for trading.

Random patterns that you observe or discover by data mining are quite often simply the inevitable result of the fact that random data is chock full of mostly meaningless patterns. Find patterns and do your best to explain them. Then make a rational determination of whether they might repeat in the future.

Indicator scanning

Indicator scanning is a process where you have specific filters that will identify trading opportunities. This might be volume or large move filters in the equity market or a dashboard that shows abnormal moves in options markets. Scanning for large moves and unusual activity can often lead you in the direction of a good idea. The markets are mostly a sea of efficient tranquility and you are looking for whirlpools and weirdness that might tell you something abnormal is happening.

•••

Once you have a trade idea, hopefully with the help of the four headings above (Surfing the narrative, News and events, Deviation from fair value and Pattern recognition), you need to filter the idea using the other criteria in the grid. You also need to figure out whether or not the trade can be structured in a way that offers compelling leverage and risk/reward.

Can you profitably put this trade on at current levels or does it make more sense to wait? Does the action in related markets support the idea, or invalidate it? Are positioning and sentiment a headwind or tailwind for your idea? Sticking with the huge grid, let's move on to the next row and talk about how we filter good ideas from bad.

2. FILTERING

Your initial idea can now be filtered using the steps listed in row 2 of the diagram. Let's go through how that works, column by column.

A. The narrative cycle

Depending on what your trade idea is, or where it came from, it may have occurred to you totally independent of the narrative cycle. Say you have seen a pattern where bonds rally at month end and you think it might make sense to go long at noon on the last day of the month and take profit at 4 p.m.

It's just a four-hour trade, surely the narrative cycle doesn't matter, right? Well, it depends. You should still have an idea of what the story is in bonds, generally, and what might disrupt that story during the short time you plan to have this trade on.

Are there any Fed speakers, for example? If so, and the narrative has been one of a dovish Fed while the most hawkish member of the committee is set to come on CNBC at 3 p.m., that could be important. Are stocks volatile these days? In bear markets, stocks often squeeze higher into the end of the day. Is this a risk to your trade? The shorter your trade, the less likely the narrative cycle will matter but it's rare that it doesn't matter at all.

Say news comes out that TSLA plans to release a battery that lasts 3X longer than its previous model. You buy TSLA on instinct, and it's immediately $8 in the money. Now, you can filter a bit here. Where are we in the TSLA narrative? Has there been chatter for weeks about a possible battery advance and has everyone been building long positions on the back of that? Is the market short TSLA because GM just came out with a battery that lasts 2X as long as the original TSLA battery?

In these two narrative scenarios, price action after the initial knee-jerk pop is going to be completely different. In scenario one, you are probably stopping out as TSLA crumbles back down through the NewsPivot while in narrative scenario two, the stock probably grinds higher all the way into the close. No matter what logic you use for a trade and what time horizon you are trading, think about where your market is in the narrative cycle and what that means for the potential upside and downside on your time horizon.

B. Positioning and sentiment

Positioning and sentiment are closely related to the narrative, usually. Is the market long or short? Are positions strong or weak? Generally, if a market has climbed significantly, the longs are confident and strong. If a market was in a bull market but has now transitioned to a correction phase, longs are going to be more nervous. If you know who has been buying or selling, that can help too. Hedge funds are generally going to be much weaker hands than real money or central banks.

Chapter 10 has a complete discussion of positioning and sentiment. For this section, just ask yourself whether your idea is made weaker or stronger by the current positioning. For example, if there is a bearish seasonal pattern, but everyone is talking about it and short because of it, that seasonal pattern becomes much less exciting. If you spot an analog to a move you remember from last year, and then remember that positioning at the time was very similar to positioning right now… Your analog just got stronger.

I want to repeat something critical here. You don't always go against positioning. It's a factor but it's not the be all/end all. Traders who go against positioning all the time miss every major trend because price loves to trend and sentiment and positioning mostly follow price. Be flexible, smart, rational and open minded when it comes to positioning.

C. Events and catalysts

What events and potential catalysts are coming up? Do they work for or against you? How will they impact liquidity? If you are bullish S&P futures for 7 good reasons but it's 2:45 p.m. on the day before non-farm payrolls, it might not be worth putting on the trade. Or you may be able to use non-farm payrolls to get an even better entry point.

Events and catalysts can create opportunity, but they can also impact liquidity and lead to discontinuous price action, random jumps and so on. Sometimes you want a position into an event because you have a strong view on that event, but often events should be avoided due to their random and illiquid nature. Once again, think about whether upcoming events and catalysts are pros or cons for your original trade idea.

D. Correlated markets

Earlier, I explained how I use correlated markets not just as a source of ideas but as a critical filter for ideas that come from other sources. Once you have your idea, flip through the most important correlated markets and figure out whether those variables are supporting or contradicting your thesis. Is there a coherent theme to those other assets that reinforces or pushes back against your idea? Smart filtering with correlated markets will help you dodge some bad trades.

E. Technical analysis

Charts are the worst place to come up with trade ideas but one of the best ways to filter ideas you come up with elsewhere. Good technical analysis (and the patience to wait for good entries) can give you the leverage that makes the difference between disappointing and amazing returns on a specific trade idea. A good idea, poorly executed is sometimes worse than a dumb idea with razor-sharp execution parameters.

As an example, say there is a bullish AUDUSD headline but I know that overall the narrative in the currency has recently turned bearish, and the market is dying to add to its small short position. I react to the news and buy some AUDUSD but then when I look at the chart I see:

1. We are mid-range with no support nearby.

2. There is a huge triple top close-by, just 20 pips above market.

3. My stop loss will need to be 80 points away for the trade to make any sense, but even if the triple top breaks, there is a trendline and the 2-year high 25 pips above that, so this is starting to look like a trade where I am risking 80 to make 45.

So, the narrative overall is bearish, people are in "sell rallies" mode and it's a poor tech setup. The market is more likely to use the bullish headline to sell more AUDUSD at better levels than it is to rip the pair higher.

This is a situation where the tech and narrative filters just don't support the trade. I get out, and move on. Don't fall in love with your trades, treat them like they are a dime-a-dozen. Every day presents new ideas, new opportunities and new trades. Don't overvalue your ideas. There will be no shortage of them going forward. Learn to love small losses.

Another example: it's 10 a.m., and as you walk to get a coffee from the kitchen, a fantastic trade idea crystallizes in your mind. You have been thinking about the spot rhodium market for a few weeks but finally realize that it's time to get long. Sentiment is at an extreme, supply is drying up and nobody has talked about rhodium in ages even though the other precious metals are all ripping higher. What are the odds that the spot rhodium market is in the perfect place to buy, at the exact moment you come up with your trade idea? Probably pretty low!

So now step back and take a look at some charts. Figure out the optimal entry point or an optimal entry band. Is there an area where multiple significant reference points converge and you can go long with maximum leverage and a reasonably tight stop? [125]

Once you have completed this filtering process, your trade idea will either be stronger, weaker or dead in the water. Do the filters support your analysis, or do they point to crosswinds? This is a critical point in your trade idea process. Do you move forward, or pause? Or do you nix the trade because it is simply not supported by enough factors? Bad trades often start out as cool ideas but then the trader ignores a series of obviously contrary information and does not filter because he is so excited about his cool trade idea that he can't accept the contrary evidence.

That's how confirmation bias works in this part of the process. Trade ideas are hard to come up with, so the last thing you want to do when you finally think of one is nix it because of a bunch of filters. But often that's exactly what you should do. While good trades have very few crosswinds, that does not mean you only take the perfect trades. There is no such thing as a perfect trade.

You go through the filtering process with an open mind and then make a sound, unbiased judgment when you're done.

The final step in the process is a critical one: *consider alternate hypotheses.* We discussed this in depth in Chapter 5 and I mentioned Richards Heuer of the CIA and his eight-step process. I said it then, and I will say it again here: you should read Heuer's book. It's free on the CIA website and is an excellent

---

125. "Tight stop in rhodium" is not really a thing, but let's not quibble over details in a theoretical scenario, OK? :]

training manual for good thinking that will benefit you not just in trading, but in any area of life that benefits from rational thought.

At this stage of the trade idea process, you need to think about the other side. If your trade idea is bearish corn futures, think about what the bulls are saying. Find research notes that are bullish corn and go through their arguments. Can you debunk them? Sometimes I read counterarguments to my view and think: "That's pretty unconvincing" and so I remain confident in my view. Sometimes I read the counterarguments and think: "Oh crap, I totally missed that."

Remember that your brain is programmed to find supporting evidence that confirms your existing hypothesis. You need to work hard to fight against that programming and honestly pursue alternative stories that might make sense.

A useful tool when attempting to embrace alternative hypotheses is to picture how the trade could go against you. What would that look like? What specific factors or events might derail your idea and stop you out? This helps you think about your idea from different angles (and hopefully with greater objectivity) and also gets you thinking about possible reassessment triggers. *If I'm wrong… What's it gonna look like?* This is sometimes called a "pre-mortem", as discussed in Chapter 7.

Bounce your trade idea off people you respect and see what comes back. Don't blindly defer to them or hope they agree with you. It doesn't really matter if they agree or disagree. What matters is any new information or evidence that they offer up. If a ton of people disagree with your idea, but you remain confident about it, that can be powerful because now you know you are not part of the consensus. You have rigorously tested your idea and it is resilient to scrutiny.

When someone smart gives me a good reason to doubt my idea and I can't really refute their argument… I am happy to toss my trade idea in the trash and wait for a better one to come along. Don't hold on to your ideas too tightly. This goes back to the idea of "strong opinions, weakly held" which I discussed earlier. You need to come up with strong trade ideas backed by significant research and multiple streams of analysis, but then have an open mind, admit error and change course if need be, as new information comes in.

This is easy to say and hard to do. Strong opinions that are too weakly held will be scared off by the first bit of noise. Determining when to give up on a trade idea is tough; we'll deal with that a bit later in this chapter.

3. TACTICS

OK, after filtering is done, it's game on. Your idea is good and now it's time to determine tactics. Don't rush to your keyboard and start pressing the BUY or SELL buttons yet. First, it's time to fine tune the tactics to maximize leverage and make the most money possible if you are right. Being right and making money are not always the same thing. You can be right and get stopped out because of a poorly chosen stop loss level. You can buy an option that expires worthless the day before your beloved asset rips to the moon. You can enter a trade mid-range and make 11bps when the guy next to you threads the needle at major support and makes 111bps. Being right is just the start.

Before you can put on your trade idea, you need to decide what to trade. In many cases, this is obvious, but not always. For example, I often have ideas driven by stock market views, but due to the nature of my role, I can't trade stocks. Therefore, once I come up with a view on where stocks are going, I need to figure out what the best FX proxy is for stocks. Often, that means AUDJPY or USDJPY but sometimes it might mean AUDUSD or even EURCHF. I analyze 90-day correlation stats and think about what makes sense going forward, then finally pick what product to trade.

If you are bearish the NASDAQ, you need to decide between QQQ, SQQQ, QID, PSQ, and NASDAQ futures. You might even decide that a specific subgroup (short FANG via FNGD?) makes sense or you might take a view in a single name like AMZN or NVDA. Which choice will give you the exposure, leverage and directional movement you want with the lowest transaction costs?

**Be thoughtful about the product you
choose to express your view. It matters.**

Once you have chosen your product, it's time to pick your entry point, stop loss and take profit. The first thing I do here is pull up a chart. What is the dream entry point? What is a realistic entry point? Is the exact place where the market is trading right now the best place to get in, or are you better off waiting? Obviously this will often come down to the type of trade it is. If you are trading news, you don't have time to wait for the ideal entry point. You get in and then determine your tactics after. But if this is a scenario where you are playing a turn in narrative and your trade is likely to last three to five days, you can finesse your entry point.

Using technical analysis, I will determine the ideal entry and stop loss at this point. Rarely will I have a stop loss closer than one day's range away unless the trade is ultra-short-term. While a risk:reward ratio of 1:2 or 1:3 is a decent rule of thumb for most trades, there is no hard and fast rule. If you think there is a 70% chance you can risk 1 to make 1, and you have high confidence in your 70% probability estimate... Do the trade! It has high expected value. On the other hand, given the significant uncertainty around probabilities in trading, higher payout ratios give you a wider margin of safety.

Solid tactics give you superior leverage because the more fine-tuned your entry point and the tighter your stop loss, the larger position you can take with the same amount of money at risk. If you buy AAPL at $100 with a stop loss at $99 you can take a 5X larger position than if you buy AAPL at $100 with a stop loss at $95. Then again, your odds of getting stopped out at $99 are clearly higher than getting stopped out at $95 so choosing a stop loss is always about the tension between 'as tight as possible' and 'lowest chance of getting stopped out'.

If you want a system that is simple and generally effective, start by risking one day's range to make two. Or, if you are day trading, risk 35% of an average day's range to make 70% of a day's range. Those are finger in the air starting points and you can adjust as you gain experience.

When things are going well and you have a strong feeling for your market, you will sometimes find trades where you can risk much less to make much more. Sometimes you can sell right against a major resistance point and risk just 20% of a day's range knowing that if you catch the turn, it might be a major top and you can extract two full day's ranges from the trade. Those trades are dreamy. Each trade will have its own ideal parameters based on technical analysis and the unique timing features of the trade.

**Tactics are just as important as strategy.
You need both to succeed in trading.**

Once you have your entry, stop loss and take profit determined, automate everything as much as possible. If AAPL is at $100 and you have determined that $101.50 is the perfect entry point, put the limit order in the system, along with your stop loss. If you don't put it in a system right away, what do you think is going to happen in two hours when AAPL spikes from $100 to $101.50? Your dumb lizard brain will say stuff like:

Whoa, it looks bid, I better check if there's some news out!

Hmmm, maybe I can sell at $103.00 and get an even better entry point.

Somebody must know something! Why is it rallying so hard???

Selling into a rally can be hard, just like buying dips is hard. Much easier is to calmly enter a limit order to sell at $101.50 when nothing is going on and the stock is bouncing around near $100.00. Automate and outsource as much of the execution process as you can and you will find you get better results. No matter how disciplined you are: computers are more disciplined than you!

The last stage in the tactics phase is to write down or record your list of reassessment triggers. A trader who clearly lays out her plan is way ahead of most traders. She has cemented a concrete process and listed specific triggers for reassessment or exit.

Reassessment triggers are important because once you have a trade on, you will be influenced by all sorts of new information that is mostly noise. Numbers jiggle on a screen. Random headlines scroll by. Your heart rate picks up. Those are not reasons to adjust your risk. It is easier to list action triggers ex-ante than to hope you will be sane and unbiased once the trade starts to move.

Reassessment triggers will always include a stop loss and a take profit but can also be other things such as:

- **Time trigger**. For example, any day trade can have a reassessment (or firm exit) time of 4 p.m. (when the main NYSE trading session ends). Many good trades have a time trigger. Another example: say you have done a ton of work on today's US Retail Sales number and you expect it will be weak. You go long bonds at 7:45 a.m. in anticipation of the release at 8:30 a.m. You believe that most of the new information from economic data gets fully priced within 10 minutes[126]. Does it make any sense to keep the trade past 8:45 a.m. or maybe 9:00 a.m. at the latest? Probably not. So you put a reassessment trigger at 8:45 a.m.

- **Level at which to tighten the stop loss**. Once a trade has made most of its gains, it makes sense to tighten up the stop loss.

---

126. This is a reasonable belief, by the way. Most studies show the directional impact (half-life) of economic data lasts five to ten minutes and then the price action after that is random.

- **New information trigger**. You need to be as specific as possible here to avoid undue reaction to noise. If a trader gets long oil on a Saudi Arabia / Russia squabble, the trader should logically have a reassessment trigger as: Truce or conciliatory Saudi Arabia and Russia headlines. That is a logical reassessment trigger. A bad reassessment trigger would be something like: "Re-evaluate if price action does not cooperate." Be specific.

- **Cross-market variable trigger**. If you are long S&P futures and one of your main reasons for entering the trade is that the VIX just dropped below the key 20 level, it makes sense to use the VIX as a potential cross-market reassessment trigger. Again, make it specific. For example: "If VIX trades above 21, I will cut the position."

Note that I am using the term "reassessment triggers" but often these are action triggers. The last example is an action trigger. I use reassessment trigger and action trigger interchangeably since often a reassessment leads to an action.

The first two reassessment triggers for any trade are always the stop loss and take profit. After that, you record anything else that might change your mind. The goal for this stage of the process is to try to guess ex-ante what might be signal and what is noise going forward.

When you have a trade on, every price movement feels like a signal or a sign of danger for your position while in reality most price movement is noise. Every time price jiggles lower or ratchets higher, you will have an emotional reaction because you are invested. The idea with reassessment triggers is to codify what will make you change your mind and what will not before the price starts flickering and jiggling around and those dumb voices in your head start to react to that flickering and jiggling.

Some other examples of good reassessment triggers:

- I am long stocks because I think the Fed has turned more dovish and the market hasn't caught on yet. There are two Fed speakers this week. If either one of those speakers is more hawkish than I expect, I should reassess my view.

- I am short bonds because I think the economy is strengthening. Any major US data point that comes in more than one standard deviation below consensus will trigger a reassessment.

- One of my main reasons for going long AUDUSD was the rebound in copper and iron ore prices. If either copper or iron ore break below their 200-hour moving average, I will reassess my AUDUSD long position.

If you take the time to record these reassessment triggers, you should find very few occasions where you make on the fly decisions mid-trade. Once you have a trade on, leave it alone and let it bake. Don't rush it. Don't keep opening the oven to peek. The market doesn't care about your time frame. A market that is not moving is boring, but it's not telling you anything. Wait for your stop loss, your take profit or one of your reassessment triggers to hit. Stop white-knuckling.

Of course, there are going to be times when you are long and bad news comes out and you hit a bid and save yourself some cash. But these are not all that common. Just as often, you will hit the bid and then find yourself buying the stock back ten minutes later after realizing the news wasn't as bad as you thought and in fact the news was actually meaningless. Remember that when you have a trade on, you are biased. Information processing is distorted by your emotional state.

The best action is almost always no action.

This is true when you have a position on and it's also true most of the time when you don't. Limit your actions as much as possible and you will put on only the best trades. Then, you will stay in those trades long enough for them to bear fruit. This is my kryptonite and the greatest strength and greatest weakness in my life.

I can do 1,000 pushups in a day every Wednesday for 10 straight weeks (action!) but have an incredibly tough time going two hours without touching the BUY or SELL buttons (inaction). This bias to action gives me the energy to write a decent macro newsletter every day and to pump out a book every year or two but it also makes it shockingly difficult for me to sit at work and keep my hands off the trading controls.

My default mode is action. I have known that for 20 years and yet it is still my greatest weakness in trading. I never stop working on it, but I also accept it is who I am. I forgive myself more easily now than I did when I was 30. I try to automate as much as possible and convince myself to sit there and do nothing as much as possible. Once you know your personal kryptonite, fine tune your process and redesign your framework to address it.

4. POSITION SIZING

Position size is a function of six factors:

1. Conviction level (TYPE I, TYPE II or TYPE III)

2. Free capital

3. YTD P&L

4. Market volatility

5. Distance from entry point to stop loss

6. Gap and liquidity risk

Here's a quick summary of how to determine position size.

a. Decide on your conviction level (Type I, II or III as discussed in chapter 11).

b. Given your YTD P&L and free capital, decide on a percentage of your capital to put at risk. This tells you how many $ (or bps) to risk on the trade.

c. Using market volatility and technical analysis, choose the appropriate stop loss.

d. Calculate the position size: ($ at risk) divided by (risk per unit) … To get the total number of units.

e. Think about liquidity. Is this a reasonable position size? Can you get in and out without much of an issue? If not, can you scale in and out and maintain the economics of the trade?

f. Think about gap risks. What major events are coming up? How has the product been trading? Do you need to worry about limit up and limit down? Is there enough liquidity for this position size? In this step, you might reduce your position size because of gap risk, or consider exiting the trade before an upcoming event.

I will go through this process again in the trade walkthrough at the end of this chapter. That should solidify your understanding.

5. EXECUTION

Good execution reduces transaction costs and improves returns. This is important at all skill levels and in all trading businesses. Remember those charts that show the impact of transaction costs in Chapter 8? Transaction costs are important. It is lazy to ignore them or minimize their importance. Take TC seriously.

Here are a few ways to reduce transaction costs and pay less spread. I discuss these approaches from the point of view of an equity trader, but these concepts apply to trading in most markets.

1. Use limit orders. If TSLA is trading 1281.00 / 1281.30 and you want to buy, you have some choices. You can:

   a. send a market order and likely get filled around $1281.30.

   b. leave a limit order at mid (if you want to buy leave a bid at 1281.15, if you want to sell leave an offer at 1281.15)

   c. leave a limit order to buy just ahead of the best bid or sell just ahead of the best offer (+@1281.01 or -@1281.29 in this case)

   The decision depends mostly on the level of urgency you feel. Option a) gets you filled every time and is the way to go if there is news, it is a fast market, or you are stopping out of a position. Option b) is less likely to get filled, but still has a high probability of execution. The risk is that you bid 1281.15, and the market goes straight up. In that case you will not get filled. Then again, if you bid or offer at mid, you will get filled the majority of the time in most markets if you show a bit of patience.

   Option c) saves you the most on transaction costs but can be riskiest since you need to wait for someone to cross a full spread. This can be a good strategy when nothing is going on, but you need to weigh the risk of the trade going hard in your direction before you get filled.

   I think people tend to use too many market orders and not enough limit orders but I have seen a change in FX markets over the past five years as more clients now use limits. Some people feel that when you leave a limit order, you give a free option to market makers or high-frequency traders (HFTs) and it is true that limit orders have some value and optionality for banks and HFTs. Still, the money you save by strategically using limit orders to minimize your transaction costs is worth it.

There is not one correct execution method for all markets and all regimes.

As a general comment, there is no strictly correct way to execute. No order type or execution style is optimal at all times. It depends on the market and situation. In a product with a wide bid/offer spread, you are more likely to miss the trade if you don't aggress, but you are also saving more by using a passive strategy. It comes down to your view of what is going to happen in the very short-term.

If you are worried about the trade ripping in a straight line before you can get it on with a limit order, use a market order. If you think nothing is going on or the market might even move against you a bit before your idea works, use a limit order or algorithm to trade. When in doubt, consult an expert or market maker in the product you trade to get an idea of liquidity, bid/offer bounce and what might be the weak side in the short term.

2. If you are a large institutional trader, don't stick to one execution style all the time. Learn about the different order types and algorithms you have at your disposal and mix in various methods depending on your urgency and on market conditions. Talk to a few market makers you trust and ask them how they transact. There is a time and a place for TWAPs[127] but there is also a time and a place to pick up the phone and do a risk transfer.

Execution strategy always comes down to the trade-off between footprint and market risk. Fast, aggressive execution has a larger footprint but less market risk. If you go slow, you pay less in TC but you take the risk the market will move against you in the meantime. When

---

127. TWAP stands for time-weighted average price. VWAP stands for volume-weighted average price. They are similar electronic strategies that take a large order and break it up into smaller pieces then execute those smaller pieces over time. For example, a client wants to buy 200 million USDCAD. That's too big of a ticket to do all at once, so they might send a TWAP to buy the 200 USDCAD over 200 minutes. Then, the computer will buy 1 million USDCAD per minute for 200 minutes (3h20m) until the order is completed. With a TWAP like this is, you reduce your footprint substantially because you spread the order out over a long period. The problem is, you are taking a ton of market risk because if you are a buyer, the market could go substantially higher in the 3 hours and 20 minutes it takes to complete the trade. TWAPs and VWAPs are best used when markets are quiet or when the user thinks the market is likely to move in their direction in the time allotted to the TWAP (i.e., if you are a buyer and you think the price is going lower, a TWAP makes sense).

it is time to execute, you need to decide how to balance the tension between minimizing footprint and market risk at the same time.

Generally for larger trades, I find a hybrid of human and electronic (algorithmic) execution is best. You run a few algorithms in the background to take care of half of your size and make sure the trade won't take all day, and you run the other half with discretion, using limit orders while absorbing any meaningful chunks of liquidity more aggressively.

One weakness with TWAP and VWAP orders is that they generally ignore the amount of liquidity available in the market. Let's say EURUSD is 1.1500 and a client wants to buy 500 million EURUSD. They decide to run a 50-minute TWAP (i.e., buy 10 million EUR per minute for 50 minutes). The computer starts buying, slowly but surely, and the market doesn't move. Drip, drip, drip, the computer buys euros slowly but surely at 1.1501 and 1.1502. After 3 minutes, a large seller appears. Someone shows a large limit order, an offer to sell 250 million euros at 1.1502.

A rational human trader would almost always buy those 250 million euros because that is a huge chunk of the order to fill just 1 pip off the bid. On the other hand, a TWAP won't care. It will just keep buying 10 euros per minute even though it could snag a huge clip of euros all at once if it was smarter. A hybrid algo/human strategy gives you the best of both worlds.

3. Are there securities or products to trade within your asset class that have lower transaction costs? Many products trade as cash, over-the-counter, futures, ETFs, and so on. ETFs are great for some traders, but futures often have tighter bid/offer spreads with the identical exposure. For example, you might be better off trading S&P futures, not the SPY ETF when you have the choice. Futures also offer more leverage than ETFs.

If you have a longer holding period, you might also discover that futures are cheaper to hold than ETFs because futures do not charge a management fee while ETFs do. For example, SLV, the silver ETF, charges 0.65% / year. This is not an epic fee by any means but if you can trade silver futures you might find that more attractive, depending on funding costs. I am not telling you which products are best, I am simply saying you should take the time to figure out the best way to trade your product if there are various expressions available.

Currencies trade over-the-counter but it is not always efficient for a hedge fund to set up credit with a bank; sometimes it's cheaper for a fund to trade currency futures. Often it is better for smaller participants to execute through an online FX broker. But sometimes they would be better off in futures. The point here is to think about the various ways of trading your asset or market, if more than one avenue exists.

4. When you trade a particular asset, ask yourself whether there is another asset or security within your asset class that will give you the same exposure with better liquidity. For example, a hedge fund PM who manages $1.4 billion expects China growth to pick up in the next few months. He decides to buy $500 million NZDUSD (long New Zealand dollars, short USD). Given AUDUSD is substantially more liquid than NZDUSD, would he have been better off just buying AUD? Very likely the answer in this scenario is yes.

Sticking with FX markets, sometimes a basket will also give you the same exposure with better liquidity and lower transaction costs. If a speculator wants to take a huge bet on a falling USD, she is better off to execute 20% of her risk across a basket of five different currencies instead of 100% short USDCHF. This situation applies to credit, too, where a basket of names can often give you bigger exposure with lower transaction costs than piling into a single name.

Retail traders rarely have to worry about liquidity and this is a huge advantage for small traders. They can trade anything, whenever it's open and never have to worry about liquidity. Yes, they need to worry about transaction costs but they don't have to worry about being able to buy or sell when they want (or need) to. I have heard retail traders complain that if they only had a bigger account, they could succeed in trading. That is almost always false. It's like saying: "I can't win this race on a jet ski… If only I had an aircraft carrier!"

A larger account is more difficult to trade, especially now that almost every asset class has minis, or fractional shares or unlimited divisibility (crypto). The only time a small account is a handicap is if you need to make X amount of money and your account size is too small to do that. Generally, smaller accounts can achieve more leverage, pay lower transaction costs, have more assets to choose from and can achieve higher returns.

In contrast, when funds grow larger than about $1 billion, the list of products they can trade slowly shrinks. Small caps and thinly-traded credits or some short-dated options (for example) become impossible to trade when you are a behemoth.

Smart execution improves performance.

Once you have executed your trade, automate your stop loss and your take profit (if you can) and record the trade in your journal. These final steps should always be part of your execution process.

Here are a few more thoughts on stop losses.

1. If you trade huge size, it is more difficult to automate your stops. This is a difficult fact of life for very large traders but does not apply to most. Even a stop loss for 100 million euros (a decent position size in FX) is perfectly manageable. If I am trading a position that is too large to automate my stop loss, I simply automate whatever percentage I can. If I'm short 200 million AUDUSD and I think anything above 50 million AUD is too much to automate, I put a stop loss for 50 million in my system. At least that is a placeholder and serves as an alert when my level triggers. Once the 50 million has been purchased automatically, I will get busy and cover the rest of the position ASAP. This is less than ideal since it relies on discipline and can lead to dumb-brain comments like: "Let me wait to see if it pulls back and maybe I can get these on the bid" or "Man, AUD has rallied so much already, I can't pay way up here!" When your stop loss level hits, you must act to get out of the position so you can survive to play again tomorrow. Don't screw around trying to get the best-possible execution. That's what you do on the way in, not on the way out.

2. Sell stops should always be below a round number and buy stops should always be above a round number. This is because of round number bias. If you ever see a trader leave a buy stop in a stock at $99.99 or $100.00… That trader probably doesn't know what he's doing. Experts always leave their stops on the correct side of the round numbers.

3. If your stop loss is in a really obvious place where a ton of stops are likely to be, it's probably going to get done! You need a bit of second-level thinking when placing stop losses. If there is a triple bottom at $101 and everyone in the market is talking about it… Expect there will be a pocket of stop losses at $100.80. Leave your stop below $100 instead. The extra space will protect you from a whipsaw through $101.00 and could be the difference between a winning and losing trade.

4. When deciding between two stop loss levels, pick the wider stop. Surviving the trade is more important than maximizing leverage, though obviously there is always an important tension between those two goals. When you get stopped out at the lows before a huge rally, it really hurts.

6. TRACKING

Once you put a trade on, take a few breaths and relax. Don't sit there staring at your screen trying to decide whether to add, cut or reverse. Your plan is in place and you should not alter course unless one of your predetermined reassessment triggers hits, or substantial new information comes in. Stick to the plan. When the risk reward has changed substantially, consider tightening up your stop loss.

7. PERFORMANCE ANALYSIS

High performing trading professionals constantly iterate through this process:

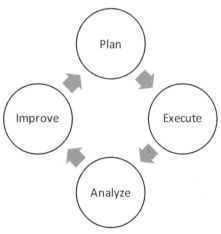

It's a never-ending cycle of action and analysis that should yield better and better results as errors are corrected and strengths are leveraged. The information and feedback from your detailed trade records and analysis will help improve your process. Each month that you trade, your process gets a bit more solid and you use these improvements to plan better and trade more successfully.

The time to analyze performance is when you are well rested and calm. After you exit a trade, record the information in your trading journal with as much detail as possible. Your journal entries should emphasize the decision-making process. Once a month, go through your journal to look for patterns. Are you sticking to your plan? Do you take profit halfway to your target because you get nervous? Do you move your stop loss for no reason or ignore it sometimes?

Compare your trading statistics to your history. Are you improving or getting worse? Focus specifically on the size of your winning days vs. the size of your losing days. This is a key metric. If it's getting better or worse, can you explain why?

The number one question you need to ask is: what is working and what is not? Search for patterns and adjust your strategy and tactics to eliminate leaks and repeat errors. Are you biased to a particular direction (i.e., are you always short S&P futures and never long)? If yes, either stop trading that product or open your mind to both sides. Directional bias is a huge weakness for short-term traders.

Once you complete your analysis and tweak your process, stop thinking about trades in the past and go back to thinking forward. What I mean by this is, you should ringfence your performance analysis and do it all at once, then move on. Don't keep thinking about trades you did in the past.

• • •

Now that you understand my process and framework in general, I want to walk you through the specifics of a real trade from start to finish, in detail. When you are done reading this example, I hope you have a clear idea of how a trade comes to life. The trade I will describe is not some epic once in a lifetime trade, it's just a good trade of the sort you should encounter fairly regularly. For confidentiality purposes, I have obscured a few specific details like exact position size but this description is a very accurate walkthrough of a real trade I did in 2020.

DETAILED TRADE WALKTHROUGH

Short EURUSD trade
September 2020

The setup

In June and July of 2020, EURUSD rallied in a steady up trend from 1.08 to 1.19 (see Figure 12.6). By the end of summer, the market was all-in on this bullish EURUSD narrative:

- Emmanuel Macron and Angela Merkel agree to a framework to bring Europe closer to fiscal union. After approval at an EU Summit in July, this removes eurozone break-up risk and makes the EUR a more attractive alternative to the USD as a reserve currency.

- ECB is quiet, saying fiscal policy (not monetary policy) needs to do the heavy lifting on COVID-19 relief. No further easing from ECB is bullish EURUSD.

- The Fed has been mega-dovish in response to COVID-19 and is ready to get even more dovish on the back of a new Average Inflation Targeting (AIT) framework. The details of the framework are not yet clear, and the market is excited to hear more from Fed Chairman Jerome Powell at Jackson Hole (late August) and the next Fed (FOMC) meeting (mid-September). The market assumes these events will be dovish and USD-negative.

- EUR long positioning (as measured the Daily Sentiment Index and many other metrics) is at a multi-year extreme.

- The stock market has rallied on global fiscal and monetary stimulus and optimism around the economic bounce back as the world economy reopens after COVID-19. Stronger global growth and world trade tend to be bullish EURUSD.

- Gold, silver, lumber and other hard assets have ripped higher in sympathy as hard assets are viewed as reflationary/anti-dollar trades and benefit from copious global liquidity.

- US twin deficits have exploded, and this worries foreign investors.

You can see the chart in Figure 12.6.

**Figure 12.6: EURUSD rallied hard after the Macron/
Merkel handshake in May 2020**

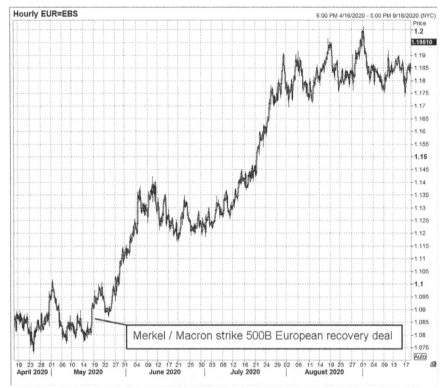

Merkel / Macron strike 500B European recovery deal

Chart courtesy of Refinitiv

This was an amazing bullish narrative and many traders (most of the FX market, actually) caught some or most of it. By the time we reached 1.1900 in July, bullish forecasters and traders were busy extrapolating as they moved their 1.2000 targets to 1.2500. Bearish forecasters meanwhile, ratcheted their forecasts up from 1.05 to 1.15. A big series of forecast revisions can often be a sign that we have come too far too fast. Strategists cannot leave stale forecasts hanging out there for too long[128]. At this stage, a great deal of good news was priced in.

Then, the narrative slowly started to shift.

---

128. For example, if your forecast was 1.05 when EURUSD was 1.08... Then EURUSD rallies to 1.1900... Your 1.05 forecast looks a bit ridiculous now. You don't want to have a ridiculous forecast. So you stay bearish and move your forecast up to 1.1500. That's how forecasting works, generally. "Forecasts" go up and down with the market price.

- Fed Chair Powell delivered an uneventful launch of the Fed's new Average Inflation Targeting regime at Jackson Hole. Markets were hoping for a strong signal that the Fed was ready to act at its September meeting. There was no such signal.

- The ECB started to push back on euro strength with Chief Economist Philip Lane and President Christine Lagarde both commenting separately that a higher euro made the inflation target more difficult to reach. When a central bank comments on its currency, pay attention. Sometimes it's irrelevant but other times it can be trend changing.

- Gold, which had been leading, was making a series of lower highs.

- Stocks were about to enter their worst month of the year (September) and were trading with a very high positive correlation to EURUSD at that time. Furthermore, I had several other reasons to feel bearish stocks. Bullish retail hysteria was strong as Davey Day Trader and the Robinhoodies gambled in stocks instead of sports. As retail bought calls, VIX went up as stocks rallied. That is unusual. When stocks are going up, volatility should be going down. If they go up in tandem, that can be a serious danger sign.

As we approached the first FOMC meeting after the Fed's announcement of Average Inflation Targeting, speculators clung to the old bullish EURUSD narrative even though it seemed fairly clear that the narrative had expired, or at least made much less sense. This was especially true as we had a 10%+ rally in EURUSD that already touched most people's original target of 1.2000. It's funny how once a trade gets to a target, many analysts and traders just raise their target instead of cashing out of the idea.

The day of the FOMC meeting, I sent a survey to my readers and responses showed a) there was a very low expectation of any major USD-negative announcement but ... b) check out the survey responses in Figure 12.7.

It was an interesting dichotomy: people didn't expect much, but mostly stayed short USD anyway. This is typical. The market will usually hold onto a position or narrative until price forces them out, regardless of how stale the narrative has become.

Since EURUSD was still near the highs then, people stuck with their USD shorts into the Fed meeting. Furthermore, this is a classic bad trade with good

Figure 12.7: What USD position will you hold into FOMC?

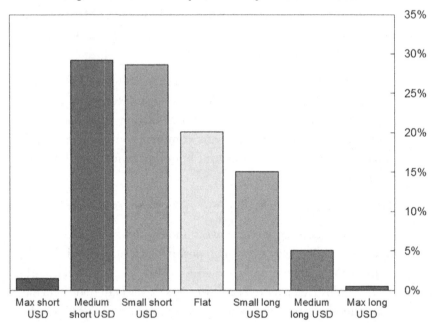

optics because the asymmetry favors short USD on the outside chance of a big policy shift and a huge move lower in the dollar. Holding short USD into the FOMC was the lottery ticket trade and speculators love lotto tickets as we discussed in the section on favorite/longshot bias.

Based on this information, I believed it was an excellent time to take the other side and go short EURUSD at the prevailing level (1.1865) the morning of the FOMC meeting. Note for the record I am not writing all this with the benefit of hindsight, this trade all happened in real-time and I wrote about it before EURUSD moved. Here is an excerpt from my pre-Fed write-up (which I published the morning of FOMC) to give you a sense of how I was thinking about the trade:

> If you want to fade the crowd and join me long USD, a good expression would be short EURUSD here with a stop at 1.1951. Here's the rationale:
>
> EURUSD is the best vanilla expression of straight USD views these days and EURUSD longs are still out there. 1.1917 was the high after Lagarde (ECB meeting) and 1.1929 was the level when Philip

Lane spoke (talking down the euro) so you have a clear stop loss level just above there.

It looks like the market does not expect much from the Fed but is going in short USD just in case. To me that means there is a good chance of a USD higher move as the meeting disappoints and weaker USD shorts / lotto tickets unwind.

The result

The Fed meeting delivered nothing special and EURUSD sold off aggressively down to 1.1788 in NY time and then hit 1.1737 in Asia time, the same night. Still, participants mesmerized by the bullish EUR narrative stayed in "buy the dip" mode and so the key 1.1700 level held again and we got one last push to 1.1850. Figure 12.8 shows the chart. See the FOMC meeting right in the middle.

Figure 12.8: EURUSD hourly chart August and September 2020

Chart courtesy of Refinitiv

You can see we rallied all the way back up to 1.1850 in the 24 hours after the FOMC. At that point, the trade was extremely frustrating because it looked to me like the narrative had clearly turned (bearish EURUSD), but price just would not cooperate. I hung on to the view but my confidence was dented by the rebound off 1.1737.

Then, the weekend after the FOMC meeting, Supreme Court Justice Ruth Bader Ginsburg died. This is a great example of a catalyst that triggers a move, even when the catalyst really makes no sense. Sometimes moves that were meant to happen just need a random bit of news to kick up volatility and then the market will go where you thought it should have gone days ago.

If anything, the vibe on the weekend RBG passed away was that the news would be bad for the USD because it increased the chances of a constitutional crisis around election time. The first clients to trade on the open sold dollars.

You can see that a few hours after Justice Ginsburg died, EURUSD entered a steep, aggressive decline. As mentioned earlier, 1.1700 was considered the bottom of the range and a major support for EURUSD so I covered (too early!) at 1.1710. Net, I risked 86 pips to make 155 pips (1.1865 entry vs. 1.1951 stop loss).

Astute observers will note that there was more money to be made in the primary trend from 1.0800 to 1.2000 than there was playing the pullback. That is true! In fact, the rally from 1.0800 was a textbook macro news trade as the good news for euro (the Macron/Merkel agreement) came out right as the market was max bearish EURUSD and still very bearish stocks.

When I went short EURUSD, I considered the possibility that it might trade symmetrically and go all the way back down to 1.0800. But I believed it was a countertrend move and the decaying US fiscal story would keep the dollar on a downward trend in the bigger picture. That is why I played the trade as a short-term pullback (not a new down trend) and took profit at 1.1710. In an ideal world, it would have been a major turn and I could try to ride the thing all the way back down to 1.0800 but in this case that is not what I believed.

I often trade countertrend and "narrative is turning" style trades but the juiciest trades occur when you identify a new trend where positioning is max short, you get in early, then you ride it all the way up until the market is max long. The EURUSD move from 1.0800 to 1.2000 fits that description and was rather tradable in real time because the pair hung around 1.0900 for a full week after the Macron/Merkel news broke. Then it finally ripped higher.

This is not meant to be a recap of one of the greatest trades of all time. It is the detailed story of a good trade that made sense and made money. But it is not some rare bird that can only be spotted once every seventy-pleven fortmoons. This is a typical short-term global macro trade you will see all the time.

Now that you have the overview of the trade, let's go through each of the seven steps in the "Lifecycle of a trade" grid to provide more granular detail.

1. IDEA GENERATION

The idea comes to me gradually as I see the market build a bigger and bigger long position in EURUSD even as it seems clear that the bull story has become patchy and much less compelling. Crosswinds blow all over the place and EUR bulls are still heading out to sea with full confidence.

The ECB pushback and the disappointment from the Fed (on the AIT story, which had generated significant market excitement and media attention) make me think we are past peak narrative and price is sure to follow. This is a classic "stale narrative" trade.

2. FILTERING

The narrative cycle, positioning and sentiment all work in favor of the short EURUSD trade idea. Correlated markets do not have much to say, though there is a huge triangle forming in gold[129] and the weakest seasonality of the year is coming up in stocks[130].

Events and catalysts work strongly in the trade's favor as the upcoming FOMC looks likely to hurt anyone hanging on to the bearish USD trade. In fact, there is a strange dichotomy where speculators expect nothing from FOMC but hold large short USD positions anyway. Technical analysis suggests two key NewsPivot highs (1.1910 and 1.1929, both on ECB comments) represent a meaningful double top.

Alternative hypotheses: the main alternative hypothesis is that the Fed might deliver something very dovish at the FOMC meeting. This is a real possibility but I rate it about a 10% chance; I am comfortable with the risk. Otherwise, I am fully aware of and steeped in the EURUSD bull narrative (I have been

---

129. Gold usually has a strong positive correlation to EURUSD and negative correlation to the USD in general.

130. Stock market correlation to EURUSD is very erratic and regime sensitive but at this point in time, the correlation was positive. So if stocks dumped, that would help my EURUSD short position.

participating in it and/or studying it for four months). Being expert in the current narrative, I feel like I can shoot down the bulls' arguments one by one, with high confidence.

That sounds a bit arrogant, but honestly, I am never as confident as that last paragraph sounds. Still, I am as confident in this case as one can reasonably be in a game where the rules and probabilities are constantly changing. It's more about being confident *enough*, not perfectly confident. If risk/reward is 1 : 1, you need supreme confidence but at 1.8 : 1, there is some margin of error to work with.

3. TACTICS

The whole story is about EURUSD so product choice here is easy. EURUSD, obv. With regard to the stop loss, I consider the 1.1910/1.1929 area important, so I place my stop at 1.1951, above those two levels, plus another 25% of a daily range (and one pip above the round number, 1.1950).

My take profit is 1.1710. There is a huge support at 1.1700 from July and August so I simply place my take profit just ahead of that. Risking 86 pips to make 155 (1: 1.8 ratio) is fine by me. As you know, I don't stick to an arbitrary ratio. Instead, I think about my expected probability of success vs. my upside.

In this case, I think I am better than 50/50 to be correct so risking 86 to make 155 is excellent leverage. My reassessment trigger is easy in this case and it is an automatic exit trigger: if the Fed meeting is unambiguously dovish, my idea is wrong and I will get out as quickly as possible. I also add "topside break of gold triangle" as a reassessment trigger (but not an automatic exit). If gold starts ripping higher, that's probably not good news for my short EURUSD trade.

4. POSITION SIZING

I have to be a bit opaque here because when you work at a bank you are not allowed to discuss specific trade details. So here I introduce a young trader with four years of experience: Phoebe. She has a yearly stop loss of $3 million. She is +$2 million P&L on the year and views this short EURUSD idea as a Type II trade. She has free capital of $5 million (max loss $3m + YTD P&L $2m) and decides to risk 4% of free capital on the trade. That is 4% of $5 million, which is $200,000. Then, she calculates:

Position size

= $ at risk / (entry point - stop loss level)

= 200,000 / (1.1951 - 1.1865)

= 23.2 million EURUSD

She rounds it off and thus plans to go short 23 million EURUSD at 1.1865. The market can easily handle both an entry and a stop loss for 23 million euros, so liquidity is not a constraint here. Her stop loss is far enough away that she believes with high certainty that she will be able to access 23 million EUR of liquidity at or before 1.1951, even on the worst possible FOMC outcome.

She thinks about the catastrophic outcome (Fed announces a massive new QE program) and runs through her memory of similar incidents in the past. She is confident that she will not blow herself up on this trade, even if the Fed fires a bazooka. There is no risk of ruin.

5. EXECUTION

Because the Fed meets in a few hours, and she wants the trade on before the meeting, there is no chance to fine tune the execution. She places a 1.1865 limit order to sell and gets a fill within a minute or two. The moment she is filled, she inputs a stop loss order to buy 23 million euros at 1.1951.

She flips open her journal and enters the details of the trade, along with a quick note saying she is nervous because she doesn't usually take positions through major events. She feels proud that she is keeping the full size (23 million euros) whereas in the past she would have cut back to 10 million euros through an event like this, just in case. Her confidence in her own judgment of event and gap risk has grown.

Once the trade is on, Phoebe literally sits on her hands to keep herself from trading. The FOMC meeting starts, the statement is released and EURUSD flies around during Powell's speech. The currency pair goes up first (for no reason?) then crumples under the weight of the disappointing outcome. Nothing new from the Fed = disappointed USD bears. Phoebe watches with minimal emotion knowing this is just one of many, many trades she will do this year. She updates her stop loss by adding a take profit OCO[131] to buy at 1.1710. She leaves the office and bicycles home.

---

131. OCO means "One cancels the other". If her stop gets done, the take profit will cancel, and vice versa. This is a standard order type.

That night, Phoebe is awoken by her loud neighbor at 2:14 a.m. and she breaks her own *sleep through the night don't check your phone* rule by checking her phone. She sees EURUSD is trading around 1.1741. She does a quick fist pump and falls back to sleep. She dreams of waking up with EURUSD at 1.1660. She dreams of giant cartoon dollar signs. She dreams of more fist pumping.

But... *Sad trombone*. When she wakes up, she sees that EURUSD has rallied back to 1.1801. By the time she leaves work the next day it's all the way back at 1.1850! GRRRRR. #disappointing.

Her conviction is not broken, just bent. She knows nothing's changed and her thesis remains valid and intact. The Fed wasn't dovish, gold has not broken the triangle, her stop loss hasn't hit and her take profit is nowhere close. So... She sticks to the plan. That is the whole point of reassessment triggers. If none of them have triggered: hands off the keyboard!

Eventually, a few days later, despite what looks like USD-negative news (Ruth Bader Ginsburg dies, triggering a possible constitutional crisis into the US election) EURUSD dumps lower and her take profit hits.

She made $356,000 profit on the trade. EURUSD keeps going straight down but she is smart and rational and doesn't much care what happens in a market after she gets out of a trade. Once you exit a trade, don't sit there saying woulda/coulda/shoulda if it keeps going. Nobody cares and neither should you. Start thinking about new trade ideas.

Think forward. Not back.

The ability to flush past trades quickly from your mind is a useful skill that will help keep you sane and productive. Like the tattoo says: *No Regerts*.

There are lessons to be extracted from most trades, but you should extract them quickly and move on. Write any impressions and lessons you take away immediately in your NOTES column and then start thinking about what's next. Here, Phoebe writes:

> Took a good-sized position through a major event. STUCK WITH THE PLAN despite some scary whipsaw moves. Good process / good outcome.

Record your trade results at the appropriate level of detail so that you can go back and analyze your trading once per month. By conducting post-mortems just once a month (and not on each trade individually), you will view your trading more holistically and will be less likely to get bogged down in the emotional joy or pain of specific trades.

• • •

That completes this walkthrough of the short EURUSD trade of September 2020. I hope it helps you understand my thought process and provides enough granular detail so that the giant grid numbered 1 to 7 makes complete sense at this point.

This concludes Chapter 12 and our discussion of the specific steps that go into finding, executing and monetizing trade ideas. The methodology and mathematics you use to develop and optimize your trading process are critical to your success as a professional trader.

Now, let's head to Part Four and dig into the two most critical aspects of trader mindset: *Adaptation and attitude.*

PART FOUR

ADAPTATION AND ATTITUDE

You can memorize every method and synthesize every strategy in this book, but if your mindset is bad, your trading will be bad. As an experienced trader and the author of two books on trading, I am intimately familiar with what needs to be done to trade successfully. Still, I go through periods of terrible performance and sometimes struggle under the weight of bad attitude or mindset. Experience helps, but even wily veterans like me are not immune to periods of poor adaptation, sluggish mental energy, sloppy trading, and frustration.

A rigid mindset, negative mental loops and low energy will derail the best-laid plans and render even the most carefully planned process, strategy, and tactics all but worthless. Without the right attitude, there can be no sustained success in trading. The next chapter will discuss the importance of adaptation and then we will close with Chapter 15 and some final thoughts on the importance of a healthy attitude.

CHAPTER 14

ADAPT OR DIE

Stay flexible and achieve long-term trading success

Adapt or perish, now as ever, is nature's inexorable imperative.

H. G. WELLS

Trading success can be fleeting or sustained. In this chapter, we discuss the mindset and approach that will allow you to thrive and survive as a trader over the course of years and then decades. Latching on to one style or overcommitting to a specific methodology is not the answer. The answer is adaptation and flexibility.

Excellent traders adapt to changes in market conditions and microstructure over time. Alpha Traders recognized, for example, that trend following was delivering lower and lower returns in the 1990s. Instead of complaining and sticking with a failing strategy, they developed new strategies and found new ways to trade in the 2000s.

When they saw algos enter the market in the mid-2000s, they did not scream: "These algos are stupid! This is dumb!" Instead, they thought "OK, this is a major change in market structure. How am I going to adapt? How can I beat the algos? How do I make money in this new regime?"

No market regime lasts forever. Profitable strategies slowly disappear because efficient markets discover them and crowd into them. If everyone is making money trading correlation, you can bet it will attract more participants. With more participants, profits shrink and strategies die.

You saw this with the high-frequency firms in the 2010s. Initially, high-frequency traders were obscenely profitable across the board but as the decade wore on, the arms race heated up (faster and smarter strategies) and by the end of the 2010s most high-frequency strategies barely generated enough returns to cover costs. A small group of highly adaptable firms crowded out all the less nimble participants.

Study and adapt to ongoing changes in market structure.

Markets are in a constant state of evolution and good traders need to be aware of this. The big structural changes happen every 5 to 7 years, and these are of epic importance. However, probably more important are the continual changes in the market that require adaptation in real time. A poker player cannot expect to win in the long run by employing the same style and strategy over and over. She must adapt as the game changes, and respond in real-time as the metagame evolves.

Here are the most important markers of market structure, and how to continually adapt to them.

ORDER VS. CHAOS

Markets alternate between order and chaos. Chaotic markets (often called "fast markets") generate temporary inefficiencies and outsized opportunities but also tend to be short-lived, dangerous, and volatile. Order and equilibrium are the market's default state, but when chaos arrives, so does disequilibrium. Dislocations present the opportunity for traders to capture abnormal returns. Fast markets are high risk and high reward. Here is a primer on trading fast markets.

Trading fast markets

In World War 1, there was a famous quote:

> Modern warfare is months of boredom punctuated by moments of extreme terror[132].

I would paraphrase here and say modern trading is hours of boredom punctuated by minutes of extreme terror. Things are quiet most of the time but what matters is how you act and react when the guano hits the rotating blades.

Crisis markets can provide the best opportunities for profit and the greatest

---

132. https://english.stackexchange.com/questions/103851/where-does-the-phrase-of-boredom-punctu-ated-by-moments-of-terror-come-from

chance of ruin. Markets can lay dormant for months, then go completely insane. A whole day can go by without excitement, then a headline hits at 4:00PM and everything boots off.

In this section, I discuss fast markets and, more specifically, trading during a crisis or extreme high volatility event. Trading crisis markets and trading idiosyncratic bursts of extreme high volatility involve most of the same skills and concepts.

It is usually easy to identify when a crisis is happening but for simplicity, I would say any time the VIX is above 40, that's a crisis market. Looking at all days since 1990, the VIX closed above 40 just 2.2% of the time. Check out Figure 14.1.

Figure 14.1: VIX marked with vertical bar any time it closed above 40

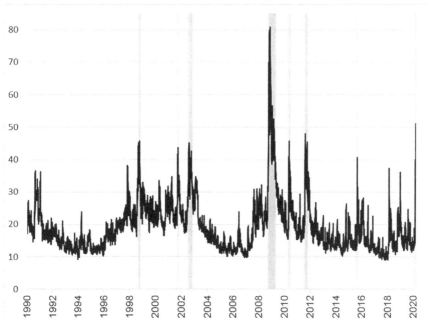

The vertical bars are all famous events in financial market history:

1998	Asian Financial Crisis, Russia Crisis, LTCM meltdown
2001/2002	September 11 / Dot com bubble burst
2008	Global Financial Crisis
2010/2011	Eurozone Crisis
2015	Energy crisis and China deval
2020	COVID-19 and Saudi / Russia oil price war

There is nothing special about the number 40, it's just a level we rarely see in the VIX.

When markets are in crisis, you need to trade differently. You need to be faster and smarter. The challenge is to be both more careful and more courageous at the same time. That is hard to balance! Fast markets are scary, but they are the best times to make money, and to truly excel at trading you need to crush fast markets.

Here are some tips to help you trade fast markets:

1. **Correct position size is the difference between winning and losing in a crisis**. Too big is not OK; you might blow up or get fired. Too small is not OK either; you need to seize the moment. Trading in fast markets is when the most money gets made and the alpha traders emerge.

   I remember as volatility went to the moon in 2008, I changed my normal trade size in USDMXN from 20 million to 3 million and I was still amazed (scared) by the volatility of my P&L. If you can size dynamically using forward-looking estimates of volatility, that is ideal. Look at what options markets are pricing for 1-week volatility. If you can't do that, look at the average daily range over the past 5, 10 or 20 days.

   As a rough logic check: for day traders, your stop loss should rarely or never be closer than within 1/3 of a day's range. For swing traders, use one full day's range. In other words, if you are trading Apple common stock and the average daily range over the past 5, 10 and 20 days is $25: day traders' stops should be $8 or more away from the entry point and swing traders stops should be at least $25 away from entry. This should be a good starting point in most markets.

   If you are getting stopped out and chopped up every day, your stops are too tight. A smaller position with a wider stop is necessary in crisis markets but you need to be mindful that you don't get so small that you are trading meaningless positions that won't move the needle on your P&L. Yes, a lot of traders get blown up in a crisis, but a lot just hide under the desk and reveal they are fundamentally risk-averse actors who are not really fit to trade moving markets.

   Striking the balance between too big and too small is vital in trading and that balance can be the difference between crushing a crisis period or getting crushed by it.

2. **Keep an open mind and use your imagination**. When COVID-19 hit in 2020, the market took oil from $65 to $50 as concerns about consumer demand knocked a market that was already bulled up on "cheap" energy stocks. Then the OPEC meeting in early March crumbled and crude plummeted from $50 to $27 in a week. The pressure from COVID-19 started the ball rolling then the Saudi pledge to pump like crazy broke the back of the oil market. Anyone watching oil go from $65 to $50 might have thought that was enough of a move. "It's a big move! I'm going the other way!" *Not a good plan.* Eventually oil went to MINUS $40. This leads to the next point about crisis markets.

3. **In crisis markets, there is no such thing as overbought and oversold**. Don't be the person that fades the whole bear market all the way down. In a crisis, stocks can stay oversold for ages and then get wildly overbought days later. You need to differentiate between run-of-the-mill risk aversion and crisis-level risk aversion.

Most risky asset sell-offs are routine affairs that should be traded using sentiment and overbought and oversold signals. When you see put/call ratios or the Greed & Fear Index or DSI or whatever positioning indicators flashing a reversal signal, it is normally time to pounce. But in a real economic or financial crisis, these signals are useless.

For example, there is a simple metric I use to calculate overbought and oversold which I call The Deviation, as discussed in Chapter 10. It measures the difference between the current price of an asset and the 100-HOUR moving average. As The Deviation gets to prior extremes, it can give a nice mean reversion signal. Figure 14.2 shows an example using EURUSD.

You can see that The Deviation (the gray line in the bottom panel) oscillated consistently between -80 pips and +80 pips[133] over the course of five months and the overbought and oversold readings offered up some decent reversal trades. Then, the COVID-19 crisis

---

133. See dark, horizontal lines. Note: 80 pips = 0.0080

**Figure 14.2: EURUSD (top, black) vs. deviation
from the 100-hour MA (gray, bottom)**
September 2019 to January 2020

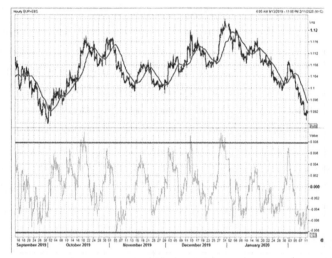

Chart courtesy of Refinitiv

**Figure 14.3: EURUSD (top, black) vs. deviation
from the 100-hour MA (gray, bottom)**
September 2019 to March 2020

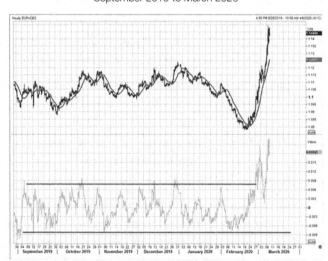

Chart courtesy of Refinitiv

hit and all hell broke loose. Now look at the same chart, adding February 2020 (see Figure 14.3).

As the crisis hit, the old measures of overbought were blown away as EURUSD ripped higher.

4. **Have courage.** Insane markets are the reason you got into this business. Don't hide under your desk and hope for the tornado to pass. Get involved and trade like you know you can. Don't put yourself in a position where you look back years later with regret. It is better to try and fail than to forever wonder what kind of trader you could have been.

By the time the 2008/2009 Global Financial Crisis was over, careers were made and lost. Some of those lost were not people that blew up but just traders that sat there doing nothing while their peers extracted insane P&L out of thin air. Most of my best trading memories are from crisis periods because these periods deliver fast, volatile, and exciting markets.

Like any high stress profession (pro sports, jet fighter pilot, professional poker...), it all comes down to how you respond in the periods of extreme stress. Don't be shy, get involved.

Recognize when your product transitions from normal trading to a fast market and adjust your position size and trading strategies accordingly.

VOLATILITY

Fast markets are temporary, but changes in volatility can be more permanent. Do you know how to size your risk correctly to reflect current levels of volatility? Does your methodology respond systematically to changes in volatility? It should. For example, higher volatility means you should be trading smaller positions. Lower volatility means larger positions.

Bad traders always put on the same position size.

Many traders are not very good at adjusting their position size and risk management strategies in response to volatility. If S&P futures are moving 1% per day, should you have the same position size or stop loss parameters as if they are moving 3% per day? Clearly the answer is no. Actively adjust your trading as volatility changes.

The easiest way to volatility-adjust (or vol-adjust, as most professionals say) is to use a spreadsheet that determines position size and stop loss parameters based on a volatility input. This does not have to be complicated.

The figure you use for volatility adjustment will never be perfect because we don't know future volatility until it happens. That said, there are many ways to estimate future volatility, and those estimates will generally be accurate enough for our purposes. For example, Figure 14.4 shows the VIX on a given day plotted against the percent range in the S&P futures the day after.

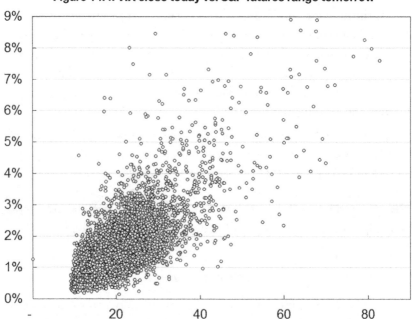

Figure 14.4: VIX close today vs. S&P futures range tomorrow

You can see from the that plot that tomorrow's range has a strong relationship with today's VIX. The relationship between VIX and S&P ranges is not linear or normal as you see by the many outliers. The point is not to be perfect here.

Here is a simplified but realistic example of how a trader can apply this information and use good thinking to determine position size.

Frank trades only S&P futures and has $1,000,000 in his account. He buys or sells on the open each day and risks 2% of his account ($20,000) on each trade. He does not believe much in technical analysis so he simply sets his stop loss and take profit this way:

STOP LOSS = (entry level) + (half of one average daily range)
TAKE PROFIT = 2 * stop loss

In other words, he risks half a day's range to make one day's range. These parameters are not unreasonable and a simple methodology like this will work in real life. The point of the example is to show that changes in volatility should change your sizing and risk management parameters.

Frank looks at yesterday's close in VIX and plugs it into a formula in Excel. Figure 14.5 shows Frank's risk in six different volatility regimes.

Figure 14.5: Vol-adjusting with Trader Frank

VIX today	Average Range SPX tomorrow	# of contracts where half day range is $20,000
Under 12	0.5%	23
12 to 15	0.7%	16
16 to 20	1.1%	10
21 to 30	1.6%	7
31 to 40	2.3%	5
above 40	3.9%	3

Assume index at 3500 so 1% = 35 points
35 points X $50 per contract = $1,750
Therefore each 1% move costs $1,750 per contract

You can see here that as volatility rises, Frank takes smaller positions. If he normally trades 50 e-mini contracts and market volatility falls substantially, he will find the volatility of his P&L falls if he doesn't adjust the number of contracts he trades. In contrast, if he sticks with the same number of contracts and the same P&L parameters as volatility rises, he will get stopped out of good trades all the time before they have a chance to work. All other things being equal, the probability that your trade hits its stop loss level is a direct function of volatility.

I cannot emphasize this enough. Your position size should change as volatility changes. This is the easiest and most automatic adaptation you can make as markets change.

Rangebound vs. Trending

While markets can be volatile or quiet, and liquid or illiquid, they can also be viewed through the lens of Rangebound vs. Trending. Rangebound markets favor mean reversion strategies (buy low/sell high) while trending markets favor breakout or "go with" strategies (buy high/sell higher). You should always have a good sense of whether each market you trade is trending, rangebound or neither. It is not always easy to tell.

It is usually straightforward to figure out whether a market has been trending or rangebound. Start by looking at the chart and making a subjective, common sense assessment. Sometimes a rangebound or trending market is easy to identify at a glance. The harder part is identifying when the market is transitioning from one to the other.

The simplest way to identify the range or trend status of a market (and a possible change) is with technical analysis tools. I prefer simple technical analysis to more esoteric methods, so here are a few simple approaches to gauge whether a market is rangebound or trending (note that this methodology is suited to short-term trading with a 1-hour to 5-day time horizon).

1. Has the price made a new 20-day high or low in the last ten days? If yes, it is trending that way; if no, rangebound.

2. Put a 100-HOUR and 200-HOUR moving average on an hourly chart and look at this matrix:

	100-HOUR above 200-HOUR	100-HOUR below 200-HOUR
Price of asset above both 100-HOUR and 200-HOUR	UP TREND	Range
Price of asset between the 100-HOUR and 200-HOUR	Range	Range
Price of asset below both 100-HOUR and 200-HOUR	Range	DOWN TREND

You can substitute different moving averages depending on what you find generally fits the trend of the product and time frame you trade. If you are trading a longer time horizon you can also put three moving averages on your daily chart. Say, 20, 50 and 100-day moving averages. When they are in order it is a trend (20 > 50 > 100 = uptrend or 20 < 50 < 100 = downtrend). When they are not in order, there is no trend or the trend is weak.

3. Eyeball it. This sounds kind of stupid but generally no advanced mathematics degree is required to determine if a market is trending

or rangebound. Often a cursory glance at a chart (or your experience sitting there trading the market for the past month or two) reveals the type of regime.

It's not difficult to figure out if you are in a range or trend regime, but the challenge is to trade appropriately and to figure out when the regime is changing. Assume trends and ranges are somewhat persistent, and wait for evidence of a regime shift before altering your approach. It is better to wait for a signal to tell you the regime has changed than to try to anticipate or front run that regime change.

Volatility, liquidity, and trend are the three features you should always be able to describe with confidence for each market you trade. You should always know where volatility is relative to recent history, whether liquidity is good, bad, or ugly and whether your market is in a trend or a range. If you update your view of these three variables daily, you will adapt in real time better than most of your competitors.

Here are some other ways to adapt to bigger macro changes in market structure.

Realize no trading method works always and forever. No matter how well your methodology works right now, there is a chance it won't work tomorrow. Be vigilant to changes in the market and monitor the success of different trading strategies. For example, if you notice that breakout trading has not been working for you over the past two years, spend some time thinking about why. Has your methodology changed? Did you stop following your own rules? Or... Are there new algorithms doing the same thing you used to do, but faster? Are the basic breakout trading strategies such common knowledge that they no longer provide any edge? **If everybody is doing the same thing, the odds are low that it will make money.**

William Faulkner's advice to fiction writers was: "Kill your darlings." What he means is no matter how much you love some paragraph or character or scene you've written, if it doesn't work in the bigger picture: *cut it*. The same applies to trading strategies. Don't be the trader that is a one-trick pony and can't drop a strategy even though he knows (and the P&L shows) that it doesn't work. Do not fall in love with strategies that made you money in the past. Kill your darlings.

I tell you this from experience because throughout my career, my bread and butter was always trading lead/lag and correlation between currencies and variables like oil, gold, interest rates and equities. This made me a pile of money from 2003 to 2013 or so, but since then it has been much more difficult to extract profit from this approach. Too many people know about the methodology, too many blogs post about it and too many algos trade it.

In 2006, very few FX traders had live feeds for gold, oil, and single name equities. Now every single trader does. In 2006 there might have been a few expensive, PhD-built algorithms trading correlation, now you can build a correlation trading algo in Excel in two hours and plug it directly into the market through an online broker.

Efficient markets eventually prevail. *Always.*

It took me a few years to transition, but now I use correlation more selectively and question the logic more aggressively before I employ it as a tactical or strategic decision-making tool. My first assumption now is to assume lead/lag will *not* work, and then see if I can find reasons why it might work in this particular instance. In the past, my base assumption was the opposite. I'd assume it would work and then try to think of reasons it might not.

When there is a major change to the structure of markets, STOP AND THINK. How is this going to impact me? Here are a few examples of major structural changes that have changed markets in my lifetime.

1996	Currency market trading moves from voice brokers to electronic brokers.
2001	US stock markets stop trading in fractions and trade in decimals instead.
2002 - 2005	Algorithmic trading becomes an important part of most markets.
2010 - 2015	Flash crashes become an important liquidity risk in many markets.
October 2019	Free stock trading for retail traders triggers several euphoric "runnings of the bulls" in US stocks.

I believe that adaptation is one of the keys to survival and professional longevity in almost every industry. A good athlete adapts as her sport changes, just like a good trader adapts as markets change. Be thoughtful about the current environment, how it is changing and how it might change in the future. Think about how you can adapt your trading to stay ahead.

As Billy Beane says to the aging baseball scout in Moneyball, "Adapt or die."

This all circles back to the discussion near the start of the book where I discussed conscientiousness and the growth mindset. Good traders adapt because they are thoughtful about adaptation and employ it as a conscious strategy in their trading. But they are also more likely to have a growth mindset in life, too. Keep adding new knowledge on the existing base and never say things like "I'm not good at that" or "I don't trade that kind of market". The market won't always be in your favorite regime. Identify and trade the reality, not the ideal.

Since the market is a huge, adaptive system, you need to constantly adapt to it. As the Red Queen in *Through the Looking-Glass* (Lewis Carroll) says:

> Now, here, you see, it takes all the running you can do, to keep in the same place. If you want to get somewhere else, you must run at least twice as fast as that!

You need to work twice as hard as everyone else if you want to get ahead. Understand the market regime and fit your trading strategy to that regime. Don't embrace a trading style and hope the market complies with it. "Trading style" should describe your time-horizon, risk management approach and preferred analysis methodology, it should *not* describe the specific strategies you prefer. Specific strategies work in specific market regimes and you need to adapt your overall style to the regime.

Like most important trading behaviors, adaptation is easy to understand, but hard to continually execute successfully. It is especially difficult to give up particular strategies that worked for many years. Think about the areas where you have been slow to adapt, and how you can catch up. Think about how your market has changed, or is changing. And change with it.

That's it for our discussion of adaptation. You are now more than 91% done this book. In the final chapter, I will give you some parting thoughts on healthy mindset and positive thinking. Your attitude and mindset will determine some part of your success and help you bounce back when the market pummels you into submission now and then.

CHAPTER 15

THANK GOD IT'S MONDAY!

*It is impossible to succeed
without the right attitude*

In this chapter, I offer some final thoughts on how proactive goal setting, self-awareness, and attitude shape our trading experience and impact trading success. Before we dive in, let's start with a Chinese fable.

> There was once a farmer in ancient China who owned a horse. "You are so lucky!" his neighbors told him, "to have a horse to pull the cart for you."
>
> "Maybe," the farmer replied.
>
> One day the farmer forgot to latch the gate and his horse bolted. "Oh no! This is terrible news!" his neighbors cried. "Such terrible misfortune!"
>
> "Maybe," the farmer replied.
>
> A few days later the horse returned, bringing with it six wild horses. "How fantastic! You are so lucky," his neighbors told him. "Now you are rich!"
>
> "Maybe," the farmer replied.
>
> The next week, the farmer's son was breaking in one of the wild horses when he fell off and broke his leg. "Oh no!" the neighbors cried, "such bad luck!"
>
> "Maybe," the farmer replied.

> The next day soldiers came and took away all the young men to fight in the war. The farmer's son was left behind due to his injury. "You are so lucky!" his neighbors cried.
>
> "Maybe," the farmer replied.

I like this story because it is a great reminder that we never know how the movie is going to end. Your life is a big, long story and everything that happens along the way is driven by six heaping spoonfuls of variance. Don't get too triggered by any specific short-term outcome.

This chapter explains what it takes to find and maintain a healthy mindset over many years of trading. It is pretty easy to come in to work all revved up when you're 23 years old and in year two of your trading career. But how do you find a state of mind that will let you trade for ten, twenty or even thirty years? What kind of mindset do you need to keep trading well into your 40s?

In this Chapter, I am going to once again ask you to complete a few quick exercises. It is easy to be lazy and just skim over exercises in books like this. Please don't. When you passively absorb information from a book it is so, soooo different from when you engage with questions, stop to think, write things down, and actively and honestly assess your strengths and weaknesses.

Self-Evaluation

Introspection can feel a bit cheesy at times and it makes some people uncomfortable. I know I used to gag when this sort of stuff came up in business school. Please, suspend your cynicism. This first exercise will take less than 10 minutes.

**Professionals who self-evaluate,
set specific goals, and create clear action
plans outperform those who do not.**

The first exercise is to complete a super-quick self-evaluation. Feel free to write directly in the book[134]. To give you a bit of inspiration and momentum, I have completed the self-evaluation myself, just now. I plan to follow through on the results. Below my responses, you'll find blank boxes for you to complete.

---

134. Unless it's not yours.

Quick self-evaluation completed by Brent Donnelly on August 17, 2020

Two strengths in trading	Two weaknesses in trading
1. Understand and love macro. Always have a ton of passion and trade ideas. 2. Unlimited risk appetite.	1. Overtrade (too many positions and/or positions too big). 2. Undisciplined when mental energy is low.
Two strengths in life 1. Rational optimism / sense of humor. 2. Writing / communication.	**Two weaknesses in life** 1. Spread myself too thin. There is not enough time in the day for everything I want to do. Sometimes I choose friends or markets over family. 2. Addicted to change and stimulation. Need to sit still and enjoy the present moment more.
A goal I can accomplish in the next 6 months that will build on one of my strengths Finish this book.	**A goal I can accomplish in the next 6 months that will improve one of my weaknesses** Find a performance coach or psychologist to work on cognitive therapy or behavioral modification to improve discipline and break bad mental habits.

Now your turn:

Quick self-evaluation completed by _____ on _____ , 20___

Two strengths in trading	Two weaknesses in trading
Two strengths in life	**Two weaknesses in life**
A goal I can accomplish in the next 6 months that will build on one of my strengths	**A goal I can accomplish in the next 6 months that will improve one of my weaknesses**

People in the business world spend a lot of time working on their weaknesses. Personally, I think working on strengths often has more value. Not to say you ignore your weaknesses, just make sure you keep levelling up your strengths, too.

It's a bit like when you coach kids in a sport. If you spend all your time focused on the weakest players, because they tend to demand more attention, you neglect the athletes with all the upside. That's clearly not good for the best players but it's also just generally bad for the team overall.

As I mentioned in Chapter 5, I am a big fan of setting just one or two goals, no more. Look at the two goals you wrote in the boxes above and put reminders in your calendar for three months and six months from now. Did you complete both goals in the six months allotted?

If you didn't fill in the assessment, go back and do it now. If you choose not to, read this angry footnote instead[135]. Now let's cover a few more facets of quality trading mindset.

Passion

What is your purpose when it comes to trading? Organizations have mission statements that help them stay on a path towards success. What is your mission statement? Why do you trade? Write a simple statement of purpose. Here's mine:

> Come in to work energized and positive. Wait for opportunity then trade as aggressively as possible within clear, rule-based risk limits. Write something interesting every day. Make clients happy. Avoid random, low EV trades.

A simple statement of purpose can serve as a compass when you are feeling lost. Print it out and stick it to your desk. Whether you are crushing it, sucking wind or something in between, circle back to the statement and ask yourself: "Am I on track?"

Now stop reading and write your statement of purpose. Don't come back until you're done.

Notice that there is nothing in my mission statement about making money. It is more about process and attitude. If I wrote a mission statement when I was 25, money would have been front and center. I am not going to pooh pooh

---

135. Are you serious about becoming a better trader? If you want to be good at something, you have to put in the work. You have invested hours into reading this book. Take 10 or 15 minutes to look inward. :]

money as a motivation. It is a great motivator! A bit later, I discuss how money was my number one motivator when I entered the business of trading. But now, it is way down the list.

Trading pays well if you are good at it. It's an outcome that derives from a process. Focus on the process and let the money take care of itself. The longer you trade, the more you will find yourself focused on becoming the best possible trader and the less you will focus on how much money you're going to make. The time to worry about compensation is when you are negotiating an employment contract. Negotiate the most lucrative contract you can, then be glad you are employed in one of the most fun jobs in the world, and get to work.

I worked at a day trading shop called SwiftTrade in the late 1990s. They had a huge banner across one wall that read: "Thank God It's Monday!" If you don't feel this excited about trading most of the time, that's a bad sign.

The role of emotions in trading

We discussed emotions in Chapter 6 and here I give you a few more thoughts. Emotions can cloud judgment and hurt your trading behavior when extreme, but overall, I don't think there is anything wrong with emotions in trading. When you watch elite athletes perform, you see plenty of emotion and yet their performance is at the highest level. The important thing is to not ignore or repress your emotions. Observe and understand them.

**Don't suppress your emotions,
observe and understand them.**

Emotions are not bad. You do not need to be a robot. In fact, you need to be something that robots are not: self-aware.

When you are too high, you get sloppy and overconfident. When you are too low, you lose confidence. Therefore, you need to be aware of these emotions and include them in your decision-making. For example, you might say:

"I just high-fived the trader next to me because we both jumped on the same headline and are hugely in the money. That is clearly a sign I am euphoric. I am going to cut half my position. Actually, I'm going to take profit on the whole thing."

Or...

"I have a lump in my throat because I am so angry about the terrible fill that bank just gave me. And now I get a voice mail saying my sprinkler system repair is going to cost $3,400? *Grrr.* My entry point on this trade sucks and I can barely think straight…" *Pauses and moves outside his body to observe himself and his raging thoughts…* "Shoot. I really *can't* think straight right now. I still like this position but given my emotional state I am better off cutting it in half and moving my stop farther away to give it some room to breathe. And to give myself a chance to breathe."

This is how good self-awareness and metacognition work. When you can think about how you are thinking, you move to the next level of trading awesomeness because you will start to see errors happen in real time and you will gain the ability to course-correct before a faulty decision hurts you.

Also note that the trader in the second quote is using time delay, a proven strategy to avoid the potentially negative affect of emotions on decision making. Time delay is the simplest and most effective way to ensure an emotion will not impact a decision. Full-blown emotions naturally dissipate over time and physiological responses fade. The best way to stop strong emotions from leading to poor decisions is to simply avoid making decisions when you are in a strong emotional state.

**If you are feeling super high or
super low, square up and go for a walk.**

Take a moment to think back over the last week. What emotions have you felt while trading? How strong were these emotions? List physiological and behavioral markers that you can readily identify. For example: my face gets flushed and hot when I am near or through my daily stop loss limit. I feel like singing and joking around more when I am up huge on the day. I feel kind of sick when I am in the process of breaking one of my own rules, especially with regard to position size or P&L tolerance.

Think about your physiology and behavior throughout every day and take note of irregularities.

Commitment, engagement, and hard work

Nobody succeeds in trading by doing it half-assed. You need to do the work. If you are too tired to do the work, get some sleep. Again, if you can't bring yourself to complete the few 5 or 10-minute exercises in this book, you are probably not ready to commit to maximum trading success. Get motivated.

In trading, hard work means **you must work to become an expert in the**

products or markets you trade. You cannot become an expert overnight; that is why I strongly advise new traders to pick a short list of products to trade (one particular currency pair, a single commodity, or maybe 3 to 5 different single name stocks in the same industry) and go as deep as possible on those products.

Healthy body leads to healthy mindset

I know you know this but I'm going to say it anyway: you can never reach peak mental performance without proper exercise. *Sluggish body = sluggish mind.* Find a way to eliminate the decision-making process when it comes to working out, and make it a regular habit that is not a choice or option. The easiest way to do this is to work out every single day, even if it's just for 20 or 30 minutes.

Soon, you will find that if you don't work out, you feel bad and you want to get back in the gym. Rely as little as possible on willpower and as much as possible on the power of habit.

Superstitions

In a book about rational trading, the section on superstition should just be three words, like: superstitions are dumb.

There, *done.*

The thing is, even a person who takes a placebo knowing it is a placebo still derives some benefit from it! The human mind is strange and complex. If you are afraid of the number 13, why mess with it? It might put you off your game. Personally, I avoid transacting in amounts of 13, even though I know technically it's not rational because I believe there is a non-zero possibility my subconscious views it as bad luck and this subconscious belief could infect my trading or confidence.

Nils Bohr, the famous atomic scientist, had a horseshoe hung above his office door. Many viewed this as surprising or confusing as they viewed Bohr as a scientist and a man of logic. When asked, "Do you, a Nobel Prize winning scientist, believe in such superstitions as the magic of a horseshoe?" His response was:

> "Of course not, but I understand it's lucky whether you believe in it or not."

This is similar to the concept of Pascal's Wager. Pascal said that no matter how tiny the odds that God actually exists, it is still worth believing in God given the huge upside (eternal life in heaven) versus the downside (a few earthly sacrifices).

Anyway, I just included this bit about superstition in case you were wondering why a book about rational thinking has no Chapter 13.

Forgive yourself

Don't be too hard on yourself. Look at your failures as objectively as possible. Analyze them but don't waste your time smashing your head against the keyboard. First of all, the sun will always come up tomorrow, no matter how badly you traded today. After a big failure you should:

Step away. Calm down. Analyze. Extract any lessons (often, there are none!) Move on. Get ready for tomorrow.

Every trade is a spoonful of water in a huge ocean. Flush your mind quickly after a failure and come in each day with thoughts like this in your mind: "Today is a new day. All I can do is work hard and do my best."

Even the Gods of Trading experience huge failures. Here's a passage from Stan Druckenmiller's famous speech at the Lost Tree Club in 2015. In this excerpt, he recalls the devastating moment in 2000 when he paid the ding dong highs for size at the peak of the dotcom bubble.

> So, like, around March, I could feel it coming. I had to play. I couldn't help myself. And three times during the same week I pick up a – don't do it. Don't do it. Anyway, I pick up the phone finally. I think I missed the top by an hour. I bought $6 billion worth of tech stocks and in six weeks I had left Soros and I had lost $3 billion in that one play.

> You ask me what I learned. I didn't learn anything. I already knew that I wasn't supposed to do that. I was just an emotional basket case and couldn't help myself. So, maybe I learned not to do it again. But I already knew that.

You are just like Stan Druckenmiller; you are human. You will make mistakes. That's OK. Hitting a baseball in the major leagues is similar to trading in that there is a high expected failure rate baked in to the process. A hall of fame hitter will get on base maybe 35% of the time. The other 65% of the time, he fails.

Billy Beane, the Oakland Athletics general manager immortalized in the book and movie "Moneyball", was asked why Lenny Dykstra succeeded in baseball while he did not. Lenny was an inferior athlete to Billy and was drafted much lower. Beane replied:

> Lenny was so perfectly designed, emotionally, to play the game of baseball. He was able to instantly forget any failure and draw strength from every success. He had no concept of failure. And he had no idea where he was. And I was the opposite.

Lenny understood, whether subconsciously or not, that failure is part of the game. You strike out; you move on. You hit a home run. You move on. Each at bat is a new test. Just like in trading. Each day is a new test.

This anonymous quote nicely sums up the inevitability of mistakes in trading:

"Good judgment comes from experience. And experience comes from bad judgment."

Find your mantra

A mantra is something we repeat over and over out loud or in our heads. Mantras can be positive or negative. For example, an insecure person's mantra might be "I'm too fat. I'm too ugly." While a positive mantra might be something like "I can succeed if I just try hard every day." Develop your own mantra and say it over and over. Use it to drown out negative thoughts.

My mantra is "stick to the plan".

P.S., I still don't always stick to the plan.

Think about your trading history

> *The strongest and most solid legs are formed by personal experiences that we have a lot of emotion attached to because they were painful or pleasurable experiences.*
>
> **TONY ROBBINS**

If you have been trading for more than a few years… Think about how your trading history and experience to date influence your current approach. If you started in a highly volatile year, are you more comfortable trading breakouts and volatile markets? If your best year was 2008, are you always hoping for a bear market? If you started in a less-volatile period, do you favor mean reversion? And so on.

Research shows that salient memories are often an important driver of future behavior. Think about your salient trading memories and how they might influence you now. I sometimes find myself thinking, "I made so much money with this strategy in the past, it's really hard to give it up." Instead of dumping a losing strategy that I know doesn't work anymore, I stick with it like you stick with that old friend who is now a bad influence and always borrows money from you but never pays it back.

You can go pretty deep into the psychology and dig into traumatic or salient moments from your past and link them to current behaviors. I'm not qualified to talk about that, plus I find it's often a bit of a stretch when I read about connecting (for example) that salient memory of being bullied in the playground (or whatever) to your current trading leaks. Do whatever works for you.

> **A true professional works hard and does their best each day, even if they don't feel like it.**

Trading requires endurance and a commitment to work hard every day. When I get sloppy or lazy, I pay the price. There is someone else out there willing to do the work every single day and they want the same money you want. The global alpha pie is a certain size and the competition for slices (and crumbs!) is epic.

When I'm finding things hard, I narrow my focus to the current day. I think about what doing a good job *today* means, and I try not to think about the medium- or long-term. The long-term is just a whole bunch of single days added together and what you do in each of those individual days determines where you end up in the long run. I am often surprised by how some random thing I did five years ago or random person I made an effort to connect with three years ago comes back to help me.

The game of life is incredibly long. Make each turn count.

Think about your personal history

Think about your history (childhood and young adult years especially) and how it might influence your trading. For example: if your dad was an electrician and your mom was an entrepreneur… Your subconscious might have trouble with the idea that in trading you magically pull money out of thin air without any traditional hard work and without producing or creating anything.

Many traders from blue-collar families struggle with this when they first find success. It is a strange and sometimes surreal feeling to generate huge income without producing anything. Clearly trading is not the only job where this is the case, but the sometimes gigantic and sudden income stream from trading make it different from most other pursuits.

I grew up in a lower middle-class family, in the second house down from the top in this row of five attached houses:

Photo circa 1980-something, courtesy of the Donnelly Archives

We had enough money to live normally and not worry about cash but when there was a school trip to Europe or whatever… No chance. There was no extra money, just the minimum required amount.

Meanwhile, my godparents successfully created and sold an advertising agency and retired when they were 40 years old. They had one child and to keep her company (she was around my age), they used to take me on their two-week trips to the Caribbean every March. I got to see a whole different world of opportunity and awesomeness. "I want that!" I thought.

A fridge with a button you can press to get water!??! A full-sized basketball hoop with fiberglass backboard, right on your driveway? I want that!

That goal (getting out of suburban Ottawa and into something exciting and new) had a huge influence on my perception of money as a giver of freedom and novelty, and kept the fire in my belly through late high school and university.

My high school years were the days of Gordon Gekko and *Wall Street* (the movie) and after I read Liar's Poker cover to cover at age 15, I knew what I wanted to do. My one and only goal was to become a trader on Wall Street[136]. I had a crystal-clear and laser-focused motivation: money. That singular focus was good.

However, as I matured and built a decent life for myself and my family, money became less important. There is a minimum level everyone must reach before they can stop worrying about money. Above that amount, the correlation between money and happiness usually flatlines. The naïve and single-minded pursuit of a high-paying job when I was young made my life pretty simple. I had one clear goal and all I had to do was work towards it. The weird thing about dreams though, is that once you achieve them, there is a hole where that dream once was.

So for many, including me, achieving a dream can produce a fleeting sense of elation followed by a deeper existential disorientation as the thing that was pushing you forward all those years no longer has any power. A feeling of: *now what?*

By the time I hit my 30s and realized that any increase in money would not give me new freedoms or happiness, I hit a bit of an existential wall. It was not as clear or obvious what my motivation was. I still sometimes have tricky thoughts about what I'm doing here still trading at age 47 when there are so many other interesting things to do out there in the world. My early-life focus on money meant I needed to find new reasons to trade as I got older.

After looking inward and thinking about things for a few years, I developed a new set of motivations.

1. I love trading. I enjoy going to work every day. Going in to an office where I enjoy what I do, I like the people I work with, and I respect the management I report to, have been the most important drivers of my happiness over the years. The constantly evolving macro picture and the ever-changing market regimes and nearly impossibly complicated process of trying to solve the market is enjoyable. If you

---

136. Not exactly true as I wanted most to be a major league infielder. But that was more of a dream than a real goal. I didn't work hard enough or lift weights or do the things necessary to become a professional baseball player. On the other hand, I did do everything possible to become a trader. There is some overlap between pro athlete and professional trader in terms of the stress and excitement. In fact, I still remember a Lehman Brothers recruitment brochure from 1993 that featured this Q&A with a senior trader: "Q: Why did you decide to work at Lehman Brothers? A: Because I wasn't good enough to play for the New York Yankees." Man, the 1990s were amazing.

enjoy coming into work each day, the money doesn't matter as much. **No job is fun all the time, but if trading isn't fun most of the time, you're not doing it right.**

2. I want to publish my writing. One of my favorite things to do is write about finance and markets. Working at a bank and writing AM/FX every day is the ideal platform to do that. Again, intellectual stimulation before money.

3. I want to maintain my current level of monetary success but do not really aspire to anything more than what I have now, financially. The idea of getting super rich does not excite me. Working as a trader at a bank is a high-paying job that involves skills that most people don't have. I should just be thankful and keep trading until the day they tap me on the shoulder or the day I don't love it anymore. Until then, I am grateful for the job I have, and I don't need to dream of making 5X what I'm making now because I know that will not make me happier.

Everyone has a money vs. happiness curve. Think about the shape of yours. There is a point for everyone (except sociopaths) where more money will not deliver more happiness. The shape of your curve will depend on where you live, how many kids you have, how you grew up, your values, your ambition and your opportunity set. Don't be one of those people that just always wants more. That will put you on a treadmill, running towards an impossible-to-reach goal. Be thoughtful about what kind of money you need to do what you want to do and aim there. Don't keep moving the goalposts or you will never be happy. Life is not a video game.

Think about your own upbringing, how you value money (or don't) and how that will influence your motivation. More money is not always the answer. In fact, it usually is not the answer unless you are struggling to pay rent or cannot afford to pursue specific, costly passions like travel or owning a boat.

Many people believe that success leads to money and money leads to happiness. I think that chain of causality is mostly wrong. In real life, if you are happy (i.e., you enjoy coming in to work each day, are passionate about what you do, and have a positive attitude) you will succeed and in trading, an inevitable output of that process will be a whole bunch of money.

The number one reason to trade is that you love trading.

FINAL MINDSET ADVICE: SPEED ROUND

Don't get too high or too low, don't be an asshole, don't burn bridges, don't sing on the desk when you are making money. Arrive on time. Do the work. Enjoy yourself. Treat the gate keepers and the back office and support staff with respect. Don't bitch about algos. Turn off your phone at night. Take cold showers. Take responsibility for everything that happens to you. Learn about the size of the universe. Lift weights. Watch less TV. Or no TV. Have outside interests. Don't look back in anger. Fast, cheap, or good, pick two. Don't talk about trades you missed. Always go to the funeral. If you have heartburn, don't take a pill to fix it, figure out what foods are causing it and stop eating them. Drink more water, especially if you are prone to headaches. Be open and transparent. In business relationships, give more than you take. If it comes down to luck, you are doing it wrong. Smile at yourself in the mirror. Be nice. Call your mom.

CONCLUSION

I hope you found this book educational and also not boring. I hope that I improved your overall knowledge of markets and gave you some interesting and random insights about trading, mathematics, and life. And I hope you can extract some useful information from this book and use that information to make more money and to achieve whatever goals you have set for yourself. If you take nothing else from this book, remember these six points:

- The first rule of trading is: Don't blow up.
- To succeed in trading, you must be rational, and you need to put in the work.
- It's OK to be wrong.
- Variance is part of trading. Deal with it.
- There is no single trading methodology that will work always and forever.
- Trading should be fun (most of the time).

Now before you go, please complete one final assignment. Flip back to the questionnaire from Chapter 1. Pick a few categories where you want to make a change, and draw small arrows from the current box to the box where you would like to be. Be realistic. If you are generally risk averse and have trouble committing to full sized positions, don't target a 10 in risk appetite. Try moving from 5 to 7 first.

You don't need to change on every metric. This is about incremental improvement. Pick traits where you think a change will make you a better trader. If you are comfortable with your discipline score at 8 and think there is not much value trying to change it: leave it. You want to find two or three traits at most, and think about how to move the needle on them.

What is the date today? Go get your phone and put a reminder in for this date, one year from now. It should read: "Redo questionnaire in Donnelly's Alpha Trader book". Come back to this book once per year on this date for as long as you are trading and do the survey again. Keep improving every month and every year. You can change, it just takes time. Play a long game. Keep pushing yourself. Do not give up, no matter how hard things get.

I almost gave up. A few times.

In December 2007, I was beaten down and frustrated. It was my worst trading year ever and it looked like I might finish negative on the year. When you work in a market making seat at a bank, it is fairly uncommon to have a down year and I was proud of never having finished in the red. After this long and frustrating period, all I wanted to do was finish the year in the black. Even by $1.

Every time I got close to zero P&L, I would lose money again. By mid-November, I had gone from down $2.5 million back to $250,000 in the black and was thinking about making one last push to finish with a number that might be at least respectable. I finally felt mildly optimistic for the first time in ages, after almost an entire year battling repeated cycles of frustration and despair.

Then, a brutal turn. A salesman slinked over to me with his tail between his legs and told me there was an out trade in my book. Negative $700,000. That put me back to minus $450,000 with less than two months in the year. *Gross.* I grinded out the next few weeks and was finally up tiny YTD, about $200k, on the very last day of the year.

At 10 a.m., our toughest client called and wished me a happy new year by ripping my face off to the tune of $600,000. Despite what felt like a heroic effort to the very last day, I ended the year in the red.

I'm done with this. I am the worst trader in the world.

I e-mailed my wife: "This is impossible. I don't think I can do it anymore."

I walked out of the office miserable that day. But the sun came up on January 1. Slowly, the frustration dissipated a bit, and the prospect of a new year gave me some hope. Despite that exhausting and disappointing year, I hung on and kept going.

Twelve months later, I was staring at my best year ever: I made more than $50 million of trading profits in 2008. Sometimes the thing is just to keep going. As Joe Mauro said in his classic 2016 e-mail to the Goldman Sachs analyst class: "Keep running"[137].

• • •

Thanks for taking the time to read my book. I really appreciate it. Please feel free to reach out with feedback, criticism, or questions. You can follow me on Twitter (@donnelly_brent) and LinkedIn.

I plan to publish future updates, fresh trading stories and new lessons, tactics and strategies, exclusively for readers of Alpha Trader. If you are interested, please sign up at brentdonnelly.com.

---

137. https://www.businessinsider.com/goldman-sachs-partner-email-2016-3#-4

ONE LAST STORY
BEFORE YOU GO

Before I sign off, I want to take you on one last trip down memory lane. Back to the year 2000, around the time of Napster and Limp Bizkit and the hanging chad. The moment, some would argue, American optimism peaked. A time before the dotcom crash and before 9/11 and the Global Financial Crisis and *waaaaay* before COVID-19. A time when the world was less cynical and bull markets were much loved and quantitative easing was a weird experimental form of monetary policy that only PhD economists knew or cared about.

• • •

Note: This story is written from the point of view of my wildly over-confident, 27-year-old self

---

JULY 26, 2000

It's 3:05 p.m.

I am sitting at my workstation in a 50-person day trading operation in Toronto, Canada. I don't have much risk on. Waiting for the 4 p.m. close.

A few months ago, in March 2000, the NASDAQ topped out just above 5,000 then crashed to 3,200. Everyone thought the tech bubble had gone permanently *Tango Uniform*. People thought: "Finally, game over."

But not so fast. Now it's summer and we're trading back above 4,000, the Fed's cutting rates and new all-time highs are within reach.

About a year ago, I deposited my entire net worth ($25,000) into a day trading account. Now I'm running $350,000+. And it is worth noting this factors in a fair number of purchases including a nice library of PS2 games, two years of rent in downtown Toronto, a sweet-ass Sony 200-disc CD player and a black 1996 BMW M3.

Many days I bail out of here by 2 p.m. because there isn't much trading to do after lunch, but today I'm here for the close. It could be a big one. JDS Uniphase, a Canadian optical networking stock and internet darling, (NASDAQ: JDSU) will be added to the S&P 500 today. When a stock is added to an index, it creates a ton of demand for the stock because many funds simply track the indexes and so they need to buy the stock that's added in order to accurately mirror the index. The JDSU inclusion was announced a few weeks ago and there has been some excitement about it. Today is the day.

The indexers are not particularly smart about how they add the stock. They just buy it at the end of the day. This leads to a situation where large S&P 500

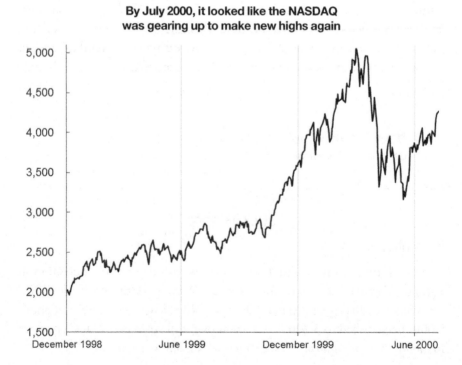

By July 2000, it looked like the NASDAQ was gearing up to make new highs again

adds create nearly impossible-to-fill demand for a stock in the closing moments of trading on the day the stock is added. Stocks close at 4:00:00 p.m.

I own 800 shares of JDSU, a decent but not super aggressive position size. Risking $4/share ($3,200 maximum loss or just under 1% of my capital).

It's 3:56 p.m.

To give you a sense of the hysteria around JDSU and Canadian tech darlings at that time… From October 1999 to March 2000, JDSU Uniphase stock rallied 600%, splitting two-for-one three times in just six months.

Meanwhile, Nortel Networks, another Canadian technology favorite, represented 35% of the *entire Toronto Stock Exchange* market capitalization in July 2000. That's right. One Canadian company accounted for 35% of the Canadian stock market, dwarfing the Big Six banks and the hugely-profitable Western Canadian oil companies.

It's 3:57 p.m.

JDSU is trading around $132 and everyone in the day trading office (around 50 traders) owns some. I'm nervous because when everyone knows something in markets, it's usually wrong. The idea is to know something before everyone else, and then get out once everyone knows it. But I don't want to miss the last push higher as every index fund in the world comes in to hoover JDSU.

It's 3:58 p.m.

The stock rallies to $136.50. I tap a few buttons and I'm out. No way am I holding on until exactly 4 p.m. It's way too dangerous. Sometimes with these index adds, too many people are positioned in advance and the buying from indexers isn't big enough to offset all the day traders trying to take profit so the price crashes right at 4 o'clock.

I am satisfied with the profits. I bought 500 shares at $129 about an hour ago and sold them at $136.50 for a profit of $3,750 minus brokerage. Brokerage is tiny so that's pretty much $3,750 in my pocket. Traders here keep 100% of P&L after brokerage fees. I settle into my seat to watch the last two minutes of fireworks. I feel like I should have a bucket of popcorn in my lap for this.

It's 3:58:40 p.m.

Tension builds in the room. There is always a ton of activity at the close, even when there is no index add, so with the JDSU thing happening, everyone is still here and everyone is locked and loaded for any last second opportunities. The greediest JDSU holders hope for one last push higher.

Our trading screen looks something like Figure QS.1. This is a sample showing Cisco Systems (NASDAQ: CSCO), not the JDSU window.

Figure QS.1: Level 2 screen for Cisco Systems circa late 1990s

CSCO	26.3 -- 26.31				

CSCO	↑	H 26.38 · L 25.76	PCL 25.56		0
Last 26.29		0.73 (2.9%)	Vol 33,458,113		
Lv1	26.3	26.31			

MMID	BID	SIZE	MMID	ASK	SIZE
SIZE	26.300	25	ISB	26.310	33
ARCA#	26.300	42	INB	26.310	44
BUB	26.300	42	BUB	26.310	53
INB	26.300	10	SIZE	26.310	16
ISB	26.300	69	ARCA#	26.310	133
JPMS	26.290	1	BTRD#	26.310	28
BOFA	26.290	1	ISB	26.320	10
LEHM	26.290	10	INB	26.320	32
BUB	26.290	68	BUB	26.320	16
INB	26.290	86	SCHB	26.320	2
ISB	26.290	210	JPMS	26.320	1
BTRD#	26.280	20	COWN	26.320	1
COWN	26.280	1	NITE	26.320	40
BUB	26.280	19	UBSW	26.320	7
INB	26.280	32	ISB	26.330	12
ISB	26.280	16	INB	26.330	33
FBCO	26.260	1	BUB	26.330	11
			FBCO	26.330	1

Execute Buy 7000 CSCO 26.33 ~ARCA~12:39:03~

| 1000 | P | | 26.33 | TMP | ? | ✓ |
| ARCAL ▼ | | DAY ▼ | ANY ▼ | 90327061 | | ▼ |

| SHRT | CXL | BUY |

This is called the NASDAQ Level 2 screen and it shows all the buyers on the left and sellers on the right. MMID means "Market Maker ID", BID is the price someone is willing to buy, SIZE is the number of shares (in 100s). Ask is the price someone is willing to sell. If the bid price matches an ask price, they match and the buyer transacts with the seller: a trade happens and both prices disappear. For reasons that I hope are obvious, the BID price is always lower than the ASK price.

The MMIDs indicate different banks and electronic communication networks (ECNs, or brokers) that place orders. For example, JPMS is JP Morgan, BOFA is Bank of America, LEHM is Lehman Brothers. ARCA, ISB, SIZE and BTRD are examples of ECN prices. ECNs are used by day traders and banks to show liquidity and execute in the market.

Our setup trades mostly with ISB, BTRD and ARCA. We trade using hot buttons assigned to the function keys. You set up your default number of shares (mine is set to 1,000) and the F keys on the left are F1: Sell on ISB, F2: Sell on BTRD, F3: Sell on ARCA. Then to buy you press F6 F7 and F8. You can operate these keys very quickly because there is no confirm dialog. You press F1 and you have instantly sold 1,000 shares of whatever stock window you are on at the best BID available on ISB.

It's 3:58:50 p.m.

I am relaxed, watching the prices spin higher and lower in the JDSU window. My PC can barely keep up with the number of quotes and trades being jammed down the pipe but somehow it manages and the information continues to flow smoothly and impossibly fast. Then I notice something weird. JDSU is $141 bid on ISB. And $140 ASK on ARCA. Impossible. And it's not just there for a microsecond. It's just sitting there.

"Guys, you see this?"

Everyone is in the zone, doing their own thing. Nobody has noticed the discrepancy.

I tap F1 and then F8 in succession, selling 1,000 shares at $141 and buying them back at $140 in less than a second. My P&L clicks $1,000 higher. I do it five more times in about 5 seconds. Still believing this is probably too good to be true, I check my P&L. This must be a mindfart right? Wrong. My P&L is $5,000 higher than it was before I made the keystrokes.

"Dude! ARBITRAAAGGGGGE!"

I yell out, to no one in particular (channeling the 1994 Beastie Boys song: Sabotage). Then I go nuts on the keyboard. F1 F8 F1 F8 F1 F8 F1 F8 F1 F8 F1 F8 F1 F8 F1 F8 F1 F8 F1 F8 as fast as I possibly can. Like a kid playing the 1980s coin-op video game "Track and Field".

I pause for breath and check my P&L. Up another $12,000 in about 12 seconds. The ISB and ARCA feeds both reset at 4:00:00 because the market makers drop out at the official close. I can only do this arbitrage 'til 4.

It's 3:59:35 p.m.

F1 F8 F1 F8 F1 F8 F1 F8 F1 F8 F1 F8 F1 F8 F1 F8 F1 F8 F1 F8 F1 F8 F1 F8 F1 F8 F1 F8 F1 F8 F1 F8 F1 F8 F1 F8 F1 F8 F1 F8 F1 F8 F1 F8

24 more times I press the F1 to F8 combo and my P&L jumps another $24,000 in less than 30 seconds.

My final P&L that day is +$48,500, the best day anyone had ever realized in that office to that point. Everyone gathers around my desk. My heart is pounding, vision pulsating. My buddy points to my P&L.

"Nice!"

POSTSCRIPT

Never before or after that day did I ever see a market inverted like that again. It was a one-time deal. JDSU stock never again traded higher than the 4:00 p.m. print on that day: July 26, 2000. It went on to lose 99% of its value in the next few years. The chart is shown in Figure QS.2.

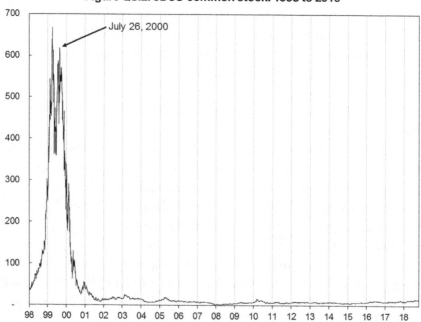

Figure QS.2: JDSU common stock: 1998 to 2019

Note that due to reverse splits, the prices on this chart don't match the prices in my story.

That day was also high water for my P&L and the peak equity for my trading account. The NASDAQ made its final last-gasp high a few weeks later. Never in my life was I more overconfident than in the weeks immediately following that day. By mid-2002, I shut down my account with a balance below $35,000 and I was out looking for a "real" job by early 2003. Insult to injury: I had to accept a ridiculous low-ball bid to sell my M3 to pay the rent.

I got crushed by a confluence of overconfidence and some epic market-altering events. The two biggest changes that killed the day trading community were decimalization (effective April 2001) and the collapse in price of every single NASDAQ stock.

My main strategy was to capture the bid/offer on high-priced stocks. Each morning, starting in 1999, I printed off sheets listing every NASDAQ stock trading above $100. In 1999, that list was four pages long. By 2002, it was *four stocks*. Four lessons learned:

- Markets don't stay inefficient forever. The NASDAQ was wildly inefficient from 1998 to 2002. If you find an inefficiency, make hay while the sun shines and then stash away as many nuts as you can for winter. Winter is always around the corner.
- If you are overconfident, the market will swiftly and harshly beat that overconfidence out of you.
- Trading can be incredibly fun.
- Indexes don't tell the full story.

Figure QS.3: The NASDAQ eventually came roaring back
Many single stocks never did

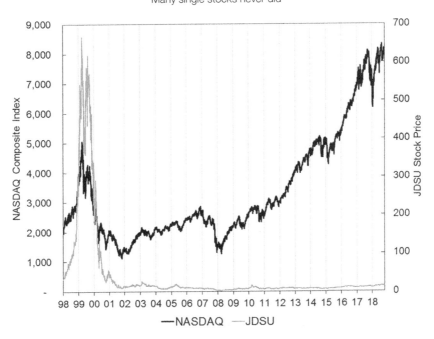

GOOD LUCK ↕ BE NIMBLE

CODA

Remember the flash crash USDJPY story from the start of this book? Now, here's the same story annotated with all the concepts I have outlined throughout. I hope this demonstrates the way good and bad decisions, great calls, dumb mistakes, and heaps of trader bias can all influence a single trading day.

● ● ●

FAIRFIELD COUNTY, CONNECTICUT
MAY 6, 2010 | 4:55AM

The Connecticut air is cold and damp. The trader moves in silence. He steps quietly through the pitch-black darkness of his Colonial McMansion and toward the door. As he disarms the home security system, the BEEP BEEP BEEP of the keypad code he enters is impossibly loud in the quiet of the pre-dawn morning. He steps out of the house, closes and locks the door, and hops into his car.

As he rolls down the driveway and into the foggy morning, he inserts a Deadmau5 CD and blasts it at high volume in an effort to wake up and get pumped for another day of trading. But this will not just be another day of trading. This will be one of the most insane trading days of his career.

It has been a frustrating year so far. The Eurozone Crisis has been smoldering for months but the trader's attempts to sell the euro have been met with massive countertrend rallies as the Fed embarks on another round of USD-negative QE. They call EURUSD a collision of two garbage trucks. The trader struggles to steer clear of the wreckage.

His strongest view recently has been lower USDJPY. There is risk aversion popping up all over the place as markets worry about a domino effect where Greece crashes out of the Eurozone, followed by Spain, Portugal, Ireland and then finally Italy. Everyone is bearish stocks as the S&P 500 rally from 666 in March 2009 to 1050 now is seen as a mirage; the side effect of a money printing magic trick performed by central bankers. Totally unsustainable. [grizzly bias]

EURUSD opened the year at 1.4500 and now trades sub-1.25 so the short trade is now hard to stomach. Even when you know it's the right thing to do, it takes a lot of courage to sell something down >15%. [anchoring bias] So the trader has shifted his attention to USDJPY and he expects it to go substantially

Figure C.1: USDJPY vs. US 10-year rates November 2009 to May 5, 2010

The chart covers the period up to May 5. This story takes place May 6.
Chart courtesy of Refinitiv

lower as global risk aversion remains elevated and safe haven currencies like the yen should find demand.

USDJPY has been inexplicably well-bid given recent risk aversion and the Fed "money printing". It just rallied from 90 to 94 on air over the last two weeks. Meanwhile, the best leading indicator for USDJPY is always US bond yields and they have been plummeting for a month. USDJPY looks completely wrong.

The trader stares at Figure C.1, which shows US 10-year bond yields and USDJPY. The black bars are USDJPY and the dotted line shows US bond yields. Note they usually follow in lockstep. The divergence is a strong signal to the trader that he should be short USDJPY. [**relative value, lead/lag trading**]

If you look in the top right corner, you can see that USDJPY is a bit off the highs, but not much. Two days in a row, the high has been 94.99 [**round number bias**] and USDJPY is now bouncing aimlessly around 93.80 as he rolls into the hedge fund's parking lot. It is still early so there are only three Porsche 911s in the lot right now. More will arrive later. [**money does not buy happiness but it does buy nice cars**]

This USDJPY trade has been tiring and painful as the trader got short at 94.00 with a stop loss at 95.05 and those two daily highs mean he has come within a hair (6 pips, or 0.064%) of getting stopped out, two days in a row. [**endurance**] Holding on to a trade like this is exhausting as the trader's fight-or-flight stress system remains activated for long stretches. *Cortisol overload.* [**ability to handle stress**]

Now, he can relax a bit and let things play out. His target is 91.00. Average daily range has been about 100 points lately so he figures we might get there in the next week or so.

10:45 AM

It has been a boring morning with USDJPY in a tight range. [**hours of boredom, moments of terror**] The sun comes out and it's almost shorts weather outside so the trader decides to go for a run before lunch. [**healthy body, healthy mindset**] Less than a mile into his run, he gets his first indication that this is not a random, ordinary day. His Blackberry rings. Bank sales on the line to tell him that USDJPY has just dumped 100 points in 15 minutes. Trading 92.80 now… Odd. He turns around and sprints back to the office, Spidey-sense tingling. [**intuition is useful, though often overrated**]

By the time he grabs a quick shower and returns to the desk, USDJPY is

91.50. He is short $100 million USDJPY so that puts his profit (aka P&L or profit and loss) around +$2.8 million on the day. That's more P&L than this trader typically makes in an excellent month. A huge haul. [**fat tails and variance**] He scans the headlines and Bloomberg chats and finds no good explanation for what is going on. The stock market is down, but not enough to explain 100 points in USDJPY. This makes no sense. [**it doesn't always have to make sense**] When a trade shows a big profit that makes no sense, he likes to cover it and move on.

The trader buys 100 million USDJPY at 91.50. He is back to flat with no position and nearly 3 bucks of P&L in the bank. [**flat is the strongest position**]

He sits there calmly and processes what has happened. He allows himself to feel happy, just for a second. He stuck to his plan and had the patience to sit with a decent-sized position for three days. [**it's OK to be happy**] He relaxes and basks in the satisfaction of a job well done. [**overconfidence**]

Then… Some dumb voice in his brain says:

2.8 million dollars is an amazing day. But…
Maybe I can make 5 million today?

And his hands, as if possessed by some mischievous or evil force, move slowly toward the BUY and SELL buttons. For no reason. And like a moron… He goes long USDJPY. [**don't bleed out on dumb trades with no rationale**]

First, he buys $50 million at 91.50 and then another $50 million at 91.25. It's an impulsive trade with no rationale. [**lizard brain**] His planned stop loss is 90.85 but before he has time to input a stop loss order, he notices S&Ps lurch lower on a huge volume surge. [**automate your risk management process**] He puts on his headset and fires up the S&P squawk to see what's going on.

> If you want to hear the soundtrack to what happens next, Google "Flash crash stock market 2010 squawk" and select one of the YouTube replay videos

The announcer's voice is strained as he narrates an unexplained fall in stocks from 1150 to 1120. USDJPY skips through 91.00 and the trader's P&L shrinks to $2.0 million. He tries to sell at 90.80 and whiffs. USDJPY is suddenly in freefall. 90.10 trades. 90.00 breaks. USDJPY has just dropped more than four percent in a few hours. A monster move. [**fast markets**] The trader's eyes flick over to his P&L which has now shrunk back to six digits. Two-thirds of three days' work, gone in 60 seconds. [**time dilation**]

And then… Stocks sell off hard out of nowhere. Like… REALLY HARD. The S&P squawk guy is losing it. Screaming. 1100 breaks in the S&P. 1080, 1070, 1060. USDJPY is a waterfall. The squawk loses his mind as he yells:

"We have some BIG paper sellers here… 7 evens are trading. 6 evens are trading! 5 EVENS ARE TRADING!!!. New lows here…" [**herding**]

USDJPY breaks 89.00 and the trader has still sold only 23 million USD, leaving him stuck with a position of 77 million USD. It is a fast market, nearly impossible to transact. He picks up a phone to two different banks and neither one answers. He tries to hit the 88.60 and gets a reject notice from the aggregator. The price feed is stale and crossed now; it shows 89.00 / 88.10, which is not possible. The trader is now down on the day. In the red. His face is hot and feels red like his P&L. Urge to slam fist on desk is rising. [**do not let emotions control you**] The trader feels like he is falling, falling:::::::::::::::::::::in cinematic slow-mo.

USDJPY stabilizes a bit even as the S&P squawk continues to go nuts.

"65 even offered! 60 trades… 60 even bid, this is the widest we have seen in years," his voice cracks, he's yelling like the announcer at Churchill Downs as the horses turn for the stretch.

"60s trading! 50s trading! 50 at 70 now! We are twenty wide!"

1060 trades in S&Ps now, just about 10% down today, on zero news. [**it doesn't always have to make sense**] Nobody knows what the hell is going on and there is panic in the air. The squawk dude continues to scream. He is pouring gasoline on the trader's agitation.

The trader's P&L is now six figures in the red. Sadness. Anger. He is furious with himself [**forgive yourself**] because he had the right trade, waited patiently for almost three days for it to work, caught the move perfectly according to plan [**stick to the plan, you win**] … And then flipped the other way on a whim, for no reason and gave everything and more back in half an hour. [**when you don't stick to the plan, you lose**] $2.8 million is a good month for this trader. He just made and lost that much in less than two hours. [**time dilation**]

I am an idiot. How did I get into this mess?

He needs to make a decision here and quick but he realizes that he is flooded. [**Alpha Traders are self-aware**] It is impossible to make a good trading decision when you're flooded. [**Alpha Traders make rational, quality decisions**] He needs a second to clear his mind. He tears off the headphones, drops them on his desk, and stands up.

He walks over to the window and tries to find a moment of lucid calm. He has been through these emotional storms before and knows how to get back to shore. **[experience is an asset]** He stares over the waters of the Long Island Sound. Gradually, his heart rate lowers. Clarity slowly, slowwwwly returns. His lizard brain retreats and his rational mind takes over. **[System 1 vs. System 2]** He talks to himself, out loud:

It doesn't matter how you got here. What are you going to do about it? 88.00 was the low in March. It's a massive level. The panic is fading. USDJPY is down 700 points in two days and now bonds are reversing lower. This is the place to buy USDJPY, not sell.

He returns to his keyboard, puts his headphones back on. The squawk guy has stopped screaming. He is noticeably more composed. S&P futures have bottomed within a whisker of limit down. They are stable but have not rebounded significantly. The bid/offer is super wide so it is hard to tell whether they are moving higher or just bouncing along the bottom. **[how to trade fast markets]**

The trader looks around the room and sees the panic and electricity levels have dropped. Not as many phones are ringing. Voices in the room are no longer frantic. **[trading requires focused, decisive action]** He buys 50 million USDJPY at 88.85. And another 73 million at 88.95. Max long now, long $200 million USDJPY. But this time it's thought out, not random and he feels good about what he is doing. He feels confident but fully in control. **[there is a time and place to be a pig]** He calmly thinks forward: *USDJPY could easily rally to 92.50 from here. When you catch a turn like this, you can be greedy.*

He leaves a stop loss for half his position (sell 100 million USDJPY at 87.94) **[automate your risk management]** and then sits back to let the thing play out. He has his plan and now he knows all he can do is watch and see if it works. There is one more frenetic whipsaw and USDJPY briefly prints to a low of 87.95. One pip from his 100 million USD stop loss. Amazing luck. **[quality decisions sometimes look like luck]** Seconds later, stocks stabilize, and then it's like everyone realizes all at once that whatever the heck just happened… It's over. **[markets are efficient most of the time, but not always]**

USDJPY is paid at 88.70, then up through 89.50. It breaks 90.00 and as it hits 90.40, the trader flicks his eyes to the P&L. It is almost exactly back to the level where it peaked earlier: $2.8 million. He praises the trading gods and squares up. NICE! **[anchoring bias]**

Figure C.2 shows the chart of that day in USDJPY:

Figure C.2: USDJPY May 3-7, 2010 (US stock market Flash Crash was May 6)

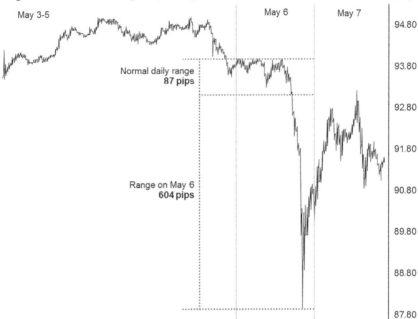

The trader made a multitude of both good and bad decisions in the three hours around the 2010 Flash Crash. The trading I describe in this story is a microcosm of everything that can go right and wrong in trading. Traders make good, careful decisions and get rewarded, they make bad decisions and get punished … but sometimes a good decision leads to a bad outcome … or a bad decision is rescued by good luck.

That's it. We're officially done. Thanks again for reading!

THE END

ACKNOWLEDGEMENTS

Many people helped me write this book. Number one on the list is Christine, who always supports me and backs my dreams. The one who continues to love me despite, and also because. Thank you for carrying all of us on your back through the endless, half-lit, mind-numbing tunnel of distorted mirrors that was 2020. You literally built a house and filled it with love, hard work, and pumpkin muffin smells (and two awesome kids). There is light at the end of the tunnel. I am pretty sure I can see it now.

Adam, you are a handsome, mature young man whose understanding of right and wrong far exceeds mine when I was your age. You make life better for everyone you come in contact with and I am proud to be your father. Oliver, you are a super-smart, funny and huggable little sloth-lover and I could not love you more than I already do. I am so glad I get to be your dad.

Thanks Mom, for playing catch with me when I was 8, for taking me to Crock and Block on Thursdays, and for giving me total freedom to choose my own life. Thanks Dad for teaching me there is extraordinary and unforgettable joy to be had from airborne pickles (in or outside the jar). I wish there was a way back to Olympic Stadium circa 1982 so I could keep score with you at just one more Expos game.

Thanks Steve for all the fun and creative interactions over the last few years and for the many gifts of Magic. Thanks Brother Craig, the last remaining unconditional optimist on earth… Sometimes it feels like the whole world is held together by your optimism (no pressure, though). Our trip to the World Series will always be one of my best ever memories.

Thank you, Ben Hunt, for the intellectual stimulation and life inspiration, the unmatched writing skill, and the non-stop original thought. Thank you for writing the foreword to this book. And thanks be to Benajah, who crushed my soul more than once with a ridiculous late-night oof-y boat over boat. So sick!

I appreciate the support of the five men who put their names on my book, backing it by blurbing on my behalf. I put them in alphabetical order because I have a ton of respect for each one and I am secretly super intimidated by all of them and don't want to make anyone mad.

- Jared Dillian, the hardest-working man in finance with new content dropping daily on the intertubes, TV, radio and SoundCloud. Your courage to talk about hard subjects makes me feel that I can do that too.

- Dave Floyd, the cool dude from the West Coast and a true student of the market.

- John Mauldin, whose long and prolific career is the epitome of the long-run success and adaptation I outline in this book.

- Ben Melkman: the man, the myth, the legend. Coolest hedge fund office art in the business. Call level at 05 in USDCAD.

- Jens Nordvig, possibly the smartest person I have ever met and definitely the most handsome.

Thanks Nick Jonas, AM/FX proofreader supreme, Aussie trader, and #1 Newcastle-born Mets fan. The man who loves trading and a Shane Warne flipper more than almost anything else. His ideas make my daily better. Nick had a major role in editing this book and our on-desk conversations inspired many sections.

Thanks Matt Thompson for his rare combo of smartness, generosity, courageous integrity, and ludicrous chart-formatting skills. Also, one of the most important things in life (to me) is working with people that are fun and interesting—and that's Matt in a nutshell. This is also Matt in a nutshell:

Illustration by Mr. Peter Little

Gus and Christina, thank you for contributing to this book and for being consistently fun to work with. Corbi thanks for your wisdom and friendship; I am sorry that you are not better at billiards. Joe Mauro: thanks for the "keep running" inspiration and Twitter hilarity. Sal, thanks for all the timely news and ideas and for being an excellent sounding board. And GM@SatskoPickles.

I am grateful for Sam, Pete, Bracco!, MG, Locky, Witz, BH, and the rest of the RNG crew who helped me survive all those numb 'rona nights while stationed abroad in Jersey City… When I was supposed to be writing this book, but longed for distraction, human interaction and a bit of fun. RAD.

Gitt and Suv helped improve portions of this book. My life is strictly better in the current timeline compared to any timeline where they do not exist. Vin Chopra helped me brainstorm a section of this book when I was stuck and he is also just one hell of a brainstormer in general (he's also really good at Googling). {VW} Saed, thanks for your camaraderie and market knowledge and for the deep dive you did on this book. And sorry I never answer the phone. :]

Thanks to B-Mac, Libardo, Clyde, Volkan and Richard for your personal and professional support, not to mention the platform and paycheck you have provided me for the past four years. Thanks to Refinitiv for all the charts.

And thank you reader, for dedicating the time to read my book. I appreciate it.

Special thanks to Stephen K. Donnelly, for all the hours he poured into editing this project.

Good luck. Be nimble.

New Canaan, Connecticut
2021

FURTHER READING

BOOKS

Trading classics
Market Wizards (series), Jack Schwager (1989)
Reminiscences of a Stock Operator, Edwin Lefèvre (1923)

Luck vs. skill, process vs. outcome
The Success Equation, Michael Mauboussin (2012)
Thinking in Bets, Annie Duke (2018)

Be disciplined
Willpower, Baumeister and Tierney (2012)
The Science of Self-Discipline, Peter Hollins (2017)
The Disciplined Trader, Mark Douglas (1990)

Behavioral finance bibles
Thinking, Fast and Slow, Daniel Kahneman (2011)
Irrational Exuberance, Robert Shiller (2000)

Get organized
The Seven Habits of Highly Effective People, Stephen Covey (1988)
The Checklist Manifesto, Atul Gawande (2009)
The Power of Habit, Charles Duhigg (2012)

Be self-aware
The Power of Now, Eckhart Tolle (1997)
Breath, James Nestor (2020)
The Hour Between Dog and Wolf, John Coates (2012)

Get quantitative

Fortune's Formula, William Poundstone (2005)

Superforecasting, Dan Gardner and Philip Tetlock (2015)

Fooled by Randomness, Nassim Taleb (2001)

Fooled by Technical Analysis, Michael Harris (2015)

A Man for All Markets, Edward Thorp (2017)

Risk, Dan Gardner (2008)

How to Lie with Statistics, Darrell Huff (1954)

BLOGS, PODCASTS AND NEWSLETTERS

Aspen Trading daily and intraday trading newsletter, Dave Floyd

Epsilon Theory website, podcast and newsletter, Ben Hunt and Rusty Guynn

Exante blog on Substack, Jens Nordvig et al.

"Outside the Box" weekly newsletter, John Mauldin

"The Daily Dirtnap" newsletter, Jared Dillian

"No mercy / No Malice" blog, Scott Galloway

"Cheap Convexity" on Substack, Jon Turek

21 WAYS TO SUCCEED AT TRADING AND 13 WAYS TO FAIL

Excellent traders:

1. Adapt.
2. Are rational.
3. Are self-aware.
4. Do not blow up.
5. Study metacognition.
6. Don't mind being wrong.
7. Can clearly describe their edge.
8. Love trading more than money.
9. Understand process vs. outcome.
10. Use the tight/aggressive approach.
11. Are experts in the markets they trade.
12. Are creative and independent thinkers.
13. Understand variance and the metagame.
14. Fall down, get back up, and keep running.
15. Work hard, even when they don't feel like it.
16. Have the discipline to both make a plan *and stick to it*.
17. Recognize biased thinking (in themselves, and others).
18. Employ a rigorous and systematic risk management process.
19. Have an unshakable belief in themselves, but are not overconfident.
20. Are intelligent problem solvers with above-average quantitative skill.
21. Have courage to put on high conviction trades in max appropriate size.

Losing traders:

1. Overtrade.
2. Have no edge.
3. Hate to be wrong.
4. Are overconfident.
5. Can't pull the trigger.
6. Rely too much on simple indicators.
7. Think much more about trade ideas than risk management.
8. Always trade the same position size.
9. Are impulsive and undisciplined.
10. Rely on System 1 thinking.
11. Don't read much.
12. Lie to themselves.
13. Gamble.

Come in to work each day with a positive attitude.
Do the work. Focus. Behave rationally.
Go home. Do it again tomorrow.

That is the 22-word recipe for trading success.

INDEX

Italicized page numbers indicate graphs and charts

ABOUT THE AUTHOR

Brent Donnelly has been trading currencies since 1995 and is currently a senior FX trader at HSBC New York. He is the author of *The Art of Currency Trading* (Wiley, 2019). He writes a widely-read, highly-respected macro and FX daily called AM/FX. Over the course of his career, he has been a market maker, trader, and senior manager at some of the top banks in foreign exchange. He trades tactical global macro.

He has extensive experience trading currencies, FX options, stock index futures, NASDAQ stocks, and commodities. Brent is a respected macro thinker with the unique perspective of a senior risk taker. He has been quoted by, or featured in, the Economist, Epsilon Theory, Real Vision, the Wall Street Journal, Financial Times, Bloomberg, and CNBC.

Before joining HSBC, Brent was head of G10 Spot Trading at Citi New York and global head of G10 FX Trading at Nomura New York. He was also a portfolio manager at a major hedge fund in Connecticut for three years. He created and wrote a cartoon called "Daft Planet," which aired on TV in Canada, and he dreams of one day winning the Man Booker Prize.

Sign up for updates at **brentdonnelly.com**

Made in the USA
Las Vegas, NV
07 February 2024

85446602R00282